COMPREHENSIVE MORTGAGE PAYMENT TABLES

Showing the monthly payment required
to amortize a loan in a given
number of years.

PUBLICATION NO. 392

Computed and
Published by

FINANCIAL
PUBLISHING
COMPANY
82 Brookline Avenue
Boston, Massachusetts 02215

SCOPE

INTEREST RATES:
> 7% to 15% by ¼%, 15½%,
> 16%, 17% and 18%

TERMS:
> 1 year to 3 years by ½ year
> 4 years to 22 years by 1 year
> 25 years to 40 years by 5 years

AMOUNTS:
> $25, $50, $75
> $100 to $1,000 by $100
> $2,000 to $35,000 by $1,000
> $40,000 to $80,000 by $5,000
> And $100,000

AUXILIARY TABLES:
> Loan Progress Charts
> Sample Schedule

FEDERAL TRUTH in LENDING

It is necessary on credit transactions (effective July 1, 1969) to disclose the charge and the annual percentage rate.

Exemption: all commercial transactions, and all transactions over $25,000 (except real estate mortgages).

I. DISCLOSURE OF CHARGE IN DOLLARS

A. On first mortgages on a dwelling it is not necessary to disclose the charge.

B. On other credit the charge must be disclosed and includes interest, finance charge, time price differential, discounts, "points", service charge, fees for credit investigation or report, appraisal fee. The charge does not include credit insurance or property insurance purchased on written order of borrower, official fees actually disbursed, taxes.

METHOD OF COMPUTATION OF CHARGE. This book does not show total charge for disclosure. If the transaction is not a first mortgage, or a commercial loan, obtain the charge by multiplication.

EXAMPLE: on a $20,000 8¼% 10 year loan the monthly payment is shown as $245.31. What is the dollar charge for disclosure?

Method: multiply the payment by the number of payments to determine the total the borrower will pay. Subtract the original loan principal and the remainder is the charge for interest.

Solution: 245.31 × 120 = 29,437.20
            original loan   20,000.00
            charge   9,437.20

II. DISCLOSURE OF ANNUAL PERCENTAGE RATE

The annual percentage rate must be disclosed both on first mortgages and other credit transactions. In the simple case the rate to be disclosed is the interest rate at which you entered this table. Where there are charges other than interest, these must be considered.

A. On mortgages secured by real property the charge includes interest, discounts, "points"; but excludes normal expenses on real estate mortgages such as title search, title insurance, credit report, appraisal fee, notary, documentary fee, preparation of deed and closing statement.

B. On other credit, the charge includes all the items listed for disclosure of charge.

METHOD OF COMPUTATION OF ANNUAL PERCENTAGE RATE: This book shows the rate for disclosure based on interest only. If the borrower did not get the full amount of loan, compute a disclosure rate.

Compute the payment per $1000 on the net cash received by borrower. Hunt in the tables for the nearest rate on the $1000 line, or interpolate.

EXAMPLE: a loan of $20,000 at 8¼% for 20 years carries a payment of $170.42 as shown in the table. In this case the lender takes 2 points or $400 and makes a charge of $186 for unusual expenses. The net cash to borrower is $19,414.

Method: divide the payment of $170.42 by $19,414 to get the payment per $1000 as $8.78. In this book for $1000 20 years you may read the payments as 8¼% 8.53
8½% 8.68
8¾% 8.84

The nearest payment to 8.78 is for 8¾%. Since Federal Reserve regulations permit disclosure at the nearest ¼%, you may disclose 8¾% as the annual percentage rate. If you prefer you may interpolate between the payments at 8½% and 8¾% and disclose 8.66%.

POINTS DISCOUNT TABLE

The following table shows the yield to maturity on a mortgage when from 1 to 5 points discount are taken.

INTEREST RATE	NET PRICE	TERM					
		5 YEARS	10 YEARS	15 YEARS	20 YEARS	25 YEARS	30 YEARS
7%	95	9.17	8.17	7.83	7.67	7.58	7.52
	96	8.73	7.93	7.66	7.53	7.46	7.41
	97	8.29	7.69	7.49	7.40	7.34	7.30
	98	7.85	7.46	7.33	7.26	7.23	7.20
	99	7.42	7.23	7.16	7.13	7.11	7.10
7½%	95	9.69	8.68	8.35	8.19	8.09	8.03
	96	9.24	8.44	8.17	8.04	7.97	7.92
	97	8.79	8.20	8.00	7.90	7.85	7.81
	98	8.36	7.96	7.83	7.77	7.73	7.71
	99	7.92	7.73	7.66	7.63	7.61	7.60
8%	95	10.20	9.19	8.86	8.70	8.61	8.55
	96	9.74	8.95	8.68	8.55	8.48	8.44
	97	9.30	8.70	8.51	8.41	8.36	8.32
	98	8.86	8.47	8.34	8.27	8.24	8.21
	99	8.43	8.23	8.17	8.14	8.12	8.11
8½%	95	10.71	9.70	9.37	9.21	9.12	9.07
	96	10.25	9.46	9.19	9.07	8.99	8.95
	97	9.80	9.21	9.02	8.92	8.87	8.83
	98	9.36	8.97	8.84	8.78	8.74	8.72
	99	8.93	8.73	8.67	8.64	8.62	8.61
9%	95	11.22	10.22	9.89	9.73	9.64	9.58
	96	10.76	9.96	9.70	9.58	9.51	9.46
	97	10.31	9.72	9.52	9.43	9.38	9.34
	98	9.87	9.48	9.35	9.28	9.25	9.23
	99	9.43	9.24	9.17	9.14	9.12	9.11
9½%	95	11.73	10.73	10.40	10.24	10.16	10.10
	96	11.27	10.47	10.21	10.09	10.02	9.98
	97	10.82	10.23	10.03	9.94	9.89	9.86
	98	10.37	9.98	9.85	9.79	9.76	9.73
	99	9.93	9.74	9.67	9.64	9.63	9.62
10%	95	12.24	11.24	10.91	10.76	10.67	10.62
	96	11.78	10.98	10.73	10.60	10.53	10.49
	97	11.32	10.73	10.54	10.45	10.40	10.37
	98	10.88	10.48	10.36	10.30	10.26	10.24
	99	10.44	10.24	10.18	10.15	10.13	10.12
10½%	95	12.75	11.75	11.43	11.27	11.19	11.14
	96	12.29	11.49	11.24	11.11	11.05	11.01
	97	11.83	11.24	11.05	10.96	10.91	10.88
	98	11.38	10.99	10.86	10.80	10.77	10.75
	99	10.94	10.74	10.68	10.65	10.63	10.62
11%	95	13.26	12.26	11.94	11.79	11.71	11.66
	96	12.80	12.00	11.75	11.63	11.56	11.52
	97	12.34	11.75	11.56	11.47	11.42	11.39
	98	11.88	11.49	11.37	11.31	11.28	11.26
	99	11.44	11.25	11.18	11.15	11.14	11.13

7%

MONTHLY PAYMENT
NECESSARY TO AMORTIZE A LOAN

TERM AMOUNT	1 YEAR	1½ YEARS	2 YEARS	2½ YEARS	3 YEARS	4 YEARS	5 YEARS
$ 25	2.17	1.47	1.12	.92	.78	.60	.50
50	4.33	2.94	2.24	1.83	1.55	1.20	1.00
75	6.49	4.41	3.36	2.74	2.32	1.80	1.49
100	8.66	5.87	4.48	3.65	3.09	2.40	1.99
200	17.31	11.74	8.96	7.29	6.18	4.79	3.97
300	25.96	17.61	13.44	10.93	9.27	7.19	5.95
400	34.62	23.48	17.91	14.58	12.36	9.58	7.93
500	43.27	29.35	22.39	18.22	15.44	11.98	9.91
600	51.92	35.22	26.87	21.86	18.53	14.37	11.89
700	60.57	41.08	31.35	25.51	21.62	16.77	13.87
800	69.23	46.95	35.82	29.15	24.71	19.16	15.85
900	77.88	52.82	40.30	32.79	27.79	21.56	17.83
1000	86.53	58.69	44.78	36.44	30.88	23.95	19.81
2000	173.06	117.37	89.55	72.87	61.76	47.90	39.61
3000	259.59	176.06	134.32	109.30	92.64	71.84	59.41
4000	346.11	234.74	179.10	145.73	123.51	95.79	79.21
5000	432.64	293.43	223.87	182.16	154.39	119.74	99.01
6000	519.17	352.11	268.64	218.60	185.27	143.68	118.81
7000	605.69	410.80	313.41	255.03	216.14	167.63	138.61
8000	692.22	469.48	358.19	291.46	247.02	191.57	158.41
9000	778.75	528.17	402.96	327.89	277.90	215.52	178.22
10000	865.27	586.85	447.73	364.32	308.78	239.47	198.02
11000	951.80	645.54	492.50	400.76	339.65	263.41	217.82
12000	1038.33	704.22	537.28	437.19	370.53	287.36	237.62
13000	1124.85	762.91	582.05	473.62	401.41	311.31	257.42
14000	1211.38	821.59	626.82	510.05	432.28	335.25	277.22
15000	1297.91	880.28	671.59	546.48	463.16	359.20	297.02
16000	1384.43	938.96	716.37	582.92	494.04	383.14	316.82
17000	1470.96	997.65	761.14	619.35	524.92	407.09	336.63
18000	1557.49	1056.33	805.91	655.78	555.79	431.04	356.43
19000	1644.01	1115.02	850.68	692.21	586.67	454.98	376.23
20000	1730.54	1173.70	895.46	728.64	617.55	478.93	396.03
21000	1817.07	1232.39	940.23	765.08	648.42	502.88	415.83
22000	1903.59	1291.07	985.00	801.51	679.30	526.82	435.63
23000	1990.12	1349.76	1029.77	837.94	710.18	550.77	455.43
24000	2076.65	1408.44	1074.55	874.37	741.06	574.71	475.23
25000	2163.17	1467.13	1119.32	910.80	771.93	598.66	495.03
26000	2249.70	1525.81	1164.09	947.23	802.81	622.61	514.84
27000	2336.23	1584.50	1208.86	983.67	833.69	646.55	534.64
28000	2422.75	1643.18	1253.64	1020.10	864.56	670.50	554.44
29000	2509.28	1701.87	1298.41	1056.53	895.44	694.45	574.24
30000	2595.81	1760.55	1343.18	1092.96	926.32	718.39	594.04
31000	2682.33	1819.24	1387.95	1129.39	957.20	742.34	613.84
32000	2768.86	1877.92	1432.73	1165.83	988.07	766.28	633.64
33000	2855.39	1936.61	1477.50	1202.26	1018.95	790.23	653.44
34000	2941.91	1995.29	1522.27	1238.69	1049.83	814.18	673.25
35000	3028.44	2053.98	1567.04	1275.12	1080.70	838.12	693.05
40000	3461.07	2347.40	1790.91	1457.28	1235.09	957.85	792.05
45000	3893.71	2640.83	2014.77	1639.44	1389.47	1077.59	891.06
50000	4326.34	2934.25	2238.63	1821.60	1543.86	1197.32	990.06
55000	4758.98	3227.68	2462.50	2003.76	1698.25	1317.05	1089.07
60000	5191.61	3521.10	2686.36	2185.92	1852.63	1436.78	1188.08
65000	5624.24	3814.53	2910.22	2368.08	2007.02	1556.51	1287.08
70000	6056.88	4107.95	3134.09	2550.24	2161.40	1676.24	1386.09
75000	6489.51	4401.38	3357.95	2732.40	2315.79	1795.97	1485.09
80000	6922.14	4694.80	3581.81	2914.56	2470.17	1915.70	1584.10
100000	8652.68	5868.50	4477.26	3643.20	3087.71	2394.63	1980.12

6

TERM AMOUNT	6 YEARS	7 YEARS	8 YEARS	9 YEARS	10 YEARS	11 YEARS	12 YEARS
$ 25	.43	.38	.35	.32	.30	.28	.26
50	.86	.76	.69	.63	.59	.55	.52
75	1.28	1.14	1.03	.94	.88	.82	.78
100	1.71	1.51	1.37	1.26	1.17	1.09	1.03
200	3.41	3.02	2.73	2.51	2.33	2.18	2.06
300	5.12	4.53	4.10	3.76	3.49	3.27	3.09
400	6.82	6.04	5.46	5.01	4.65	4.36	4.12
500	8.53	7.55	6.82	6.26	5.81	5.45	5.15
600	10.23	9.06	8.19	7.51	6.97	6.54	6.18
700	11.94	10.57	9.55	8.76	8.13	7.62	7.20
800	13.64	12.08	10.91	10.01	9.29	8.71	8.23
900	15.35	13.59	12.28	11.26	10.45	9.80	9.26
1000	17.05	15.10	13.64	12.51	11.62	10.89	10.29
2000	34.10	30.19	27.27	25.02	23.23	21.77	20.57
3000	51.15	45.28	40.91	37.52	34.84	32.66	30.86
4000	68.20	60.38	54.54	50.03	46.45	43.54	41.14
5000	85.25	75.47	68.17	62.54	58.06	54.43	51.42
6000	102.30	90.56	81.81	75.04	69.67	65.31	61.71
7000	119.35	105.65	95.44	87.55	81.28	76.19	71.99
8000	136.40	120.75	109.07	100.06	92.89	87.08	82.28
9000	153.45	135.84	122.71	112.56	104.50	97.96	92.56
10000	170.50	150.93	136.34	125.07	116.11	108.85	102.84
11000	187.54	166.02	149.98	137.57	127.72	119.73	113.13
12000	204.59	181.12	163.61	150.08	139.34	130.61	123.41
13000	221.64	196.21	177.24	162.59	150.95	141.50	133.69
14000	238.69	211.30	190.88	175.09	162.56	152.38	143.98
15000	255.74	226.40	204.51	187.60	174.17	163.27	154.26
16000	272.79	241.49	218.14	200.11	185.78	174.15	164.55
17000	289.84	256.58	231.78	212.61	197.39	185.03	174.83
18000	306.89	271.67	245.41	225.12	209.00	195.92	185.11
19000	323.94	286.77	259.05	237.62	220.61	206.80	195.40
20000	340.99	301.86	272.68	250.13	232.22	217.69	205.68
21000	358.03	316.95	286.31	262.64	243.83	228.57	215.97
22000	375.08	332.04	299.95	275.14	255.44	239.46	226.25
23000	392.13	347.14	313.58	287.65	267.05	250.34	236.53
24000	409.18	362.23	327.21	300.16	278.67	261.22	246.82
25000	426.23	377.32	340.85	312.66	290.28	272.11	257.10
26000	443.28	392.41	354.48	325.17	301.89	282.99	267.38
27000	460.33	407.51	368.12	337.67	313.50	293.88	277.67
28000	477.38	422.60	381.75	350.18	325.11	304.76	287.95
29000	494.43	437.69	395.38	362.69	336.72	315.64	298.24
30000	511.48	452.79	409.02	375.19	348.33	326.53	308.52
31000	528.52	467.88	422.65	387.70	359.94	337.41	318.80
32000	545.57	482.97	436.28	400.21	371.55	348.30	329.09
33000	562.62	498.06	449.92	412.71	383.16	359.18	339.37
34000	579.67	513.16	463.55	425.22	394.77	370.06	349.65
35000	596.72	528.25	477.19	437.72	406.38	380.95	359.94
40000	681.97	603.71	545.35	500.26	464.44	435.37	411.36
45000	767.21	679.18	613.52	562.79	522.49	489.79	462.78
50000	852.46	754.64	681.69	625.32	580.55	544.21	514.20
55000	937.70	830.10	749.86	687.85	638.60	598.63	565.61
60000	1022.95	905.57	818.03	750.38	696.66	653.05	617.03
65000	1108.19	981.03	886.20	812.91	754.71	707.47	668.45
70000	1193.44	1056.49	954.37	875.44	812.76	761.89	719.87
75000	1278.68	1131.96	1022.53	937.98	870.82	816.31	771.29
80000	1363.93	1207.42	1090.70	1000.51	928.87	870.73	822.71
100000	1704.91	1509.27	1363.38	1250.63	1161.09	1088.42	1028.39

7

7%

TERM AMOUNT	13 YEARS	14 YEARS	15 YEARS	16 YEARS	17 YEARS	18 YEARS	19 YEARS
$ 25	.25	.24	.23	.22	.21	.21	.20
50	.49	.47	.45	.44	.42	.41	.40
75	.74	.71	.68	.66	.63	.62	.60
100	.98	.94	.90	.87	.84	.82	.80
200	1.96	1.88	1.80	1.74	1.68	1.64	1.59
300	2.94	2.81	2.70	2.61	2.52	2.45	2.39
400	3.92	3.75	3.60	3.47	3.36	3.27	3.18
500	4.90	4.68	4.50	4.34	4.20	4.08	3.98
600	5.87	5.62	5.40	5.21	5.04	4.90	4.77
700	6.85	6.55	6.30	6.08	5.88	5.71	5.56
800	7.83	7.49	7.20	6.94	6.72	6.53	6.36
900	8.81	8.42	8.09	7.81	7.56	7.34	7.15
1000	9.79	9.36	8.99	8.68	8.40	8.16	7.95
2000	19.57	18.71	17.98	17.35	16.80	16.32	15.89
3000	29.35	28.07	26.97	26.02	25.19	24.47	23.83
4000	39.13	37.42	35.96	34.69	33.59	32.63	31.77
5000	48.91	46.78	44.95	43.37	41.99	40.78	39.71
6000	58.69	56.13	53.93	52.04	50.38	48.94	47.66
7000	68.47	65.48	62.92	60.71	58.78	57.09	55.60
8000	78.25	74.84	71.91	69.38	67.18	65.25	63.54
9000	88.03	84.19	80.90	78.05	75.57	73.40	71.48
10000	97.81	93.55	89.89	86.73	83.97	81.56	79.42
11000	107.59	102.90	98.88	95.40	92.37	89.71	87.37
12000	117.37	112.25	107.86	104.07	100.76	97.87	95.31
13000	127.15	121.61	116.85	112.74	109.16	106.02	103.25
14000	136.94	130.96	125.84	121.41	117.56	114.18	111.19
15000	146.72	140.32	134.83	130.09	125.95	122.33	119.13
16000	156.50	149.67	143.82	138.76	134.35	130.49	127.08
17000	166.28	159.02	152.81	147.43	142.75	138.64	135.02
18000	176.06	168.38	161.79	156.10	151.14	146.80	142.96
19000	185.84	177.73	170.78	164.77	159.54	154.95	150.90
20000	195.62	187.09	179.77	173.45	167.94	163.11	158.84
21000	205.40	196.44	188.76	182.12	176.33	171.26	166.79
22000	215.18	205.79	197.75	190.79	184.73	179.42	174.73
23000	224.96	215.15	206.74	199.46	193.13	187.57	182.67
24000	234.74	224.50	215.72	208.13	201.52	195.73	190.61
25000	244.52	233.86	224.71	216.81	209.92	203.88	198.55
26000	254.30	243.21	233.70	225.48	218.32	212.04	206.50
27000	264.09	252.56	242.69	234.15	226.71	220.19	214.44
28000	273.87	261.92	251.68	242.82	235.11	228.35	222.38
29000	283.65	271.27	260.67	251.50	243.51	236.50	230.32
30000	293.43	280.63	269.65	260.17	251.90	244.66	238.26
31000	303.21	289.98	278.64	268.84	260.30	252.81	246.20
32000	312.99	299.33	287.63	277.51	268.70	260.97	254.15
33000	322.77	308.69	296.62	286.18	277.09	269.12	262.09
34000	332.55	318.04	305.61	294.86	285.49	277.28	270.03
35000	342.33	327.40	314.59	303.53	293.89	285.43	277.97
40000	391.23	374.17	359.54	346.89	335.87	326.21	317.68
45000	440.14	420.94	404.48	390.25	377.85	366.98	357.39
50000	489.04	467.71	449.42	433.61	419.84	407.76	397.10
55000	537.95	514.48	494.36	476.97	461.82	448.53	436.81
60000	586.85	561.25	539.30	520.33	503.80	489.31	476.52
65000	635.75	608.02	584.24	563.69	545.78	530.08	516.23
70000	684.66	654.79	629.18	607.05	587.77	570.86	555.94
75000	733.56	701.56	674.13	650.41	629.75	611.63	595.65
80000	782.46	748.33	719.07	693.77	671.73	652.41	635.36
100000	978.08	935.41	898.83	867.21	839.67	815.51	794.20

8

TERM AMOUNT	20 YEARS	21 YEARS	22 YEARS	25 YEARS	30 YEARS	35 YEARS	40 YEARS
$ 25	.20	.19	.19	.18	.17	.16	.16
50	.39	.38	.38	.36	.34	.32	.32
75	.59	.57	.56	.54	.50	.48	.47
100	.78	.76	.75	.71	.67	.64	.63
200	1.56	1.52	1.49	1.42	1.34	1.28	1.25
300	2.33	2.28	2.24	2.13	2.00	1.92	1.87
400	3.11	3.04	2.98	2.83	2.67	2.56	2.49
500	3.88	3.80	3.72	3.54	3.33	3.20	3.11
600	4.66	4.56	4.47	4.25	4.00	3.84	3.73
700	5.43	5.31	5.21	4.95	4.66	4.48	4.36
800	6.21	6.07	5.95	5.66	5.33	5.12	4.98
900	6.98	6.83	6.70	6.37	5.99	5.75	5.60
1000	7.76	7.59	7.44	7.07	6.66	6.39	6.22
2000	15.51	15.17	14.87	14.14	13.31	12.78	12.43
3000	23.26	22.76	22.31	21.21	19.96	19.17	18.65
4000	31.02	30.34	29.74	28.28	26.62	25.56	24.86
5000	38.77	37.93	37.18	35.34	33.27	31.95	31.08
6000	46.52	45.51	44.61	42.41	39.92	38.34	37.29
7000	54.28	53.10	52.04	49.48	46.58	44.72	43.51
8000	62.03	60.68	59.48	56.55	53.23	51.11	49.72
9000	69.78	68.27	66.91	63.62	59.88	57.50	55.93
10000	77.53	75.85	74.35	70.68	66.54	63.89	62.15
11000	85.29	83.44	81.78	77.75	73.19	70.28	68.36
12000	93.04	91.02	89.22	84.82	79.84	76.67	74.58
13000	100.79	98.61	96.65	91.89	86.49	83.06	80.79
14000	108.55	106.19	104.08	98.95	93.15	89.44	87.01
15000	116.30	113.78	111.52	106.02	99.80	95.83	93.22
16000	124.05	121.36	118.95	113.09	106.45	102.22	99.43
17000	131.81	128.95	126.39	120.16	113.11	108.61	105.65
18000	139.56	136.53	133.82	127.23	119.76	115.00	111.86
19000	147.31	144.11	141.26	134.29	126.41	121.39	118.08
20000	155.06	151.70	148.69	141.36	133.07	127.78	124.29
21000	162.82	159.28	156.12	148.43	139.72	134.16	130.51
22000	170.57	166.87	163.56	155.50	146.37	140.55	136.72
23000	178.32	174.45	170.99	162.56	153.02	146.94	142.93
24000	186.08	182.04	178.43	169.63	159.68	153.33	149.15
25000	193.83	189.62	185.86	176.70	166.33	159.72	155.36
26000	201.58	197.21	193.30	183.77	172.98	166.11	161.58
27000	209.34	204.79	200.73	190.84	179.64	172.50	167.79
28000	217.09	212.38	208.16	197.90	186.29	178.88	174.01
29000	224.84	219.96	215.60	204.97	192.94	185.27	180.22
30000	232.59	227.55	223.03	212.04	199.60	191.66	186.43
31000	240.35	235.13	230.47	219.11	206.25	198.05	192.65
32000	248.10	242.72	237.90	226.17	212.90	204.44	198.86
33000	255.85	250.30	245.33	233.24	219.55	210.83	205.08
34000	263.61	257.89	252.77	240.31	226.21	217.22	211.29
35000	271.36	265.47	260.20	247.38	232.86	223.60	217.51
40000	310.12	303.39	297.37	282.72	266.13	255.55	248.58
45000	348.89	341.32	334.55	318.05	299.39	287.49	279.65
50000	387.65	379.24	371.72	353.39	332.66	319.43	310.72
55000	426.42	417.16	408.89	388.73	365.92	351.38	341.79
60000	465.18	455.09	446.06	424.07	399.19	383.32	372.86
65000	503.95	493.01	483.23	459.41	432.45	415.26	403.94
70000	542.71	530.94	520.40	494.75	465.72	447.20	435.01
75000	581.48	568.86	557.57	530.09	498.98	479.15	466.08
80000	620.24	606.78	594.74	565.43	532.25	511.09	497.15
100000	775.30	758.48	743.43	706.78	665.31	638.86	621.44

9

7¼%

MONTHLY PAYMENT
NECESSARY TO AMORTIZE A LOAN

TERM AMOUNT	1 YEAR	1½ YEARS	2 YEARS	2½ YEARS	3 YEARS	4 YEARS	5 YEARS
$ 25	2.17	1.47	1.13	.92	.78	.61	.50
50	4.34	2.94	2.25	1.83	1.55	1.21	1.00
75	6.50	4.41	3.37	2.75	2.33	1.81	1.50
100	8.67	5.88	4.49	3.66	3.10	2.41	2.00
200	17.33	11.76	8.98	7.31	6.20	4.82	3.99
300	26.00	17.64	13.47	10.97	9.30	7.22	5.98
400	34.66	23.52	17.96	14.62	12.40	9.63	7.97
500	43.33	29.40	22.45	18.28	15.50	12.04	9.96
600	51.99	35.28	26.94	21.93	18.60	14.44	11.96
700	60.65	41.16	31.43	25.59	21.70	16.85	13.95
800	69.32	47.04	35.91	29.24	24.80	19.25	15.94
900	77.98	52.92	40.40	32.90	27.90	21.66	17.93
1000	86.65	58.80	44.89	36.55	31.00	24.07	19.92
2000	173.29	117.60	89.78	73.10	61.99	48.13	39.84
3000	259.93	176.40	134.66	109.64	92.98	72.19	59.76
4000	346.57	235.20	179.55	146.19	123.97	96.25	79.68
5000	433.22	294.00	224.44	182.73	154.96	120.32	99.60
6000	519.86	352.80	269.32	219.28	185.95	144.38	119.52
7000	606.50	411.60	314.21	255.82	216.95	168.44	139.44
8000	693.14	470.39	359.09	292.37	247.94	192.50	159.36
9000	779.78	529.19	403.98	328.92	278.93	216.57	179.28
10000	866.43	587.99	448.87	365.46	309.92	240.63	199.20
11000	953.07	646.79	493.75	402.01	340.91	264.69	219.12
12000	1039.71	705.59	538.64	438.55	371.90	288.75	239.04
13000	1126.35	764.39	583.52	475.10	402.89	312.82	258.96
14000	1212.99	823.19	628.41	511.64	433.89	336.88	278.88
15000	1299.64	881.98	673.30	548.19	464.88	360.94	298.80
16000	1386.28	940.78	718.18	584.74	495.87	385.00	318.71
17000	1472.92	999.58	763.07	621.28	526.86	409.07	338.63
18000	1559.56	1058.38	807.95	657.83	557.85	433.13	358.55
19000	1646.20	1117.18	852.84	694.37	588.84	457.19	378.47
20000	1732.85	1175.98	897.73	730.92	619.84	481.25	398.39
21000	1819.49	1234.78	942.61	767.46	650.83	505.32	418.31
22000	1906.13	1293.57	987.50	804.01	681.82	529.38	438.23
23000	1992.77	1352.37	1032.38	840.56	712.81	553.44	458.15
24000	2079.41	1411.17	1077.27	877.10	743.80	577.50	478.07
25000	2166.06	1469.97	1122.16	913.65	774.79	601.57	497.99
26000	2252.70	1528.77	1167.04	950.19	805.78	625.63	517.91
27000	2339.34	1587.57	1211.93	986.74	836.78	649.69	537.83
28000	2425.98	1646.37	1256.81	1023.28	867.77	673.75	557.75
29000	2512.62	1705.17	1301.70	1059.83	898.76	697.81	577.67
30000	2599.27	1763.96	1346.59	1096.38	929.75	721.88	597.59
31000	2685.91	1822.76	1391.47	1132.92	960.74	745.94	617.51
32000	2772.55	1861.56	1436.36	1169.47	991.73	770.00	637.42
33000	2859.19	1940.36	1481.24	1206.01	1022.73	794.06	657.34
34000	2945.83	1999.16	1526.13	1242.56	1053.72	818.13	677.26
35000	3032.48	2057.96	1571.02	1279.10	1084.71	842.19	697.18
40000	3465.69	2351.95	1795.45	1461.83	1239.67	962.50	796.78
45000	3898.90	2645.94	2019.88	1644.56	1394.62	1082.81	896.38
50000	4332.11	2939.94	2244.31	1827.29	1549.58	1203.13	995.97
55000	4765.32	3233.93	2468.74	2010.02	1704.54	1323.44	1095.57
60000	5198.53	3527.92	2693.17	2192.75	1859.50	1443.75	1195.17
65000	5631.74	3821.92	2917.60	2375.47	2014.45	1564.06	1294.76
70000	6064.95	4115.91	3142.03	2558.20	2169.41	1684.37	1394.36
75000	6498.16	4409.90	3366.46	2740.93	2324.37	1804.69	1493.96
80000	6931.37	4703.89	3590.89	2923.66	2479.33	1925.00	1593.55
100000	8664.21	5879.87	4488.61	3654.57	3099.16	2406.25	1991.94

10

TERM AMOUNT	6 YEARS	7 YEARS	8 YEARS	9 YEARS	10 YEARS	11 YEARS	12 YEARS
$ 25	.43	.39	.35	.32	.30	.28	.27
50	.86	.77	.69	.64	.59	.56	.53
75	1.29	1.15	1.04	.95	.89	.83	.79
100	1.72	1.53	1.38	1.27	1.18	1.11	1.05
200	3.44	3.05	2.76	2.53	2.35	2.21	2.09
300	5.16	4.57	4.13	3.79	3.53	3.31	3.13
400	6.87	6.09	5.51	5.06	4.70	4.41	4.17
500	8.59	7.61	6.88	6.32	5.88	5.51	5.21
600	10.31	9.13	8.26	7.58	7.05	6.61	6.26
700	12.02	10.66	9.64	8.85	8.22	7.72	7.30
800	13.74	12.18	11.01	10.11	9.40	8.82	8.34
900	15.46	13.70	12.39	11.37	10.57	9.92	9.38
1000	17.17	15.22	13.76	12.64	11.75	11.02	10.42
2000	34.34	30.44	27.52	25.27	23.49	22.04	20.84
3000	51.51	45.65	41.28	37.90	35.23	33.05	31.26
4000	68.68	60.87	55.04	50.54	46.97	44.07	41.68
5000	85.85	76.08	68.80	63.17	58.71	55.08	52.09
6000	103.02	91.30	82.56	75.80	70.45	66.10	62.51
7000	120.19	106.51	96.31	88.44	82.19	77.11	72.93
8000	137.36	121.73	110.07	101.07	93.93	88.13	83.35
9000	154.53	136.94	123.83	113.70	105.67	99.15	93.76
10000	171.70	152.16	137.59	126.34	117.41	110.16	104.18
11000	188.87	167.37	151.35	138.97	129.15	121.18	114.60
12000	206.04	182.59	165.11	151.60	140.89	132.19	125.02
13000	223.21	197.80	178.86	164.24	152.63	143.21	135.43
14000	240.38	213.02	192.62	176.87	164.37	154.22	145.85
15000	257.54	228.23	206.38	189.50	176.11	165.24	156.27
16000	274.71	243.45	220.14	202.14	187.85	176.25	166.69
17000	291.88	258.66	233.90	214.77	199.59	187.27	177.10
18000	309.05	273.88	247.66	227.40	211.33	198.29	187.52
19000	326.22	289.09	261.42	240.04	223.07	209.30	197.94
20000	343.39	304.31	275.17	252.67	234.81	220.32	208.36
21000	360.56	319.52	288.93	265.30	246.55	231.33	218.77
22000	377.73	334.74	302.69	277.94	258.29	242.35	229.19
23000	394.90	349.95	316.45	290.57	270.03	253.36	239.61
24000	412.07	365.17	330.21	303.20	281.77	264.38	250.03
25000	429.24	380.38	343.97	315.84	293.51	275.40	260.44
26000	446.41	395.60	357.72	328.47	305.25	286.41	270.86
27000	463.58	410.81	371.48	341.10	316.99	297.43	281.28
28000	480.75	426.03	385.24	353.74	328.73	308.44	291.70
29000	497.91	441.25	399.00	366.37	340.47	319.46	302.11
30000	515.08	456.46	412.76	379.00	352.21	330.47	312.53
31000	532.25	471.68	426.52	391.64	363.95	341.49	322.95
32000	549.42	486.89	440.28	404.27	375.69	352.50	333.37
33000	566.59	502.11	454.03	416.90	387.43	363.52	343.78
34000	583.76	517.32	467.79	429.54	399.17	374.54	354.20
35000	600.93	532.54	481.55	442.17	410.91	385.55	364.62
40000	686.78	608.61	550.34	505.34	469.61	440.63	416.71
45000	772.62	664.69	619.14	568.50	528.31	495.71	468.80
50000	858.47	760.76	687.93	631.67	587.01	550.79	520.88
55000	944.32	836.84	756.72	694.84	645.71	605.86	572.97
60000	1030.16	912.92	825.51	758.00	704.41	660.94	625.06
65000	1116.01	988.99	894.30	821.17	763.11	716.02	677.15
70000	1201.86	1065.07	963.10	884.33	821.81	771.10	729.23
75000	1287.70	1141.14	1031.89	947.50	880.51	826.18	781.32
80000	1373.55	1217.22	1100.68	1010.67	939.21	881.25	833.41
100000	1716.94	1521.52	1375.85	1263.33	1174.02	1101.57	1041.76

MONTHLY PAYMENT
NECESSARY TO AMORTIZE A LOAN

TERM AMOUNT	13 YEARS	14 YEARS	15 YEARS	16 YEARS	17 YEARS	18 YEARS	19 YEARS
$ 25	.25	.24	.23	.23	.22	.21	.21
50	.50	.48	.46	.45	.43	.42	.41
75	.75	.72	.69	.67	.65	.63	.61
100	1.00	.95	.92	.89	.86	.84	.81
200	1.99	1.90	1.83	1.77	1.71	1.67	1.62
300	2.98	2.85	2.74	2.65	2.57	2.50	2.43
400	3.97	3.80	3.66	3.53	3.42	3.33	3.24
500	4.96	4.75	4.57	4.41	4.28	4.16	4.05
600	5.96	5.70	5.48	5.29	5.13	4.99	4.86
700	6.95	6.65	6.40	6.18	5.98	5.82	5.67
800	7.94	7.60	7.31	7.06	6.84	6.65	6.48
900	8.93	8.55	8.22	7.94	7.69	7.48	7.29
1000	9.92	9.50	9.13	8.82	8.55	8.31	8.10
2000	19.84	18.99	18.26	17.63	17.09	16.61	16.19
3000	29.76	28.48	27.39	26.45	25.63	24.91	24.28
4000	39.67	37.97	36.52	35.26	34.17	33.21	32.37
5000	49.59	47.47	45.65	44.08	42.71	41.51	40.46
6000	59.51	56.96	54.78	52.89	51.25	49.82	48.55
7000	69.42	66.45	63.91	61.71	59.79	58.12	56.64
8000	79.34	75.94	73.03	70.52	68.33	66.42	64.73
9000	89.26	85.43	82.16	79.34	76.88	74.72	72.82
10000	99.17	94.93	91.29	88.15	85.42	83.02	80.91
11000	109.09	104.42	100.42	96.97	93.96	91.32	89.00
12000	119.01	113.91	109.55	105.78	102.50	99.63	97.09
13000	128.92	123.40	118.68	114.59	111.04	107.93	105.18
14000	138.84	132.90	127.81	123.41	119.58	116.23	113.27
15000	148.76	142.39	136.93	132.22	128.12	124.53	121.37
16000	158.67	151.88	146.06	141.04	136.66	132.83	129.46
17000	168.59	161.37	155.19	149.85	145.21	141.13	137.55
18000	178.51	170.86	164.32	158.67	153.75	149.44	145.64
19000	188.42	180.36	173.45	167.48	162.29	157.74	153.73
20000	198.34	189.85	182.58	176.30	170.83	166.04	161.82
21000	208.26	199.34	191.71	185.11	179.37	174.34	169.91
22000	218.17	208.83	200.83	193.93	187.91	182.64	178.00
23000	228.09	218.33	209.96	202.74	196.45	190.94	186.09
24000	238.01	227.82	219.09	211.55	204.99	199.25	194.18
25000	247.92	237.31	228.22	220.37	213.54	207.55	202.27
26000	257.84	246.80	237.35	229.18	222.08	215.85	210.36
27000	267.76	256.29	246.48	238.00	230.62	224.15	218.45
28000	277.67	265.79	255.61	246.81	239.16	232.45	226.54
29000	287.59	275.28	264.74	255.63	247.70	240.75	234.63
30000	297.51	284.77	273.86	264.44	256.24	249.06	242.73
31000	307.42	294.26	282.99	273.26	264.78	257.36	250.82
32000	317.34	303.75	292.12	282.07	273.32	265.66	258.91
33000	327.26	313.25	301.25	290.89	281.87	273.96	267.00
34000	337.17	322.74	310.38	299.70	290.41	282.26	275.09
35000	347.09	332.23	319.51	308.52	298.95	290.57	283.18
40000	396.67	379.69	365.15	352.59	341.65	332.07	323.63
45000	446.26	427.15	410.79	396.66	384.36	373.58	364.09
50000	495.84	474.61	456.44	440.73	427.07	415.09	404.54
55000	545.42	522.07	502.08	484.81	469.77	456.60	444.99
60000	595.01	569.54	547.72	528.88	512.48	498.11	485.45
65000	644.59	617.00	593.37	572.95	555.18	539.62	525.90
70000	694.17	664.46	639.01	617.03	597.89	581.13	566.35
75000	743.76	711.92	684.65	661.10	640.60	622.63	606.81
80000	793.34	759.38	730.30	705.17	683.30	664.14	647.26
100000	991.68	949.22	912.87	881.46	854.13	830.18	809.07

12

TERM AMOUNT	20 YEARS	21 YEARS	22 YEARS	25 YEARS	30 YEARS	35 YEARS	40 YEARS
$ 25	.20	.20	.19	.19	.18	.17	.16
50	.40	.39	.38	.37	.35	.33	.32
75	.60	.59	.57	.55	.52	.50	.48
100	.80	.78	.76	.73	.69	.66	.64
200	1.59	1.55	1.52	1.45	1.37	1.32	1.28
300	2.38	2.33	2.28	2.17	2.05	1.97	1.92
400	3.17	3.10	3.04	2.90	2.73	2.63	2.56
500	3.96	3.87	3.80	3.62	3.42	3.29	3.20
600	4.75	4.65	4.56	4.34	4.10	3.94	3.84
700	5.54	5.42	5.32	5.06	4.78	4.60	4.48
800	6.33	6.19	6.08	5.79	5.46	5.26	5.12
900	7.12	6.97	6.84	6.51	6.14	5.91	5.76
1000	7.91	7.74	7.59	7.23	6.83	6.57	6.40
2000	15.81	15.48	15.18	14.46	13.65	13.13	12.80
3000	23.72	23.22	22.77	21.69	20.47	19.70	19.20
4000	31.62	30.95	30.36	28.92	27.29	26.26	25.59
5000	39.52	38.69	37.95	36.15	34.11	32.83	31.99
6000	47.43	46.43	45.54	43.37	40.94	39.39	38.39
7000	55.33	54.17	53.13	50.60	47.76	45.96	44.78
8000	63.24	61.90	60.72	57.83	54.58	52.52	51.18
9000	71.14	69.64	68.31	65.06	61.40	59.09	57.58
10000	79.04	77.38	75.89	72.29	68.22	65.65	63.97
11000	86.95	85.12	83.48	79.51	75.04	72.22	70.37
12000	94.85	92.85	91.07	86.74	81.87	78.78	76.77
13000	102.75	100.59	98.66	93.97	88.69	85.35	83.16
14000	110.66	108.33	106.25	101.20	95.51	91.91	89.56
15000	118.56	116.07	113.84	108.43	102.33	98.48	95.96
16000	126.47	123.80	121.43	115.65	109.15	105.04	102.35
17000	134.37	131.54	129.02	122.88	115.97	111.60	108.75
18000	142.27	139.28	136.61	130.11	122.80	118.17	115.15
19000	150.18	147.02	144.19	137.34	129.62	124.73	121.54
20000	158.08	154.75	151.78	144.57	136.44	131.30	127.94
21000	165.98	162.49	159.37	151.79	143.26	137.86	134.34
22000	173.89	170.23	166.96	159.02	150.08	144.43	140.73
23000	181.79	177.97	174.55	166.25	156.91	150.99	147.13
24000	189.70	185.70	182.14	173.48	163.73	157.56	153.53
25000	197.60	193.44	189.73	180.71	170.55	164.12	159.92
26000	205.50	201.18	197.32	187.93	177.37	170.69	166.32
27000	213.41	208.92	204.91	195.16	184.19	177.25	172.72
28000	221.31	216.65	212.50	202.39	191.01	183.82	179.11
29000	229.21	224.39	220.08	209.62	197.84	190.38	185.51
30000	237.12	232.13	227.67	216.85	204.66	196.95	191.91
31000	245.02	239.87	235.26	224.08	211.48	203.51	198.30
32000	252.93	247.60	242.85	231.30	218.30	210.07	204.70
33000	260.83	255.34	250.44	238.53	225.12	216.64	211.10
34000	268.73	263.08	258.03	245.76	231.94	223.20	217.49
35000	276.64	270.82	265.62	252.99	238.77	229.77	223.89
40000	316.16	309.50	303.56	289.13	272.88	262.59	255.87
45000	355.67	348.19	341.51	325.27	306.98	295.42	287.86
50000	395.19	386.88	379.45	361.41	341.09	328.24	319.84
55000	434.71	425.57	417.40	397.55	375.20	361.06	351.82
60000	474.23	464.25	455.34	433.69	409.31	393.89	383.81
65000	513.75	502.94	493.29	469.83	443.42	426.71	415.79
70000	553.27	541.63	531.23	505.97	477.53	459.53	447.78
75000	592.79	580.32	569.18	542.11	511.64	492.36	479.76
80000	632.31	619.00	607.12	578.25	545.75	525.18	511.74
100000	790.38	773.75	758.90	722.81	682.18	656.47	639.68

7 1/2%

TERM AMOUNT	1 YEAR	1 1/2 YEARS	2 YEARS	2 1/2 YEARS	3 YEARS	4 YEARS	5 YEARS
$ 25	2.17	1.48	1.13	.92	.78	.61	.51
50	4.34	2.95	2.25	1.84	1.56	1.21	1.01
75	6.51	4.42	3.38	2.75	2.34	1.82	1.51
100	8.68	5.90	4.50	3.67	3.12	2.42	2.01
200	17.36	11.79	9.00	7.34	6.23	4.84	4.01
300	26.03	17.68	13.50	11.00	9.34	7.26	6.02
400	34.71	23.57	18.00	14.67	12.45	9.68	8.02
500	43.38	29.46	22.50	18.33	15.56	12.09	10.02
600	52.06	35.35	27.00	22.00	18.67	14.51	12.03
700	60.74	41.24	31.50	25.67	21.78	16.93	14.03
800	69.41	47.13	36.00	29.33	24.89	19.35	16.04
900	78.09	53.03	40.50	33.00	28.00	21.77	18.04
1000	86.76	58.92	45.00	36.66	31.11	24.18	20.04
2000	173.52	117.83	90.00	73.32	62.22	48.36	40.08
3000	260.28	176.74	135.00	109.98	93.32	72.54	60.12
4000	347.03	235.65	180.00	146.64	124.43	96.72	80.16
5000	433.79	294.57	225.00	183.30	155.54	120.90	100.19
6000	520.55	353.48	270.00	219.96	186.64	145.08	120.23
7000	607.31	412.39	315.00	256.62	217.75	169.26	140.27
8000	694.06	471.30	360.00	293.28	248.85	193.44	160.31
9000	780.82	530.22	405.00	329.94	279.96	217.62	180.35
10000	867.58	589.13	450.00	366.60	311.07	241.79	200.38
11000	954.34	648.04	495.00	403.26	342.17	265.97	220.42
12000	1041.09	706.95	540.00	439.92	373.28	290.15	240.46
13000	1127.85	765.87	585.00	476.58	404.39	314.33	260.50
14000	1214.61	824.78	630.00	513.24	435.49	338.51	280.54
15000	1301.37	883.69	675.00	549.90	466.60	362.69	300.57
16000	1388.12	942.60	720.00	586.56	497.70	386.87	320.61
17000	1474.88	1001.52	765.00	623.22	528.81	411.05	340.65
18000	1561.64	1060.43	810.00	659.88	559.92	435.23	360.69
19000	1648.40	1119.34	855.00	696.54	591.02	459.40	380.73
20000	1735.15	1178.25	900.00	733.20	622.13	483.58	400.76
21000	1821.91	1237.17	945.00	769.86	653.24	507.76	420.80
22000	1908.67	1296.08	990.00	806.52	684.34	531.94	440.84
23000	1995.43	1354.99	1035.00	843.18	715.45	556.12	460.88
24000	2082.18	1413.90	1080.00	879.84	746.55	580.30	480.92
25000	2168.94	1472.81	1124.99	916.50	777.66	604.48	500.95
26000	2255.70	1531.73	1169.99	953.16	808.77	628.66	520.99
27000	2342.46	1590.64	1214.99	989.82	839.87	652.84	541.03
28000	2429.21	1649.55	1259.99	1026.48	870.98	677.01	561.07
29000	2515.97	1708.46	1304.99	1063.14	902.09	701.19	581.11
30000	2602.73	1767.38	1349.99	1099.80	933.19	725.37	601.14
31000	2689.48	1826.29	1394.99	1136.46	964.30	749.55	621.18
32000	2776.24	1885.20	1439.99	1173.12	995.41	773.73	641.22
33000	2863.00	1944.11	1484.99	1209.77	1026.51	797.91	661.26
34000	2949.76	2003.03	1529.99	1246.43	1057.62	822.09	681.30
35000	3036.51	2061.94	1574.99	1283.09	1088.72	846.27	701.33
40000	3470.30	2356.50	1799.99	1466.39	1244.25	967.16	801.52
45000	3904.09	2651.06	2024.99	1649.69	1399.78	1088.06	901.71
50000	4337.88	2945.62	2249.98	1832.99	1555.32	1208.95	1001.90
55000	4771.66	3240.19	2474.98	2016.29	1710.85	1329.84	1102.09
60000	5205.45	3534.75	2699.98	2199.59	1866.38	1450.74	1202.28
65000	5639.24	3829.31	2924.98	2382.88	2021.91	1571.63	1302.47
70000	6073.02	4123.87	3149.98	2566.18	2177.44	1692.53	1402.66
75000	6506.81	4418.43	3374.97	2749.48	2332.97	1813.42	1502.85
80000	6940.60	4713.00	3599.97	2932.78	2488.50	1934.32	1603.04
100000	8675.75	5891.24	4499.96	3665.97	3110.63	2417.90	2003.80

14

TERM AMOUNT	6 YEARS	7 YEARS	8 YEARS	9 YEARS	10 YEARS	11 YEARS	12 YEARS
$ 25	.44	.39	.35	.32	.30	.28	.27
50	.87	.77	.70	.64	.60	.56	.53
75	1.30	1.16	1.05	.96	.90	.84	.80
100	1.73	1.54	1.39	1.28	1.19	1.12	1.06
200	3.46	3.07	2.78	2.56	2.38	2.23	2.12
300	5.19	4.61	4.17	3.83	3.57	3.35	3.17
400	6.92	6.14	5.56	5.11	4.75	4.46	4.23
500	8.65	7.67	6.95	6.39	5.94	5.58	5.28
600	10.38	9.21	8.34	7.66	7.13	6.69	6.34
700	12.11	10.74	9.72	8.94	8.31	7.81	7.39
800	13.84	12.28	11.11	10.21	9.50	8.92	8.45
900	15.57	13.81	12.50	11.49	10.69	10.04	9.50
1000	17.30	15.34	13.89	12.77	11.88	11.15	10.56
2000	34.59	30.68	27.77	25.53	23.75	22.30	21.11
3000	51.88	46.02	41.66	38.29	35.62	33.45	31.66
4000	69.17	61.36	55.54	51.05	47.49	44.60	42.21
5000	86.46	76.70	69.42	63.81	59.36	55.75	52.77
6000	103.75	92.03	83.31	76.57	71.23	66.89	63.32
7000	121.04	107.37	97.19	89.33	83.10	78.04	73.87
8000	138.33	122.71	111.08	102.09	94.97	89.19	84.42
9000	155.62	138.05	124.96	114.85	106.84	100.34	94.98
10000	172.91	153.39	138.84	127.62	118.71	111.49	105.53
11000	190.20	168.73	152.73	140.38	130.58	122.63	116.08
12000	207.49	184.06	166.61	153.14	142.45	133.78	126.63
13000	224.78	199.40	180.50	165.90	154.32	144.93	137.18
14000	242.07	214.74	194.38	178.66	166.19	156.08	147.74
15000	259.36	230.08	208.26	191.42	178.06	167.23	158.29
16000	276.65	245.42	222.15	204.18	189.93	178.37	168.84
17000	293.94	260.76	236.03	216.94	201.80	189.52	179.39
18000	311.23	276.09	249.91	229.70	213.67	200.67	189.95
19000	328.52	291.43	263.80	242.46	225.54	211.82	200.50
20000	345.81	306.77	277.68	255.23	237.41	222.97	211.05
21000	363.10	322.11	291.57	267.99	249.28	234.11	221.60
22000	380.39	337.45	305.45	280.75	261.15	245.26	232.15
23000	397.68	352.79	319.33	293.51	273.02	256.41	242.71
24000	414.97	368.12	333.22	306.27	284.89	267.56	253.26
25000	432.26	383.46	347.10	319.03	296.76	278.71	263.81
26000	449.55	398.80	360.99	331.79	308.63	289.85	274.36
27000	466.84	414.14	374.87	344.55	320.50	301.00	284.92
28000	484.13	429.48	388.75	357.31	332.37	312.15	295.47
29000	501.42	444.81	402.64	370.07	344.24	323.30	306.02
30000	518.71	460.15	416.52	382.84	356.11	334.45	316.57
31000	536.00	475.49	430.40	395.60	367.98	345.59	327.13
32000	553.29	490.83	444.29	408.36	379.85	356.74	337.68
33000	570.58	506.17	458.17	421.12	391.72	367.89	348.23
34000	587.87	521.51	472.06	433.88	403.59	379.04	358.78
35000	605.16	536.84	485.94	446.64	415.46	390.19	369.33
40000	691.61	613.54	555.36	510.45	474.81	445.93	422.10
45000	778.06	690.23	624.78	574.25	534.16	501.67	474.86
50000	864.51	766.92	694.20	638.06	593.51	557.41	527.62
55000	950.96	843.61	763.62	701.86	652.86	613.15	580.38
60000	1037.41	920.30	833.04	765.67	712.22	668.89	633.14
65000	1123.86	996.99	902.46	829.47	771.57	724.63	685.90
70000	1210.31	1073.68	971.88	893.28	830.92	780.37	738.66
75000	1296.76	1150.38	1041.30	957.08	890.27	836.11	791.42
80000	1383.21	1227.07	1110.71	1020.89	949.62	891.85	844.19
100000	1729.02	1533.83	1388.39	1276.11	1187.02	1114.81	1055.23

MONTHLY PAYMENT
NECESSARY TO AMORTIZE A LOAN

TERM AMOUNT	13 YEARS	14 YEARS	15 YEARS	16 YEARS	17 YEARS	18 YEARS	19 YEARS
$ 25	.26	.25	.24	.23	.22	.22	.21
50	.51	.49	.47	.45	.44	.43	.42
75	.76	.73	.70	.68	.66	.64	.62
100	1.01	.97	.93	.90	.87	.85	.83
200	2.02	1.93	1.86	1.80	1.74	1.69	1.65
300	3.02	2.89	2.79	2.69	2.61	2.54	2.48
400	4.03	3.86	3.71	3.59	3.48	3.38	3.30
500	5.03	4.82	4.64	4.48	4.35	4.23	4.13
600	6.04	5.78	5.57	5.38	5.22	5.07	4.95
700	7.04	6.75	6.49	6.28	6.09	5.92	5.77
800	8.05	7.71	7.42	7.17	6.95	6.76	6.60
900	9.05	8.67	8.35	8.07	7.82	7.61	7.42
1000	10.06	9.64	9.28	8.96	8.69	8.45	8.25
2000	20.11	19.27	18.55	17.92	17.38	16.90	16.49
3000	30.17	28.90	27.82	26.88	26.07	25.35	24.73
4000	40.22	38.53	37.09	35.84	34.75	33.80	32.97
5000	50.27	48.16	46.36	44.80	43.44	42.25	41.21
6000	60.33	57.79	55.63	53.75	52.13	50.70	49.45
7000	70.38	67.43	64.90	62.71	60.81	59.15	57.69
8000	80.43	77.06	74.17	71.67	69.50	67.60	65.93
9000	90.49	86.69	83.44	80.63	78.19	76.05	74.17
10000	100.54	96.32	92.71	89.59	86.88	84.50	82.41
11000	110.60	105.95	101.98	98.55	95.56	92.95	90.65
12000	120.65	115.58	111.25	107.50	104.25	101.40	98.89
13000	130.70	125.21	120.52	116.46	112.94	109.85	107.14
14000	140.76	134.85	129.79	125.42	121.62	118.30	115.38
15000	150.81	144.48	139.06	134.38	130.31	126.75	123.62
16000	160.86	154.11	148.33	143.34	139.00	135.20	131.86
17000	170.92	163.74	157.60	152.30	147.69	143.65	140.10
18000	180.97	173.37	166.87	161.25	156.37	152.10	148.34
19000	191.03	183.00	176.14	170.21	165.06	160.55	156.58
20000	201.08	192.63	185.41	179.17	173.75	169.00	164.82
21000	211.13	202.27	194.68	188.13	182.43	177.45	173.06
22000	221.19	211.90	203.95	197.09	191.12	185.90	181.30
23000	231.24	221.53	213.22	206.05	199.81	194.35	189.54
24000	241.29	231.16	222.49	215.00	208.50	202.80	197.78
25000	251.35	240.79	231.76	223.96	217.18	211.25	206.02
26000	261.40	250.42	241.03	232.92	225.87	219.70	214.27
27000	271.46	260.05	250.30	241.88	234.56	228.15	222.51
28000	281.51	269.69	259.57	250.84	243.24	236.60	230.75
29000	291.56	279.32	268.84	259.80	251.93	245.05	238.99
30000	301.62	288.95	278.11	268.75	260.62	253.50	247.23
31000	311.67	298.58	287.38	277.71	269.30	261.95	255.47
32000	321.72	308.21	296.65	286.67	277.99	270.40	263.71
33000	331.78	317.84	305.92	295.63	286.68	278.85	271.95
34000	341.83	327.47	315.19	304.59	295.37	287.30	280.19
35000	351.88	337.11	324.45	313.54	304.05	295.75	288.43
40000	402.15	385.26	370.81	358.34	347.49	337.99	329.64
45000	452.42	433.42	417.16	403.13	390.92	380.24	370.84
50000	502.69	481.58	463.51	447.92	434.36	422.49	412.04
55000	552.96	529.73	509.86	492.71	477.80	464.74	453.25
60000	603.23	577.89	556.21	537.50	521.23	506.99	494.45
65000	653.50	626.05	602.56	582.29	564.67	549.24	535.66
70000	703.76	674.21	648.91	627.08	608.10	591.49	576.86
75000	754.03	722.36	695.26	671.88	651.54	633.73	618.06
80000	804.30	770.52	741.61	716.67	694.97	675.98	659.27
100000	1005.38	963.15	927.02	895.83	868.71	844.98	824.08

16

TERM AMOUNT	20 YEARS	21 YEARS	22 YEARS	25 YEARS	30 YEARS	35 YEARS	40 YEARS
$ 25	.21	.20	.20	.19	.18	.17	.17
50	.41	.40	.39	.37	.35	.34	.33
75	.61	.60	.59	.56	.53	.51	.50
100	.81	.79	.78	.74	.70	.68	.66
200	1.62	1.58	1.55	1.48	1.40	1.35	1.32
300	2.42	2.37	2.33	2.22	2.10	2.03	1.98
400	3.23	3.16	3.10	2.96	2.80	2.70	2.64
500	4.03	3.95	3.88	3.70	3.50	3.38	3.30
600	4.84	4.74	4.65	4.44	4.20	4.05	3.95
700	5.64	5.53	5.43	5.18	4.90	4.72	4.61
800	6.45	6.32	6.20	5.92	5.60	5.40	5.27
900	7.26	7.11	6.98	6.66	6.30	6.07	5.93
1000	8.06	7.90	7.75	7.39	7.00	6.75	6.59
2000	16.12	15.79	15.50	14.78	13.99	13.49	13.17
3000	24.17	23.68	23.24	22.17	20.98	20.23	19.75
4000	32.23	31.57	30.99	29.56	27.97	26.97	26.33
5000	40.28	39.46	38.73	36.95	34.97	33.72	32.91
6000	48.34	47.35	46.48	44.34	41.96	40.46	39.49
7000	56.40	55.25	54.22	51.73	48.95	47.20	46.07
8000	64.45	63.14	61.97	59.12	55.94	53.94	52.65
9000	72.51	71.03	69.71	66.51	62.93	60.69	59.23
10000	80.56	78.92	77.46	73.90	69.93	67.43	65.81
11000	88.62	86.81	85.20	81.29	76.92	74.17	72.39
12000	96.68	94.70	92.95	88.68	83.91	80.91	78.97
13000	104.73	102.60	100.69	96.07	90.90	87.66	85.55
14000	112.79	110.49	108.44	103.46	97.90	94.40	92.13
15000	120.84	118.38	116.18	110.85	104.89	101.14	98.72
16000	128.90	126.27	123.93	118.24	111.88	107.88	105.30
17000	136.96	134.16	131.67	125.63	118.87	114.63	111.88
18000	145.01	142.05	139.42	133.02	125.86	121.37	118.46
19000	153.07	149.95	147.16	140.41	132.86	128.11	125.04
20000	161.12	157.84	154.91	147.80	139.85	134.85	131.62
21000	169.18	165.73	162.65	155.19	146.84	141.60	138.20
22000	177.24	173.62	170.40	162.58	153.83	148.34	144.78
23000	185.29	181.51	178.14	169.97	160.82	155.08	151.36
24000	193.35	189.40	185.89	177.36	167.82	161.82	157.94
25000	201.40	197.30	193.63	184.75	174.81	168.57	164.52
26000	209.46	205.19	201.38	192.14	181.80	175.31	171.10
27000	217.52	213.08	209.12	199.53	188.79	182.05	177.68
28000	225.57	220.97	216.87	206.92	195.79	188.79	184.26
29000	233.63	228.86	224.61	214.31	202.78	195.54	190.85
30000	241.68	236.75	232.36	221.70	209.77	202.28	197.43
31000	249.74	244.65	240.10	229.09	216.76	209.02	204.01
32000	257.79	252.54	247.85	236.48	223.75	215.76	210.59
33000	265.85	260.43	255.59	243.87	230.75	222.51	217.17
34000	273.91	268.32	263.34	251.26	237.74	229.25	223.75
35000	281.96	276.21	271.08	258.65	244.73	235.99	230.33
40000	322.24	315.67	309.81	295.60	279.69	269.70	263.23
45000	362.52	355.13	348.53	332.55	314.65	303.41	296.14
50000	402.80	394.59	387.26	369.50	349.61	337.13	329.04
55000	443.08	434.05	425.99	406.45	384.57	370.84	361.94
60000	483.36	473.50	464.71	443.40	419.53	404.55	394.85
65000	523.64	512.96	503.44	480.35	454.49	438.26	427.75
70000	563.92	552.42	542.16	517.30	489.46	471.97	460.65
75000	604.20	591.88	580.89	554.25	524.42	505.69	493.56
80000	644.48	631.34	619.61	591.20	559.38	539.40	526.46
100000	805.60	789.17	774.52	739.00	699.22	674.25	658.08

17

MONTHLY PAYMENT
NECESSARY TO AMORTIZE A LOAN

TERM AMOUNT	1 YEAR	1½ YEARS	2 YEARS	2½ YEARS	3 YEARS	4 YEARS	5 YEARS
$ 25	2.18	1.48	1.13	.92	.79	.61	.51
50	4.35	2.96	2.26	1.84	1.57	1.22	1.01
75	6.52	4.43	3.39	2.76	2.35	1.83	1.52
100	8.69	5.91	4.52	3.68	3.13	2.43	2.02
200	17.38	11.81	9.03	7.36	6.25	4.86	4.04
300	26.07	17.71	13.54	11.04	9.37	7.29	6.05
400	34.75	23.62	18.05	14.71	12.49	9.72	8.07
500	43.44	29.52	22.56	18.39	15.62	12.15	10.08
600	52.13	35.42	27.07	22.07	18.74	14.58	12.10
700	60.82	41.32	31.58	25.75	21.86	17.01	14.11
800	69.50	47.23	36.10	29.42	24.98	19.44	16.13
900	78.19	53.13	40.61	33.10	28.10	21.87	18.15
1000	86.88	59.03	45.12	36.78	31.23	24.30	20.16
2000	173.75	118.06	90.23	73.55	62.45	48.60	40.32
3000	260.62	177.08	135.35	110.33	93.67	72.89	60.48
4000	347.50	236.11	180.46	147.10	124.89	97.19	80.63
5000	434.37	295.14	225.57	183.87	156.11	121.48	100.79
6000	521.24	354.16	270.69	220.65	187.33	145.78	120.95
7000	608.12	413.19	315.80	257.42	218.55	170.08	141.10
8000	694.99	472.22	360.91	294.20	249.77	194.37	161.26
9000	781.86	531.24	406.03	330.97	281.00	218.67	181.42
10000	868.73	590.27	451.14	367.74	312.22	242.96	201.57
11000	955.61	649.29	496.25	404.52	343.44	267.26	221.73
12000	1042.48	708.32	541.37	441.29	374.66	291.55	241.89
13000	1129.35	767.35	586.48	478.07	405.88	315.85	262.05
14000	1216.23	826.37	631.59	514.84	437.10	340.15	282.20
15000	1303.10	885.40	676.71	551.61	468.32	364.44	302.36
16000	1389.97	944.43	721.82	588.39	499.54	388.74	322.52
17000	1476.84	1003.45	766.93	625.16	530.76	413.03	342.67
18000	1563.72	1062.48	812.05	661.94	561.99	437.33	362.83
19000	1650.59	1121.50	857.16	698.71	593.21	461.62	382.99
20000	1737.46	1180.53	902.27	735.48	624.43	485.92	403.14
21000	1824.34	1239.56	947.39	772.26	655.65	510.22	423.30
22000	1911.21	1298.58	992.50	809.03	686.87	534.51	443.46
23000	1998.08	1357.61	1037.61	845.80	718.09	558.81	463.62
24000	2084.95	1416.64	1082.73	882.58	749.31	583.10	483.77
25000	2171.83	1475.66	1127.84	919.35	780.53	607.40	503.93
26000	2258.70	1534.69	1172.95	956.13	811.76	631.69	524.09
27000	2345.57	1593.71	1218.07	992.90	842.98	655.99	544.24
28000	2432.45	1652.74	1263.18	1029.67	874.20	680.29	564.40
29000	2519.32	1711.77	1308.29	1066.45	905.42	704.58	584.56
30000	2606.19	1770.79	1353.41	1103.22	936.64	728.88	604.71
31000	2693.06	1829.82	1398.52	1140.00	967.86	753.17	624.87
32000	2779.94	1888.85	1443.63	1176.77	999.08	777.47	645.03
33000	2866.81	1947.87	1488.75	1213.54	1030.30	801.76	665.18
34000	2953.68	2006.90	1533.86	1250.32	1061.52	826.06	685.34
35000	3040.56	2065.92	1578.97	1287.09	1092.75	850.36	705.50
40000	3474.92	2361.06	1804.54	1470.96	1248.85	971.83	806.28
45000	3909.28	2656.19	2030.11	1654.83	1404.96	1093.31	907.07
50000	4343.65	2951.32	2255.69	1838.70	1561.06	1214.79	1007.85
55000	4778.01	3246.45	2481.24	2022.57	1717.17	1336.27	1108.64
60000	5212.38	3541.58	2706.82	2206.44	1873.27	1457.75	1209.42
65000	5646.74	3836.71	2932.37	2390.31	2029.37	1579.23	1310.21
70000	6081.11	4131.84	3157.94	2574.18	2185.49	1700.71	1410.99
75000	6515.47	4426.98	3383.51	2758.05	2341.59	1822.19	1511.78
80000	6949.84	4722.11	3609.07	2941.92	2497.70	1943.66	1612.56
100000	8687.29	5902.63	4511.34	3677.39	3122.12	2429.58	2015.70

TERM AMOUNT	6 YEARS	7 YEARS	8 YEARS	9 YEARS	10 YEARS	11 YEARS	12 YEARS
$ 25	.44	.39	.36	.33	.31	.29	.27
50	.88	.78	.71	.65	.61	.57	.54
75	1.31	1.16	1.06	.97	.91	.85	.81
100	1.75	1.55	1.41	1.29	1.21	1.13	1.07
200	3.49	3.10	2.81	2.58	2.41	2.26	2.14
300	5.23	4.64	4.21	3.87	3.61	3.39	3.21
400	6.97	6.19	5.61	5.16	4.81	4.52	4.28
500	8.71	7.74	7.01	6.45	6.01	5.65	5.35
600	10.45	9.28	8.41	7.74	7.21	6.77	6.42
700	12.19	10.83	9.81	9.03	8.41	7.90	7.49
800	13.93 ·	12.37	11.21	1C.32	9.61	9.03	8.56
900	15.68	13.92	12.61	11.61	10.81	10.16	9.62
1000	17.42	15.47	14.01	12.89	12.01	11.29	10.69
2000	34.83	30.93	28.02	25.78	24.01	22.57	21.38
3000	52.24	46.39	42.03	38.67	36.01	33.85	32.07
4000	69.65	61.85	56.04	51.56	48.01	45.13	42.76
5000	87.06	77.31	70.05	64.45	60.01	56.41	53.44
6000	104.47	92.78	84.06	77.34	72.01	67.69	64.13
7000	121.88	108.24	98.07	9C.23	84.01	78.97	74.82
8000	139.30	123.70	112.08	103.12	96.01	90.26	85.51
9000	156.71	139.16	126.09	116.01	108.01	101.54	96.20
10000	174.12	154.62	140.10	128.90	120.02	112.82	106.88
11000	191.53	170.09	154.11	141.79	132.02	124.10	117.57
12000	208.94	185.55	168.12	154.68	144.02	135.38	128.26
13000	226.35	201.01	182.13	167.57	156.02	146.66	138.95
14000	243.76	216.47	196.14	180.46	168.02	157.94	149.64
15000	261.18	231.93	210.15	193.35	180.02	169.22	160.32
16000	278.59	247.40	224.16	206.24	192.02	180.51	171.01
17000	296.00	262.86	238.17	219.13	204.02	191.79	181.70
18000	313.41	278.32	252.18	232.C2	216.02	203.07	192.39
19000	330.82	293.78	266.19	244.91	228.03	214.35	203.08
20000	348.23	309.24	280.20	257.79	240.03	225.63	213.76
21000	365.64	324.71	294.21	27C.68	252.03	236.91	224.45
22000	383.06	340.17	308.22	283.57	264.03	248.19	235.14
23000	400.47	355.63	322.23	296.46	276.03	259.47	245.83
24000	417.88	371.09	336.24	309.35	288.03	270.76	256.52
25000	435.29	386.55	350.25	322.24	300.03	282.04	267.20
26000	452.70	402.02	364.26	335.13	312.03	293.32	277.89
27000	470.11	417.48	378.27	348.C2	324.03	304.60	288.58
28000	487.52	432.94	392.28	360.91	336.03	315.88	299.27
29000	504.94	448.40	406.29	373.80	348.04	327.16	309.95
30000	522.35	463.86	420.30	386.69	360.04	338.44	320.64
31000	539.76	479.33	434.31	399.58	372.04	349.72	331.33
32000	557.17	494.79	448.32	412.47	384.04	361.01	342.02
33000	574.58	510.25	462.33	425.36	396.04	372.29	352.71
34000	591.99	525.71	476.34	438.25	408.04	383.57	363.39
35000	609.40	541.17	490.35	451.14	420.04	394.85	374.08
40000	696.46	618.48	560.40	515.58	480.05	451.26	427.52
45000	783.52	695.79	630.45	580.03	540.05	507.66	480.96
50000	870.58	773.10	700.50	644.48	600.06	564.07	534.40
55000	957.63	850.41	770.55	708.93	660.06	620.48	587.84
60000	1044.69	927.72	840.60	773.37	720.07	676.88	641.28
65000	1131.75	1005.03	910.65	837.82	780.07	733.29	694.72
70000	1218.80	1082.34	980.70	902.27	840.08	789.70	748.16
75000	1305.86	1159.65	1050.75	966.72	900.08	846.10	801.60
80000	1392.92	1236.96	1120.80	1031.16	960.09	902.51	855.04
100000	1741.15	1546.20	1401.00	1288.95	1200.11	1128.13	1068.80

MONTHLY PAYMENT
NECESSARY TO AMORTIZE A LOAN

TERM AMOUNT	13 YEARS	14 YEARS	15 YEARS	16 YEARS	17 YEARS	18 YEARS	19 YEARS
$ 25	.26	.25	.24	.23	.23	.22	.21
50	.51	.49	.48	.46	.45	.43	.42
75	.77	.74	.71	.69	.67	.65	.63
100	1.02	.98	.95	.92	.89	.86	.84
200	2.04	1.96	1.89	1.83	1.77	1.72	1.68
300	3.06	2.94	2.83	2.74	2.66	2.58	2.52
400	4.08	3.91	3.77	3.65	3.54	3.44	3.36
500	5.10	4.89	4.71	4.56	4.42	4.30	4.20
600	6.12	5.87	5.65	5.47	5.31	5.16	5.04
700	7.14	6.85	6.59	6.38	6.19	6.02	5.88
800	8.16	7.82	7.54	7.29	7.07	6.88	6.72
900	9.18	8.80	8.48	8.20	7.96	7.74	7.56
1000	10.20	9.78	9.42	9.11	8.84	8.60	8.40
2000	20.39	19.55	18.83	18.21	17.67	17.20	16.79
3000	30.58	29.32	28.24	27.31	26.51	25.80	25.18
4000	40.77	39.09	37.66	36.42	35.34	34.40	33.57
5000	50.96	48.86	47.07	45.52	44.18	43.00	41.97
6000	61.16	58.64	56.48	54.62	53.01	51.60	50.36
7000	71.35	68.41	65.89	63.73	61.84	60.20	58.75
8000	81.54	78.18	75.31	72.83	70.68	68.80	67.14
9000	91.73	87.95	84.72	81.93	79.51	77.40	75.54
10000	101.92	97.72	94.13	91.04	88.35	86.00	83.93
11000	112.11	107.49	103.55	100.14	98.18	94.59	92.32
12000	122.31	117.27	112.96	109.24	106.02	103.19	100.71
13000	132.50	127.04	122.37	118.35	114.85	111.79	109.10
14000	142.69	136.81	131.78	127.45	123.68	120.39	117.50
15000	152.88	146.58	141.20	136.55	132.52	128.99	125.89
16000	163.07	156.35	150.61	145.66	141.35	137.59	134.28
17000	173.26	166.13	160.02	154.76	150.19	146.19	142.67
18000	183.46	175.90	169.43	163.86	159.02	154.79	151.07
19000	193.65	185.67	178.85	172.97	167.86	163.39	159.46
20000	203.84	195.44	188.26	182.07	176.69	171.99	167.85
21000	214.03	205.21	197.67	191.17	185.52	180.59	176.24
22000	224.22	214.98	207.09	200.27	194.36	189.18	184.63
23000	234.41	224.76	216.50	209.38	203.19	197.78	193.03
24000	244.61	234.53	225.91	218.48	212.03	206.38	201.42
25000	254.80	244.30	235.32	227.58	220.86	214.98	209.81
26000	264.99	254.07	244.74	236.69	229.69	223.58	218.20
27000	275.18	263.84	254.15	245.79	238.53	232.18	226.60
28000	285.37	273.61	263.56	254.89	247.36	240.78	234.99
29000	295.56	283.39	272.97	264.00	256.20	249.38	243.38
30000	305.76	293.16	282.39	273.10	265.03	257.98	251.77
31000	315.95	302.93	291.80	282.20	273.87	266.57	260.16
32000	326.14	312.70	301.21	291.31	282.70	275.17	268.56
33000	336.33	322.47	310.63	300.41	291.53	283.77	276.95
34000	346.52	332.25	320.04	309.51	300.37	292.37	285.34
35000	356.72	342.02	329.45	318.62	309.20	300.97	293.73
40000	407.67	390.88	376.52	364.13	353.37	343.97	335.69
45000	458.63	439.73	423.58	409.65	397.54	386.96	377.66
50000	509.59	488.59	470.64	455.15	441.72	429.96	419.62
55000	560.55	537.45	517.71	500.68	485.89	472.95	461.58
60000	611.51	586.31	564.78	546.20	530.06	515.95	503.54
65000	662.47	635.17	611.83	591.71	574.23	558.94	545.50
70000	713.43	684.03	658.90	637.23	618.40	601.94	587.46
75000	764.38	732.89	705.96	682.74	662.57	644.93	629.42
80000	815.34	781.75	753.03	728.26	706.74	687.93	671.38
100000	1019.18	977.18	941.28	910.32	883.43	859.91	839.23

TERM AMOUNT	20 YEARS	21 YEARS	22 YEARS	25 YEARS	30 YEARS	35 YEARS	40 YEARS
$ 25	.21	.21	.20	.19	.18	.18	.17
50	.42	.41	.40	.38	.36	.35	.34
75	.62	.61	.60	.57	.54	.52	.51
100	.83	.81	.80	.76	.72	.70	.68
200	1.65	1.61	1.59	1.52	1.44	1.39	1.36
300	2.47	2.42	2.38	2.27	2.15	2.08	2.03
400	3.29	3.22	3.17	3.03	2.87	2.77	2.71
500	4.11	4.03	3.96	3.78	3.59	3.47	3.39
600	4.93	4.83	4.75	4.54	4.30	4.16	4.06
700	5.75	5.64	5.54	5.29	5.02	4.85	4.74
800	6.57	6.44	6.33	6.05	5.74	5.54	5.42
900	7.39	7.25	7.12	6.80	6.45	6.23	6.09
1000	8.21	8.05	7.91	7.56	7.17	6.93	6.77
2000	16.42	16.10	15.81	15.11	14.33	13.85	13.54
3000	24.63	24.15	23.71	22.66	21.50	20.77	20.30
4000	32.84	32.19	31.62	30.22	28.66	27.69	27.07
5000	41.05	40.24	39.52	37.77	35.83	34.61	33.84
6000	49.26	48.29	47.42	45.32	42.99	41.54	40.60
7000	57.47	56.34	55.32	52.88	50.15	48.46	47.37
8000	65.68	64.38	63.23	60.43	57.32	55.38	54.13
9000	73.89	72.43	71.13	67.98	64.48	62.30	60.90
10000	82.10	80.48	79.03	75.54	71.65	69.22	67.67
11000	90.31	88.52	86.94	83.09	78.81	76.14	74.43
12000	98.52	96.57	94.84	90.64	85.97	83.07	81.20
13000	106.73	104.62	102.74	98.20	93.14	89.99	87.97
14000	114.94	112.67	110.64	105.75	100.30	96.91	94.73
15000	123.15	120.71	118.55	113.30	107.47	103.83	101.50
16000	131.36	128.76	126.45	120.86	114.63	110.76	108.26
17000	139.57	136.81	134.35	128.41	121.80	117.67	115.03
18000	147.78	144.86	142.25	135.96	128.96	124.60	121.80
19000	155.99	152.90	150.16	143.52	136.12	131.52	128.56
20000	164.19	160.95	158.06	151.07	143.29	138.44	135.33
21000	172.40	169.00	165.96	158.62	150.45	145.36	142.10
22000	180.61	177.04	173.87	166.18	157.62	152.28	148.86
23000	188.82	185.09	181.77	173.73	164.78	159.21	155.63
24000	197.03	193.14	189.67	181.28	171.94	166.13	162.39
25000	205.24	201.19	197.57	188.84	179.11	173.05	169.16
26000	213.45	209.23	205.48	196.39	186.27	179.97	175.93
27000	221.66	217.28	213.38	203.94	193.44	186.89	182.69
28000	229.87	225.33	221.28	211.50	200.60	193.81	189.46
29000	238.08	233.38	229.18	219.05	207.76	200.74	196.22
30000	246.29	241.42	237.09	226.60	214.93	207.66	202.99
31000	254.50	249.47	244.99	234.16	222.09	214.58	209.76
32000	262.71	257.52	252.89	241.71	229.26	221.50	216.52
33000	270.92	265.56	260.80	249.26	236.42	228.42	223.29
34000	279.13	273.61	268.70	256.82	243.59	235.34	230.06
35000	287.34	281.66	276.60	264.37	250.75	242.27	236.82
40000	328.38	321.90	316.11	302.14	286.57	276.88	270.65
45000	369.43	362.13	355.63	339.90	322.39	311.48	304.48
50000	410.48	402.37	395.14	377.67	358.21	346.09	338.31
55000	451.53	442.60	434.66	415.44	394.03	380.70	372.15
60000	492.57	482.84	474.17	453.20	429.85	415.31	405.98
65000	533.62	523.08	513.68	490.97	465.67	449.92	439.81
70000	574.67	563.31	553.20	528.74	501.49	484.53	473.64
75000	615.72	603.55	592.71	566.50	537.31	519.14	507.47
80000	656.76	643.79	632.22	604.27	573.13	553.75	541.30
100000	820.95	804.73	790.28	755.33	716.42	692.18	676.62

8%

MONTHLY PAYMENT
NECESSARY TO AMORTIZE A LOAN

TERM AMOUNT	1 YEAR	1½ YEARS	2 YEARS	2½ YEARS	3 YEARS	4 YEARS	5 YEARS
$ 25	2.18	1.48	1.14	.93	.79	.62	.51
50	4.35	2.96	2.27	1.85	1.57	1.23	1.02
75	6.53	4.44	3.40	2.77	2.36	1.84	1.53
100	8.70	5.92	4.53	3.69	3.14	2.45	2.03
200	17.40	11.83	9.05	7.38	6.27	4.89	4.06
300	26.10	17.75	13.57	11.07	9.41	7.33	6.09
400	34.80	23.66	18.10	14.76	12.54	9.77	8.12
500	43.50	29.58	22.62	18.45	15.67	12.21	10.14
600	52.20	35.49	27.14	22.14	18.81	14.65	12.17
700	60.90	41.40	31.66	25.83	21.94	17.09	14.20
800	69.60	47.32	36.19	29.52	25.07	19.54	16.23
900	78.29	53.23	40.71	33.20	28.21	21.98	18.25
1000	86.99	59.15	45.23	36.89	31.34	24.42	20.28
2000	173.98	118.29	90.46	73.78	62.68	48.83	40.56
3000	260.97	177.43	135.69	110.67	94.01	73.24	60.83
4000	347.96	236.57	180.91	147.56	125.35	97.66	81.11
5000	434.95	295.71	226.14	184.45	156.69	122.07	101.39
6000	521.94	354.85	271.37	221.33	188.02	146.48	121.66
7000	608.92	413.99	316.60	258.22	219.36	170.90	141.94
8000	695.91	473.13	361.82	295.11	250.70	195.31	162.22
9000	782.90	532.27	407.05	332.00	282.03	219.72	182.49
10000	869.89	591.41	452.28	368.89	313.37	244.13	202.77
11000	956.88	650.55	497.51	405.78	344.71	268.55	223.05
12000	1043.87	709.69	542.73	442.66	376.04	292.96	243.32
13000	1130.85	768.83	587.96	479.55	407.38	317.37	263.60
14000	1217.84	827.97	633.19	516.44	438.71	341.79	283.87
15000	1304.83	887.11	678.41	553.33	470.05	366.20	304.15
16000	1391.82	946.25	723.64	590.22	501.39	390.61	324.43
17000	1478.81	1005.39	768.87	627.11	532.72	415.02	344.70
18000	1565.80	1064.53	814.10	663.99	564.06	439.44	364.98
19000	1652.79	1123.67	859.32	700.88	595.40	463.85	385.26
20000	1739.77	1182.81	904.55	737.77	626.73	488.26	405.53
21000	1826.76	1241.95	949.78	774.66	658.07	512.68	425.81
22000	1913.75	1301.09	995.01	811.55	689.41	537.09	446.09
23000	2000.74	1360.23	1040.23	848.44	720.74	561.50	466.36
24000	2087.73	1419.37	1085.46	885.32	752.08	585.92	486.64
25000	2174.72	1478.51	1130.69	922.21	783.41	610.33	506.91
26000	2261.70	1537.65	1175.91	959.10	814.75	634.74	527.19
27000	2348.69	1596.79	1221.14	995.99	846.09	659.15	547.47
28000	2435.68	1655.93	1266.37	1032.88	877.42	683.57	567.74
29000	2522.67	1715.07	1311.60	1069.77	908.76	707.98	588.02
30000	2609.66	1774.21	1356.82	1106.65	940.10	732.39	608.30
31000	2696.65	1833.35	1402.05	1143.54	971.43	756.81	628.57
32000	2783.63	1892.49	1447.28	1180.43	1002.77	781.22	648.85
33000	2870.62	1951.63	1492.51	1217.32	1034.11	805.63	669.13
34000	2957.61	2010.78	1537.73	1254.21	1065.44	830.04	689.40
35000	3044.60	2069.92	1582.96	1291.10	1096.78	854.46	709.68
40000	3479.54	2365.62	1809.10	1475.54	1253.46	976.52	811.06
45000	3914.48	2661.32	2035.23	1659.98	1410.14	1098.59	912.44
50000	4349.43	2957.02	2261.37	1844.42	1566.82	1220.65	1013.82
55000	4784.37	3252.72	2487.51	2028.86	1723.51	1342.72	1115.21
60000	5219.31	3548.42	2713.64	2213.30	1880.19	1464.78	1216.59
65000	5654.25	3844.12	2939.78	2397.75	2036.87	1586.84	1317.97
70000	6089.20	4139.83	3165.92	2582.19	2193.55	1708.91	1419.35
75000	6524.14	4435.53	3392.05	2766.63	2350.23	1830.97	1520.73
80000	6959.08	4731.23	3618.19	2951.07	2506.91	1953.04	1622.12
100000	8698.85	5914.03	4522.73	3688.84	3133.64	2441.30	2027.64

TERM AMOUNT	6 YEARS	7 YEARS	8 YEARS	9 YEARS	10 YEARS	11 YEARS	12 YEARS
$ 25	.44	.39	.36	.33	.31	.29	.28
50	.88	.78	.71	.66	.61	.58	.55
75	1.32	1.17	1.07	.98	.91	.86	.82
100	1.76	1.56	1.42	1.31	1.22	1.15	1.09
200	3.51	3.12	2.83	2.61	2.43	2.29	2.17
300	5.26	4.68	4.25	3.91	3.64	3.43	3.25
400	7.02	6.24	5.66	5.21	4.86	4.57	4.33
500	8.77	7.80	7.07	6.51	6.07	5.71	5.42
600	10.52	9.36	8.49	7.82	7.28	6.85	6.50
700	12.28	10.92	9.90	9.12	8.50	8.00	7.58
800	14.03	12.47	11.31	10.42	9.71	9.14	8.66
900	15.78	14.03	12.73	11.72	10.92	10.28	9.75
1000	17.54	15.59	14.14	13.02	12.14	11.42	10.83
2000	35.07	31.18	28.28	26.04	24.27	22.84	21.65
3000	52.60	46.76	42.42	39.06	36.40	34.25	32.48
4000	70.14	62.35	56.55	52.08	48.54	45.67	43.30
5000	87.67	77.94	70.69	65.10	60.67	57.08	54.13
6000	105.20	93.52	84.83	78.12	72.80	68.50	64.95
7000	122.74	109.11	98.96	91.14	84.93	79.91	75.78
8000	140.27	124.69	113.10	104.15	97.07	91.33	86.60
9000	157.80	140.28	127.24	117.17	109.20	102.74	97.43
10000	175.34	155.87	141.37	130.19	121.33	114.16	108.25
11000	192.87	171.45	155.51	143.21	133.47	125.57	119.07
12000	210.40	187.04	169.65	156.23	145.60	136.99	129.90
13000	227.94	202.63	183.78	169.25	157.73	148.41	140.72
14000	245.47	218.21	197.92	182.27	169.86	159.82	151.55
15000	263.00	233.80	212.06	195.29	182.00	171.24	162.37
16000	280.54	249.38	226.19	208.30	194.13	182.65	173.20
17000	298.07	264.97	240.33	221.32	206.26	194.07	184.02
18000	315.60	280.56	254.47	234.34	218.39	205.48	194.85
19000	333.14	296.14	268.60	247.36	230.53	216.90	205.67
20000	350.67	311.73	282.74	260.38	242.66	228.31	216.50
21000	368.20	327.32	296.88	273.40	254.79	239.73	227.32
22000	385.74	342.90	311.01	286.42	266.93	251.14	238.14
23000	403.27	358.49	325.15	299.44	279.06	262.56	248.97
24000	420.80	374.07	339.29	312.45	291.19	273.98	259.79
25000	438.34	389.66	353.42	325.47	303.32	285.39	270.62
26000	455.87	405.25	367.56	338.49	315.46	296.81	281.44
27000	473.40	420.83	381.70	351.51	327.59	308.22	292.27
28000	490.94	436.42	395.83	364.53	339.72	319.64	303.09
29000	508.47	452.01	409.97	377.55	351.86	331.05	313.92
30000	526.00	467.59	424.11	390.57	363.99	342.47	324.74
31000	543.54	483.18	438.24	403.59	376.12	353.88	335.57
32000	561.07	498.76	452.38	416.60	388.25	365.30	346.39
33000	578.60	514.35	466.52	429.62	400.39	376.71	357.21
34000	596.14	529.94	460.65	442.64	412.52	388.13	368.04
35000	613.67	545.52	494.79	455.66	424.65	399.55	378.86
40000	701.33	623.45	565.47	520.75	485.32	456.62	432.99
45000	789.00	701.38	636.16	585.85	545.98	513.70	487.11
50000	876.67	779.32	706.84	650.94	606.64	570.78	541.23
55000	964.33	857.25	777.52	716.03	667.31	627.85	595.35
60000	1052.00	935.18	848.21	781.13	727.97	684.93	649.48
65000	1139.67	1013.11	918.89	846.22	788.63	742.01	703.60
70000	1227.33	1091.04	989.57	911.32	849.30	799.09	757.72
75000	1315.00	1168.97	1060.26	976.41	909.96	856.16	811.84
80000	1402.66	1246.90	1130.94	1041.50	970.63	913.24	865.97
100000	1753.33	1558.63	1413.67	1301.88	1213.28	1141.55	1082.46

MONTHLY PAYMENT
NECESSARY TO AMORTIZE A LOAN

TERM AMOUNT	13 YEARS	14 YEARS	15 YEARS	16 YEARS	17 YEARS	18 YEARS	19 YEARS
$ 25	.26	.25	.24	.24	.23	.22	.22
50	.52	.50	.48	.47	.45	.44	.43
75	.78	.75	.72	.70	.68	.66	.65
100	1.04	1.00	.96	.93	.90	.88	.86
200	2.07	1.99	1.92	1.85	1.80	1.75	1.71
300	3.10	2.98	2.87	2.78	2.70	2.63	2.57
400	4.14	3.97	3.83	3.70	3.60	3.50	3.42
500	5.17	4.96	4.78	4.63	4.50	4.38	4.28
600	6.20	5.95	5.74	5.55	5.39	5.25	5.13
700	7.24	6.94	6.69	6.48	6.29	6.13	5.99
800	8.27	7.94	7.65	7.40	7.19	7.00	6.84
900	9.30	8.93	8.61	8.33	8.09	7.88	7.70
1000	10.34	9.92	9.56	9.25	8.99	8.75	8.55
2000	20.67	19.83	19.12	18.50	17.97	17.50	17.10
3000	31.00	29.74	28.67	27.75	26.95	26.25	25.64
4000	41.33	39.66	38.23	37.00	35.94	35.00	34.19
5000	51.66	49.57	47.79	46.25	44.92	43.75	42.73
6000	61.99	59.48	57.34	55.50	53.90	52.50	51.28
7000	72.32	69.40	66.90	64.75	62.88	61.25	59.82
8000	82.65	79.31	76.46	74.00	71.87	70.00	68.37
9000	92.98	89.22	86.01	83.25	80.85	78.75	76.91
10000	103.31	99.14	95.57	92.50	89.83	87.50	85.46
11000	113.64	109.05	105.13	101.74	98.81	96.25	94.00
12000	123.97	118.96	114.68	111.00	107.80	105.00	102.55
13000	134.30	128.88	124.24	120.25	116.78	113.75	111.09
14000	144.64	138.79	133.80	129.49	125.76	122.50	119.64
15000	154.97	148.70	143.35	138.74	134.74	131.25	128.18
16000	165.30	158.62	152.91	147.99	143.73	140.00	136.73
17000	175.63	168.53	162.47	157.24	152.71	148.75	145.27
18000	185.96	178.44	172.02	166.49	161.69	157.50	153.82
19000	196.29	188.36	181.58	175.74	170.67	166.25	162.36
20000	206.62	198.27	191.14	184.99	179.66	175.00	170.91
21000	216.95	208.18	200.69	194.24	188.64	183.75	179.45
22000	227.28	218.10	210.25	203.49	197.62	192.50	188.00
23000	237.61	228.01	219.80	212.74	206.60	201.25	196.54
24000	247.94	237.92	229.36	221.99	215.59	210.00	205.09
25000	258.27	247.83	238.92	231.24	224.57	218.75	213.63
26000	268.60	257.75	248.47	240.49	233.55	227.50	222.18
27000	278.93	267.66	258.03	249.73	242.53	236.24	230.72
28000	289.27	277.57	267.59	258.98	251.52	244.99	239.27
29000	299.60	287.49	277.14	268.23	260.50	253.74	247.81
30000	309.93	297.40	286.70	277.48	269.48	262.49	256.36
31000	320.26	307.31	296.26	286.73	278.46	271.24	264.90
32000	330.59	317.23	305.81	295.98	287.45	279.99	273.45
33000	340.92	327.14	315.37	305.23	296.43	288.74	281.99
34000	351.25	337.05	324.93	314.48	305.41	297.49	290.54
35000	361.58	346.97	334.48	323.73	314.39	306.24	299.08
40000	413.23	396.53	382.27	369.98	359.31	349.99	341.81
45000	464.89	446.10	430.05	416.22	404.22	393.74	384.53
50000	516.54	495.66	477.83	462.47	449.13	437.49	427.26
55000	568.20	545.23	525.61	508.71	494.05	481.23	469.98
60000	619.85	594.80	573.40	554.96	538.96	524.98	512.71
65000	671.50	644.36	621.18	601.21	583.87	568.73	555.43
70000	723.16	693.93	668.96	647.45	628.78	612.48	598.16
75000	774.81	743.49	716.74	693.70	673.70	656.23	640.88
80000	826.46	793.06	764.53	739.95	718.61	699.98	683.61
100000	1033.08	991.32	955.66	924.93	898.26	874.97	854.51

TERM AMOUNT	20 YEARS	21 YEARS	22 YEARS	25 YEARS	30 YEARS	35 YEARS	40 YEARS
$ 25	.21	.21	.21	.20	.19	.18	.18
50	.42	.42	.41	.39	.37	.36	.35
75	.63	.62	.61	.58	.56	.54	.53
100	.84	.83	.81	.78	.74	.72	.70
200	1.68	1.65	1.62	1.55	1.47	1.43	1.40
300	2.51	2.47	2.42	2.32	2.21	2.14	2.09
400	3.35	3.29	3.23	3.09	2.94	2.85	2.79
500	4.19	4.11	4.04	3.86	3.67	3.56	3.48
600	5.02	4.93	4.84	4.64	4.41	4.27	4.18
700	5.86	5.75	5.65	5.41	5.14	4.98	4.87
800	6.70	6.57	6.45	6.18	5.88	5.69	5.57
900	7.53	7.39	7.26	6.95	6.61	6.40	6.26
1000	8.37	8.21	8.07	7.72	7.34	7.11	6.96
2000	16.73	16.41	16.13	15.44	14.68	14.21	13.91
3000	25.10	24.62	24.19	23.16	22.02	21.31	20.86
4000	33.46	32.82	32.25	30.88	29.36	28.42	27.82
5000	41.83	41.03	40.31	38.60	36.69	35.52	34.77
6000	50.19	49.23	48.38	46.31	44.03	42.62	41.72
7000	58.56	57.43	56.44	54.03	51.37	49.72	48.68
8000	66.92	65.64	64.50	61.75	58.71	56.83	55.63
9000	75.28	73.84	72.56	69.47	66.04	63.93	62.58
10000	83.65	82.05	80.62	77.19	73.38	71.03	69.54
11000	92.01	90.25	88.68	84.90	80.72	78.13	76.49
12000	100.38	98.46	96.75	92.62	88.06	85.24	83.44
13000	108.74	106.66	104.81	100.34	95.39	92.34	90.40
14000	117.11	114.86	112.87	108.06	102.73	99.44	97.35
15000	125.47	123.07	120.93	115.78	110.07	106.54	104.30
16000	133.84	131.27	128.99	123.50	117.41	113.65	111.25
17000	142.20	139.48	137.06	131.21	124.74	120.75	118.21
18000	150.56	147.68	145.12	138.93	132.08	127.85	125.16
19000	158.93	155.89	153.18	146.65	139.42	134.95	132.11
20000	167.29	164.09	161.24	154.37	146.76	142.06	139.07
21000	175.66	172.29	169.30	162.09	154.10	149.16	146.02
22000	184.02	180.50	177.36	169.80	161.43	156.26	152.97
23000	192.39	188.70	185.43	177.52	168.77	163.37	159.93
24000	200.75	196.91	193.49	185.24	176.11	170.47	166.88
25000	209.12	205.11	201.55	192.96	183.45	177.57	173.83
26000	217.48	213.32	209.61	200.68	190.78	184.67	180.79
27000	225.84	221.52	217.67	208.40	198.12	191.78	187.74
28000	234.21	229.72	225.73	216.11	205.46	198.88	194.69
29000	242.57	237.93	233.80	223.83	212.80	205.98	201.65
30000	250.94	246.13	241.86	231.55	220.13	213.08	208.60
31000	259.30	254.34	249.92	239.27	227.47	220.19	215.55
32000	267.67	262.54	257.98	246.99	234.81	227.29	222.50
33000	276.03	270.75	266.04	254.70	242.15	234.39	229.46
34000	284.39	278.95	274.11	262.42	249.48	241.49	236.41
35000	292.76	287.15	282.17	270.14	256.82	248.60	243.36
40000	334.58	328.18	322.48	308.73	293.51	284.11	278.13
45000	376.40	369.20	362.79	347.32	330.20	319.62	312.90
50000	418.23	410.22	403.09	385.91	366.89	355.14	347.66
55000	460.05	451.24	443.40	424.50	403.58	390.65	382.43
60000	501.87	492.26	483.71	463.09	440.26	426.16	417.19
65000	543.69	533.28	524.02	501.69	476.95	461.67	451.96
70000	585.51	574.30	564.33	540.28	513.64	497.19	486.72
75000	627.34	615.33	604.64	578.87	550.33	532.70	521.49
80000	669.16	656.35	644.95	617.46	587.02	568.21	556.25
100000	836.45	820.43	806.18	771.82	733.77	710.27	695.32

TERM AMOUNT	1 YEAR	1½ YEARS	2 YEARS	2½ YEARS	3 YEARS	4 YEARS	5 YEARS
$ 25	2·18	1·49	1.14	·93	·79	·62	·51
50	4.36	2.97	2.27	1.86	1.58	1.23	1.02
75	6.54	4.45	3.41	2.78	2.36	1.84	1.53
100	8.72	5.93	4.54	3.71	3.15	2.46	2.04
200	17.43	11.86	9.07	7.41	6.30	4.91	4.08
300	26.14	17.78	13.61	11.11	9.44	7.36	6.12
400	34.85	23.71	18.14	14.81	12.59	9.82	8.16
500	43.56	29.63	22.68	18.51	15.73	12.27	10.20
600	52.27	35.56	27.21	22.21	18.88	14.72	12.24
700	60.98	41.48	31.74	25.91	22.02	17.18	14.28
800	69.69	47.41	36.28	29.61	25.17	19.63	16.32
900	78.40	53.33	40.81	33.31	28.31	22.08	18.36
1000	87.11	59.26	45.35	37.01	31.46	24.54	20.40
2000	174.21	118.51	90.69	74.01	62.91	49.07	40.80
3000	261.32	177.77	136.03	111.01	94.36	73.60	61.19
4000	348.42	237.02	181.37	148.02	125.81	98.13	81.59
5000	435.53	296.28	226.71	185.02	157.26	122.66	101.99
6000	522.63	355.53	272.05	222.02	188.72	147.19	122.38
7000	609.73	414.79	317.39	259.03	220.17	171.72	142.78
8000	696.84	474.04	362.74	296.03	251.62	196.25	163.18
9000	783.94	533.30	408.08	333.03	283.07	220.78	183.57
10000	871.05	592.55	453.42	370.03	314.52	245.31	203.97
11000	958.15	651.80	498.76	407.04	345.98	269.84	224.37
12000	1045.25	711.06	544.10	444.04	377.43	294.37	244.76
13000	1132.36	770.31	589.44	481.04	408.88	318.90	265.16
14000	1219.46	829.57	634.78	518.05	440.33	343.43	285.55
15000	1306.57	888.82	680.13	555.05	471.78	367.96	305.95
16000	1393.67	948.08	725.47	592.05	503.23	392.49	326.35
17000	1480.77	1007.33	770.81	629.06	534.69	417.02	346.74
18000	1567.88	1066.59	816.15	666.06	566.14	441.55	367.14
19000	1654.98	1125.84	861.49	703.06	597.59	466.08	387.53
20000	1742.09	1185.09	906.83	740.06	629.04	490.61	407.93
21000	1829.19	1244.35	952.17	777.07	660.49	515.14	428.33
22000	1916.29	1303.60	997.52	814.07	691.95	539.67	448.72
23000	2003.40	1362.86	1042.86	851.07	723.40	564.21	469.12
24000	2090.50	1422.11	1088.20	888.08	754.85	588.74	489.52
25000	2177.61	1481.37	1133.54	925.08	786.30	613.27	509.91
26000	2264.71	1540.62	1178.88	962.08	817.75	637.80	530.31
27000	2351.81	1599.88	1224.22	999.08	849.20	662.33	550.70
28000	2438.92	1659.13	1269.56	1036.09	880.66	686.86	571.10
29000	2526.02	1718.38	1314.91	1073.09	912.11	711.39	591.50
30000	2613.13	1777.64	1360.25	1110.09	943.56	735.92	611.89
31000	2700.23	1836.89	1405.59	1147.10	975.01	760.45	632.29
32000	2787.34	1896.15	1450.93	1184.10	1006.46	784.98	652.69
33000	2874.44	1955.40	1496.27	1221.10	1037.92	809.51	673.08
34000	2961.54	2014.66	1541.61	1258.11	1069.37	834.04	693.48
35000	3048.65	2073.91	1586.95	1295.11	1100.82	858.57	713.87
40000	3484.17	2370.18	1813.66	1480.12	1258.08	981.22	815.86
45000	3919.69	2666.46	2040.37	1665.14	1415.34	1103.87	917.84
50000	4355.21	2962.73	2267.07	1850.15	1572.60	1226.53	1019.82
55000	4790.73	3259.00	2493.78	2035.17	1729.86	1349.18	1121.80
60000	5226.25	3555.27	2720.49	2220.18	1887.11	1471.83	1223.78
65000	5661.77	3851.54	2947.20	2405.20	2044.37	1594.48	1325.76
70000	6097.29	4147.82	3173.90	2590.21	2201.63	1717.14	1427.74
75000	6532.81	4444.09	3400.61	2775.23	2358.89	1839.79	1529.72
80000	6968.33	4740.36	3627.32	2960.24	2516.15	1962.44	1631.71
100000	8710.41	5925.45	4534.14	3700.30	3145.19	2453.05	2039.63

TERM AMOUNT	6 YEARS	7 YEARS	8 YEARS	9 YEARS	10 YEARS	11 YEARS	12 YEARS
$ 25	.45	.40	.36	.33	.31	.29	.28
50	.89	.79	.72	.66	.62	.58	.55
75	1.33	1.18	1.07	.99	.92	.87	.83
100	1.77	1.58	1.43	1.32	1.23	1.16	1.10
200	3.54	3.15	2.86	2.63	2.46	2.32	2.20
300	5.30	4.72	4.28	3.95	3.68	3.47	3.29
400	7.07	6.29	5.71	5.26	4.91	4.63	4.39
500	8.83	7.86	7.14	6.58	6.14	5.78	5.49
600	10.60	9.43	8.56	7.89	7.36	6.94	6.58
700	12.36	11.00	9.99	9.21	8.59	8.09	7.68
800	14.13	12.57	11.42	1C.52	9.82	9.25	8.77
900	15.90	14.14	12.84	11.84	11.04	10.40	9.87
1000	17.66	15.72	14.27	13.15	12.27	11.56	10.97
2000	35.32	31.43	28.53	26.30	24.54	23.11	21.93
3000	52.97	47.14	42.80	39.45	36.80	34.66	32.89
4000	70.63	62.85	57.06	52.60	49.07	46.21	43.85
5000	88.28	78.56	71.33	65.75	61.33	57.76	54.82
6000	105.94	94.27	85.59	78.90	73.60	69.31	65.78
7000	123.59	109.98	99.85	92.05	85.86	80.86	76.74
8000	141.25	125.69	114.12	105.19	98.13	92.41	87.70
9000	158.91	141.40	128.38	118.34	110.39	103.96	98.66
10000	176.56	157.12	142.65	131.49	122.66	115.51	109.63
11000	194.22	172.83	156.91	144.64	134.92	127.06	120.59
12000	211.87	188.54	171.17	157.79	147.19	138.61	131.55
13000	229.53	204.25	185.44	170.94	159.45	150.16	142.51
14000	247.18	219.96	199.70	184.09	171.72	161.71	153.47
15000	264.84	235.67	213.97	197.24	183.98	173.26	164.44
16000	282.49	251.38	228.23	210.38	196.25	184.81	175.40
17000	300.15	267.09	242.49	223.53	208.51	196.36	186.36
18000	317.81	282.80	256.76	236.68	220.78	207.91	197.32
19000	335.46	298.52	271.02	249.83	233.04	219.46	208.28
20000	353.12	314.23	285.29	262.98	245.31	231.01	219.25
21000	370.77	329.94	299.55	276.13	257.58	242.57	230.21
22000	388.43	345.65	313.81	289.28	269.84	254.12	241.17
23000	406.08	361.36	328.08	302.42	282.11	265.67	252.13
24000	423.74	377.07	342.34	315.57	294.37	277.22	263.09
25000	441.39	392.78	356.61	328.72	306.64	288.77	274.06
26000	459.05	408.49	370.87	341.87	318.90	300.32	285.02
27000	476.71	424.20	385.14	355.02	331.17	311.87	295.98
28000	494.36	439.91	399.40	368.17	343.43	323.42	306.94
29000	512.02	455.63	413.66	381.32	355.70	334.97	317.91
30000	529.67	471.34	427.93	394.47	367.96	346.52	328.87
31000	547.33	487.05	442.19	407.61	380.23	358.07	339.83
32000	564.98	502.76	456.46	420.76	392.49	369.62	350.79
33000	582.64	518.47	470.72	433.91	404.76	381.17	361.75
34000	600.29	534.18	484.98	447.06	417.02	392.72	372.72
35000	617.95	549.89	499.25	46C.21	429.29	404.27	383.68
40000	706.23	628.45	570.57	525.95	490.62	462.02	438.49
45000	794.51	707.00	641.89	591.70	551.94	519.78	493.30
50000	882.78	785.56	713.21	657.44	613.27	577.53	548.11
55000	971.06	864.11	784.53	723.18	674.59	635.28	602.92
60000	1059.34	942.67	855.85	788.93	735.92	693.03	657.73
65000	1147.62	1021.22	927.17	854.67	797.25	750.79	712.54
70000	1235.89	1099.78	998.49	920.41	858.57	808.54	767.35
75000	1324.17	1178.33	1069.81	986.16	919.90	866.29	822.16
80000	1412.45	1256.89	1141.13	1051.90	981.23	924.04	876.97
100000	1765.56	1571.11	1426.41	1314.87	1226.53	1155.05	1096.21

8¼%

MONTHLY PAYMENT
NECESSARY TO AMORTIZE A LOAN

TERM AMOUNT	13 YEARS	14 YEARS	15 YEARS	16 YEARS	17 YEARS	18 YEARS	19 YEARS
$ 25	.27	.26	.25	.24	.23	.23	.22
50	.53	.51	.49	.47	.46	.45	.44
75	.79	.76	.73	.71	.69	.67	.66
100	1.05	1.01	.98	.94	.92	.90	.87
200	2.10	2.02	1.95	1.88	1.83	1.79	1.74
300	3.15	3.02	2.92	2.82	2.74	2.68	2.61
400	4.19	4.03	3.89	3.76	3.66	3.57	3.48
500	5.24	5.03	4.86	4.70	4.57	4.46	4.35
600	6.29	6.04	5.83	5.64	5.48	5.35	5.22
700	7.33	7.04	6.80	6.58	6.40	6.24	6.09
800	8.38	8.05	7.77	7.52	7.31	7.13	6.96
900	9.43	9.06	8.74	8.46	8.22	8.02	7.83
1000	10.48	10.06	9.71	9.40	9.14	8.91	8.70
2000	20.95	20.12	19.41	18.80	18.27	17.81	17.40
3000	31.42	30.17	29.11	28.19	27.40	26.71	26.10
4000	41.89	40.23	38.81	37.59	36.53	35.61	34.80
5000	52.36	50.28	48.51	46.99	45.67	44.51	43.50
6000	62.83	60.34	58.21	56.38	54.80	53.41	52.20
7000	73.30	70.39	67.91	65.78	63.93	62.32	60.90
8000	83.77	80.45	77.62	75.18	73.06	71.22	69.60
9000	94.24	90.51	87.32	84.57	82.19	80.12	78.30
10000	104.71	100.56	97.02	93.97	91.33	89.02	87.00
11000	115.18	110.62	106.72	103.37	100.46	97.92	95.70
12000	125.65	120.67	116.42	112.76	109.59	106.82	104.39
13000	136.12	130.73	126.12	122.16	118.72	115.72	113.09
14000	146.60	140.78	135.82	131.56	127.85	124.63	121.79
15000	157.07	150.84	145.53	140.95	136.99	133.53	130.49
16000	167.54	160.90	155.23	150.35	146.12	142.43	139.19
17000	178.01	170.95	164.93	159.75	155.25	151.33	147.89
18000	188.48	181.01	174.63	169.14	164.38	160.23	156.59
19000	198.95	191.06	184.33	178.54	173.52	169.13	165.29
20000	209.42	201.12	194.03	187.94	182.65	178.03	173.99
21000	219.89	211.17	203.73	197.33	191.78	186.94	182.69
22000	230.36	221.23	213.44	206.73	200.91	195.84	191.39
23000	240.83	231.29	223.14	216.12	210.04	204.74	200.08
24000	251.30	241.34	232.84	225.52	219.18	213.64	208.78
25000	261.77	251.40	242.54	234.92	228.31	222.54	217.48
26000	272.24	261.45	252.24	244.31	237.44	231.44	226.18
27000	282.72	271.51	261.94	253.71	246.57	240.34	234.88
28000	293.19	281.56	271.64	263.11	255.70	249.25	243.58
29000	303.66	291.62	281.35	272.50	264.84	258.15	252.28
30000	314.13	301.67	291.05	281.90	273.97	267.05	260.98
31000	324.60	311.73	300.75	291.30	283.10	275.95	269.68
32000	335.07	321.79	310.45	300.69	292.23	284.85	278.38
33000	345.54	331.84	320.15	310.09	301.37	293.75	287.08
34000	356.01	341.90	329.85	319.49	310.50	302.66	295.77
35000	366.48	351.95	339.55	328.88	319.63	311.56	304.47
40000	418.84	402.23	388.06	375.87	365.29	356.06	347.97
45000	471.19	452.51	436.57	422.85	410.95	400.57	391.46
50000	523.54	502.79	485.08	469.83	456.61	445.08	434.96
55000	575.90	553.07	533.58	516.81	502.27	489.59	478.46
60000	628.25	603.34	582.09	563.80	547.93	534.10	521.95
65000	680.60	653.62	630.60	610.78	593.59	578.60	565.45
70000	732.96	703.90	679.10	657.76	639.25	623.11	608.94
75000	785.31	754.18	727.61	704.74	684.92	667.62	652.44
80000	837.67	804.46	776.12	751.73	730.58	712.12	695.93
100000	1047.08	1005.57	970.15	939.66	913.22	890.15	869.91

28

TERM AMOUNT	20 YEARS	21 YEARS	22 YEARS	25 YEARS	30 YEARS	35 YEARS	40 YEARS
$ 25	.22	.21	.21	.20	.19	.19	.18
50	.43	.42	.42	.40	.38	.37	.36
75	.64	.63	.62	.60	.57	.55	.54
100	.86	.84	.83	.79	.76	.73	.72
200	1.71	1.68	1.65	1.58	1.51	1.46	1.43
300	2.56	2.51	2.47	2.47	2.26	2.19	2.15
400	3.41	3.35	3.29	3.16	3.01	2.92	2.86
500	4.27	4.19	4.12	3.95	3.76	3.65	3.58
600	5.12	5.02	4.94	4.74	4.51	4.38	4.29
700	5.97	5.86	5.76	5.52	5.26	5.10	5.00
800	6.82	6.70	6.58	6.31	6.02	5.83	5.72
900	7.67	7.53	7.41	7.10	6.77	6.56	6.43
1000	8.53	8.37	8.23	7.89	7.52	7.29	7.15
2000	17.05	16.73	16.45	15.77	15.03	14.57	14.29
3000	25.57	25.09	24.67	23.66	22.54	21.86	21.43
4000	34.09	33.46	32.89	31.54	30.06	29.14	28.57
5000	42.61	41.82	41.12	39.43	37.57	36.43	35.71
6000	51.13	50.18	49.34	47.31	45.08	43.71	42.85
7000	59.65	58.54	57.56	55.20	52.59	51.00	49.99
8000	68.17	66.91	65.78	63.08	60.11	58.28	57.14
9000	76.69	75.27	74.01	70.97	67.62	65.57	64.28
10000	85.21	83.63	82.23	78.85	75.13	72.85	71.42
11000	93.73	91.99	90.45	86.73	82.64	80.14	78.56
12000	102.25	100.36	98.67	94.62	90.16	87.42	85.70
13000	110.77	108.72	106.89	102.50	97.67	94.71	92.84
14000	119.29	117.08	115.12	110.39	105.18	101.99	99.98
15000	127.81	125.44	123.34	118.27	112.69	109.28	107.13
16000	136.34	133.81	131.56	126.16	120.21	116.56	114.27
17000	144.86	142.17	139.78	134.04	127.72	123.85	121.41
18000	153.38	150.53	148.01	141.93	135.23	131.13	128.55
19000	161.90	158.90	156.23	149.81	142.75	138.42	135.69
20000	170.42	167.26	164.45	157.70	150.26	145.70	142.83
21000	178.94	175.62	172.67	165.58	157.77	152.99	149.97
22000	187.46	183.98	180.89	173.46	165.28	160.27	157.12
23000	195.98	192.35	189.12	181.35	172.80	167.56	164.26
24000	204.50	200.71	197.34	189.23	180.31	174.84	171.40
25000	213.02	209.07	205.56	197.12	187.82	182.13	178.54
26000	221.54	217.43	213.78	205.00	195.33	189.41	185.68
27000	230.06	225.80	222.01	212.89	202.85	196.70	192.82
28000	238.58	234.16	230.23	220.77	210.36	203.98	199.96
29000	247.10	242.52	238.45	228.66	217.87	211.27	207.11
30000	255.62	250.88	246.67	236.54	225.38	218.55	214.25
31000	264.15	259.25	254.89	244.42	232.90	225.84	221.39
32000	272.67	267.61	263.12	252.31	240.41	233.12	228.53
33000	281.19	275.97	271.34	260.19	247.92	240.41	235.67
34000	289.71	284.34	279.56	268.08	255.44	247.69	242.81
35000	298.23	292.70	287.78	275.96	262.95	254.98	249.95
40000	340.83	334.51	328.89	315.39	300.51	291.40	285.66
45000	383.43	376.32	370.01	354.81	338.07	327.83	321.37
50000	426.04	418.14	411.12	394.23	375.64	364.25	357.07
55000	468.64	459.95	452.23	433.65	413.20	400.68	392.78
60000	511.24	501.76	493.34	473.08	450.76	437.10	428.49
65000	553.85	543.58	534.45	512.50	488.33	473.52	464.20
70000	596.45	585.39	575.56	551.92	525.89	509.95	499.90
75000	639.05	627.20	616.67	591.34	563.45	546.37	535.61
80000	681.66	669.02	657.78	630.77	601.02	582.80	571.32
100000	852.07	836.27	822.23	788.46	751.27	728.50	714.14

MONTHLY PAYMENT
NECESSARY TO AMORTIZE A LOAN

TERM AMOUNT	1 YEAR	1½ YEARS	2 YEARS	2½ YEARS	3 YEARS	4 YEARS	5 YEARS
$ 25	2.19	1.49	1.14	.93	.79	.62	.52
50	4.37	2.97	2.28	1.86	1.58	1.24	1.03
75	6.55	4.46	3.41	2.79	2.37	1.85	1.54
100	8.73	5.94	4.55	3.72	3.16	2.47	2.06
200	17.45	11.88	9.10	7.43	6.32	4.93	4.11
300	26.17	17.82	13.64	11.14	9.48	7.40	6.16
400	34.89	23.75	18.19	14.85	12.63	9.86	8.21
500	43.61	29.69	22.73	18.56	15.79	12.33	10.26
600	52.34	35.63	27.28	22.28	18.95	14.79	12.31
700	61.06	41.56	31.82	25.99	22.10	17.26	14.37
800	69.78	47.50	36.37	29.70	25.26	19.72	16.42
900	78.50	53.44	40.92	33.41	28.42	22.19	18.47
1000	87.22	59.37	45.46	37.12	31.57	24.65	20.52
2000	174.44	118.74	90.92	74.24	63.14	49.30	41.04
3000	261.66	178.11	136.37	111.36	94.71	73.95	61.55
4000	348.88	237.48	181.83	148.48	126.28	98.60	82.07
5000	436.10	296.85	227.28	185.59	157.84	123.25	102.59
6000	523.32	356.22	272.74	222.71	189.41	147.89	123.10
7000	610.54	415.59	318.19	259.83	220.98	172.54	143.62
8000	697.76	474.95	363.65	296.95	252.55	197.19	164.14
9000	784.98	534.32	409.11	334.07	284.11	221.84	184.65
10000	872.20	593.69	454.56	371.18	315.68	246.49	205.17
11000	959.42	653.06	500.02	408.30	347.25	271.14	225.69
12000	1046.64	712.43	545.47	445.42	378.82	295.78	246.20
13000	1133.86	771.80	590.93	482.54	410.38	320.43	266.72
14000	1221.08	831.17	636.38	519.65	441.95	345.08	287.24
15000	1308.30	890.54	681.84	556.77	473.52	369.73	307.75
16000	1395.52	949.90	727.30	593.89	505.09	394.38	328.27
17000	1482.74	1009.27	772.75	631.01	536.65	419.03	348.79
18000	1569.96	1068.64	818.21	668.13	568.22	443.67	369.30
19000	1657.18	1128.01	863.66	705.24	599.79	468.32	389.82
20000	1744.40	1187.38	909.12	742.36	631.36	492.97	410.34
21000	1831.62	1246.75	954.57	779.48	662.92	517.62	430.85
22000	1918.84	1306.12	1000.03	816.60	694.49	542.27	451.37
23000	2006.06	1365.49	1045.49	853.71	726.06	566.92	471.89
24000	2093.28	1424.85	1090.94	890.83	757.63	591.56	492.40
25000	2180.50	1484.22	1136.40	927.95	789.19	616.21	512.92
26000	2267.72	1543.59	1181.85	965.07	820.76	640.86	533.43
27000	2354.94	1602.96	1227.31	1002.19	852.33	665.51	553.95
28000	2442.16	1662.33	1272.76	1039.30	883.90	690.16	574.47
29000	2529.38	1721.70	1318.22	1076.42	915.46	714.81	594.98
30000	2616.60	1781.07	1363.68	1113.54	947.03	739.45	615.50
31000	2703.82	1840.44	1409.13	1150.66	978.60	764.10	636.02
32000	2791.04	1899.80	1454.59	1187.78	1010.17	788.75	656.53
33000	2878.26	1959.17	1500.04	1224.89	1041.73	813.40	677.05
34000	2965.48	2018.54	1545.50	1262.01	1073.30	838.05	697.57
35000	3052.70	2077.91	1590.95	1299.13	1104.87	862.70	718.08
40000	3488.80	2374.75	1818.24	1484.72	1262.71	985.94	820.67
45000	3924.90	2671.60	2045.51	1670.31	1420.54	1109.18	923.25
50000	4360.99	2968.44	2272.79	1855.90	1578.38	1232.42	1025.83
55000	4797.09	3265.28	2500.07	2041.48	1736.22	1355.66	1128.41
60000	5233.19	3562.13	2727.35	2227.07	1894.06	1478.90	1231.00
65000	5669.29	3858.97	2954.62	2412.66	2051.89	1602.14	1333.58
70000	6105.39	4155.82	3181.90	2598.25	2209.73	1725.39	1436.16
75000	6541.49	4452.66	3409.18	2783.84	2367.57	1848.63	1538.74
80000	6977.59	4749.50	3636.46	2969.43	2525.41	1971.87	1641.33
100000	8721.98	5936.88	4545.57	3711.79	3156.76	2464.84	2051.66

TERM AMOUNT	6 YEARS	7 YEARS	8 YEARS	9 YEARS	10 YEARS	11 YEARS	12 YEARS
$ 25	.45	.40	.36	.34	.31	.30	.28
50	.89	.80	.72	.67	.62	.59	.56
75	1.34	1.19	1.08	1.00	.93	.88	.84
100	1.78	1.59	1.44	1.33	1.24	1.17	1.12
200	3.56	3.17	2.88	2.66	2.48	2.34	2.23
300	5.34	4.76	4.32	3.99	3.72	3.51	3.34
400	7.12	6.34	5.76	5.32	4.96	4.68	4.45
500	8.89	7.92	7.20	6.64	6.20	5.85	5.56
600	10.67	9.51	8.64	7.97	7.44	7.02	6.67
700	12.45	11.09	10.08	9.30	8.68	8.19	7.78
800	14.23	12.67	11.52	10.63	9.92	9.35	8.89
900	16.01	14.26	12.96	11.96	11.16	10.52	10.00
1000	17.78	15.84	14.40	13.28	12.40	11.69	11.11
2000	35.56	31.68	28.79	26.56	24.00	23.38	22.21
3000	53.34	47.51	43.18	39.84	37.20	35.06	33.31
4000	71.12	63.35	57.57	53.12	49.60	46.75	44.41
5000	88.90	79.19	71.97	66.40	62.00	58.44	55.51
6000	106.68	95.02	86.36	79.68	74.40	70.12	66.61
7000	124.45	110.86	100.75	92.96	86.79	81.81	77.71
8000	142.23	126.70	115.14	106.24	99.19	93.50	88.81
9000	160.01	142.53	129.53	119.52	111.59	105.18	99.91
10000	177.79	158.37	143.93	132.80	123.99	116.87	111.01
11000	195.57	174.21	158.32	146.08	136.39	128.56	122.11
12000	213.35	190.04	172.71	159.36	148.79	140.24	133.21
13000	231.12	205.88	187.10	172.64	161.19	151.93	144.31
14000	248.90	221.72	201.49	185.92	173.58	163.61	155.41
15000	266.68	237.55	215.89	199.20	185.98	175.30	166.51
16000	284.46	253.39	230.28	212.47	198.38	186.99	177.61
17000	302.24	269.23	244.67	225.75	210.78	198.67	188.71
18000	320.02	285.06	259.06	239.03	223.18	210.36	199.82
19000	337.79	300.90	273.46	252.31	235.58	222.05	210.92
20000	355.57	316.73	287.85	265.59	247.98	233.73	222.02
21000	373.35	332.57	302.24	278.87	260.37	245.42	233.12
22000	391.13	348.41	316.63	292.15	272.77	257.11	244.22
23000	408.91	364.24	331.02	305.43	285.17	268.79	255.32
24000	426.69	380.08	345.42	318.71	297.57	280.48	266.42
25000	444.46	395.92	359.81	331.99	309.97	292.16	277.52
26000	462.24	411.75	374.20	345.27	322.37	303.85	288.62
27000	480.02	427.59	388.59	358.55	334.77	315.54	299.72
28000	497.80	443.43	402.98	371.83	347.16	327.22	310.82
29000	515.58	459.26	417.38	385.11	359.56	338.91	321.92
30000	533.36	475.10	431.77	398.39	371.96	350.60	333.02
31000	551.13	490.94	446.16	411.66	384.36	362.28	344.12
32000	568.91	506.77	460.55	424.94	396.76	373.97	355.22
33000	586.69	522.61	474.95	438.22	409.16	385.66	366.32
34000	604.47	538.45	489.34	451.50	421.56	397.34	377.42
35000	622.25	554.28	503.73	464.78	433.95	409.03	388.52
40000	711.14	633.46	575.69	531.18	495.95	467.46	444.03
45000	800.03	712.65	647.65	597.58	557.94	525.89	499.53
50000	888.92	791.83	719.61	663.97	619.93	584.32	555.03
55000	977.82	871.01	791.57	730.37	681.93	642.76	610.54
60000	1066.71	950.19	863.53	796.77	743.92	701.19	666.04
65000	1155.60	1029.38	935.49	863.16	805.91	759.62	721.54
70000	1244.49	1108.56	1007.45	929.56	867.90	818.05	777.04
75000	1333.38	1187.74	1079.41	995.96	929.90	876.48	832.55
80000	1422.28	1266.92	1151.38	1062.35	991.89	934.92	888.05
100000	1777.84	1583.65	1439.22	1327.94	1239.86	1168.64	1110.06

MONTHLY PAYMENT
NECESSARY TO AMORTIZE A LOAN

TERM AMOUNT	13 YEARS	14 YEARS	15 YEARS	16 YEARS	17 YEARS	18 YEARS	19 YEARS
$ 25	.27	.26	.25	.24	.24	.23	.23
50	.54	.51	.50	.48	.47	.46	.45
75	.80	.77	.74	.72	.70	.68	.67
100	1.07	1.02	.99	.96	.93	.91	.89
200	2.13	2.04	1.97	1.91	1.86	1.82	1.78
300	3.19	3.06	2.96	2.87	2.79	2.72	2.66
400	4.25	4.08	3.94	3.82	3.72	3.63	3.55
500	5.31	5.10	4.93	4.78	4.65	4.53	4.43
600	6.37	6.12	5.91	5.73	5.57	5.44	5.32
700	7.43	7.14	6.90	6.69	6.50	6.34	6.20
800	8.49	8.16	7.88	7.64	7.43	7.25	7.09
900	9.56	9.18	8.87	8.60	8.36	8.15	7.97
1000	10.62	10.20	9.85	9.55	9.29	9.06	8.86
2000	21.23	20.40	19.70	19.09	18.57	18.11	17.71
3000	31.84	30.60	29.55	28.64	27.85	27.17	26.57
4000	42.45	40.80	39.39	38.18	37.14	36.22	35.42
5000	53.06	51.00	49.24	47.73	46.42	45.28	44.28
6000	63.68	61.20	59.09	57.27	55.70	54.33	53.13
7000	74.29	71.40	68.94	66.82	64.99	63.39	61.99
8000	84.90	81.60	78.78	76.36	74.27	72.44	70.84
9000	95.51	91.80	88.63	85.91	83.55	81.50	79.70
10000	106.12	102.00	98.48	95.45	92.83	90.55	88.55
11000	116.73	112.20	108.33	105.00	102.12	99.61	97.40
12000	127.35	122.40	118.17	114.54	111.40	108.66	106.26
13000	137.96	132.59	128.02	124.09	120.68	117.71	115.11
14000	148.57	142.79	137.87	133.63	129.97	126.77	123.97
15000	159.18	152.99	147.72	143.18	139.25	135.82	132.82
16000	169.79	163.19	157.56	152.72	148.53	144.88	141.68
17000	180.41	173.39	167.41	162.27	157.81	153.93	150.53
18000	191.02	183.59	177.26	171.81	167.10	162.99	159.39
19000	201.63	193.79	187.11	181.36	176.38	172.04	168.24
20000	212.24	203.99	196.95	190.90	185.66	181.10	177.09
21000	222.85	214.19	206.80	200.45	194.95	190.15	185.95
22000	233.46	224.39	216.65	209.99	204.23	199.21	194.80
23000	244.08	234.59	226.50	219.54	213.51	208.26	203.66
24000	254.69	244.79	236.34	229.08	222.80	217.31	212.51
25000	265.30	254.98	246.19	238.63	232.08	226.37	221.37
26000	275.91	265.18	256.04	248.17	241.36	235.42	230.22
27000	286.52	275.38	265.88	257.72	250.64	244.48	239.08
28000	297.14	285.58	275.73	267.26	259.93	253.53	247.93
29000	307.75	295.78	285.58	276.81	269.21	262.59	256.78
30000	318.36	305.98	295.43	286.35	278.49	271.64	265.64
31000	328.97	316.18	305.27	295.90	287.78	280.70	274.49
32000	339.58	326.38	315.12	305.44	297.06	289.75	283.35
33000	350.19	336.58	324.97	314.99	306.34	298.81	292.20
34000	360.81	346.78	334.82	324.53	315.62	307.86	301.06
35000	371.42	356.98	344.66	334.08	324.91	316.92	309.91
40000	424.48	407.97	393.90	381.80	371.32	362.19	354.18
45000	477.54	458.97	443.14	429.53	417.74	407.46	398.46
50000	530.59	509.96	492.37	477.25	464.15	452.73	442.73
55000	583.65	560.96	541.61	524.98	510.57	498.01	487.00
60000	636.71	611.96	590.85	572.70	556.98	543.28	531.27
65000	689.77	662.95	640.09	620.42	603.39	588.55	575.54
70000	742.83	713.95	689.32	668.15	649.81	633.83	619.82
75000	795.89	764.94	738.56	715.87	696.22	679.10	664.09
80000	848.95	815.94	787.80	763.60	742.64	724.37	708.36
100000	1061.18	1019.92	984.74	954.50	928.30	905.46	885.45

32

TERM AMOUNT	20 YEARS	21 YEARS	22 YEARS	25 YEARS	30 YEARS	35 YEARS	40 YEARS
$ 25	.22	.22	.21	.21	.20	.19	.19
50	.44	.43	.42	.41	.39	.38	.37
75	.66	.64	.63	.61	.58	.57	.55
100	.87	.86	.84	.81	.77	.75	.74
200	1.74	1.71	1.68	1.62	1.54	1.50	1.47
300	2.61	2.56	2.52	2.42	2.31	2.25	2.20
400	3.48	3.41	3.36	3.23	3.08	2.99	2.94
500	4.34	4.27	4.20	4.03	3.85	3.74	3.67
600	5.21	5.12	5.04	4.84	4.62	4.49	4.40
700	6.08	5.97	5.87	5.64	5.39	5.23	5.14
800	6.95	6.82	6.71	6.45	6.16	5.98	5.87
900	7.82	7.68	7.55	7.25	6.93	6.73	6.60
1000	8.68	8.53	8.39	8.06	7.69	7.47	7.34
2000	17.36	17.05	16.77	16.11	15.38	14.94	14.67
3000	26.04	25.57	25.16	24.16	23.07	22.41	22.00
4000	34.72	34.09	33.54	32.21	30.76	29.88	29.33
5000	43.40	42.62	41.93	40.27	38.45	37.35	36.66
6000	52.07	51.14	50.31	48.32	46.14	44.82	43.99
7000	60.75	59.66	58.69	56.37	53.83	52.29	51.32
8000	69.43	68.18	67.08	64.42	61.52	59.75	58.65
9000	78.11	76.71	75.46	72.48	69.21	67.22	65.98
10000	86.79	85.23	83.85	80.53	76.90	74.69	73.31
11000	95.47	93.75	92.23	88.58	84.59	82.16	80.65
12000	104.14	102.27	100.61	96.63	92.27	89.63	87.98
13000	112.82	110.80	109.00	104.68	99.96	97.10	95.31
14000	121.50	119.32	117.38	112.74	107.65	104.57	102.64
15000	130.18	127.84	125.77	120.79	115.34	112.03	109.97
16000	138.86	136.36	134.15	128.84	123.03	119.50	117.30
17000	147.53	144.89	142.53	136.89	130.72	126.97	124.63
18000	156.21	153.41	150.92	144.95	138.41	134.44	131.96
19000	164.89	161.93	159.30	153.00	146.10	141.91	139.29
20000	173.57	170.45	167.69	161.05	153.79	149.38	146.62
21000	182.25	178.98	176.07	169.10	161.48	156.85	153.95
22000	190.93	187.50	184.45	177.15	169.17	164.31	161.29
23000	199.60	196.02	192.84	185.21	176.86	171.78	168.62
24000	208.28	204.54	201.22	193.26	184.54	179.25	175.95
25000	216.96	213.06	209.61	201.31	192.23	186.72	183.28
26000	225.64	221.59	217.99	209.36	199.92	194.19	190.61
27000	234.32	230.11	226.37	217.42	207.61	201.66	197.94
28000	243.00	238.63	234.76	225.47	215.30	209.13	205.27
29000	251.67	247.15	243.14	233.52	222.99	216.59	212.60
30000	260.35	255.68	251.53	241.57	230.68	224.06	219.93
31000	269.03	264.20	259.91	249.63	238.37	231.53	227.26
32000	277.71	272.72	268.29	257.68	246.06	239.00	234.60
33000	286.39	281.24	276.68	265.73	253.75	246.47	241.93
34000	295.06	289.77	285.06	273.78	261.44	253.94	249.26
35000	303.74	298.29	293.45	281.83	269.12	261.41	256.59
40000	347.13	340.90	335.37	322.10	307.00	298.75	293.24
45000	390.53	383.51	377.29	362.36	346.02	336.09	329.90
50000	433.92	426.12	419.21	402.62	384.46	373.44	366.55
55000	477.31	468.74	461.13	442.88	422.91	410.78	403.21
60000	520.70	511.35	503.05	483.14	461.35	448.12	439.86
65000	564.09	553.96	544.97	523.40	499.80	485.46	476.52
70000	607.48	596.57	586.89	563.66	538.24	522.81	513.17
75000	650.87	639.18	628.81	603.93	576.69	560.15	549.83
80000	694.26	681.80	670.73	644.19	615.14	597.49	586.48
100000	867.83	852.24	838.41	805.23	768.92	746.87	733.10

33

8¾%

MONTHLY PAYMENT
NECESSARY TO AMORTIZE A LOAN

TERM AMOUNT	1 YEAR	1½ YEARS	2 YEARS	2½ YEARS	3 YEARS	4 YEARS	5 YEARS
$ 25	2.19	1.49	1.14	.94	.80	.62	.52
50	4.37	2.98	2.28	1.87	1.59	1.24	1.04
75	6.56	4.47	3.42	2.80	2.38	1.86	1.55
100	8.74	5.95	4.56	3.73	3.17	2.48	2.07
200	17.47	11.90	9.12	7.45	6.34	4.96	4.13
300	26.21	17.85	13.68	11.17	9.51	7.43	6.20
400	34.94	23.80	18.23	14.90	12.68	9.91	8.26
500	43.67	29.75	22.79	18.62	15.85	12.39	10.32
600	52.41	35.69	27.35	22.34	19.02	14.86	12.39
700	61.14	41.64	31.90	26.07	22.18	17.34	14.45
800	69.87	47.59	36.46	29.79	25.35	19.82	16.51
900	78.61	53.54	41.02	33.51	28.52	22.29	18.58
1000	87.34	59.49	45.58	37.24	31.69	24.77	20.64
2000	174.68	118.97	91.15	74.47	63.37	49.54	41.28
3000	262.01	178.45	136.72	111.70	95.06	74.30	61.92
4000	349.35	237.94	182.29	148.94	126.74	99.07	82.55
5000	436.68	297.42	227.86	186.17	158.42	123.34	103.19
6000	524.02	356.90	273.43	223.40	190.11	148.60	123.83
7000	611.35	416.39	319.00	260.64	221.79	173.37	144.47
8000	698.69	475.87	364.57	297.87	253.47	198.14	165.10
9000	786.03	535.35	410.14	335.10	285.16	222.90	185.74
10000	873.36	594.84	455.72	372.33	316.84	247.67	206.38
11000	960.70	654.32	501.28	409.57	348.52	272.44	227.01
12000	1048.03	713.80	546.85	446.80	380.21	297.20	247.65
13000	1135.37	773.29	592.42	484.03	411.89	321.97	268.29
14000	1222.70	832.77	637.99	521.27	443.57	346.74	288.93
15000	1310.04	892.25	683.56	558.50	475.26	371.50	309.56
16000	1397.37	951.74	729.13	595.73	506.94	396.27	330.20
17000	1484.71	1011.22	774.70	632.96	538.62	421.04	350.84
18000	1572.05	1070.70	820.27	670.20	570.31	445.80	371.48
19000	1659.38	1130.18	865.84	707.43	601.99	470.57	392.11
20000	1746.72	1189.67	911.41	744.66	633.68	495.34	412.75
21000	1834.05	1249.15	956.98	781.90	665.36	520.10	433.39
22000	1921.39	1308.63	1002.55	819.13	697.04	544.87	454.02
23000	2008.72	1368.12	1048.12	856.36	728.73	569.63	474.66
24000	2096.06	1427.60	1093.69	893.59	760.41	594.40	495.30
25000	2183.39	1487.08	1139.26	930.83	792.09	619.17	515.94
26000	2270.73	1546.57	1184.83	968.06	823.78	643.93	536.57
27000	2358.07	1606.05	1230.40	1005.29	855.46	668.70	557.21
28000	2445.40	1665.53	1275.97	1042.53	887.14	693.47	577.85
29000	2532.74	1725.02	1321.54	1079.76	918.83	718.23	598.48
30000	2620.07	1784.50	1367.11	1116.99	950.51	743.00	619.12
31000	2707.41	1843.98	1412.68	1154.22	982.19	767.77	639.76
32000	2794.74	1903.47	1458.25	1191.46	1013.88	792.53	660.40
33000	2882.08	1962.95	1503.82	1228.69	1045.56	817.30	681.03
34000	2969.41	2022.43	1549.39	1265.92	1077.24	842.07	701.67
35000	3056.75	2081.91	1594.96	1303.16	1108.93	866.83	722.31
40000	3493.43	2379.33	1822.81	1489.32	1267.35	990.67	825.49
45000	3930.11	2676.75	2050.66	1675.48	1425.76	1114.50	928.68
50000	4366.78	2974.16	2278.51	1861.65	1584.18	1238.33	1031.87
55000	4803.46	3271.58	2506.36	2047.81	1742.60	1362.16	1135.05
60000	5240.14	3568.99	2734.21	2233.98	1901.02	1486.00	1238.24
65000	5676.82	3866.41	2962.06	2420.14	2059.43	1609.83	1341.43
70000	6113.50	4163.82	3189.91	2606.31	2217.85	1733.66	1444.61
75000	6550.17	4461.24	3417.76	2792.47	2376.27	1857.49	1547.80
80000	6986.85	4758.66	3645.61	2978.64	2534.69	1981.33	1650.98
100000	8733.56	5948.32	4557.02	3723.29	3168.36	2476.66	2063.73

34

TERM AMOUNT	6 YEARS	7 YEARS	8 YEARS	9 YEARS	10 YEARS	11 YEARS	12 YEARS
$ 25	.45	.40	.37	.34	.32	.30	.29
50	.90	.80	.73	.68	.63	.60	.57
75	1.35	1.20	1.09	1.01	.94	.89	.85
100	1.80	1.60	1.46	1.35	1.26	1.19	1.13
200	3.59	3.20	2.91	2.69	2.51	2.37	2.25
300	5.38	4.79	4.36	4.03	3.76	3.55	3.38
400	7.17	6.39	5.81	5.37	5.02	4.73	4.50
500	8.96	7.99	7.27	6.71	6.27	5.92	5.62
600	10.75	9.58	8.72	8.05	7.52	7.10	6.75
700	12.54	11.18	10.17	9.39	8.78	8.28	7.87
800	14.33	12.77	11.62	10.73	10.03	9.46	9.00
900	16.12	14.37	13.07	12.07	11.28	10.65	10.12
1000	17.91	15.97	14.53	13.42	12.54	11.83	11.24
2000	35.81	31.93	29.05	26.83	25.07	23.65	22.48
3000	53.71	47.89	43.57	40.24	37.60	35.47	33.72
4000	71.61	63.85	58.09	53.65	50.14	47.30	44.96
5000	89.51	79.82	72.61	67.06	62.67	59.12	56.20
6000	107.42	95.78	87.13	80.47	75.20	70.94	67.44
7000	125.32	111.74	101.65	93.88	87.73	82.77	78.68
8000	143.22	127.70	116.17	107.29	100.27	94.59	89.92
9000	161.12	143.67	130.69	120.70	112.80	106.41	101.16
10000	179.02	159.63	145.21	134.11	125.33	118.24	112.40
11000	196.92	175.59	159.73	147.52	137.86	130.06	123.64
12000	214.83	191.55	174.26	160.93	150.40	141.88	134.88
13000	232.73	207.52	188.78	174.34	162.93	153.71	146.12
14000	250.63	223.48	203.30	187.76	175.46	165.53	157.36
15000	268.53	239.44	217.82	201.17	188.00	177.35	168.60
16000	286.43	255.40	232.34	214.58	200.53	189.18	179.84
17000	304.33	271.37	246.86	227.99	213.06	201.00	191.08
18000	322.24	287.33	261.38	241.40	225.59	212.82	202.32
19000	340.14	303.29	275.90	254.81	238.13	224.65	213.56
20000	358.04	319.25	290.42	268.22	250.66	236.47	224.80
21000	375.94	335.22	304.94	281.63	263.19	248.29	236.04
22000	393.84	351.18	319.46	295.04	275.72	260.11	247.28
23000	411.74	367.14	333.98	308.45	288.26	271.94	258.52
24000	429.65	383.10	348.51	321.86	300.79	283.76	269.76
25000	447.55	399.07	363.03	335.27	313.32	295.58	281.00
26000	465.45	415.03	377.55	348.68	325.85	307.41	292.24
27000	483.35	430.99	392.07	362.10	338.39	319.23	303.48
28000	501.25	446.95	406.59	375.51	350.92	331.05	314.72
29000	519.15	462.92	421.11	388.92	363.45	342.88	325.96
30000	537.06	478.88	435.63	402.33	375.99	354.70	337.20
31000	554.96	494.84	450.15	415.74	388.52	366.52	348.44
32000	572.86	510.80	464.67	429.15	401.05	378.35	359.68
33000	590.76	526.77	479.19	442.56	413.58	390.17	370.92
34000	608.66	542.73	493.71	455.97	426.12	401.99	382.16
35000	626.56	558.69	508.23	469.38	438.65	413.82	393.40
40000	716.07	638.50	580.84	536.44	501.31	472.93	449.60
45000	805.58	718.32	653.44	603.49	563.98	532.05	505.80
50000	895.09	798.13	726.05	670.54	626.64	591.16	562.00
55000	984.60	877.94	798.65	737.60	689.30	650.28	618.20
60000	1074.11	957.75	871.26	804.65	751.97	709.40	674.40
65000	1163.62	1037.57	943.86	871.70	814.63	768.51	730.60
70000	1253.12	1117.38	1016.46	938.76	877.29	827.63	786.80
75000	1342.63	1197.19	1089.07	1005.81	939.96	886.74	843.00
80000	1432.14	1277.00	1161.67	1072.87	1002.62	945.86	899.20
100000	1790.18	1596.25	1452.09	1341.08	1253.28	1182.32	1124.00

8¾%

MONTHLY PAYMENT
NECESSARY TO AMORTIZE A LOAN

TERM AMOUNT	13 YEARS	14 YEARS	15 YEARS	16 YEARS	17 YEARS	18 YEARS	19 YEARS
$ 25	.27	.26	.25	.25	.24	.24	.23
50	.54	.52	.50	.49	.48	.47	.46
75	.81	.78	.75	.73	.71	.70	.68
100	1.08	1.04	1.00	.97	.95	.93	.91
200	2.16	2.07	2.00	1.94	1.89	1.85	1.81
300	3.23	3.11	3.00	2.91	2.84	2.77	2.71
400	4.31	4.14	4.00	3.88	3.78	3.69	3.61
500	5.38	5.18	5.00	4.85	4.72	4.61	4.51
600	6.46	6.21	6.00	5.82	5.67	5.53	5.41
700	7.53	7.25	7.00	6.79	6.61	6.45	6.31
800	8.61	8.28	8.00	7.76	7.55	7.37	7.21
900	9.68	9.31	9.00	8.73	8.50	8.29	8.11
1000	10.76	10.35	10.00	9.70	9.44	9.21	9.02
2000	21.51	20.69	19.99	19.39	18.87	18.42	18.03
3000	32.27	31.04	29.99	29.09	28.31	27.62	27.04
4000	43.02	41.38	39.98	38.78	37.74	36.84	36.05
5000	53.77	51.72	49.98	48.48	47.18	46.05	45.06
6000	64.53	62.07	59.97	58.17	56.61	55.26	54.07
7000	75.28	72.41	69.97	67.87	66.05	64.47	63.08
8000	86.04	82.76	79.96	77.56	75.48	73.68	72.09
9000	96.79	93.10	89.96	87.26	84.92	82.89	81.10
10000	107.55	103.44	99.95	96.95	94.35	92.09	90.12
11000	118.30	113.79	109.94	106.64	103.79	101.30	99.13
12000	129.05	124.13	119.94	116.34	113.22	110.51	108.14
13000	139.80	134.47	129.93	126.03	122.66	119.72	117.15
14000	150.56	144.82	139.93	135.73	132.09	128.93	126.16
15000	161.31	155.16	149.92	145.42	141.53	138.14	135.17
16000	172.07	165.51	159.92	155.12	150.96	147.35	144.18
17000	182.82	175.85	169.91	164.81	160.40	156.56	153.19
18000	193.57	186.19	179.91	174.51	169.83	165.77	162.20
19000	204.33	196.54	189.90	184.20	179.27	174.97	171.22
20000	215.08	206.88	199.89	193.89	188.70	184.18	180.23
21000	225.83	217.22	209.89	203.59	198.14	193.39	189.24
22000	236.59	227.57	219.88	213.28	207.57	202.60	198.25
23000	247.34	237.91	229.88	222.98	217.01	211.81	207.26
24000	258.10	248.26	239.87	232.67	226.44	221.02	216.27
25000	268.85	258.60	249.87	242.37	235.88	230.23	225.28
26000	279.60	268.94	259.86	252.06	245.31	239.44	234.29
27000	290.36	279.29	269.86	261.76	254.75	248.65	243.30
28000	301.11	289.63	279.85	271.45	264.18	257.85	252.32
29000	311.87	299.97	289.85	281.14	273.62	267.06	261.33
30000	322.62	310.32	299.84	290.84	283.05	276.27	270.34
31000	333.37	320.66	309.83	300.53	292.49	285.48	279.35
32000	344.13	331.01	319.83	310.23	301.92	294.69	288.36
33000	354.88	341.35	329.82	319.92	311.36	303.90	297.37
34000	365.63	351.69	339.82	329.62	320.79	313.11	306.38
35000	376.39	362.04	349.81	339.31	330.23	322.32	315.39
40000	430.16	413.76	399.78	387.78	377.40	368.36	360.45
45000	483.93	465.47	449.76	436.26	424.58	414.41	405.50
50000	537.70	517.19	499.73	484.73	471.75	460.45	450.56
55000	591.46	568.91	549.70	533.20	518.92	506.49	495.61
60000	645.23	620.63	599.67	581.67	566.10	552.54	540.67
65000	699.00	672.35	649.65	630.15	613.27	598.58	585.73
70000	752.77	724.07	699.62	678.62	660.45	644.63	630.78
75000	806.54	775.79	749.59	727.09	707.62	690.67	675.84
80000	860.31	827.51	799.56	775.56	754.80	736.72	720.89
100000	1075.39	1034.38	999.45	969.45	943.49	920.90	901.11

36

TERM AMOUNT	20 YEARS	21 YEARS	22 YEARS	25 YEARS	30 YEARS	35 YEARS	40 YEARS
$ 25	.23	.22	.22	.21	.20	.20	.19
50	.45	.44	.43	.42	.40	.39	.38
75	.67	.66	.65	.62	.60	.58	.57
100	.89	.87	.86	.83	.79	.77	.76
200	1.77	1.74	1.71	1.65	1.58	1.54	1.51
300	2.66	2.61	2.57	2.47	2.37	2.30	2.26
400	3.54	3.48	3.42	3.29	3.15	3.07	3.01
500	4.42	4.35	4.28	4.12	3.94	3.83	3.77
600	5.31	5.22	5.13	4.94	4.73	4.60	4.52
700	6.19	6.08	5.99	5.76	5.51	5.36	5.27
800	7.07	6.95	6.84	6.58	6.30	6.13	6.02
900	7.96	7.82	7.70	7.40	7.09	6.89	6.77
1000	8.84	8.69	8.55	8.23	7.87	7.66	7.53
2000	17.68	17.37	17.10	16.45	15.74	15.31	15.05
3000	26.52	26.06	25.65	24.67	23.61	22.97	22.57
4000	35.35	34.74	34.19	32.89	31.47	30.62	30.09
5000	44.19	43.42	42.74	41.11	39.34	38.27	37.61
6000	53.03	52.11	51.29	49.33	47.21	45.93	45.14
7000	61.86	60.79	59.84	57.56	55.07	53.58	52.66
8000	70.70	69.47	68.38	65.78	62.94	61.23	60.18
9000	79.54	78.16	76.93	74.00	70.81	68.89	67.70
10000	88.38	86.84	85.48	82.22	78.68	76.54	75.22
11000	97.21	95.52	94.02	90.44	86.54	84.19	82.74
12000	106.05	104.21	102.57	98.66	94.41	91.85	90.27
13000	114.89	112.89	111.12	106.88	102.28	99.50	97.79
14000	123.72	121.57	119.67	115.11	110.14	107.16	105.31
15000	132.56	130.26	128.21	123.33	118.01	114.81	112.83
16000	141.40	138.94	136.76	131.55	125.88	122.46	120.35
17000	150.24	147.62	145.31	139.77	133.74	130.12	127.87
18000	159.07	156.31	153.86	147.99	141.61	137.77	135.40
19000	167.91	164.99	162.40	156.21	149.48	145.42	142.92
20000	176.75	173.67	170.95	164.43	157.35	153.08	150.44
21000	185.58	182.36	179.50	172.66	165.21	160.73	157.96
22000	194.42	191.04	188.04	180.88	173.08	168.38	165.48
23000	203.26	199.72	196.59	189.10	180.95	176.04	173.00
24000	212.10	208.41	205.14	197.32	188.81	183.69	180.53
25000	220.93	217.09	213.69	205.54	196.68	191.35	188.05
26000	229.77	225.77	222.23	213.76	204.55	199.00	195.57
27000	238.61	234.46	230.78	221.98	212.41	206.65	203.09
28000	247.44	243.14	239.33	230.21	220.28	214.31	210.61
29000	256.28	251.83	247.87	238.43	228.15	221.96	218.13
30000	265.12	260.51	256.42	246.65	236.02	229.61	225.66
31000	273.96	269.19	264.97	254.87	243.88	237.27	233.18
32000	282.79	277.88	273.52	263.09	251.75	244.92	240.70
33000	291.63	286.56	282.06	271.31	259.62	252.57	248.22
34000	300.47	295.24	290.61	279.53	267.48	260.23	255.74
35000	309.30	303.93	299.16	287.76	275.35	267.88	263.26
40000	353.49	347.34	341.89	328.86	314.69	306.15	300.87
45000	397.67	390.76	384.63	369.97	354.02	344.42	338.48
50000	441.86	434.18	427.37	411.08	393.36	382.69	376.09
55000	486.05	477.59	470.10	452.18	432.69	420.95	413.70
60000	530.23	521.01	512.84	493.29	472.03	459.22	451.31
65000	574.42	564.43	555.58	534.40	511.36	497.49	488.92
70000	618.60	607.85	598.31	575.51	550.70	535.76	526.52
75000	662.79	651.26	641.05	616.61	590.03	574.03	564.13
80000	706.97	694.68	683.78	657.72	629.37	612.30	601.74
100000	883.72	868.35	854.73	822.15	786.71	765.37	752.18

MONTHLY PAYMENT
NECESSARY TO AMORTIZE A LOAN

TERM AMOUNT	1 YEAR	1½ YEARS	2 YEARS	2½ YEARS	3 YEARS	4 YEARS	5 YEARS
$ 25	2.19	1.49	1.15	.94	.80	.63	.52
50	4.38	2.98	2.29	1.87	1.59	1.25	1.04
75	6.56	4.47	3.43	2.81	2.39	1.87	1.56
100	8.75	5.96	4.57	3.74	3.18	2.49	2.08
200	17.50	11.92	9.14	7.47	6.36	4.98	4.16
300	26.24	17.88	13.71	11.21	9.54	7.47	6.23
400	34.99	23.84	18.28	14.94	12.72	9.96	8.31
500	43.73	29.80	22.85	18.68	15.90	12.45	10.38
600	52.48	35.76	27.42	22.41	19.08	14.94	12.46
700	61.22	41.72	31.98	26.15	22.26	17.42	14.54
800	69.97	47.68	36.55	29.88	25.44	19.91	16.61
900	78.71	53.64	41.12	33.62	28.62	22.40	18.69
1000	87.46	59.60	45.69	37.35	31.80	24.89	20.76
2000	174.91	119.20	91.37	74.70	63.60	49.78	41.52
3000	262.36	178.80	137.06	112.05	95.40	74.66	62.28
4000	349.81	238.40	182.74	149.40	127.20	99.55	83.04
5000	437.26	297.99	228.43	186.75	159.00	124.43	103.80
6000	524.71	357.59	274.11	224.09	190.80	149.32	124.56
7000	612.17	417.19	319.80	261.44	222.60	174.20	145.31
8000	699.62	476.79	365.48	298.79	254.40	199.09	166.07
9000	787.07	536.38	411.17	336.14	286.20	223.97	186.83
10000	874.52	595.98	456.85	373.49	318.00	248.86	207.59
11000	961.97	655.58	502.54	410.83	349.80	273.74	228.35
12000	1049.42	715.18	548.22	448.18	381.60	298.63	249.11
13000	1136.87	774.77	593.91	485.53	413.40	323.51	269.86
14000	1224.33	834.37	639.59	522.88	445.20	348.40	290.62
15000	1311.78	893.97	685.28	560.23	477.00	373.28	311.38
16000	1399.23	953.57	730.96	597.58	508.80	398.17	332.14
17000	1486.68	1013.17	776.65	634.92	540.60	423.05	352.90
18000	1574.13	1072.76	822.33	672.27	572.40	447.94	373.66
19000	1661.58	1132.36	868.02	709.62	604.20	472.82	394.41
20000	1749.03	1191.96	913.70	746.97	636.00	497.71	415.17
21000	1836.49	1251.56	959.38	784.32	667.80	522.59	435.93
22000	1923.94	1311.15	1005.07	821.66	699.60	547.48	456.69
23000	2011.39	1370.75	1050.75	859.01	731.40	572.36	477.45
24000	2098.84	1430.35	1096.44	896.36	763.20	597.25	498.21
25000	2186.29	1489.95	1142.12	933.71	795.00	622.13	518.96
26000	2273.74	1549.54	1187.81	971.06	826.80	647.02	539.72
27000	2361.19	1609.14	1233.49	1008.41	858.60	671.90	560.48
28000	2448.65	1668.74	1279.18	1045.75	890.40	696.79	581.24
29000	2536.10	1728.34	1324.86	1083.10	922.20	721.67	602.00
30000	2623.55	1787.93	1370.55	1120.45	954.00	746.56	622.76
31000	2711.00	1847.53	1416.23	1157.80	985.80	771.44	643.51
32000	2798.45	1907.13	1461.92	1195.15	1017.60	796.33	664.27
33000	2885.90	1966.73	1507.60	1232.49	1049.40	821.21	685.03
34000	2973.36	2026.33	1553.29	1269.84	1081.20	846.10	705.79
35000	3060.81	2085.92	1598.97	1307.19	1113.00	870.98	726.55
40000	3498.06	2383.91	1827.39	1493.93	1271.99	995.41	830.34
45000	3935.32	2681.90	2055.82	1680.67	1430.99	1119.83	934.13
50000	4372.58	2979.89	2284.24	1867.41	1589.99	1244.26	1037.92
55000	4809.84	3277.88	2512.67	2054.15	1748.99	1368.68	1141.71
60000	5247.09	3575.86	2741.09	2240.89	1907.99	1493.11	1245.51
65000	5684.35	3873.85	2969.51	2427.64	2066.99	1617.53	1349.30
70000	6121.61	4171.84	3197.94	2614.38	2225.99	1741.96	1453.09
75000	6558.87	4469.83	3426.36	2801.12	2384.98	1866.38	1556.88
80000	6996.12	4767.82	3654.78	2987.86	2543.98	1990.81	1660.67
100000	8745.15	5959.77	4568.48	3734.82	3179.98	2488.51	2075.84

9%

TERM AMOUNT	6 YEARS	7 YEARS	8 YEARS	9 YEARS	10 YEARS	11 YEARS	12 YEARS
$ 25	.46	.41	.37	.34	.32	.30	.29
50	.91	.81	.74	.68	.64	.60	.57
75	1.36	1.21	1.10	1.02	.96	.90	.86
100	1.81	1.61	1.47	1.36	1.27	1.20	1.14
200	3.61	3.22	2.94	2.71	2.54	2.40	2.28
300	5.41	4.83	4.40	4.07	3.81	3.59	3.42
400	7.22	6.44	5.87	5.42	5.07	4.79	4.56
500	9.02	8.05	7.33	6.78	6.34	5.99	5.70
600	10.82	9.66	8.80	8.13	7.61	7.18	6.83
700	12.62	11.27	10.26	9.49	8.87	8.38	7.97
800	14.43	12.88	11.73	10.84	10.14	9.57	9.11
900	16.23	14.49	13.19	12.19	11.41	10.77	10.25
1000	18.03	16.09	14.66	13.55	12.67	11.97	11.39
2000	36.06	32.18	29.31	27.09	25.34	23.93	22.77
3000	54.08	48.27	43.96	40.63	38.01	35.89	34.15
4000	72.11	64.36	58.61	54.18	50.68	47.85	45.53
5000	90.13	80.45	73.26	67.72	63.34	59.81	56.91
6000	108.16	96.54	87.91	81.26	76.01	71.77	68.29
7000	126.18	112.63	102.56	94.81	88.68	83.73	79.67
8000	144.21	128.72	117.21	108.35	101.35	95.69	91.05
9000	162.23	144.81	131.86	121.89	114.01	107.65	102.43
10000	180.26	160.90	146.51	135.43	126.68	119.61	113.81
11000	198.29	176.98	161.16	148.98	139.35	131.57	125.19
12000	216.31	193.07	175.81	162.52	152.02	143.53	136.57
13000	234.34	209.16	190.46	176.06	164.68	155.50	147.95
14000	252.36	225.25	205.11	189.61	177.35	167.46	159.33
15000	270.39	241.34	219.76	203.15	190.02	179.42	170.71
16000	288.41	257.43	234.41	216.69	202.69	191.38	182.09
17000	306.44	273.52	249.06	230.23	215.35	203.34	193.47
18000	324.46	289.61	263.71	243.78	228.02	215.30	204.85
19000	342.49	305.70	278.36	257.32	240.69	227.26	216.23
20000	360.52	321.79	293.01	270.86	253.36	239.22	227.61
21000	378.54	337.88	307.66	284.41	266.02	251.18	238.99
22000	396.57	353.96	322.31	297.95	278.69	263.14	250.37
23000	414.59	370.05	336.96	311.49	291.36	275.10	261.75
24000	432.62	386.14	351.61	325.03	304.03	287.06	273.13
25000	450.64	402.23	366.26	338.58	316.69	299.03	284.51
26000	468.67	418.32	380.91	352.12	329.36	310.99	295.89
27000	486.69	434.41	395.56	365.66	342.03	322.95	307.27
28000	504.72	450.50	410.21	379.21	354.70	334.91	318.65
29000	522.75	466.59	424.86	392.75	367.36	346.87	330.03
30000	540.77	482.68	439.51	406.29	380.03	358.83	341.41
31000	558.80	498.77	454.16	419.84	392.70	370.79	352.79
32000	576.82	514.86	468.81	433.38	405.37	382.75	364.17
33000	594.85	530.94	483.46	446.92	418.04	394.71	375.56
34000	612.87	547.03	498.11	460.46	430.70	406.67	386.94
35000	630.90	563.12	512.76	474.01	443.37	418.63	398.32
40000	721.03	643.57	586.01	541.72	506.71	478.44	455.22
45000	811.15	724.01	659.26	609.44	570.05	538.24	512.12
50000	901.28	804.46	732.52	677.15	633.38	598.05	569.02
55000	991.41	884.90	805.77	744.86	696.72	657.85	625.92
60000	1081.54	965.35	879.02	812.58	760.06	717.65	682.82
65000	1171.66	1045.80	952.27	880.29	823.40	777.46	739.72
70000	1261.79	1126.24	1025.52	948.01	886.74	837.26	796.63
75000	1351.92	1206.69	1098.77	1015.72	950.07	897.07	853.53
80000	1442.05	1287.13	1172.02	1083.44	1013.41	956.87	910.43
100000	1802.56	1608.91	1465.03	1354.30	1266.76	1196.09	1138.04

MONTHLY PAYMENT
NECESSARY TO AMORTIZE A LOAN

TERM AMOUNT	13 YEARS	14 YEARS	15 YEARS	16 YEARS	17 YEARS	18 YEARS	19 YEARS
$ 25	.28	.27	.26	.25	.24	.24	.23
50	.55	.53	.51	.50	.48	.47	.46
75	.82	.79	.77	.74	.72	.71	.69
100	1.09	1.05	1.02	.99	.96	.94	.92
200	2.18	2.10	2.03	1.97	1.92	1.88	1.84
300	3.27	3.15	3.05	2.96	2.88	2.81	2.76
400	4.36	4.20	4.06	3.94	3.84	3.75	3.67
500	5.45	5.25	5.08	4.93	4.80	4.69	4.59
600	6.54	6.30	6.09	5.91	5.76	5.62	5.51
700	7.63	7.35	7.10	6.90	6.72	6.56	6.42
800	8.72	8.40	8.12	7.88	7.68	7.50	7.34
900	9.81	9.45	9.13	8.87	8.63	8.43	8.26
1000	10.90	10.49	10.15	9.85	9.59	9.37	9.17
2000	21.80	20.98	20.29	19.70	19.18	18.73	18.34
3000	32.70	31.47	30.43	29.54	28.77	28.10	27.51
4000	43.59	41.96	40.58	39.39	38.36	37.46	36.68
5000	54.49	52.45	50.72	49.23	47.95	46.83	45.85
6000	65.39	62.94	60.86	59.08	57.53	56.19	55.02
7000	76.28	73.43	71.00	68.92	67.12	65.56	64.19
8000	87.18	83.92	81.15	78.77	76.71	74.92	73.36
9000	98.08	94.41	91.29	88.61	86.30	84.29	82.53
10000	108.97	104.90	101.43	98.46	95.89	93.65	91.69
11000	119.87	115.39	111.57	108.30	105.47	103.01	100.86
12000	130.77	125.88	121.72	118.15	115.06	112.38	110.03
13000	141.66	136.37	131.86	127.99	124.65	121.74	119.20
14000	152.56	146.86	142.00	137.84	134.24	131.11	128.37
15000	163.46	157.35	152.14	147.68	143.83	140.47	137.54
16000	174.35	167.84	162.29	157.53	153.41	149.84	146.71
17000	185.25	178.32	172.43	167.37	163.00	159.20	155.88
18000	196.15	188.81	182.57	177.22	172.59	168.57	165.05
19000	207.04	199.30	192.72	187.06	182.18	177.93	174.22
20000	217.94	209.79	202.86	196.91	191.77	187.29	183.38
21000	228.84	220.28	213.00	206.75	201.35	196.66	192.55
22000	239.73	230.77	223.14	216.60	210.94	206.02	201.72
23000	250.63	241.26	233.29	226.44	220.53	215.39	210.89
24000	261.53	251.75	243.43	236.29	230.12	224.75	220.06
25000	272.43	262.24	253.57	246.13	239.71	234.12	229.23
26000	283.32	272.73	263.71	255.98	249.29	243.48	238.40
27000	294.22	283.22	273.86	265.82	258.88	252.85	247.57
28000	305.12	293.71	284.00	275.67	268.47	262.21	256.74
29000	316.01	304.20	294.14	285.51	278.06	271.57	265.91
30000	326.91	314.69	304.28	295.36	287.65	280.94	275.07
31000	337.81	325.18	314.43	305.20	297.23	290.30	284.24
32000	348.70	335.67	324.57	315.05	306.82	299.67	293.41
33000	359.60	346.15	334.71	324.90	316.41	309.03	302.58
34000	370.50	356.64	344.86	334.74	326.00	318.40	311.75
35000	381.39	367.13	355.00	344.59	335.59	327.76	320.92
40000	435.88	419.58	405.71	393.81	383.53	374.58	366.76
45000	490.36	472.03	456.42	443.04	431.47	421.41	412.61
50000	544.85	524.47	507.14	492.26	479.41	468.23	458.45
55000	599.33	576.92	557.85	541.49	527.35	515.05	504.30
60000	653.81	629.37	608.56	590.71	575.29	561.87	550.14
65000	708.30	681.81	659.28	639.94	623.23	608.69	595.99
70000	762.78	734.26	709.99	689.17	671.17	655.52	641.83
75000	817.27	786.71	760.70	738.39	719.11	702.34	687.68
80000	871.75	839.16	811.42	787.62	767.05	749.16	733.52
100000	1089.69	1048.94	1014.27	984.52	958.81	936.45	916.90

TERM AMOUNT	20 YEARS	21 YEARS	22 YEARS	25 YEARS	30 YEARS	35 YEARS	40 YEARS
$ 25	.23	.23	.22	.21	.21	.20	.20
50	.45	.45	.44	.42	.41	.40	.39
75	.68	.67	.66	.63	.61	.59	.58
100	.90	.89	.88	.84	.81	.79	.78
200	1.80	1.77	1.75	1.68	1.61	1.57	1.55
300	2.70	2.66	2.62	2.52	2.42	2.36	2.32
400	3.60	3.54	3.49	3.36	3.22	3.14	3.09
500	4.50	4.43	4.36	4.20	4.03	3.92	3.86
600	5.40	5.31	5.23	5.04	4.83	4.71	4.63
700	6.30	6.20	6.10	5.88	5.64	5.49	5.40
800	7.20	7.08	6.97	6.72	6.44	6.28	6.18
900	8.10	7.97	7.85	7.56	7.25	7.06	6.95
1000	9.00	8.85	8.72	8.40	8.05	7.84	7.72
2000	18.00	17.70	17.43	16.79	16.10	15.68	15.43
3000	27.00	26.54	26.14	25.18	24.14	23.52	23.15
4000	35.99	35.39	34.85	33.57	32.19	31.36	30.86
5000	44.99	44.23	43.56	41.96	40.24	39.20	38.57
6000	53.99	53.08	52.28	50.36	48.28	47.04	46.29
7000	62.99	61.93	60.99	58.75	56.33	54.88	54.00
8000	71.98	70.77	69.70	67.14	64.37	62.72	61.71
9000	80.98	79.62	78.41	75.53	72.42	70.56	69.43
10000	89.98	88.46	87.12	83.92	80.47	78.40	77.14
11000	98.97	97.31	95.83	92.32	88.51	86.24	84.85
12000	107.97	106.15	104.55	100.71	96.56	94.08	92.57
13000	116.97	115.00	113.26	109.10	104.61	101.92	100.28
14000	125.97	123.85	121.97	117.49	112.65	109.76	108.00
15000	134.96	132.69	130.68	125.88	120.70	117.60	115.71
16000	143.96	141.54	139.39	134.28	128.74	125.44	123.42
17000	152.96	150.38	148.10	142.67	136.79	133.28	131.14
18000	161.96	159.23	156.82	151.06	144.84	141.12	138.85
19000	170.95	168.08	165.53	159.45	152.88	148.96	146.56
20000	179.95	176.92	174.24	167.84	160.93	156.80	154.28
21000	188.95	185.77	182.95	176.24	168.98	164.64	161.99
22000	197.94	194.61	191.66	184.63	177.02	172.48	169.70
23000	206.94	203.46	200.38	193.02	185.07	180.32	177.42
24000	215.94	212.30	209.09	201.41	193.11	188.16	185.13
25000	224.94	221.15	217.80	209.80	201.16	196.00	192.85
26000	233.93	230.00	226.51	218.20	209.21	203.84	200.56
27000	242.93	238.84	235.22	226.59	217.25	211.68	208.27
28000	251.93	247.69	243.93	234.98	225.30	219.52	215.99
29000	260.93	256.53	252.65	243.37	233.35	227.36	223.70
30000	269.92	265.38	261.36	251.76	241.39	235.20	231.41
31000	278.92	274.23	270.07	260.16	249.44	243.04	239.13
32000	287.92	283.07	278.78	268.55	257.48	250.88	246.84
33000	296.91	291.92	287.49	276.94	265.53	258.72	254.55
34000	305.91	300.76	296.20	285.33	273.58	266.56	262.27
35000	314.91	309.61	304.92	293.72	281.62	274.40	269.98
40000	359.90	353.84	348.47	335.68	321.85	313.60	308.55
45000	404.88	398.07	392.03	377.64	362.09	352.80	347.12
50000	449.87	442.30	435.59	419.60	402.32	392.00	385.69
55000	494.85	486.52	479.15	461.56	442.55	431.20	424.25
60000	539.84	530.75	522.71	503.52	482.78	470.40	462.82
65000	584.83	574.98	566.27	545.48	523.01	509.60	501.39
70000	629.81	619.21	609.83	587.44	563.24	548.80	539.96
75000	674.80	663.44	653.39	629.40	603.47	588.00	578.53
80000	719.79	707.67	696.94	671.36	643.70	627.20	617.09
100000	899.73	884.59	871.18	839.20	804.63	784.00	771.37

9¼%

MONTHLY PAYMENT
NECESSARY TO AMORTIZE A LOAN

TERM AMOUNT	1 YEAR	1½ YEARS	2 YEARS	2½ YEARS	3 YEARS	4 YEARS	5 YEARS
$ 25	2.19	1.50	1.15	.94	.80	.63	.53
50	4.38	2.99	2.29	1.88	1.60	1.26	1.05
75	6.57	4.48	3.44	2.81	2.40	1.88	1.57
100	8.76	5.98	4.58	3.75	3.20	2.51	2.09
200	17.52	11.95	9.16	7.50	6.39	5.01	4.18
300	26.28	17.92	13.74	11.24	9.58	7.51	6.27
400	35.03	23.89	18.32	14.99	12.77	10.01	8.36
500	43.79	29.86	22.90	18.74	15.96	12.51	10.44
600	52.55	35.83	27.48	22.48	19.15	15.01	12.53
700	61.30	41.80	32.06	26.23	22.35	17.51	14.62
800	70.06	47.77	36.64	29.98	25.54	20.01	16.71
900	78.82	53.75	41.22	33.72	28.73	22.51	18.80
1000	87.57	59.72	45.80	37.47	31.92	25.01	20.88
2000	175.14	119.43	91.60	74.93	63.84	50.01	41.76
3000	262.71	179.14	137.40	112.40	95.75	75.02	62.64
4000	350.27	238.85	183.20	149.86	127.67	100.02	83.52
5000	437.84	298.57	229.00	187.32	159.59	125.02	104.40
6000	525.41	358.28	274.80	224.79	191.50	150.03	125.28
7000	612.98	417.99	320.60	262.25	223.42	175.03	146.16
8000	700.54	477.70	366.40	299.71	255.33	200.04	167.04
9000	788.11	537.42	412.20	337.18	287.25	225.04	187.92
10000	875.68	597.13	458.00	374.64	319.17	250.04	208.80
11000	963.25	656.84	503.80	412.11	351.08	275.05	229.68
12000	1050.81	716.55	549.60	449.57	383.00	300.05	250.56
13000	1138.38	776.27	595.40	487.03	414.92	325.06	271.44
14000	1225.95	835.98	641.20	524.50	446.83	350.06	292.32
15000	1313.52	895.69	687.00	561.96	478.75	375.06	313.20
16000	1401.08	955.40	732.80	599.42	510.66	400.07	334.08
17000	1488.65	1015.11	778.60	636.89	542.58	425.07	354.96
18000	1576.22	1074.83	824.40	674.35	574.50	450.08	375.84
19000	1663.79	1134.54	870.20	711.81	606.41	475.08	396.72
20000	1751.35	1194.25	916.00	749.28	638.33	500.08	417.60
21000	1838.92	1253.96	961.80	786.74	670.25	525.09	438.48
22000	1926.49	1313.68	1007.59	824.21	702.16	550.09	459.36
23000	2014.06	1373.39	1053.39	861.67	734.08	575.10	480.24
24000	2101.62	1433.10	1099.19	899.13	765.99	600.10	501.12
25000	2189.19	1492.81	1144.99	936.60	797.91	625.10	522.00
26000	2276.76	1552.53	1190.79	974.06	829.83	650.11	542.88
27000	2364.33	1612.24	1236.59	1011.52	861.74	675.11	563.76
28000	2451.89	1671.95	1282.39	1048.99	893.66	700.11	584.64
29000	2539.46	1731.66	1328.19	1086.45	925.58	725.12	605.52
30000	2627.03	1791.37	1373.99	1123.91	957.49	750.12	626.40
31000	2714.60	1851.09	1419.79	1161.38	989.41	775.13	647.28
32000	2802.16	1910.80	1465.59	1198.84	1021.32	800.13	668.16
33000	2889.73	1970.51	1511.39	1236.31	1053.24	825.13	689.04
34000	2977.30	2030.22	1557.19	1273.77	1085.16	850.14	709.92
35000	3064.87	2089.94	1602.99	1311.23	1117.07	875.14	730.80
40000	3502.70	2388.50	1831.99	1498.55	1276.65	1000.16	835.20
45000	3940.54	2687.06	2060.98	1685.87	1436.23	1125.18	939.60
50000	4378.38	2985.62	2289.98	1873.19	1595.82	1250.20	1044.00
55000	4816.21	3284.18	2518.98	2060.51	1755.40	1375.22	1148.40
60000	5254.05	3582.74	2747.98	2247.82	1914.98	1500.24	1252.80
65000	5691.89	3881.31	2976.97	2435.14	2074.56	1625.26	1357.20
70000	6129.73	4179.87	3205.97	2622.46	2234.14	1750.28	1461.60
75000	6567.56	4478.43	3434.97	2809.78	2393.72	1875.30	1566.00
80000	7005.40	4776.99	3663.97	2997.10	2553.30	2000.32	1670.40
100000	8756.75	5971.24	4579.96	3746.37	3191.63	2500.40	2087.99

42

TERM AMOUNT	6 YEARS	7 YEARS	8 YEARS	9 YEARS	10 YEARS	11 YEARS	12 YEARS
$ 25	.46	.41	.37	.35	.33	.31	.29
50	.91	.82	.74	.69	.65	.61	.58
75	1.37	1.22	1.11	1.03	.97	.91	.87
100	1.82	1.63	1.48	1.37	1.29	1.21	1.16
200	3.63	3.25	2.96	2.74	2.57	2.42	2.31
300	5.45	4.87	4.44	4.11	3.85	3.63	3.46
400	7.26	6.49	5.92	5.48	5.13	4.84	4.61
500	9.08	8.11	7.40	6.84	6.41	6.05	5.77
600	10.89	9.73	8.87	8.21	7.69	7.26	6.92
700	12.71	11.36	10.35	9.58	8.97	8.47	8.07
800	14.52	12.98	11.83	10.95	10.25	9.68	9.22
900	16.34	14.60	13.31	12.31	11.53	10.89	10.37
1000	18.15	16.22	14.79	13.68	12.81	12.10	11.53
2000	36.30	32.44	29.57	27.36	25.61	24.20	23.05
3000	54.45	48.65	44.35	41.03	38.41	36.30	34.57
4000	72.60	64.87	59.13	54.71	51.22	48.40	46.09
5000	90.75	81.09	73.91	68.38	64.02	60.50	57.61
6000	108.90	97.30	88.69	82.06	76.82	72.60	69.13
7000	127.05	113.52	103.47	95.74	89.63	84.70	80.66
8000	145.20	129.73	118.25	109.41	102.43	96.80	92.18
9000	163.35	145.95	133.03	123.09	115.23	108.90	103.70
10000	181.50	162.17	147.81	136.76	128.04	121.00	115.22
11000	199.65	178.38	162.59	150.44	140.84	133.10	126.74
12000	217.80	194.60	177.37	164.11	153.64	145.20	138.26
13000	235.95	210.82	192.15	177.79	166.45	157.30	149.79
14000	254.10	227.03	206.93	191.47	179.25	169.40	161.31
15000	272.25	243.25	221.71	205.14	192.05	181.49	172.83
16000	290.40	259.46	236.49	218.82	204.86	193.59	184.35
17000	308.55	275.68	251.27	232.49	217.66	205.69	195.87
18000	326.70	291.90	266.05	246.17	230.46	217.79	207.39
19000	344.85	308.11	280.83	259.84	243.27	229.89	218.91
20000	363.00	324.33	295.61	273.52	256.07	241.99	230.44
21000	381.15	340.55	310.39	287.20	268.87	254.09	241.96
22000	399.30	356.76	325.17	300.87	281.68	266.19	253.48
23000	417.45	372.98	339.95	314.55	294.48	278.29	265.00
24000	435.60	389.19	354.73	328.22	307.28	290.39	276.52
25000	453.75	405.41	369.51	341.90	320.09	302.49	288.04
26000	471.90	421.63	384.29	355.58	332.89	314.59	299.57
27000	490.05	437.84	399.07	369.25	345.69	326.69	311.09
28000	508.20	454.06	413.85	382.93	358.50	338.79	322.61
29000	526.35	470.28	428.63	396.60	371.30	350.88	334.13
30000	544.50	486.49	443.41	410.28	384.10	362.98	345.65
31000	562.65	502.71	458.19	423.95	396.91	375.08	357.17
32000	580.80	518.92	472.97	437.63	409.71	387.18	368.70
33000	598.95	535.14	487.75	451.31	422.51	399.28	380.22
34000	617.10	551.36	502.53	464.98	435.32	411.38	391.74
35000	635.25	567.57	517.31	478.66	448.12	423.48	403.26
40000	726.00	648.65	591.21	547.04	512.14	483.98	460.87
45000	816.75	729.74	665.11	615.41	576.15	544.47	518.48
50000	907.50	810.82	739.02	683.79	640.17	604.97	576.08
55000	998.25	891.90	812.92	752.17	704.18	665.47	633.69
60000	1089.00	972.98	886.82	820.55	768.20	725.96	691.30
65000	1179.75	1054.06	960.72	888.93	832.22	786.46	748.91
70000	1270.50	1135.14	1034.62	957.31	896.23	846.96	806.51
75000	1361.24	1216.22	1108.52	1025.69	960.25	907.45	864.12
80000	1451.99	1297.30	1182.42	1094.07	1024.27	967.95	921.73
100000	1814.99	1621.63	1478.03	1367.58	1280.33	1209.93	1152.16

MONTHLY PAYMENT
NECESSARY TO AMORTIZE A LOAN

TERM AMOUNT	13 YEARS	14 YEARS	15 YEARS	16 YEARS	17 YEARS	18 YEARS	19 YEARS
$ 25	.28	.27	.26	.25	.25	.24	.24
50	.56	.54	.52	.50	.49	.48	.47
75	.83	.80	.78	.75	.74	.72	.70
100	1.11	1.07	1.03	1.00	.98	.96	.94
200	2.21	2.13	2.06	2.00	1.95	1.91	1.87
300	3.32	3.20	3.09	3.00	2.93	2.86	2.80
400	4.42	4.26	4.12	4.00	3.90	3.81	3.74
500	5.53	5.32	5.15	5.00	4.88	4.77	4.67
600	6.63	6.39	6.18	6.00	5.85	5.72	5.60
700	7.73	7.45	7.21	7.00	6.82	6.67	6.53
800	8.84	8.51	8.24	8.00	7.80	7.62	7.47
900	9.94	9.58	9.27	9.00	8.77	8.57	8.40
1000	11.05	10.64	10.30	10.00	9.75	9.53	9.33
2000	22.09	21.28	20.59	20.00	19.49	19.05	18.66
3000	33.13	31.91	30.88	30.00	29.23	28.57	27.99
4000	44.17	42.55	41.17	39.99	38.97	38.09	37.32
5000	55.21	53.19	51.46	49.99	48.72	47.61	46.65
6000	66.25	63.82	61.76	59.99	58.46	57.13	55.97
7000	77.29	74.46	72.05	69.98	68.20	66.65	65.30
8000	88.33	85.09	82.34	79.98	77.94	76.17	74.63
9000	99.37	95.73	92.63	89.98	87.69	85.70	83.96
10000	110.41	106.37	102.92	99.97	97.43	95.22	93.29
11000	121.45	117.00	113.22	109.97	107.17	104.74	102.61
12000	132.49	127.64	123.51	119.97	116.91	114.26	111.94
13000	143.54	138.27	133.80	129.97	126.66	123.78	121.27
14000	154.58	148.91	144.09	139.96	136.40	133.30	130.60
15000	165.62	159.55	154.38	149.96	146.14	142.82	139.93
16000	176.66	170.18	164.68	159.96	155.88	152.34	149.25
17000	187.70	180.82	174.97	169.95	165.62	161.87	158.58
18000	198.74	191.45	185.26	179.95	175.37	171.39	167.91
19000	209.78	202.09	195.55	189.95	185.11	180.91	177.24
20000	220.82	212.73	205.84	199.94	194.85	190.43	186.57
21000	231.86	223.36	216.14	209.94	204.59	199.95	195.89
22000	242.90	234.00	226.43	219.94	214.34	209.47	205.22
23000	253.94	244.63	236.72	229.94	224.08	218.99	214.55
24000	264.98	255.27	247.01	239.93	233.82	228.51	223.88
25000	276.02	265.91	257.30	249.93	243.56	238.03	233.21
26000	287.07	276.54	267.59	259.93	253.31	247.56	242.53
27000	298.11	287.18	277.89	269.92	263.05	257.08	251.86
28000	309.15	297.81	288.18	279.92	272.79	266.60	261.19
29000	320.19	308.45	298.47	289.92	282.53	276.12	270.52
30000	331.23	319.09	308.76	299.91	292.28	285.64	279.85
31000	342.27	329.72	319.05	309.91	302.02	295.16	289.18
32000	353.31	340.36	329.35	319.91	311.76	304.68	298.50
33000	364.35	350.99	339.64	329.91	321.50	314.20	307.83
34000	375.39	361.63	349.93	339.90	331.24	323.73	317.16
35000	386.43	372.27	360.22	349.90	340.99	333.25	326.49
40000	441.64	425.45	411.68	399.88	389.70	380.85	373.13
45000	496.84	478.63	463.14	449.87	438.41	428.46	419.77
50000	552.04	531.81	514.60	499.85	487.12	476.06	466.41
55000	607.25	584.99	566.06	549.84	535.83	523.67	513.05
60000	662.45	638.17	617.52	599.82	584.55	571.28	559.69
65000	717.66	691.35	668.98	649.81	633.26	618.88	606.33
70000	772.86	744.53	720.44	699.79	681.97	666.49	652.97
75000	828.06	797.71	771.90	749.78	730.68	714.09	699.61
80000	883.27	850.89	823.36	799.76	779.39	761.70	746.25
100000	1104.08	1063.61	1029.20	999.70	974.24	952.12	932.81

TERM AMOUNT	20 YEARS	21 YEARS	22 YEARS	25 YEARS	30 YEARS	35 YEARS	40 YEARS
$ 25	.23	.23	.23	.22	.21	.21	.20
50	.46	.46	.45	.43	.42	.41	.40
75	.69	.68	.67	.65	.62	.61	.60
100	.92	.91	.89	.86	.83	.81	.80
200	1.84	1.81	1.78	1.72	1.65	1.61	1.59
300	2.75	2.71	2.67	2.57	2.47	2.41	2.38
400	3.67	3.61	3.56	3.43	3.30	3.22	3.17
500	4.58	4.51	4.44	4.29	4.12	4.02	3.96
600	5.50	5.41	5.33	5.14	4.94	4.82	4.75
700	6.42	6.31	6.22	6.00	5.76	5.62	5.54
800	7.33	7.21	7.11	6.86	6.59	6.43	6.33
900	8.25	8.11	7.99	7.71	7.41	7.23	7.12
1000	9.16	9.01	8.88	8.57	8.23	8.03	7.91
2000	18.32	18.02	17.76	17.13	16.46	16.06	15.82
3000	27.48	27.03	26.64	25.70	24.69	24.09	23.72
4000	36.64	36.04	35.52	34.26	32.91	32.11	31.63
5000	45.80	45.05	44.39	42.82	41.14	40.14	39.54
6000	54.96	54.06	53.27	51.39	49.37	48.17	47.44
7000	64.12	63.07	62.15	59.95	57.59	56.20	55.35
8000	73.27	72.08	71.03	68.52	65.82	64.22	63.26
9000	82.43	81.09	79.90	77.08	74.05	72.25	71.16
10000	91.59	90.10	88.78	85.64	82.27	80.28	79.07
11000	100.75	99.11	97.66	94.21	90.50	88.31	86.98
12000	109.91	108.12	106.54	102.77	98.73	96.33	94.88
13000	119.07	117.13	115.41	111.33	106.95	104.36	102.79
14000	128.23	126.14	124.29	119.90	115.18	112.39	110.70
15000	137.39	135.15	133.17	128.46	123.41	120.42	118.60
16000	146.54	144.16	142.05	137.03	131.63	128.44	126.51
17000	155.70	153.17	150.92	145.59	139.86	136.47	134.42
18000	164.86	162.18	159.80	154.15	148.09	144.50	142.32
19000	174.02	171.18	168.68	162.72	156.31	152.53	150.23
20000	183.18	180.19	177.56	171.28	164.54	160.55	158.14
21000	192.34	189.20	186.43	179.85	172.77	168.58	166.04
22000	201.50	198.21	195.31	188.41	180.99	176.61	173.95
23000	210.65	207.22	204.19	196.97	189.22	184.64	181.86
24000	219.81	216.23	213.07	205.54	197.45	192.66	189.76
25000	228.97	225.24	221.94	214.10	205.67	200.69	197.67
26000	238.13	234.25	230.82	222.66	213.90	208.72	205.58
27000	247.29	243.26	239.70	231.23	222.13	216.75	213.48
28000	256.45	252.27	248.58	239.79	230.35	224.77	221.39
29000	265.61	261.28	257.45	248.36	238.58	232.80	229.30
30000	274.77	270.29	266.33	256.92	246.81	240.83	237.20
31000	283.92	279.30	275.21	265.48	255.04	248.86	245.11
32000	293.08	288.31	284.09	274.05	263.26	256.88	253.02
33000	302.24	297.32	292.96	282.61	271.49	264.91	260.92
34000	311.40	306.33	301.84	291.17	279.71	272.94	268.83
35000	320.56	315.34	310.72	299.74	287.94	280.97	276.74
40000	366.35	360.38	355.11	342.56	329.02	321.10	316.27
45000	412.15	405.43	399.49	385.38	370.21	361.24	355.80
50000	457.94	450.48	443.88	428.20	411.34	401.38	395.34
55000	503.73	495.52	488.27	471.02	452.48	441.51	434.87
60000	549.53	540.57	532.66	513.83	493.61	481.65	474.40
65000	595.32	585.62	577.05	556.65	534.74	521.79	513.93
70000	641.11	630.67	621.43	599.47	575.88	561.93	553.47
75000	686.91	675.71	665.82	642.29	617.01	602.06	593.00
80000	732.70	720.76	710.21	685.11	658.15	642.20	632.53
100000	915.87	900.95	887.76	856.39	822.68	802.75	790.67

9½%

MONTHLY PAYMENT
NECESSARY TO AMORTIZE A LOAN

TERM AMOUNT	1 YEAR	1½ YEARS	2 YEARS	2½ YEARS	3 YEARS	4 YEARS	5 YEARS
$ 25	2.20	1.50	1.15	.94	.81	.63	.53
50	4.39	3.00	2.30	1.88	1.61	1.26	1.06
75	6.58	4.49	3.45	2.82	2.41	1.89	1.58
100	8.77	5.99	4.60	3.76	3.21	2.52	2.11
200	17.54	11.97	9.19	7.52	6.41	5.03	4.21
300	26.31	17.95	13.78	11.28	9.61	7.54	6.31
400	35.08	23.94	18.37	15.04	12.82	10.05	8.41
500	43.85	29.92	22.96	18.79	16.02	12.57	10.51
600	52.62	35.90	27.55	22.55	19.22	15.08	12.61
700	61.38	41.88	32.15	26.31	22.43	17.59	14.71
800	70.15	47.87	36.74	30.07	25.63	20.10	16.81
900	78.92	53.85	41.33	33.83	28.83	22.62	18.91
1000	87.69	59.83	45.92	37.58	32.04	25.13	21.01
2000	175.37	119.66	91.83	75.16	64.07	50.25	42.01
3000	263.06	179.49	137.75	112.74	96.10	75.37	63.01
4000	350.74	239.31	183.66	150.32	128.14	100.50	84.01
5000	438.42	299.14	229.58	187.90	160.17	125.62	105.01
6000	526.11	358.97	275.49	225.48	192.20	150.74	126.02
7000	613.79	418.79	321.41	263.06	224.24	175.87	147.02
8000	701.47	478.62	367.32	300.64	256.27	200.99	168.02
9000	789.16	538.45	413.24	338.22	288.30	226.11	189.02
10000	876.84	598.28	459.15	375.80	320.33	251.24	210.02
11000	964.52	658.10	505.06	413.38	352.37	276.36	231.03
12000	1052.21	717.93	550.98	450.96	384.40	301.48	252.03
13000	1139.89	777.76	596.89	488.54	416.43	326.61	273.03
14000	1227.57	837.58	642.81	526.12	448.47	351.73	294.03
15000	1315.26	897.41	688.72	563.70	480.50	376.85	315.03
16000	1402.94	957.24	734.64	601.27	512.53	401.98	336.03
17000	1490.62	1017.07	780.55	638.85	544.57	427.10	357.04
18000	1578.31	1076.89	826.47	676.43	576.60	452.22	378.04
19000	1665.99	1136.72	872.38	714.01	608.63	477.34	399.04
20000	1753.68	1196.55	918.29	751.59	640.66	502.47	420.04
21000	1841.36	1256.38	964.21	789.17	672.70	527.59	441.04
22000	1929.04	1316.20	1010.12	826.75	704.73	552.71	462.05
23000	2016.73	1376.03	1056.04	864.33	736.76	577.84	483.05
24000	2104.41	1435.86	1101.95	901.91	768.80	602.96	504.05
25000	2192.09	1495.68	1147.87	939.49	800.83	628.08	525.05
26000	2279.78	1555.51	1193.78	977.07	832.86	653.21	546.05
27000	2367.46	1615.34	1239.70	1014.65	864.89	678.33	567.06
28000	2455.14	1675.16	1285.61	1052.23	896.93	703.45	588.06
29000	2542.83	1734.99	1331.53	1089.81	928.96	728.58	609.06
30000	2630.51	1794.82	1377.44	1127.39	960.99	753.70	630.06
31000	2718.19	1854.65	1423.36	1164.97	993.03	778.82	651.06
32000	2805.88	1914.47	1469.27	1202.54	1025.06	803.95	672.06
33000	2893.56	1974.30	1515.18	1240.12	1057.09	829.07	693.07
34000	2981.24	2034.13	1561.10	1277.70	1089.13	854.19	714.07
35000	3068.93	2093.95	1607.01	1315.28	1121.16	879.31	735.07
40000	3507.35	2393.09	1836.58	1503.18	1281.32	1004.93	840.08
45000	3945.76	2692.23	2066.16	1691.08	1441.69	1130.55	945.09
50000	4384.18	2991.36	2295.73	1878.97	1601.65	1256.16	1050.10
55000	4822.60	3290.50	2525.30	2066.87	1761.82	1381.78	1155.11
60000	5261.02	3589.63	2754.87	2254.77	1921.98	1507.39	1260.12
65000	5699.43	3888.77	2984.45	2442.66	2082.15	1633.01	1365.13
70000	6137.85	4187.90	3214.02	2630.56	2242.31	1758.62	1470.14
75000	6576.27	4487.04	3443.59	2818.46	2402.48	1884.24	1575.14
80000	7014.69	4786.17	3673.16	3006.35	2562.64	2009.86	1680.15
100000	8768.36	5982.72	4591.46	3757.94	3203.30	2512.32	2100.19

46

TERM AMOUNT	6 YEARS	7 YEARS	8 YEARS	9 YEARS	10 YEARS	11 YEARS	12 YEARS
$ 25	.46	.41	.38	.35	.33	.31	.30
50	.92	.82	.75	.70	.65	.62	.59
75	1.38	1.23	1.12	1.04	.98	.92	.88
100	1.83	1.64	1.50	1.39	1.30	1.23	1.17
200	3.66	3.27	2.99	2.77	2.59	2.45	2.34
300	5.49	4.91	4.48	4.15	3.89	3.68	3.50
400	7.31	6.54	5.97	5.53	5.18	4.90	4.67
500	9.14	8.18	7.46	6.91	6.47	6.12	5.84
600	10.97	9.81	8.95	8.29	7.77	7.35	7.00
700	12.80	11.45	10.44	9.67	9.06	8.57	8.17
800	14.62	13.08	11.93	11.05	10.36	9.80	9.34
900	16.45	14.71	13.42	12.43	11.65	11.02	10.50
1000	18.28	16.35	14.92	13.81	12.94	12.24	11.67
2000	36.55	32.69	29.83	27.62	25.88	24.48	23.33
3000	54.83	49.04	44.74	41.43	38.82	36.72	35.00
4000	73.10	65.38	59.65	55.24	51.76	48.96	46.66
5000	91.38	81.72	74.56	69.05	64.70	61.20	58.32
6000	109.65	98.07	89.47	82.86	77.64	73.44	69.99
7000	127.93	114.41	104.38	96.67	90.58	85.68	81.65
8000	146.20	130.76	119.29	110.48	103.52	97.91	93.31
9000	164.48	147.10	134.20	124.29	116.46	110.15	104.98
10000	182.75	163.44	149.11	138.10	129.40	122.39	116.64
11000	201.03	179.79	164.02	151.91	142.34	134.63	128.31
12000	219.30	196.13	178.94	165.72	155.28	146.87	139.97
13000	237.58	212.48	193.85	179.53	168.22	159.11	151.63
14000	255.85	228.82	208.76	193.34	181.16	171.35	163.30
15000	274.13	245.16	223.67	207.15	194.10	183.58	174.96
16000	292.40	261.51	238.58	220.95	207.04	195.82	186.62
17000	310.67	277.85	253.49	234.76	219.98	208.06	198.29
18000	328.95	294.20	268.40	248.57	232.92	220.30	209.95
19000	347.22	310.54	283.31	262.38	245.86	232.54	221.62
20000	365.50	326.88	298.22	276.19	258.80	244.78	233.28
21000	383.77	343.23	313.13	290.00	271.74	257.02	244.94
22000	402.05	359.57	328.04	303.81	284.68	269.26	256.61
23000	420.32	375.92	342.96	317.62	297.62	281.49	268.27
24000	438.60	392.26	357.87	331.43	310.56	293.73	279.93
25000	456.87	408.60	372.78	345.24	323.50	305.97	291.60
26000	475.15	424.95	387.69	359.05	336.44	318.21	303.26
27000	493.42	441.29	402.60	372.86	349.38	330.45	314.93
28000	511.70	457.64	417.51	386.67	362.32	342.69	326.59
29000	529.97	473.98	432.42	400.48	375.26	354.93	338.25
30000	548.25	490.32	447.33	414.29	388.20	367.16	349.92
31000	566.52	506.67	462.24	428.10	401.14	379.40	361.58
32000	584.80	523.01	477.15	441.90	414.08	391.64	373.24
33000	603.07	539.36	492.06	455.71	427.02	403.88	384.91
34000	621.34	555.70	506.98	469.52	439.96	416.12	396.57
35000	639.62	572.04	521.89	483.33	452.90	428.36	408.24
40000	730.99	653.76	596.44	552.38	517.60	489.55	466.55
45000	822.37	735.48	670.99	621.43	582.29	550.74	524.87
50000	913.74	817.20	745.55	690.47	646.99	611.94	583.19
55000	1005.11	898.92	820.10	759.52	711.69	673.13	641.51
60000	1096.49	980.64	894.66	828.57	776.39	734.32	699.83
65000	1187.86	1062.36	969.21	897.61	841.09	795.52	758.15
70000	1279.23	1144.08	1043.77	966.66	905.79	856.71	816.47
75000	1370.61	1225.80	1118.32	1035.71	970.49	917.90	874.78
80000	1461.98	1307.52	1192.88	1104.75	1035.19	979.10	933.10
100000	1827.47	1634.40	1491.09	1380.94	1293.98	1223.87	1166.38

47

9½%

TERM AMOUNT	13 YEARS	14 YEARS	15 YEARS	16 YEARS	17 YEARS	18 YEARS	19 YEARS
$ 25	.28	.27	.27	.26	.25	.25	.24
50	.56	.54	.53	.51	.50	.49	.48
75	.84	.81	.79	.77	.75	.73	.72
100	1.12	1.08	1.05	1.02	.99	.97	.95
200	2.24	2.16	2.09	2.03	1.98	1.94	1.90
300	3.36	3.24	3.14	3.05	2.97	2.91	2.85
400	4.48	4.32	4.18	4.06	3.96	3.88	3.80
500	5.60	5.40	5.23	5.08	4.95	4.84	4.75
600	6.72	6.48	6.27	6.09	5.94	5.81	5.70
700	7.84	7.55	7.31	7.11	6.93	6.78	6.65
800	8.95	8.63	8.36	8.12	7.92	7.75	7.60
900	10.07	9.71	9.40	9.14	8.91	8.72	8.54
1000	11.19	10.79	10.45	10.15	9.90	9.68	9.49
2000	22.38	21.57	20.89	20.30	19.80	19.36	18.98
3000	33.56	32.36	31.33	30.45	29.70	29.04	28.47
4000	44.75	43.14	41.77	40.80	39.60	38.72	37.96
5000	55.93	53.92	52.22	50.75	49.49	48.40	47.45
6000	67.12	64.71	62.66	60.90	59.39	58.08	56.94
7000	78.31	75.49	73.10	71.05	69.29	67.76	66.42
8000	89.49	86.27	83.54	81.20	79.19	77.44	75.91
9000	100.68	97.06	93.99	91.35	89.09	87.12	85.40
10000	111.86	107.84	104.43	101.50	98.98	96.80	94.89
11000	123.05	118.63	114.87	111.65	108.88	106.48	104.38
12000	134.23	129.41	125.31	121.80	118.78	116.15	113.87
13000	145.42	140.19	135.75	131.95	128.68	125.83	123.35
14000	156.61	150.98	146.20	142.10	138.57	135.51	132.84
15000	167.79	161.76	156.64	152.25	148.47	145.19	142.33
16000	178.98	172.54	167.08	162.40	158.37	154.87	151.82
17000	190.16	183.33	177.52	172.55	168.27	164.55	161.31
18000	201.35	194.11	187.97	182.70	178.17	174.23	170.80
19000	212.53	204.89	198.41	192.85	188.06	183.91	180.28
20000	223.72	215.68	208.85	203.00	197.96	193.59	189.77
21000	234.91	226.46	219.29	213.15	207.86	203.27	199.26
22000	246.09	237.25	229.73	223.30	217.76	212.95	208.75
23000	257.28	248.03	240.18	233.45	227.65	222.62	218.24
24000	268.46	258.81	250.62	243.60	237.55	232.30	227.73
25000	279.65	269.60	261.06	253.75	247.45	241.98	237.21
26000	290.83	280.38	271.50	263.90	257.35	251.66	246.70
27000	302.02	291.16	281.95	274.05	267.25	261.34	256.19
28000	313.21	301.95	292.39	284.20	277.14	271.02	265.68
29000	324.39	312.73	302.83	294.35	287.04	280.70	275.17
30000	335.58	323.52	313.27	304.50	296.94	290.38	284.66
31000	346.76	334.30	323.71	314.65	306.84	300.06	294.15
32000	357.95	345.08	334.16	324.80	316.73	309.74	303.63
33000	369.13	355.87	344.60	334.95	326.63	319.42	313.12
34000	380.32	366.65	355.04	345.10	336.53	329.09	322.61
35000	391.51	377.43	365.48	355.25	346.43	338.77	332.10
40000	447.43	431.35	417.69	406.00	395.92	387.17	379.54
45000	503.36	485.27	469.91	456.75	445.41	435.57	426.98
50000	559.29	539.19	522.12	507.50	494.90	483.96	474.42
55000	615.22	593.11	574.33	558.25	544.38	532.36	521.87
60000	671.15	647.03	626.54	609.00	593.87	580.75	569.31
65000	727.08	700.94	678.75	659.75	643.36	629.15	616.75
70000	783.01	754.86	730.96	710.50	692.85	677.54	664.19
75000	838.93	808.78	783.17	761.25	742.34	725.94	711.63
80000	894.86	862.70	835.38	812.00	791.83	774.33	759.08
100000	1118.58	1078.37	1044.23	1014.99	989.79	967.92	948.84

TERM AMOUNT	20 YEARS	21 YEARS	22 YEARS	25 YEARS	30 YEARS	35 YEARS	40 YEARS
$ 25	.24	.23	.23	.22	.22	.21	.21
50	.47	.46	.46	.44	.43	.42	.41
75	.70	.69	.68	.66	.64	.62	.61
100	.94	.92	.91	.88	.85	.83	.82
200	1.87	1.84	1.81	1.75	1.69	1.65	1.63
300	2.80	2.76	2.72	2.63	2.53	2.47	2.44
400	3.73	3.67	3.62	3.50	3.37	3.29	3.25
500	4.67	4.59	4.53	4.37	4.21	4.11	4.06
600	5.60	5.51	5.43	5.25	5.05	4.93	4.87
700	6.53	6.43	6.34	6.12	5.89	5.76	5.68
800	7.46	7.34	7.24	6.99	6.73	6.58	6.49
900	8.39	8.26	8.15	7.87	7.57	7.40	7.30
1000	9.33	9.18	9.05	8.74	8.41	8.22	8.11
2000	18.65	18.35	18.09	17.48	16.82	16.44	16.21
3000	27.97	27.53	27.14	26.22	25.23	24.65	24.31
4000	37.29	36.70	36.18	34.95	33.64	32.87	32.41
5000	46.61	45.88	45.23	43.69	42.05	41.09	40.51
6000	55.93	55.05	54.27	52.43	50.46	49.30	48.61
7000	65.25	64.23	63.32	61.16	58.86	57.52	56.71
8000	74.58	73.40	72.36	69.90	67.27	65.73	64.81
9000	83.90	82.57	81.41	78.64	75.68	73.95	72.91
10000	93.22	91.75	90.45	87.37	84.09	82.17	81.01
11000	102.54	100.92	99.50	96.11	92.50	90.38	89.11
12000	111.86	110.10	108.54	104.85	100.91	98.60	97.21
13000	121.18	119.27	117.58	113.59	109.32	106.81	105.31
14000	130.50	128.45	126.63	122.32	117.72	115.03	113.41
15000	139.82	137.62	135.67	131.06	126.13	123.25	121.51
16000	149.15	146.79	144.72	139.80	134.54	131.46	129.61
17000	158.47	155.97	153.76	148.53	142.95	139.68	137.72
18000	167.79	165.14	162.81	157.27	151.36	147.90	145.82
19000	177.11	174.32	171.85	166.01	159.77	156.11	153.92
20000	186.43	183.49	180.90	174.74	168.18	164.33	162.02
21000	195.75	192.67	189.94	183.48	176.58	172.54	170.12
22000	205.07	201.84	198.99	192.22	184.99	180.76	178.22
23000	214.40	211.01	208.03	200.96	193.40	188.98	186.32
24000	223.72	220.19	217.08	209.69	201.81	197.19	194.42
25000	233.04	229.36	226.12	218.43	210.22	205.41	202.52
26000	242.36	238.54	235.16	227.17	218.63	213.62	210.62
27000	251.68	247.71	244.21	235.90	227.04	221.84	218.72
28000	261.00	256.89	253.25	244.64	235.44	230.06	226.82
29000	270.32	266.06	262.30	253.38	243.85	238.27	234.92
30000	279.64	275.24	271.34	262.11	252.26	246.49	243.02
31000	288.97	284.41	280.39	270.85	260.67	254.70	251.12
32000	298.29	293.58	289.43	279.59	269.08	262.92	259.22
33000	307.61	302.76	298.48	288.32	277.49	271.14	267.33
34000	316.93	311.93	307.52	297.06	285.90	279.35	275.43
35000	326.25	321.11	316.57	305.80	294.30	287.57	283.53
40000	372.86	366.98	361.79	349.48	336.35	328.65	324.03
45000	419.46	412.85	407.01	393.17	378.39	369.73	364.53
50000	466.07	458.72	452.24	436.85	420.43	410.81	405.04
55000	512.68	504.59	497.46	480.54	462.47	451.89	445.54
60000	559.28	550.47	542.68	524.22	504.52	492.97	486.04
65000	605.89	596.34	587.90	567.91	546.56	534.05	526.55
70000	652.50	642.21	633.13	611.59	588.60	575.13	567.05
75000	699.10	688.08	678.35	655.28	630.65	616.21	607.55
80000	745.71	733.95	723.57	698.96	672.69	657.29	648.05
100000	932.14	917.44	904.47	873.70	840.86	821.62	810.07

49

TERM AMOUNT	1 YEAR	1½ YEARS	2 YEARS	2½ YEARS	3 YEARS	4 YEARS	5 YEARS
$ 25	2.20	1.50	1.16	.95	.81	.64	.53
50	4.39	3.00	2.31	1.89	1.61	1.27	1.06
75	6.59	4.50	3.46	2.83	2.42	1.90	1.59
100	8.78	6.00	4.61	3.77	3.22	2.53	2.12
200	17.56	11.99	9.21	7.54	6.43	5.05	4.23
300	26.34	17.99	13.81	11.31	9.65	7.58	6.34
400	35.12	23.98	18.42	15.08	12.86	10.10	8.45
500	43.90	29.98	23.02	18.85	16.08	12.63	10.57
600	52.68	35.97	27.62	22.62	19.29	15.15	12.68
700	61.46	41.96	32.23	26.39	22.51	17.67	14.79
800	70.24	47.96	36.83	30.16	25.72	20.20	16.90
900	79.02	53.95	41.43	33.93	28.94	22.72	19.02
1000	87.80	59.95	46.03	37.70	32.15	25.25	21.13
2000	175.60	119.89	92.06	75.40	64.30	50.49	42.25
3000	263.40	179.83	138.09	113.09	96.45	75.73	63.38
4000	351.20	239.77	184.12	150.79	128.60	100.98	84.50
5000	439.00	299.72	230.15	188.48	160.75	126.22	105.63
6000	526.80	359.66	276.18	226.18	192.90	151.46	126.75
7000	614.60	419.60	322.21	263.87	225.05	176.70	147.87
8000	702.40	479.54	368.24	301.57	257.20	201.95	169.00
9000	790.20	539.48	414.27	339.26	289.35	227.19	190.12
10000	878.00	599.43	460.30	376.96	321.50	252.43	211.25
11000	965.80	659.37	506.33	414.65	353.65	277.67	232.37
12000	1053.60	719.31	552.36	452.35	385.80	302.92	253.50
13000	1141.40	779.25	598.39	490.04	417.95	328.16	274.62
14000	1229.20	839.19	644.42	527.74	450.10	353.40	295.74
15000	1317.00	899.14	690.45	565.43	482.25	378.65	316.87
16000	1404.80	959.08	736.48	603.13	514.40	403.89	337.99
17000	1492.60	1019.02	782.51	640.82	546.55	429.13	359.12
18000	1580.40	1078.96	828.54	678.52	578.70	454.37	380.24
19000	1668.20	1138.90	874.57	716.22	610.85	479.62	401.37
20000	1756.00	1198.85	920.60	753.91	643.00	504.86	422.49
21000	1843.80	1258.79	966.63	791.61	675.15	530.10	443.61
22000	1931.60	1318.73	1012.66	829.30	707.30	555.34	464.74
23000	2019.40	1378.67	1058.69	867.00	739.45	580.59	485.86
24000	2107.20	1438.61	1104.72	904.69	771.60	605.83	506.99
25000	2195.00	1498.56	1150.75	942.39	803.75	631.07	528.11
26000	2282.80	1558.50	1196.78	980.08	835.90	656.31	549.24
27000	2370.60	1618.44	1242.80	1017.78	868.05	681.56	570.36
28000	2458.40	1678.38	1288.83	1055.47	900.20	706.80	591.48
29000	2546.20	1738.32	1334.86	1093.17	932.35	732.04	612.61
30000	2633.99	1798.27	1380.89	1130.86	964.50	757.29	633.73
31000	2721.79	1858.21	1426.92	1168.56	996.65	782.53	654.86
32000	2809.59	1918.15	1472.95	1206.25	1028.80	807.77	675.98
33000	2897.39	1978.09	1518.98	1243.95	1060.95	833.01	697.11
34000	2985.19	2038.03	1565.01	1281.64	1093.10	858.26	718.23
35000	3072.99	2097.98	1611.04	1319.34	1125.25	883.50	739.35
40000	3511.99	2397.69	1841.19	1507.82	1286.00	1009.71	844.97
45000	3950.99	2697.40	2071.34	1696.29	1446.75	1135.93	950.60
50000	4389.99	2997.11	2301.49	1884.77	1607.50	1262.14	1056.22
55000	4828.99	3296.82	2531.63	2073.25	1768.25	1388.35	1161.84
60000	5267.98	3596.53	2761.78	2261.72	1929.00	1514.57	1267.46
65000	5706.98	3896.24	2991.93	2450.20	2089.75	1640.78	1373.08
70000	6145.98	4195.95	3222.08	2638.67	2250.50	1766.99	1478.70
75000	6584.98	4495.66	3452.23	2827.15	2411.25	1893.21	1584.32
80000	7023.98	4795.37	3682.37	3015.63	2572.00	2019.42	1689.94
100000	8779.97	5994.21	4602.97	3769.53	3215.00	2524.27	2112.43

TERM AMOUNT	6 YEARS	7 YEARS	8 YEARS	9 YEARS	10 YEARS	11 YEARS	12 YEARS
$ 25	.47	.42	.38	.35	.33	.31	.30
50	.93	.83	.76	.70	.66	.62	.60
75	1.39	1.24	1.13	1.05	.99	.93	.89
100	1.85	1.65	1.51	1.40	1.31	1.24	1.19
200	3.69	3.30	3.01	2.79	2.62	2.48	2.37
300	5.53	4.95	4.52	4.19	3.93	3.72	3.55
400	7.37	6.59	6.02	5.58	5.24	4.96	4.73
500	9.21	8.24	7.53	6.98	6.54	6.19	5.91
600	11.05	9.89	9.03	8.37	7.85	7.43	7.09
700	12.89	11.54	10.53	9.77	9.16	8.67	8.27
800	14.73	13.18	12.04	11.16	10.47	9.91	9.45
900	16.57	14.83	13.54	12.55	11.77	11.15	10.63
1000	18.41	16.48	15.05	13.95	13.08	12.38	11.81
2000	36.81	32.95	30.09	27.89	26.16	24.76	23.62
3000	55.21	49.42	45.13	41.84	39.24	37.14	35.43
4000	73.61	65.89	60.17	55.78	52.31	49.52	47.23
5000	92.01	82.37	75.22	69.72	65.39	61.90	59.04
6000	110.41	98.84	90.26	83.67	78.47	74.28	70.85
7000	128.81	115.31	105.30	97.61	91.54	86.66	82.65
8000	147.21	131.78	120.34	111.55	104.62	99.04	94.46
9000	165.61	148.25	135.38	125.50	117.70	111.41	106.27
10000	184.01	164.73	150.43	139.44	130.78	123.79	118.07
11000	202.41	181.20	165.47	153.39	143.85	136.17	129.88
12000	220.81	197.67	180.51	167.33	156.93	148.55	141.69
13000	239.21	214.14	195.55	181.27	170.01	160.93	153.49
14000	257.61	230.62	210.60	195.22	183.08	173.31	165.30
15000	276.01	247.09	225.64	209.16	196.16	185.69	177.11
16000	294.41	263.56	240.68	223.10	209.24	198.07	188.91
17000	312.81	280.03	255.72	237.05	222.31	210.45	200.72
18000	331.21	296.51	270.76	250.99	235.39	222.82	212.53
19000	349.61	312.98	285.81	264.93	248.47	235.20	224.33
20000	368.01	329.45	300.85	278.88	261.55	247.58	236.14
21000	386.41	345.92	315.89	292.82	274.62	259.96	247.95
22000	404.81	362.40	330.93	306.77	287.70	272.34	259.75
23000	423.21	378.87	345.98	320.71	300.78	284.72	271.56
24000	441.61	395.34	361.02	334.65	313.85	297.10	283.37
25000	460.01	411.81	376.06	348.60	326.93	309.48	295.18
26000	478.41	428.28	391.10	362.54	340.01	321.85	306.98
27000	496.81	444.76	406.14	376.48	353.08	334.23	318.79
28000	515.21	461.23	421.19	390.43	366.16	346.61	330.60
29000	533.61	477.70	436.23	404.37	379.24	358.99	342.40
30000	552.01	494.17	451.27	418.31	392.32	371.37	354.21
31000	570.41	510.65	466.31	432.26	405.39	383.75	366.02
32000	588.81	527.12	481.36	446.20	418.47	396.13	377.82
33000	607.21	543.59	496.40	460.15	431.55	408.51	389.63
34000	625.61	560.06	511.44	474.09	444.62	420.89	401.44
35000	644.01	576.54	526.48	488.03	457.70	433.26	413.24
40000	736.01	658.90	601.69	557.75	523.09	495.16	472.28
45000	828.01	741.26	676.90	627.47	588.47	557.05	531.31
50000	920.01	823.62	752.12	697.19	653.86	618.95	590.35
55000	1012.01	905.98	827.33	766.91	719.24	680.84	649.38
60000	1104.01	988.34	902.54	836.62	784.63	742.74	708.41
65000	1196.01	1070.70	977.75	906.34	850.01	804.63	767.45
70000	1288.01	1153.07	1052.96	976.06	915.40	866.52	826.48
75000	1380.01	1235.43	1128.17	1045.78	980.78	928.42	885.52
80000	1472.01	1317.79	1203.38	1115.50	1046.17	990.31	944.55
100000	1840.01	1647.23	1504.23	1394.37	1307.71	1237.89	1180.69

51

TERM AMOUNT	13 YEARS	14 YEARS	15 YEARS	16 YEARS	17 YEARS	18 YEARS	19 YEARS
$ 25	.29	.28	.27	.26	.26	.25	.25
50	.57	.55	.53	.52	.51	.50	.49
75	.85	.82	.80	.78	.76	.74	.73
100	1.14	1.10	1.06	1.04	1.01	.99	.97
200	2.27	2.19	2.12	2.07	2.02	1.97	1.93
300	3.40	3.28	3.18	3.10	3.02	2.96	2.90
400	4.54	4.38	4.24	4.13	4.03	3.94	3.86
500	5.67	5.47	5.30	5.16	5.03	4.92	4.83
600	6.80	6.56	6.36	6.19	6.04	5.91	5.79
700	7.94	7.66	7.42	7.22	7.04	6.89	6.76
800	9.07	8.75	8.48	8.25	8.05	7.88	7.72
900	10.20	9.84	9.54	9.28	9.05	8.86	8.69
1000	11.34	10.94	10.60	10.31	10.06	9.84	9.65
2000	22.67	21.87	21.19	20.61	20.11	19.68	19.30
3000	34.00	32.80	31.79	30.92	30.17	29.52	28.95
4000	45.33	43.73	42.38	41.22	40.22	39.36	38.60
5000	56.66	54.67	52.97	51.52	50.28	49.20	48.25
6000	67.99	65.60	63.57	61.83	60.33	59.03	57.90
7000	79.33	76.53	74.16	72.13	70.39	68.87	67.55
8000	90.66	87.46	84.75	82.44	80.44	78.71	77.20
9000	101.99	98.40	95.35	92.74	90.49	88.55	86.85
10000	113.32	109.33	105.94	103.04	100.55	98.39	96.50
11000	124.65	120.26	116.53	113.35	110.60	108.23	106.15
12000	135.98	131.19	127.13	123.65	120.66	118.06	115.80
13000	147.32	142.13	137.72	133.96	130.71	127.90	125.45
14000	158.65	153.06	148.32	144.26	140.77	137.74	135.10
15000	169.98	163.99	158.91	154.56	150.82	147.58	144.75
16000	181.31	174.92	169.50	164.87	160.88	157.42	154.40
17000	192.64	185.85	180.10	175.17	170.93	167.25	164.05
18000	203.97	196.79	190.69	185.48	180.98	177.09	173.70
19000	215.31	207.72	201.28	195.78	191.04	186.93	183.35
20000	226.64	218.65	211.88	206.08	201.09	196.77	193.00
21000	237.97	229.58	222.47	216.39	211.15	206.61	202.65
22000	249.30	240.52	233.06	226.69	221.20	216.45	212.30
23000	260.63	251.45	243.66	237.00	231.26	226.28	221.95
24000	271.96	262.38	254.25	247.30	241.31	236.12	231.60
25000	283.30	273.31	264.85	257.60	251.36	245.96	241.25
26000	294.63	284.25	275.44	267.91	261.42	255.80	250.90
27000	305.96	295.18	286.03	278.21	271.47	265.64	260.55
28000	317.29	306.11	296.63	288.51	281.53	275.47	270.20
29000	328.62	317.04	307.22	298.82	291.58	285.31	279.85
30000	339.95	327.98	317.81	309.12	301.64	295.15	289.50
31000	351.29	338.91	328.41	319.43	311.69	304.99	299.15
32000	362.62	349.84	339.00	329.73	321.75	314.83	308.80
33000	373.95	360.77	349.59	340.03	331.80	324.67	318.45
34000	385.28	371.70	360.19	350.34	341.85	334.50	328.10
35000	396.61	382.64	370.78	360.64	351.91	344.34	337.75
40000	453.27	437.30	423.75	412.16	402.18	393.53	386.00
45000	509.93	491.96	476.72	463.68	452.45	442.72	434.25
50000	566.59	546.62	529.69	515.20	502.72	491.92	482.50
55000	623.24	601.28	582.65	566.72	553.00	541.11	530.75
60000	679.90	655.95	635.62	618.24	603.27	590.30	579.00
65000	736.56	710.61	688.59	669.76	653.54	639.49	627.25
70000	793.22	765.27	741.56	721.28	703.81	688.68	675.50
75000	849.88	819.93	794.53	772.80	754.08	737.87	723.75
80000	906.54	874.59	847.50	824.32	804.36	787.06	772.00
100000	1133.17	1093.24	1059.37	1030.40	1005.44	983.83	965.00

MONTHLY PAYMENT 9¾%
NECESSARY TO AMORTIZE A LOAN

TERM AMOUNT	20 YEARS	21 YEARS	22 YEARS	25 YEARS	30 YEARS	35 YEARS	40 YEARS
$ 25	.24	.24	.24	.23	.22	.22	.21
50	.48	.47	.47	.45	.43	.43	.42
75	.72	.71	.70	.67	.65	.64	.63
100	.95	.94	.93	.90	.86	.85	.83
200	1.90	1.87	1.85	1.79	1.72	1.69	1.66
300	2.85	2.81	2.77	2.68	2.58	2.53	2.49
400	3.80	3.74	3.69	3.57	3.44	3.37	3.32
500	4.75	4.68	4.61	4.46	4.30	4.21	4.15
600	5.70	5.61	5.53	5.35	5.16	5.05	4.98
700	6.64	6.54	6.45	6.24	6.02	5.89	5.81
800	7.59	7.48	7.38	7.13	6.88	6.73	6.64
900	8.54	8.41	8.30	8.03	7.74	7.57	7.47
1000	9.49	9.35	9.22	8.92	8.60	8.41	8.30
2000	18.98	18.69	18.43	17.83	17.19	16.82	16.60
3000	28.46	28.03	27.64	26.74	25.78	25.22	24.89
4000	37.95	37.37	36.86	35.65	34.37	33.63	33.19
5000	47.43	46.71	46.07	44.56	42.96	42.03	41.48
6000	56.92	56.05	55.28	53.47	51.55	50.44	49.78
7000	66.40	65.39	64.50	62.38	60.15	58.85	58.07
8000	75.89	74.73	73.71	71.30	68.74	67.25	66.37
9000	85.37	84.07	82.92	80.21	77.33	75.66	74.67
10000	94.86	93.41	92.13	89.12	85.92	84.06	82.96
11000	104.34	102.75	101.35	98.03	94.51	92.47	91.26
12000	113.83	112.09	110.56	106.94	103.10	100.88	99.55
13000	123.31	121.43	119.77	115.85	111.70	109.28	107.85
14000	132.80	130.77	128.99	124.76	120.29	117.69	116.14
15000	142.28	140.11	138.20	133.68	128.88	126.09	124.44
16000	151.77	149.45	147.41	142.59	137.47	134.50	132.73
17000	161.25	158.79	156.62	151.50	146.06	142.91	141.03
18000	170.74	168.13	165.84	160.41	154.65	151.31	149.33
19000	180.22	177.47	175.05	169.32	163.24	159.72	157.62
20000	189.71	186.81	184.26	178.23	171.84	168.12	165.92
21000	199.19	196.15	193.48	187.14	180.43	176.53	174.21
22000	208.68	205.50	202.69	196.06	189.02	184.93	182.51
23000	218.16	214.84	211.90	204.97	197.61	193.34	190.80
24000	227.65	224.18	221.12	213.88	206.20	201.75	199.10
25000	237.13	233.52	230.33	222.79	214.79	210.15	207.39
26000	246.62	242.86	239.54	231.70	223.39	218.56	215.69
27000	256.10	252.20	248.75	240.61	231.98	226.96	223.99
28000	265.59	261.54	257.97	249.52	240.57	235.37	232.28
29000	275.07	270.88	267.18	258.43	249.16	243.78	240.58
30000	284.56	280.22	276.39	267.35	257.75	252.18	248.87
31000	294.05	289.56	285.61	276.26	266.34	260.59	257.17
32000	303.53	298.90	294.82	285.17	274.93	268.99	265.46
33000	313.02	308.24	304.03	294.08	283.53	277.40	273.76
34000	322.50	317.58	313.24	302.99	292.12	285.81	282.05
35000	331.99	326.92	322.46	311.90	300.71	294.21	290.35
40000	379.41	373.62	368.52	356.46	343.67	336.24	331.83
45000	426.84	420.33	414.59	401.02	386.62	378.27	373.31
50000	474.26	467.03	460.65	445.57	429.58	420.30	414.78
55000	521.69	513.73	506.72	490.13	472.54	462.33	456.26
60000	569.12	560.44	552.78	534.69	515.50	504.36	497.74
65000	616.54	607.14	598.85	579.24	558.46	546.39	539.22
70000	663.97	653.84	644.91	623.80	601.41	588.42	580.70
75000	711.39	700.54	690.97	668.36	644.37	630.45	622.17
80000	758.82	747.24	737.04	712.91	687.33	672.48	663.65
100000	948.52	934.05	921.30	891.14	859.16	840.59	829.56

53

10%   MONTHLY PAYMENT
NECESSARY TO AMORTIZE A LOAN

TERM AMOUNT	1 YEAR	1½ YEARS	2 YEARS	2½ YEARS	3 YEARS	4 YEARS	5 YEARS
$ 25	2.20	1.51	1.16	.95	.81	.64	.54
50	4.40	3.01	2.31	1.90	1.62	1.27	1.07
75	6.60	4.51	3.47	2.84	2.43	1.91	1.60
100	8.80	6.01	4.62	3.79	3.23	2.54	2.13
200	17.59	12.02	9.23	7.57	6.46	5.08	4.25
300	26.38	18.02	13.85	11.35	9.69	7.61	6.38
400	35.17	24.03	18.46	15.13	12.91	10.15	8.50
500	43.96	30.03	23.08	18.91	16.14	12.69	10.63
600	52.75	36.04	27.69	22.69	19.37	15.22	12.75
700	61.55	42.04	32.31	26.47	22.59	17.76	14.88
800	70.34	48.05	36.92	30.25	25.82	20.30	17.00
900	79.13	54.06	41.54	34.04	29.05	22.83	19.13
1000	87.92	60.06	46.15	37.82	32.27	25.37	21.25
2000	175.84	120.12	92.29	75.63	64.54	50.73	42.50
3000	263.75	180.18	138.44	113.44	96.81	76.09	63.75
4000	351.67	240.23	184.58	151.25	129.07	101.46	84.99
5000	439.58	300.29	230.73	189.06	161.34	126.82	106.24
6000	527.50	360.35	276.87	226.87	193.61	152.18	127.49
7000	615.42	420.40	323.02	264.68	225.88	177.54	148.73
8000	703.33	480.46	369.16	302.50	258.14	202.91	169.98
9000	791.25	540.52	415.31	340.31	290.41	228.27	191.23
10000	879.16	600.58	461.45	378.12	322.68	253.63	212.48
11000	967.08	660.63	507.60	415.93	354.94	278.99	233.72
12000	1055.00	720.69	553.74	453.74	387.21	304.36	254.97
13000	1142.91	780.75	599.89	491.55	419.48	329.72	276.22
14000	1230.83	840.80	646.03	529.36	451.75	355.08	297.46
15000	1318.74	900.86	692.18	567.18	484.01	380.44	318.71
16000	1406.66	960.92	738.32	604.99	516.28	405.81	339.96
17000	1494.58	1020.98	784.47	642.80	548.55	431.17	361.20
18000	1582.49	1081.03	830.61	680.61	580.81	456.53	382.45
19000	1670.41	1141.09	876.76	718.42	613.08	481.89	403.70
20000	1758.32	1201.15	922.90	756.23	645.35	507.26	424.95
21000	1846.24	1261.20	969.05	794.04	677.62	532.62	446.19
22000	1934.15	1321.26	1015.19	831.86	709.88	557.98	467.44
23000	2022.07	1381.32	1061.34	869.67	742.15	583.34	488.69
24000	2109.99	1441.37	1107.48	907.48	774.42	608.71	509.93
25000	2197.90	1501.43	1153.63	945.29	806.68	634.07	531.18
26000	2285.82	1561.49	1199.77	983.10	838.95	659.43	552.43
27000	2373.73	1621.55	1245.92	1020.91	871.22	684.79	573.68
28000	2461.65	1681.60	1292.06	1058.72	903.49	710.16	594.92
29000	2549.57	1741.66	1338.21	1096.54	935.75	735.52	616.17
30000	2637.48	1801.72	1384.35	1134.35	963.02	760.88	637.42
31000	2725.40	1861.77	1430.50	1172.16	1000.29	786.25	658.66
32000	2813.31	1921.83	1476.64	1209.97	1032.55	811.61	679.91
33000	2901.23	1981.89	1522.79	1247.78	1064.82	836.97	701.16
34000	2989.15	2041.95	1568.93	1285.59	1097.09	862.33	722.40
35000	3077.06	2102.00	1615.08	1323.40	1129.36	887.70	743.65
40000	3516.64	2402.29	1845.80	1512.46	1290.69	1014.51	849.89
45000	3956.22	2702.57	2076.53	1701.52	1452.03	1141.32	956.12
50000	4395.80	3002.86	2307.25	1890.58	1613.36	1268.13	1062.36
55000	4835.38	3303.14	2537.98	2079.63	1774.70	1394.95	1168.59
60000	5274.96	3603.43	2768.70	2268.69	1936.04	1521.76	1274.83
65000	5714.54	3903.72	2999.43	2457.75	2097.37	1648.57	1381.06
70000	6154.12	4204.00	3230.15	2646.80	2258.71	1775.39	1487.30
75000	6593.70	4504.29	3460.87	2835.86	2420.04	1902.20	1593.53
80000	7033.28	4804.57	3691.60	3024.92	2581.38	2029.01	1699.77
100000	8791.59	6005.71	4614.50	3781.15	3226.72	2536.26	2124.71

TERM AMOUNT	6 YEARS	7 YEARS	8 YEARS	9 YEARS	10 YEARS	11 YEARS	12 YEARS
$ 25	.47	.42	.38	.36	.34	.32	.30
50	.93	.84	.76	.71	.67	.63	.60
75	1.39	1.25	1.14	1.06	1.00	.94	.90
100	1.86	1.67	1.52	1.41	1.33	1.26	1.20
200	3.71	3.33	3.04	2.82	2.65	2.51	2.40
300	5.56	4.99	4.56	4.23	3.97	3.76	3.59
400	7.42	6.65	6.07	5.64	5.29	5.01	4.79
500	9.27	8.31	7.59	7.04	6.61	6.26	5.98
600	11.12	9.97	9.11	8.45	7.93	7.52	7.18
700	12.97	11.63	10.63	9.86	9.26	8.77	8.37
800	14.83	13.29	12.14	11.27	10.58	10.02	9.57
900	16.68	14.95	13.66	12.68	11.90	11.27	10.76
1000	18.53	16.61	15.18	14.08	13.22	12.52	11.96
2000	37.06	33.21	30.35	28.16	26.44	25.04	23.91
3000	55.58	49.81	45.53	42.24	39.65	37.56	35.86
4000	74.11	66.41	60.70	56.32	52.87	50.08	47.81
5000	92.63	83.01	75.88	70.40	66.08	62.60	59.76
6000	111.16	99.61	91.05	84.48	79.30	75.12	71.71
7000	129.69	116.21	106.22	98.56	92.51	87.64	83.66
8000	148.21	132.81	121.40	112.63	105.73	100.16	95.61
9000	166.74	149.42	136.57	126.71	118.94	112.68	107.56
10000	185.26	166.02	151.75	140.79	132.16	125.20	119.51
11000	203.79	182.62	166.92	154.87	145.37	137.72	131.46
12000	222.32	199.22	182.09	168.95	158.59	150.24	143.41
13000	240.84	215.82	197.27	183.03	171.80	162.76	155.37
14000	259.37	232.42	212.44	197.11	185.02	175.28	167.32
15000	277.89	249.02	227.62	211.19	198.23	187.80	179.27
16000	296.42	265.62	242.79	225.26	211.45	200.32	191.22
17000	314.94	282.23	257.97	239.34	224.66	212.84	203.17
18000	333.47	298.83	273.14	253.42	237.88	225.36	215.12
19000	352.00	315.43	288.31	267.50	251.09	237.88	227.07
20000	370.52	332.03	303.49	281.58	264.31	250.40	239.02
21000	389.05	348.63	318.66	295.66	277.52	262.92	250.97
22000	407.57	365.23	333.84	309.74	290.74	275.44	262.92
23000	426.10	381.83	349.01	323.81	303.95	287.96	274.87
24000	444.63	398.43	364.18	337.89	317.17	300.48	286.82
25000	463.15	415.03	379.36	351.97	330.38	313.00	298.77
26000	481.68	431.64	394.53	366.05	343.60	325.52	310.73
27000	500.20	448.24	409.71	380.13	356.81	338.04	322.68
28000	518.73	464.84	424.88	394.21	370.03	350.56	334.63
29000	537.25	481.44	440.06	408.29	383.24	363.08	346.58
30000	555.78	498.04	455.23	422.37	396.46	375.60	358.53
31000	574.31	514.64	470.40	436.44	409.67	388.12	370.48
32000	592.83	531.24	485.58	450.52	422.89	400.64	382.43
33000	611.36	547.84	500.75	464.60	436.10	413.16	394.38
34000	629.88	564.45	515.93	478.68	449.32	425.68	406.33
35000	648.41	581.05	531.10	492.76	462.53	438.20	418.28
40000	741.04	664.05	606.97	563.15	528.61	500.80	478.04
45000	833.67	747.06	682.84	633.55	594.68	563.40	537.79
50000	926.30	830.06	758.71	703.94	660.76	626.00	597.54
55000	1018.93	913.07	834.58	774.33	726.83	688.60	657.30
60000	1111.56	996.08	910.45	844.73	792.91	751.20	717.05
65000	1204.18	1079.08	986.33	915.12	858.98	813.80	776.81
70000	1296.81	1162.09	1062.20	985.51	925.06	876.40	836.56
75000	1389.44	1245.09	1138.07	1055.91	991.14	939.00	896.31
80000	1482.07	1328.10	1213.94	1126.30	1057.21	1001.60	956.07
100000	1852.59	1660.12	1517.42	1407.87	1321.51	1251.99	1195.08

TERM AMOUNT	13 YEARS	14 YEARS	15 YEARS	16 YEARS	17 YEARS	18 YEARS	19 YEARS
$ 25	.29	.28	.27	.27	.26	.25	.25
50	.58	.56	.54	.53	.52	.50	.50
75	.87	.84	.81	.79	.77	.75	.74
100	1.15	1.11	1.08	1.05	1.03	1.00	.99
200	2.30	2.22	2.15	2.10	2.05	2.00	1.97
300	3.45	3.33	3.23	3.14	3.07	3.00	2.95
400	4.60	4.44	4.30	4.19	4.09	4.00	3.93
500	5.74	5.55	5.38	5.23	5.11	5.00	4.91
600	6.89	6.65	6.45	6.28	6.13	6.00	5.89
700	8.04	7.76	7.53	7.33	7.15	7.00	6.87
800	9.19	8.87	8.60	8.37	8.17	8.00	7.86
900	10.34	9.98	9.68	9.42	9.20	9.00	8.84
1000	11.48	11.09	10.75	10.46	10.22	10.00	9.82
2000	22.96	22.17	21.50	20.92	20.43	20.00	19.63
3000	34.44	33.25	32.24	31.38	30.64	30.00	29.44
4000	45.92	44.33	42.99	41.84	40.85	40.00	39.26
5000	57.40	55.42	53.74	52.30	51.07	50.00	49.07
6000	68.88	66.50	64.48	62.76	61.28	60.00	58.88
7000	80.35	77.58	75.23	73.22	71.49	69.99	68.69
8000	91.83	88.66	85.97	83.68	81.70	79.99	78.51
9000	103.31	99.74	96.72	94.14	91.91	89.99	88.32
10000	114.79	110.83	107.47	104.60	102.13	99.99	98.13
11000	126.27	121.91	118.21	115.05	112.34	109.99	107.94
12000	137.75	132.99	128.96	125.51	122.55	119.99	117.76
13000	149.23	144.07	139.70	135.97	132.76	129.98	127.57
14000	160.70	155.15	150.45	146.43	142.97	139.98	137.38
15000	172.18	166.24	161.20	156.89	153.19	149.98	147.19
16000	183.66	177.32	171.94	167.35	163.40	159.98	157.01
17000	195.14	188.40	182.69	177.81	173.61	169.98	166.82
18000	206.62	199.48	193.43	188.27	183.82	179.98	176.63
19000	218.10	210.56	204.18	198.73	194.03	189.98	186.44
20000	229.57	221.65	214.93	209.19	204.25	199.97	196.26
21000	241.05	232.73	225.67	219.64	214.46	209.97	206.07
22000	252.53	243.81	236.42	230.10	224.67	219.97	215.88
23000	264.01	254.89	247.16	240.56	234.88	229.97	225.69
24000	275.49	265.97	257.91	251.02	245.10	239.97	235.51
25000	286.97	277.06	268.66	261.48	255.31	249.97	245.32
26000	298.45	288.14	279.40	271.94	265.52	259.96	255.13
27000	309.92	299.22	290.15	282.40	275.73	269.96	264.94
28000	321.40	310.30	300.89	292.86	285.94	279.96	274.76
29000	332.88	321.38	311.64	303.32	296.16	289.96	284.57
30000	344.36	332.47	322.39	313.78	306.37	299.96	294.38
31000	355.84	343.55	333.13	324.23	316.58	309.96	304.20
32000	367.32	354.63	343.88	334.69	326.79	319.95	314.01
33000	378.79	365.71	354.62	345.15	337.00	329.95	323.82
34000	390.27	376.79	365.37	355.61	347.22	339.95	333.63
35000	401.75	387.88	376.12	366.07	357.43	349.95	343.45
40000	459.14	443.29	429.85	418.37	408.49	399.94	392.51
45000	516.54	498.70	483.58	470.66	459.55	449.93	441.57
50000	573.93	554.11	537.31	522.96	510.61	499.93	490.63
55000	631.32	609.52	591.04	575.25	561.67	549.92	539.70
60000	688.71	664.93	644.77	627.55	612.73	599.91	588.76
65000	746.11	720.34	698.50	679.84	663.79	649.90	637.82
70000	803.50	775.75	752.23	732.14	714.85	699.90	686.89
75000	860.89	831.16	805.96	784.43	765.91	749.89	735.95
80000	918.28	886.57	859.69	836.73	816.97	799.88	785.01
100000	1147.85	1108.21	1074.61	1045.91	1021.22	999.85	981.26

56

TERM AMOUNT	20 YEARS	21 YEARS	22 YEARS	25 YEARS	30 YEARS	35 YEARS	40 YEARS
$ 25	.25	.24	.24	.23	.22	.22	.22
50	.49	.48	.47	.46	.44	.43	.43
75	.73	.72	.71	.69	.66	.65	.64
100	.97	.96	.94	.91	.88	.86	.85
200	1.94	1.91	1.88	1.82	1.76	1.72	1.70
300	2.90	2.86	2.82	2.73	2.64	2.58	2.55
400	3.87	3.81	3.76	3.64	3.52	3.44	3.40
500	4.83	4.76	4.70	4.55	4.39	4.30	4.25
600	5.80	5.71	5.63	5.46	5.27	5.16	5.10
700	6.76	6.66	6.57	6.37	6.15	6.02	5.95
800	7.73	7.61	7.51	7.27	7.03	6.88	6.80
900	8.69	8.56	8.45	8.18	7.90	7.74	7.65
1000	9.66	9.51	9.39	9.09	8.78	8.60	8.50
2000	19.31	19.02	18.77	18.18	17.56	17.20	16.99
3000	28.96	28.53	28.15	27.27	26.33	25.80	25.48
4000	38.61	38.04	37.53	36.35	35.11	34.39	33.97
5000	48.26	47.54	46.92	45.44	43.88	42.99	42.46
6000	57.91	57.05	56.30	54.53	52.66	51.59	50.95
7000	67.56	66.56	65.68	63.61	61.44	60.18	59.45
8000	77.21	76.07	75.06	72.70	70.21	68.78	67.94
9000	86.86	85.58	84.45	81.79	78.99	77.38	76.43
10000	96.51	95.08	93.83	90.88	87.76	85.97	84.92
11000	106.16	104.59	103.21	99.96	96.54	94.57	93.41
12000	115.81	114.10	112.59	109.05	105.31	103.17	101.90
13000	125.46	123.61	121.98	118.14	114.09	111.76	110.39
14000	135.11	133.11	131.36	127.22	122.87	120.36	118.89
15000	144.76	142.62	140.74	136.31	131.64	128.96	127.38
16000	154.41	152.13	150.12	145.40	140.42	137.55	135.87
17000	164.06	161.64	159.51	154.48	149.19	146.15	144.36
18000	173.71	171.15	168.89	163.57	157.97	154.75	152.85
19000	183.36	180.65	178.27	172.66	166.74	163.34	161.34
20000	193.01	190.16	187.65	181.75	175.52	171.94	169.83
21000	202.66	199.67	197.04	190.83	184.30	180.54	178.33
22000	212.31	209.18	206.42	199.92	193.07	189.13	186.82
23000	221.96	218.68	215.80	209.01	201.85	197.73	195.31
24000	231.61	228.19	225.18	218.09	210.62	206.33	203.80
25000	241.26	237.70	234.57	227.18	219.40	214.92	212.29
26000	250.91	247.21	243.95	236.27	228.17	223.52	220.78
27000	260.56	256.72	253.33	245.35	236.95	232.12	229.27
28000	270.21	266.22	262.71	254.44	245.73	240.71	237.77
29000	279.86	275.73	272.10	263.53	254.50	249.31	246.26
30000	289.51	285.24	281.48	272.62	263.28	257.91	254.75
31000	299.16	294.75	290.86	281.70	272.05	266.50	263.24
32000	308.81	304.25	300.24	290.79	280.83	275.10	271.73
33000	318.46	313.76	309.63	299.88	289.60	283.70	280.22
34000	328.11	323.27	319.01	308.96	298.38	292.29	288.71
35000	337.76	332.78	328.39	318.05	307.16	300.89	297.21
40000	386.01	380.32	375.30	363.49	351.03	343.87	339.66
45000	434.26	427.86	422.22	408.92	394.91	386.86	382.12
50000	482.52	475.40	469.13	454.36	438.79	429.84	424.58
55000	530.77	522.93	516.04	499.79	482.67	472.82	467.04
60000	579.02	570.47	562.95	545.23	526.55	515.81	509.49
65000	627.27	618.01	609.86	590.66	570.43	558.79	551.95
70000	675.52	665.55	656.78	636.10	614.31	601.78	594.41
75000	723.77	713.09	703.69	681.53	658.18	644.76	636.86
80000	772.02	760.63	750.60	726.97	702.06	687.74	679.32
100000	965.03	950.79	938.25	908.71	877.58	859.68	849.15

MONTHLY PAYMENT
NECESSARY TO AMORTIZE A LOAN

TERM AMOUNT	1 YEAR	1½ YEARS	2 YEARS	2½ YEARS	3 YEARS	4 YEARS	5 YEARS
$ 25	2.21	1.51	1.16	.95	.81	.64	.54
50	4.41	3.01	2.32	1.90	1.62	1.28	1.07
75	6.61	4.52	3.47	2.85	2.43	1.92	1.61
100	8.81	6.02	4.63	3.80	3.24	2.55	2.14
200	17.61	12.04	9.26	7.59	6.48	5.10	4.28
300	26.41	18.06	13.88	11.38	9.72	7.65	6.42
400	35.22	24.07	18.51	15.18	12.96	10.20	8.55
500	44.02	30.09	23.14	18.97	16.20	12.75	10.69
600	52.82	36.11	27.76	22.76	19.44	15.29	12.83
700	61.63	42.13	32.39	26.55	22.67	17.84	14.96
800	70.43	48.14	37.01	30.35	25.91	20.39	17.10
900	79.23	54.16	41.64	34.14	29.15	22.94	19.24
1000	88.04	60.18	46.27	37.93	32.39	25.49	21.38
2000	176.07	120.35	92.53	75.86	64.77	50.97	42.75
3000	264.10	180.52	138.79	113.79	97.16	76.45	64.12
4000	352.13	240.69	185.05	151.72	129.54	101.94	85.49
5000	440.17	300.87	231.31	189.64	161.93	127.42	106.86
6000	528.20	361.04	277.57	227.57	194.31	152.90	128.23
7000	616.23	421.21	323.83	265.50	226.70	178.38	149.60
8000	704.26	481.38	370.09	303.43	259.08	203.87	170.97
9000	792.29	541.56	416.35	341.35	291.47	229.35	192.34
10000	880.33	601.73	462.61	379.28	323.85	254.83	213.71
11000	968.36	661.90	508.87	417.21	356.24	280.32	235.08
12000	1056.39	722.07	555.13	455.14	388.62	305.80	256.45
13000	1144.42	782.24	601.39	493.07	421.01	331.28	277.82
14000	1232.46	842.42	647.65	530.99	453.39	356.76	299.19
15000	1320.49	902.59	693.91	568.92	485.78	382.25	320.56
16000	1408.52	962.76	740.17	606.85	518.16	407.73	341.93
17000	1496.55	1022.93	786.43	644.78	550.54	433.21	363.30
18000	1584.58	1083.11	832.69	682.70	582.93	458.70	384.67
19000	1672.62	1143.28	878.95	720.63	615.31	484.18	406.04
20000	1760.65	1203.45	925.21	758.56	647.70	509.66	427.41
21000	1848.68	1263.62	971.47	796.49	680.08	535.14	448.78
22000	1936.71	1323.79	1017.73	834.42	712.47	560.63	470.15
23000	2024.75	1383.97	1063.99	872.34	744.85	586.11	491.52
24000	2112.78	1444.14	1110.25	910.27	777.24	611.59	512.89
25000	2200.81	1504.31	1156.51	948.20	809.62	637.08	534.26
26000	2288.84	1564.48	1202.78	986.13	842.01	662.56	555.63
27000	2376.87	1624.66	1249.04	1024.05	874.39	688.04	577.00
28000	2464.91	1684.83	1295.30	1061.98	906.78	713.52	598.37
29000	2552.94	1745.00	1341.56	1099.91	939.16	739.01	619.74
30000	2640.97	1805.17	1387.82	1137.84	971.55	764.49	641.11
31000	2729.00	1865.34	1434.08	1175.77	1003.93	789.97	662.48
32000	2817.04	1925.52	1480.34	1213.69	1036.32	815.46	683.85
33000	2905.07	1985.69	1526.60	1251.62	1068.70	840.94	705.22
34000	2993.10	2045.86	1572.86	1289.55	1101.08	866.42	726.59
35000	3081.13	2106.03	1619.12	1327.48	1133.47	891.90	747.96
40000	3521.29	2406.90	1850.42	1517.12	1295.39	1019.32	854.82
45000	3961.45	2707.76	2081.72	1706.75	1457.32	1146.73	961.67
50000	4401.62	3008.62	2313.02	1896.39	1619.24	1274.15	1068.52
55000	4841.78	3309.48	2544.33	2086.03	1781.16	1401.56	1175.37
60000	5281.94	3610.34	2775.63	2275.67	1943.09	1528.97	1282.22
65000	5722.10	3911.20	3006.93	2465.31	2105.01	1656.39	1389.07
70000	6162.26	4212.06	3238.23	2654.95	2266.93	1783.80	1495.92
75000	6602.42	4512.92	3469.53	2844.59	2428.86	1911.22	1602.77
80000	7042.58	4813.79	3700.84	3034.23	2590.78	2038.63	1709.63
100000	8803.23	6017.23	4626.04	3792.78	3238.47	2548.29	2137.03

TERM AMOUNT	6 YEARS	7 YEARS	8 YEARS	9 YEARS	10 YEARS	11 YEARS	12 YEARS
$ 25	.47	.42	.39	.36	.34	.32	.31
50	.94	.84	.77	.72	.67	.64	.61
75	1.40	1.26	1.15	1.07	1.01	.95	.91
100	1.87	1.68	1.54	1.43	1.34	1.27	1.21
200	3.74	3.35	3.07	2.85	2.68	2.54	2.42
300	5.60	5.02	4.60	4.27	4.01	3.80	3.63
400	7.47	6.70	6.13	5.69	5.35	5.07	4.84
500	9.33	8.37	7.66	7.11	6.68	6.34	6.05
600	11.20	10.04	9.19	8.53	8.02	7.60	7.26
700	13.06	11.72	10.72	9.96	9.35	8.87	8.47
800	14.93	13.39	12.25	11.38	10.69	10.13	9.68
900	16.79	15.06	13.78	12.80	12.02	11.40	10.89
1000	18.66	16.74	15.31	14.22	13.36	12.67	12.10
2000	37.31	33.47	30.62	28.43	26.71	25.33	24.20
3000	55.96	50.20	45.93	42.65	40.07	37.99	36.29
4000	74.61	66.93	61.23	56.86	53.42	50.65	48.39
5000	93.27	83.66	76.54	71.08	66.77	63.31	60.48
6000	111.92	100.39	91.85	85.29	80.13	75.98	72.58
7000	130.57	117.12	107.15	99.51	93.48	88.64	84.67
8000	149.22	133.85	122.46	113.72	106.84	101.30	96.77
9000	167.87	150.58	137.77	127.93	120.19	113.96	108.87
10000	186.53	167.31	153.07	142.15	133.54	126.62	120.96
11000	205.18	184.04	168.38	156.36	146.90	139.28	133.06
12000	223.83	200.77	183.69	170.58	160.25	151.95	145.15
13000	242.48	217.50	198.99	184.79	173.61	164.61	157.25
14000	261.14	234.23	214.30	199.01	186.96	177.27	169.34
15000	279.79	250.96	229.61	213.22	200.31	189.93	181.44
16000	298.44	267.69	244.91	227.44	213.67	202.59	193.54
17000	317.09	284.43	260.22	241.65	227.02	215.25	205.63
18000	335.74	301.16	275.53	255.86	240.38	227.92	217.73
19000	354.40	317.89	290.83	270.08	253.73	240.58	229.82
20000	373.05	334.62	306.14	284.29	267.08	253.24	241.92
21000	391.70	351.35	321.45	298.51	280.44	265.90	254.01
22000	410.35	368.08	336.75	312.72	293.79	278.56	266.11
23000	429.00	384.81	352.06	326.94	307.14	291.23	278.20
24000	447.66	401.54	367.37	341.15	320.50	303.89	290.30
25000	466.31	418.27	382.67	355.37	333.85	316.55	302.40
26000	484.96	435.00	397.98	369.58	347.21	329.21	314.49
27000	503.61	451.73	413.29	383.79	360.56	341.87	326.59
28000	522.27	468.46	428.59	398.01	373.91	354.53	338.68
29000	540.92	485.19	443.90	412.22	387.27	367.20	350.78
30000	559.57	501.92	459.21	426.44	400.62	379.86	362.87
31000	578.22	518.65	474.51	440.65	413.98	392.52	374.97
32000	596.87	535.39	489.82	454.87	427.33	405.18	387.07
33000	615.53	552.12	505.13	469.08	440.68	417.84	399.16
34000	634.18	568.85	520.44	483.30	454.04	430.50	411.26
35000	652.83	585.58	535.74	497.51	467.39	443.17	423.35
40000	746.09	669.23	612.28	568.58	534.16	506.48	483.83
45000	839.35	752.88	688.81	639.65	600.93	569.78	544.31
50000	932.61	836.54	765.34	710.73	667.70	633.09	604.79
55000	1025.87	920.19	841.88	781.80	734.47	696.40	665.27
60000	1119.13	1003.84	918.41	852.87	801.24	759.71	725.74
65000	1212.40	1087.50	994.95	923.94	868.01	823.02	786.22
70000	1305.66	1171.15	1071.48	995.01	934.78	886.33	846.70
75000	1398.92	1254.80	1148.01	1066.09	1001.55	949.64	907.18
80000	1492.18	1338.46	1224.55	1137.16	1068.32	1012.95	967.66
100000	1865.22	1673.07	1530.68	1421.45	1335.40	1266.18	1209.57

10¼%

MONTHLY PAYMENT
NECESSARY TO AMORTIZE A LOAN

TERM AMOUNT	13 YEARS	14 YEARS	15 YEARS	16 YEARS	17 YEARS	18 YEARS	19 YEARS
$ 25	.30	.29	.28	.27	.26	.26	.25
50	.59	.57	.55	.54	.52	.51	.50
75	.88	.85	.82	.80	.78	.77	.75
100	1.17	1.13	1.09	1.07	1.04	1.02	1.00
200	2.33	2.25	2.18	2.13	2.08	2.04	2.00
300	3.49	3.37	3.27	3.19	3.12	3.05	3.00
400	4.66	4.50	4.36	4.25	4.15	4.07	4.00
500	5.82	5.62	5.45	5.31	5.19	5.08	4.99
600	6.98	6.74	6.54	6.37	6.23	6.10	5.99
700	8.14	7.87	7.63	7.44	7.26	7.12	6.99
800	9.31	8.99	8.72	8.50	8.30	8.13	7.99
900	10.47	10.11	9.81	9.56	9.34	9.15	8.98
1000	11.63	11.24	10.90	10.62	10.38	10.16	9.98
2000	23.26	22.47	21.80	21.24	20.75	20.32	19.96
3000	34.88	33.70	32.70	31.85	31.12	30.48	29.93
4000	46.51	44.94	43.60	42.47	41.49	40.64	39.91
5000	58.14	56.17	54.50	53.08	51.86	50.80	49.89
6000	69.76	67.40	65.40	63.70	62.23	60.96	59.86
7000	81.39	78.63	76.30	74.31	72.60	71.12	69.84
8000	93.02	89.87	87.20	84.93	82.97	81.28	79.82
9000	104.64	101.10	98.10	95.54	93.34	91.44	89.79
10000	116.27	112.33	109.00	106.16	103.71	101.60	99.77
11000	127.89	123.56	119.90	116.77	114.09	111.76	109.75
12000	139.52	134.80	130.80	127.39	124.46	121.92	119.72
13000	151.15	146.03	141.70	138.00	134.83	132.08	129.70
14000	162.77	157.26	152.60	148.62	145.20	142.24	139.67
15000	174.40	168.50	163.50	159.23	155.57	152.40	149.65
16000	186.03	179.73	174.40	169.85	165.94	162.56	159.63
17000	197.65	190.96	185.30	180.46	176.31	172.72	169.60
18000	209.28	202.19	196.20	191.08	186.68	182.88	179.58
19000	220.90	213.43	207.10	201.69	197.05	193.04	189.56
20000	232.53	224.66	218.00	212.31	207.42	203.20	199.53
21000	244.16	235.89	228.89	222.92	217.79	213.36	209.51
22000	255.78	247.12	239.79	233.54	228.17	223.52	219.49
23000	267.41	258.36	250.69	244.15	238.54	233.68	229.46
24000	279.04	269.59	261.59	254.77	248.91	243.84	239.44
25000	290.66	280.82	272.49	265.38	259.28	254.00	249.42
26000	302.29	292.06	283.39	276.00	269.65	264.16	259.39
27000	313.91	303.29	294.29	286.62	280.02	274.32	269.37
28000	325.54	314.52	305.19	297.23	290.39	284.48	279.34
29000	337.17	325.75	316.09	307.85	300.76	294.64	289.32
30000	348.79	336.99	326.99	318.46	311.13	304.80	299.30
31000	360.42	348.22	337.89	329.08	321.50	314.96	309.27
32000	372.05	359.45	348.79	339.69	331.87	325.12	319.25
33000	383.67	370.68	359.69	350.31	342.25	335.28	329.23
34000	395.30	381.92	370.59	360.92	352.62	345.44	339.20
35000	406.92	393.15	381.49	371.54	362.99	355.60	349.18
40000	465.06	449.31	435.99	424.61	414.84	406.40	399.06
45000	523.19	505.48	490.48	477.69	466.70	457.20	448.94
50000	581.32	561.64	544.98	530.76	518.55	508.00	498.83
55000	639.45	617.80	599.48	583.84	570.41	558.79	548.71
60000	697.58	673.97	653.98	636.92	622.26	609.59	598.59
65000	755.71	730.13	708.47	689.99	674.11	660.39	648.47
70000	813.84	786.29	762.97	743.07	725.97	711.19	698.35
75000	871.98	842.46	817.47	796.14	777.82	761.99	748.24
80000	930.11	898.62	871.97	849.22	829.68	812.79	798.12
100000	1162.63	1123.27	1089.96	1061.52	1037.10	1015.99	997.65

60

MONTHLY PAYMENT 10¼%
NECESSARY TO AMORTIZE A LOAN

TERM AMOUNT	20 YEARS	21 YEARS	22 YEARS	25 YEARS	30 YEARS	35 YEARS	40 YEARS
$ 25	.25	.25	.24	.24	.23	.22	.22
50	.50	.49	.48	.47	.45	.44	.44
75	.74	.73	.72	.70	.68	.66	.66
100	.99	.97	.96	.93	.90	.88	.87
200	1.97	1.94	1.92	1.86	1.80	1.76	1.74
300	2.95	2.91	2.87	2.78	2.69	2.64	2.61
400	3.93	3.88	3.83	3.71	3.59	3.52	3.48
500	4.91	4.84	4.78	4.64	4.49	4.40	4.35
600	5.89	5.81	5.74	5.56	5.38	5.28	5.22
700	6.88	6.78	6.69	6.49	6.28	6.16	6.09
800	7.86	7.75	7.65	7.42	7.17	7.04	6.96
900	8.84	8.71	8.60	8.34	8.07	7.91	7.82
1000	9.82	9.68	9.56	9.27	8.97	8.79	8.69
2000	19.64	19.36	19.11	18.53	17.93	17.58	17.38
3000	29.45	29.03	28.66	27.80	26.89	26.37	26.07
4000	39.27	38.71	38.22	37.06	35.85	35.16	34.76
5000	49.09	48.39	47.77	46.32	44.81	43.95	43.45
6000	58.90	58.06	57.32	55.59	53.77	52.74	52.13
7000	68.72	67.74	66.88	64.85	62.73	61.52	60.82
8000	78.54	77.42	76.43	74.12	71.69	70.31	69.51
9000	88.35	87.09	85.98	83.38	80.65	79.10	78.20
10000	98.17	96.77	95.54	92.64	89.62	87.89	86.89
11000	107.99	106.44	105.09	101.91	98.58	96.68	95.58
12000	117.80	116.12	114.64	111.17	107.54	105.47	104.26
13000	127.62	125.80	124.20	120.43	116.50	114.26	112.95
14000	137.44	135.47	133.75	129.70	125.46	123.04	121.64
15000	147.25	145.15	143.30	138.96	134.42	131.83	130.33
16000	157.07	154.83	152.86	148.23	143.38	140.62	139.02
17000	166.88	164.50	162.41	157.49	152.34	149.41	147.70
18000	176.70	174.18	171.96	166.75	161.30	158.20	156.39
19000	186.52	183.85	181.52	176.02	170.26	166.99	165.08
20000	196.33	193.53	191.07	185.28	179.23	175.78	173.77
21000	206.15	203.21	200.62	194.55	188.19	184.56	182.46
22000	215.97	212.88	210.18	203.81	197.15	193.35	191.15
23000	225.78	222.56	219.73	213.07	206.11	202.14	199.83
24000	235.60	232.24	229.28	222.34	215.07	210.93	208.52
25000	245.42	241.91	238.83	231.60	224.03	219.72	217.21
26000	255.23	251.59	248.39	240.86	232.99	228.51	225.90
27000	265.05	261.27	257.94	250.13	241.95	237.30	234.59
28000	274.87	270.94	267.49	259.39	250.91	246.08	243.27
29000	284.68	280.62	277.05	268.66	259.87	254.87	251.96
30000	294.50	290.29	286.60	277.92	268.84	263.66	260.65
31000	304.31	299.97	296.15	287.18	277.80	272.45	269.34
32000	314.13	309.65	305.71	296.45	286.76	281.24	278.03
33000	323.95	319.32	315.26	305.71	295.72	290.03	286.72
34000	333.76	329.00	324.81	314.98	304.68	298.82	295.40
35000	343.58	338.68	334.37	324.24	313.64	307.60	304.09
40000	392.66	387.06	382.13	370.56	358.45	351.55	347.53
45000	441.74	435.44	429.90	416.88	403.25	395.49	390.97
50000	490.83	483.82	477.66	463.20	448.06	439.43	434.41
55000	539.91	532.20	525.43	509.52	492.86	483.38	477.86
60000	588.99	580.58	573.20	555.83	537.67	527.32	521.30
65000	638.07	628.97	620.96	602.15	582.47	571.26	564.74
70000	687.16	677.35	668.73	648.47	627.28	615.20	608.18
75000	736.24	725.73	716.49	694.79	672.09	659.15	651.62
80000	785.32	774.11	764.26	741.11	716.89	703.09	695.06
100000	981.65	967.64	955.32	926.39	896.11	878.86	868.82

10½%

TERM AMOUNT	1 YEAR	1½ YEARS	2 YEARS	2½ YEARS	3 YEARS	4 YEARS	5 YEARS
$ 25	2.21	1.51	1.16	.96	.82	.65	.54
50	4.41	3.02	2.32	1.91	1.63	1.29	1.08
75	6.62	4.53	3.48	2.86	2.44	1.93	1.62
100	8.82	6.03	4.64	3.81	3.26	2.57	2.15
200	17.63	12.06	9.28	7.61	6.51	5.13	4.30
300	26.45	18.09	13.92	11.42	9.76	7.69	6.45
400	35.26	24.12	18.56	15.22	13.01	10.25	8.60
500	44.08	30.15	23.19	19.03	16.26	12.81	10.75
600	52.89	36.18	27.83	22.83	19.51	15.37	12.90
700	61.71	42.21	32.47	26.64	22.76	17.93	15.05
800	70.52	48.24	37.11	30.44	26.01	20.49	17.20
900	79.34	54.26	41.74	34.24	29.26	23.05	19.35
1000	88.15	60.29	46.38	38.05	32.51	25.61	21.50
2000	176.30	120.58	92.76	76.09	65.01	51.21	42.99
3000	264.45	180.87	139.13	114.14	97.51	76.82	64.49
4000	352.60	241.16	185.51	152.18	130.01	102.42	85.98
5000	440.75	301.44	231.89	190.23	162.52	128.02	107.47
6000	528.90	361.73	278.26	228.27	195.02	153.63	128.97
7000	617.05	422.02	324.64	266.32	227.52	179.23	150.46
8000	705.19	482.31	371.01	304.36	260.02	204.83	171.96
9000	793.34	542.59	417.39	342.40	292.53	230.44	193.45
10000	881.49	602.88	463.77	380.45	325.03	256.04	214.94
11000	969.64	663.17	510.14	418.49	357.53	281.64	236.44
12000	1057.79	723.46	556.52	456.54	390.03	307.25	257.93
13000	1145.94	783.74	602.89	494.58	422.54	332.85	279.43
14000	1234.09	844.03	649.27	532.63	455.04	358.45	300.92
15000	1322.23	904.32	695.65	570.67	487.54	384.06	322.41
16000	1410.38	964.61	742.02	608.71	520.04	409.66	343.91
17000	1498.53	1024.89	788.40	646.76	552.55	435.26	365.40
18000	1586.68	1085.18	834.77	684.80	585.05	460.87	386.90
19000	1674.83	1145.47	881.15	722.85	617.55	486.47	408.39
20000	1762.98	1205.76	927.53	760.89	650.05	512.07	429.88
21000	1851.13	1266.04	973.90	798.94	682.56	537.68	451.38
22000	1939.27	1326.33	1020.28	836.98	715.06	563.28	472.87
23000	2027.42	1386.62	1066.65	875.02	747.56	588.88	494.36
24000	2115.57	1446.91	1113.03	913.07	780.06	614.49	515.86
25000	2203.72	1507.19	1159.41	951.11	812.57	640.09	537.35
26000	2291.87	1567.48	1205.78	989.16	845.07	665.69	558.85
27000	2380.02	1627.77	1252.16	1027.20	877.57	691.30	580.34
28000	2468.17	1688.06	1298.53	1065.25	910.07	716.90	601.83
29000	2556.31	1748.34	1344.91	1103.29	942.58	742.50	623.33
30000	2644.46	1808.63	1391.29	1141.33	975.08	768.11	644.82
31000	2732.61	1868.92	1437.66	1179.38	1007.58	793.71	666.32
32000	2820.76	1929.21	1484.04	1217.42	1040.08	819.31	687.81
33000	2908.91	1989.49	1530.41	1255.47	1072.59	844.92	709.30
34000	2997.06	2049.78	1576.79	1293.51	1105.09	870.52	730.80
35000	3085.21	2110.07	1623.17	1331.56	1137.59	896.12	752.29
40000	3525.95	2411.51	1855.05	1521.78	1300.10	1024.14	859.76
45000	3966.69	2712.95	2086.93	1712.00	1462.61	1152.16	967.23
50000	4407.44	3014.38	2318.81	1902.22	1625.13	1280.17	1074.70
55000	4848.18	3315.82	2550.69	2092.44	1787.64	1408.19	1182.17
60000	5288.92	3617.26	2782.57	2282.66	1950.15	1536.21	1289.64
65000	5729.66	3918.70	3014.45	2472.89	2112.66	1664.22	1397.11
70000	6170.41	4220.13	3246.33	2663.11	2275.18	1792.24	1504.58
75000	6611.15	4521.57	3478.21	2853.33	2437.69	1920.26	1612.05
80000	7051.89	4823.01	3710.09	3043.55	2600.20	2048.28	1719.52
100000	8814.87	6028.76	4637.61	3804.44	3250.25	2560.34	2149.40

TERM AMOUNT	6 YEARS	7 YEARS	8 YEARS	9 YEARS	10 YEARS	11 YEARS	12 YEARS
$ 25	.47	.43	.39	.36	.34	.33	.31
50	.94	.85	.78	.72	.68	.65	.62
75	1.41	1.27	1.16	1.08	1.02	.97	.92
100	1.88	1.69	1.55	1.44	1.35	1.29	1.23
200	3.76	3.38	3.09	2.88	2.70	2.57	2.45
300	5.64	5.06	4.64	4.31	4.05	3.85	3.68
400	7.52	6.75	6.18	5.75	5.40	5.13	4.90
500	9.39	8.44	7.73	7.18	6.75	6.41	6.13
600	11.27	10.12	9.27	8.62	8.10	7.69	7.35
700	13.15	11.81	10.81	10.05	9.45	8.97	8.57
800	15.03	13.49	12.36	11.49	10.80	10.25	9.80
900	16.91	15.18	13.90	12.92	12.15	11.53	11.02
1000	18.78	16.87	15.45	14.35	13.50	12.81	12.25
2000	37.56	33.73	30.89	28.71	26.99	25.61	24.49
3000	56.34	50.59	46.33	43.06	40.49	38.42	36.73
4000	75.12	67.45	61.77	57.41	53.98	51.22	48.97
5000	93.90	84.31	77.21	71.76	67.47	64.03	61.21
6000	112.68	101.17	92.65	86.11	80.97	76.83	73.45
7000	131.46	118.03	108.09	100.46	94.46	89.64	85.69
8000	150.24	134.89	123.53	114.81	107.95	102.44	97.94
9000	169.02	151.75	138.97	129.16	121.45	115.25	110.18
10000	187.79	168.61	154.41	143.51	134.94	128.05	122.42
11000	206.57	185.47	169.85	157.86	148.43	140.85	134.66
12000	225.35	202.33	185.29	172.22	161.93	153.66	146.90
13000	244.13	219.19	200.73	186.57	175.42	166.46	159.14
14000	262.91	236.05	216.17	200.92	188.91	179.27	171.38
15000	281.69	252.92	231.61	215.27	202.41	192.07	183.63
16000	300.47	269.78	247.05	229.62	215.90	204.88	195.87
17000	319.25	286.64	262.49	243.97	229.39	217.68	208.11
18000	338.03	303.50	277.93	258.32	242.89	230.49	220.35
19000	356.81	320.36	293.37	272.67	256.38	243.29	232.59
20000	375.58	337.22	308.81	287.02	269.87	256.09	244.83
21000	394.36	354.08	324.25	301.37	283.37	268.90	257.07
22000	413.14	370.94	339.69	315.72	296.86	281.70	269.32
23000	431.92	387.80	355.13	330.07	310.36	294.51	281.56
24000	450.70	404.66	370.57	344.43	323.85	307.31	293.80
25000	469.48	421.52	386.01	358.78	337.34	320.12	306.04
26000	488.26	438.38	401.45	373.13	350.84	332.92	318.28
27000	507.04	455.24	416.89	387.48	364.33	345.73	330.52
28000	525.82	472.10	432.33	401.83	377.82	358.53	342.76
29000	544.60	488.96	447.77	416.18	391.32	371.33	355.01
30000	563.37	505.83	463.21	430.53	404.81	384.14	367.25
31000	582.15	522.69	478.65	444.88	418.30	396.94	379.49
32000	600.93	539.55	494.09	459.23	431.80	409.75	391.73
33000	619.71	556.41	509.53	473.58	445.29	422.55	403.97
34000	638.49	573.27	524.97	487.93	458.78	435.36	416.21
35000	657.27	590.13	540.41	502.29	472.28	448.16	428.45
40000	751.16	674.43	617.61	574.04	539.74	512.18	489.66
45000	845.06	758.74	694.81	645.79	607.21	576.21	550.87
50000	938.95	843.04	772.01	717.55	674.68	640.23	612.08
55000	1032.85	927.34	849.21	789.30	742.15	704.25	673.28
60000	1126.74	1011.65	926.41	861.06	809.61	768.27	734.49
65000	1220.64	1095.95	1003.61	932.81	877.08	832.29	795.70
70000	1314.53	1180.25	1080.81	1004.57	944.55	896.32	856.90
75000	1408.43	1264.56	1158.01	1076.32	1012.02	960.34	918.11
80000	1502.32	1348.86	1235.21	1148.07	1079.48	1024.36	979.32
100000	1877.90	1686.07	1544.01	1435.09	1349.35	1280.45	1224.15

MONTHLY PAYMENT
NECESSARY TO AMORTIZE A LOAN

TERM AMOUNT	13 YEARS	14 YEARS	15 YEARS	16 YEARS	17 YEARS	18 YEARS	19 YEARS
$ 25	.30	.29	.28	.27	.27	.26	.26
50	.59	.57	.56	.54	.53	.52	.51
75	.89	.86	.83	.81	.79	.78	.77
100	1.18	1.14	1.11	1.08	1.06	1.04	1.02
200	2.36	2.28	2.22	2.16	2.11	2.07	2.03
300	3.54	3.42	3.32	3.24	3.16	3.10	3.05
400	4.72	4.56	4.43	4.31	4.22	4.13	4.06
500	5.89	5.70	5.53	5.39	5.27	5.17	5.08
600	7.07	6.84	6.64	6.47	6.32	6.20	6.09
700	8.25	7.97	7.74	7.55	7.38	7.23	7.10
800	9.43	9.11	8.85	8.62	8.43	8.26	8.12
900	10.60	10.25	9.95	9.70	9.48	9.30	9.13
1000	11.78	11.39	11.06	10.78	10.54	10.33	10.15
2000	23.56	22.77	22.11	21.55	21.07	20.65	20.29
3000	35.33	34.16	33.17	32.32	31.60	30.97	30.43
4000	47.11	45.54	44.22	43.09	42.13	41.29	40.57
5000	58.88	56.93	55.27	53.87	52.66	51.62	50.71
6000	70.66	68.31	66.33	64.64	63.19	61.94	60.85
7000	82.43	79.70	77.38	75.41	73.72	72.26	70.99
8000	94.21	91.08	88.44	86.18	84.25	82.58	81.14
9000	105.98	102.46	99.49	96.96	94.78	92.91	91.28
10000	117.76	113.85	110.54	107.73	105.31	103.23	101.42
11000	129.53	125.23	121.60	118.50	115.84	113.55	111.56
12000	141.31	136.62	132.65	129.27	126.37	123.87	121.70
13000	153.08	148.00	143.71	140.05	136.91	134.19	131.84
14000	164.86	159.39	154.76	150.82	147.44	144.52	141.98
15000	176.63	170.77	165.81	161.59	157.97	154.84	152.13
16000	188.41	182.15	176.87	172.36	168.50	165.16	162.27
17000	200.18	193.54	187.92	183.14	179.03	175.48	172.41
18000	211.96	204.92	198.98	193.91	189.56	185.81	182.55
19000	223.73	216.31	210.03	204.68	200.09	196.13	192.69
20000	235.51	227.69	221.08	215.45	210.62	206.45	202.83
21000	247.28	239.08	232.14	226.23	221.15	216.77	212.97
22000	259.06	250.46	243.19	237.00	231.68	227.10	223.12
23000	270.83	261.84	254.25	247.77	242.21	237.42	233.26
24000	282.61	273.23	265.30	258.54	252.74	247.74	243.40
25000	294.38	284.61	276.35	269.32	263.28	258.06	253.54
26000	306.16	296.00	287.41	280.09	273.81	268.38	263.68
27000	317.93	307.38	298.46	290.86	284.34	278.71	273.82
28000	329.71	318.77	309.52	301.63	294.87	289.03	283.96
29000	341.48	330.15	320.57	312.41	305.40	299.35	294.11
30000	353.26	341.54	331.62	323.18	315.93	309.67	304.25
31000	365.03	352.92	342.68	333.95	326.46	320.00	314.39
32000	376.81	364.30	353.73	344.72	336.99	330.32	324.53
33000	388.58	375.69	364.79	355.50	347.52	340.64	334.67
34000	400.36	387.07	375.84	366.27	358.05	350.96	344.81
35000	412.13	398.46	386.89	377.04	368.58	361.28	354.95
40000	471.01	455.38	442.16	430.90	421.24	412.90	405.66
45000	529.88	512.30	497.43	484.65	473.89	464.51	456.37
50000	588.76	569.22	552.70	538.63	526.55	516.12	507.07
55000	647.63	626.14	607.97	592.49	579.20	567.73	557.78
60000	706.51	683.07	663.24	646.35	631.85	619.34	608.49
65000	765.38	739.99	718.51	700.21	684.51	670.95	659.20
70000	824.26	796.91	773.78	754.07	737.16	722.56	709.90
75000	883.13	853.83	829.05	807.94	789.82	774.18	760.61
80000	942.01	910.75	884.32	861.80	842.47	825.79	811.32
100000	1177.51	1138.44	1105.40	1077.25	1053.09	1032.23	1014.14

TERM AMOUNT	20 YEARS	21 YEARS	22 YEARS	25 YEARS	30 YEARS	35 YEARS	40 YEARS
$ 25	.25	.25	.25	.24	.23	.23	.23
50	.50	.50	.49	.48	.46	.45	.45
75	.75	.74	.73	.71	.69	.68	.67
100	1.00	.99	.98	.95	.92	.90	.89
200	2.00	1.97	1.95	1.89	1.83	1.80	1.78
300	3.00	2.96	2.92	2.84	2.75	2.70	2.67
400	4.00	3.94	3.90	3.78	3.66	3.60	3.56
500	5.00	4.93	4.87	4.73	4.58	4.50	4.45
600	6.00	5.91	5.84	5.67	5.49	5.39	5.34
700	6.99	6.90	6.81	6.61	6.41	6.29	6.22
800	7.99	7.88	7.79	7.56	7.32	7.19	7.11
900	8.99	8.87	8.76	8.50	8.24	8.09	8.00
1000	9.99	9.85	9.73	9.45	9.15	8.99	8.89
2000	19.97	19.70	19.46	18.89	18.30	17.97	17.78
3000	29.96	29.54	29.18	28.33	27.45	26.95	26.66
4000	39.94	39.39	38.91	37.77	36.59	35.93	35.55
5000	49.92	49.23	48.63	47.21	45.74	44.91	44.43
6000	59.91	59.08	58.36	56.66	54.89	53.89	53.32
7000	69.89	68.93	68.08	66.10	64.04	62.87	62.20
8000	79.88	78.77	77.81	75.54	73.18	71.86	71.09
9000	89.86	88.62	87.53	84.98	82.33	80.84	79.98
10000	99.84	98.46	97.26	94.42	91.48	89.82	88.86
11000	109.83	108.31	106.98	103.86	100.63	98.80	97.75
12000	119.81	118.16	116.71	113.31	109.77	107.78	106.63
13000	129.79	128.00	126.43	122.75	118.92	116.76	115.52
14000	139.78	137.85	136.16	132.19	128.07	125.74	124.40
15000	149.76	147.69	145.88	141.63	137.22	134.73	133.29
16000	159.75	157.54	155.61	151.07	146.36	143.71	142.18
17000	169.73	167.39	165.33	160.52	155.51	152.69	151.06
18000	179.71	177.23	175.06	169.96	164.66	161.67	159.95
19000	189.70	187.08	184.78	179.40	173.81	170.65	168.83
20000	199.68	196.92	194.51	188.84	182.95	179.64	177.72
21000	209.66	206.77	204.23	198.28	192.10	188.61	186.60
22000	219.65	216.62	213.96	207.72	201.25	197.59	195.49
23000	229.63	226.46	223.68	217.17	210.40	206.58	204.38
24000	239.62	236.31	233.41	226.61	219.54	215.56	213.26
25000	249.60	246.15	243.13	236.05	228.69	224.54	222.15
26000	259.58	256.00	252.86	245.49	237.84	233.52	231.03
27000	269.57	265.85	262.58	254.93	246.98	242.50	239.92
28000	279.55	275.69	272.31	264.38	256.13	251.48	248.80
29000	289.54	285.54	282.03	273.82	265.28	260.46	257.69
30000	299.52	295.38	291.76	283.26	274.43	269.45	266.58
31000	309.50	305.23	301.48	292.70	283.57	278.43	275.46
32000	319.49	315.08	311.21	302.14	292.72	287.41	284.35
33000	329.47	324.92	320.93	311.58	301.87	296.39	293.23
34000	339.45	334.77	330.66	321.03	311.02	305.37	302.12
35000	349.44	344.61	340.38	330.47	320.16	314.35	311.00
40000	399.36	393.84	389.01	377.68	365.90	359.26	355.43
45000	449.28	443.07	437.63	424.89	411.64	404.17	399.86
50000	499.19	492.30	486.26	472.10	457.37	449.07	444.29
55000	549.11	541.53	534.88	519.30	503.11	493.98	488.72
60000	599.03	590.76	583.51	566.51	548.85	538.89	533.15
65000	648.95	639.99	632.13	613.72	594.59	583.79	577.58
70000	698.87	689.22	680.76	660.93	640.32	628.70	622.00
75000	748.79	738.45	729.39	708.14	686.06	673.61	666.43
80000	798.71	787.68	778.01	755.35	731.80	718.51	710.86
100000	998.38	984.60	972.51	944.19	914.74	898.14	888.58

10¾%

TERM AMOUNT	1 YEAR	1½ YEARS	2 YEARS	2½ YEARS	3 YEARS	4 YEARS	5 YEARS
$ 25	2.21	1.52	1.17	.96	.82	.65	.55
50	4.42	3.03	2.33	1.91	1.64	1.29	1.09
75	6.62	4.54	3.49	2.87	2.45	1.93	1.63
100	8.83	6.05	4.65	3.82	3.27	2.58	2.17
200	17.66	12.09	9.30	7.64	6.53	5.15	4.33
300	26.48	18.13	13.95	11.45	9.79	7.72	6.49
400	35.31	24.17	18.60	15.27	13.05	10.29	8.65
500	44.14	30.21	23.25	19.09	16.32	12.87	10.81
600	52.96	36.25	27.90	22.90	19.58	15.44	12.98
700	61.79	42.29	32.55	26.72	22.84	18.01	15.14
800	70.62	48.33	37.20	30.53	26.10	20.58	17.30
900	79.44	54.37	41.85	34.35	29.36	23.16	19.46
1000	88.27	60.41	46.50	38.17	32.63	25.73	21.62
2000	176.54	120.81	92.99	76.33	65.25	51.45	43.24
3000	264.80	181.21	139.48	114.49	97.87	77.18	64.85
4000	353.07	241.62	185.97	152.65	130.49	102.90	86.48
5000	441.33	302.02	232.46	190.81	163.11	128.63	108.09
6000	529.60	362.43	278.96	228.97	195.73	154.35	129.71
7000	617.86	422.83	325.45	267.13	228.35	180.07	151.33
8000	706.13	483.23	371.94	305.29	260.97	205.80	172.95
9000	794.39	543.63	418.43	343.45	293.59	231.52	194.57
10000	882.66	604.03	464.92	381.62	326.21	257.25	216.18
11000	970.92	664.44	511.41	419.78	358.83	282.97	237.80
12000	1059.19	724.84	557.91	457.94	391.45	308.70	259.42
13000	1147.45	785.24	604.40	496.10	424.07	334.42	281.04
14000	1235.72	845.65	650.89	534.26	456.69	360.14	302.66
15000	1323.98	906.05	697.38	572.42	489.31	385.87	324.27
16000	1412.25	966.45	743.87	610.58	521.93	411.59	345.89
17000	1500.51	1026.86	790.37	648.74	554.55	437.32	367.51
18000	1588.78	1087.26	836.86	686.90	587.17	463.04	389.13
19000	1677.04	1147.66	883.35	725.07	619.79	488.77	410.75
20000	1765.31	1208.06	929.84	763.23	652.41	514.49	432.36
21000	1853.57	1268.47	976.33	801.39	685.03	540.21	453.98
22000	1941.84	1328.87	1022.83	839.55	717.65	565.94	475.60
23000	2030.10	1389.27	1069.32	877.71	750.28	591.66	497.22
24000	2118.37	1449.68	1115.81	915.87	782.90	617.39	518.84
25000	2206.63	1510.08	1162.30	954.03	815.52	643.11	540.45
26000	2294.90	1570.48	1208.79	992.19	848.14	668.84	562.07
27000	2383.16	1630.89	1255.29	1030.35	880.76	694.56	583.69
28000	2471.43	1691.29	1301.78	1068.52	913.38	720.28	605.31
29000	2559.69	1751.69	1348.27	1106.68	946.00	746.01	626.93
30000	2647.96	1812.09	1394.76	1144.84	978.62	771.73	648.54
31000	2736.22	1872.50	1441.25	1183.00	1011.24	797.46	670.16
32000	2824.49	1932.90	1487.74	1221.16	1043.86	823.18	691.78
33000	2912.75	1993.30	1534.24	1259.32	1076.49	848.91	713.40
34000	3001.02	2053.71	1580.73	1297.48	1109.10	874.63	735.02
35000	3089.28	2114.11	1627.22	1335.64	1141.72	900.35	756.63
40000	3530.61	2416.12	1859.68	1526.45	1304.82	1028.97	864.72
45000	3971.93	2718.14	2092.14	1717.25	1467.93	1157.60	972.81
50000	4413.26	3020.15	2324.60	1908.06	1631.03	1286.22	1080.90
55000	4854.58	3322.17	2557.06	2098.86	1794.13	1414.84	1188.99
60000	5295.91	3624.18	2789.52	2289.67	1957.23	1543.46	1297.08
65000	5737.24	3926.20	3021.98	2480.48	2120.33	1672.08	1405.17
70000	6178.56	4228.21	3254.43	2671.28	2283.44	1800.70	1513.26
75000	6619.89	4530.23	3486.89	2862.09	2446.54	1929.33	1621.35
80000	7061.21	4832.24	3719.35	3052.89	2609.64	2057.95	1729.44
100000	8826.51	6040.30	4649.19	3816.11	3262.05	2572.43	2161.80

66

MONTHLY PAYMENT
NECESSARY TO AMORTIZE A LOAN   10¾%

TERM AMOUNT	6 YEARS	7 YEARS	8 YEARS	9 YEARS	10 YEARS	11 YEARS	12 YEARS
$ 25	.48	.43	.39	.37	.35	.33	.31
50	.95	.85	.78	.73	.69	.65	.62
75	1.42	1.28	1.17	1.09	1.03	.98	.93
100	1.90	1.70	1.56	1.45	1.37	1.30	1.24
200	3.79	3.40	3.12	2.90	2.73	2.59	2.48
300	5.68	5.10	4.68	4.35	4.10	3.89	3.72
400	7.57	6.80	6.23	5.80	5.46	5.18	4.96
500	9.46	8.50	7.79	7.25	6.82	6.48	6.20
600	11.35	10.20	9.35	8.70	8.19	7.77	7.44
700	13.24	11.90	10.91	10.15	9.55	9.07	8.68
800	15.13	13.60	12.46	11.60	10.91	10.36	9.92
900	17.02	15.30	14.02	13.04	12.28	11.66	11.15
1000	18.91	17.00	15.58	14.49	13.64	12.95	12.39
2000	37.82	33.99	31.15	28.98	27.27	25.90	24.78
3000	56.72	50.98	46.73	43.47	40.91	38.85	37.17
4000	75.63	67.97	62.30	57.96	54.54	51.80	49.56
5000	94.54	84.96	77.87	72.45	68.17	64.74	61.95
6000	113.44	101.95	93.45	86.93	81.81	77.69	74.33
7000	132.35	118.94	109.02	101.42	95.44	90.64	86.72
8000	151.26	135.94	124.60	115.91	109.08	103.59	99.11
9000	170.16	152.93	140.17	130.40	122.71	116.54	111.50
10000	189.07	169.92	155.74	144.89	136.34	129.48	123.89
11000	207.97	186.91	171.32	159.37	149.98	142.43	136.27
12000	226.88	203.90	186.89	173.86	163.61	155.38	148.66
13000	245.79	220.89	202.47	188.35	177.25	168.33	161.05
14000	264.69	237.88	218.04	202.84	190.88	181.28	173.44
15000	283.60	254.87	233.61	217.33	204.51	194.22	185.83
16000	302.51	271.87	249.19	231.81	218.15	207.17	198.21
17000	321.41	288.86	264.76	246.30	231.78	220.12	210.60
18000	340.32	305.85	280.34	260.79	245.41	233.07	222.99
19000	359.22	322.84	295.91	275.28	259.05	246.02	235.38
20000	378.13	339.83	311.48	289.77	272.68	258.96	247.77
21000	397.04	356.82	327.06	304.25	286.32	271.91	260.15
22000	415.94	373.81	342.63	318.74	299.95	284.86	272.54
23000	434.85	390.80	358.20	333.23	313.58	297.81	284.93
24000	453.76	407.80	373.78	347.12	327.22	310.76	297.32
25000	472.66	424.79	389.35	362.21	340.85	323.70	309.71
26000	491.57	441.78	404.93	376.69	354.49	336.65	322.09
27000	510.47	458.77	420.50	391.18	368.12	349.60	334.48
28000	529.38	475.76	436.07	405.67	381.75	362.55	346.87
29000	548.29	492.75	451.65	420.16	395.39	375.50	359.26
30000	567.19	509.74	467.22	434.65	409.02	388.44	371.65
31000	586.10	526.73	482.80	449.13	422.65	401.39	384.03
32000	605.01	543.73	498.37	463.62	436.29	414.34	396.42
33000	623.91	560.72	513.94	478.11	449.92	427.29	408.81
34000	642.82	577.71	529.52	492.60	463.56	440.24	421.20
35000	661.72	594.70	545.09	507.09	477.19	453.18	433.59
40000	756.26	679.66	622.96	579.53	545.36	517.92	495.53
45000	850.79	764.61	700.83	651.97	613.53	582.66	557.47
50000	945.32	849.57	778.70	724.41	681.70	647.40	619.41
55000	1039.85	934.52	856.57	796.85	749.87	712.14	681.35
60000	1134.38	1019.48	934.44	869.29	818.04	776.88	743.29
65000	1228.91	1104.44	1012.31	941.73	886.21	841.62	805.23
70000	1323.44	1189.39	1090.18	1014.17	954.38	906.36	867.17
75000	1417.98	1274.35	1168.05	1086.61	1022.55	971.10	929.11
80000	1512.51	1359.41	1245.92	1159.05	1090.71	1035.84	991.05
100000	1890.63	1699.13	1557.40	1448.81	1363.39	1294.80	1238.81

MONTHLY PAYMENT
NECESSARY TO AMORTIZE A LOAN

TERM AMOUNT	13 YEARS	14 YEARS	15 YEARS	16 YEARS	17 YEARS	18 YEARS	19 YEARS
$ 25	.30	.29	.29	.28	.27	.27	.26
50	.60	.58	.57	.55	.54	.53	.52
75	.90	.87	.85	.82	.81	.79	.78
100	1.20	1.16	1.13	1.10	1.07	1.05	1.04
200	2.39	2.31	2.25	2.19	2.14	2.10	2.07
300	3.58	3.47	3.37	3.28	3.21	3.15	3.10
400	4.77	4.62	4.49	4.38	4.28	4.20	4.13
500	5.97	5.77	5.61	5.47	5.35	5.25	5.16
600	7.16	6.93	6.73	6.56	6.42	6.30	6.19
700	8.35	8.08	7.85	7.66	7.49	7.35	7.22
800	9.54	9.23	8.97	8.75	8.56	8.39	8.25
900	10.74	10.39	10.09	9.84	9.63	9.44	9.28
1000	11.93	11.54	11.21	1C.93	10.70	10.49	10.31
2000	23.85	23.08	22.42	21.87	21.39	20.98	20.62
3000	35.78	34.62	33.63	32.80	32.08	31.46	30.93
4000	47.70	46.15	44.84	43.73	42.77	41.95	41.23
5000	59.63	57.69	56.05	54.66	53.46	52.43	51.54
6000	71.55	69.23	67.26	65.59	64.16	62.92	61.85
7000	83.48	80.76	78.47	76.52	74.85	73.41	72.16
8000	95.40	92.30	89.68	87.45	85.54	83.89	82.46
9000	107.33	103.84	100.89	98.38	96.23	94.38	92.77
10000	119.25	115.37	112.10	109.31	106.92	104.86	103.08
11000	131.18	126.91	123.31	120.24	117.61	115.35	113.39
12000	143.10	138.45	134.52	131.17	128.31	125.84	123.69
13000	155.03	149.99	145.73	142.10	139.00	136.32	134.00
14000	166.95	161.52	156.94	153.03	149.69	146.81	144.31
15000	178.88	173.06	168.15	163.97	160.38	157.29	154.62
16000	190.80	184.60	179.36	174.90	171.07	167.78	164.92
17000	202.72	196.13	190.57	185.83	181.77	178.26	175.23
18000	214.65	207.67	201.78	196.76	192.46	188.75	185.54
19000	226.57	219.21	212.99	207.69	203.15	199.24	195.85
20000	238.50	230.74	224.19	218.62	213.84	209.72	206.15
21000	250.42	242.28	235.40	229.55	224.53	220.21	216.46
22000	262.35	253.82	246.61	240.48	235.22	230.69	226.77
23000	274.27	265.36	257.82	251.41	245.92	241.18	237.08
24000	286.20	276.89	269.03	262.34	256.61	251.67	247.38
25000	298.12	288.43	280.24	273.27	267.30	262.15	257.69
26000	310.05	299.97	291.45	284.20	277.99	272.64	268.00
27000	321.97	311.50	302.66	295.13	288.68	283.12	278.31
28000	333.90	323.04	313.87	306.06	299.37	293.61	288.61
29000	345.82	334.58	325.08	317.00	310.07	304.09	298.92
30000	357.75	346.11	336.29	327.93	320.76	314.58	309.23
31000	369.67	357.65	347.50	338.86	331.45	325.07	319.54
32000	381.59	369.19	358.71	349.79	342.14	335.55	329.84
33000	393.52	380.72	369.92	360.72	352.83	346.04	340.15
34000	405.44	392.26	381.13	371.65	363.53	356.52	350.46
35000	417.37	403.80	392.34	382.58	374.22	367.01	360.77
40000	476.99	461.48	448.38	437.23	427.68	419.44	412.30
45000	536.62	519.17	504.43	491.89	481.14	471.87	463.84
50000	596.24	576.85	560.48	546.54	534.59	524.30	515.38
55000	655.86	634.54	616.53	601.19	588.05	576.73	566.92
60000	715.49	692.22	672.57	655.85	641.51	629.16	618.45
65000	775.11	749.91	728.62	710.50	694.97	681.59	669.99
70000	834.73	807.59	784.67	765.15	748.43	734.01	721.53
75000	894.36	865.28	840.72	819.81	801.89	786.44	773.07
80000	953.98	922.96	896.76	874.46	855.35	838.87	824.60
100000	1192.47	1153.70	1120.95	1093.07	1069.18	1048.59	1030.75

TERM AMOUNT	20 YEARS	21 YEARS	22 YEARS	25 YEARS	30 YEARS	35 YEARS	40 YEARS
$ 25	.26	.26	.25	.25	.24	.23	.23
50	.51	.51	.50	.49	.47	.46	.46
75	.77	.76	.75	.73	.71	.69	.69
100	1.02	1.01	.99	.97	.94	.92	.91
200	2.04	2.01	1.98	1.93	1.87	1.84	1.82
300	3.05	3.01	2.97	2.89	2.81	2.76	2.73
400	4.07	4.01	3.96	3.85	3.74	3.68	3.64
500	5.08	5.01	4.95	4.82	4.67	4.59	4.55
600	6.10	6.02	5.94	5.78	5.61	5.51	5.46
700	7.11	7.02	6.93	6.74	6.54	6.43	6.36
800	8.13	8.02	7.92	7.70	7.47	7.35	7.27
900	9.14	9.02	8.91	8.66	8.41	8.26	8.18
1000	10.16	10.02	9.90	9.63	9.34	9.18	9.09
2000	20.31	20.04	19.80	19.25	18.67	18.36	18.17
3000	30.46	30.06	29.70	28.87	28.01	27.53	27.26
4000	40.61	40.07	39.60	38.49	37.34	36.71	36.34
5000	50.77	50.09	49.50	48.11	46.68	45.88	45.42
6000	60.92	60.11	59.39	57.73	56.01	55.06	54.51
7000	71.07	70.12	69.29	67.35	65.35	64.23	63.59
8000	81.22	80.14	79.19	76.97	74.68	73.41	72.68
9000	91.38	90.16	89.09	86.59	84.02	82.58	81.76
10000	101.53	100.17	98.99	96.21	93.35	91.76	90.84
11000	111.68	110.19	108.88	105.84	102.69	100.93	99.93
12000	121.83	120.21	118.78	115.46	112.02	110.11	109.01
13000	131.98	130.22	128.68	125.08	121.36	119.28	118.10
14000	142.14	140.24	138.58	134.70	130.69	128.46	127.18
15000	152.29	150.26	148.48	144.32	140.03	137.63	136.26
16000	162.44	160.27	158.37	153.94	149.36	146.81	145.35
17000	172.59	170.29	168.27	163.56	158.70	155.98	154.43
18000	182.75	180.31	178.17	173.18	168.03	165.16	163.52
19000	192.90	190.32	188.07	182.80	177.37	174.33	172.60
20000	203.05	200.34	197.97	192.42	186.70	183.51	181.68
21000	213.20	210.36	207.87	202.04	196.04	192.68	190.77
22000	223.36	220.37	217.76	211.67	205.37	201.86	199.85
23000	233.51	230.39	227.66	221.29	214.71	211.03	208.94
24000	243.66	240.41	237.56	230.91	224.04	220.21	218.02
25000	253.81	250.42	247.46	240.53	233.38	229.38	227.10
26000	263.96	260.44	257.36	250.15	242.71	238.56	236.19
27000	274.12	270.46	267.25	259.77	252.04	247.73	245.27
28000	284.27	280.48	277.15	269.39	261.38	256.91	254.36
29000	294.42	290.49	287.05	279.01	270.71	266.08	263.44
30000	304.57	300.51	296.95	288.63	280.05	275.26	272.52
31000	314.73	310.53	306.85	298.25	289.38	284.43	281.61
32000	324.88	320.54	316.74	307.87	298.72	293.61	290.69
33000	335.03	330.56	326.64	317.50	308.05	302.78	299.78
34000	345.18	340.58	336.54	327.12	317.39	311.96	308.86
35000	355.34	350.59	346.44	336.74	326.72	321.13	317.94
40000	406.10	400.68	395.93	384.84	373.40	367.01	363.36
45000	456.86	450.76	445.42	432.95	420.07	412.88	408.78
50000	507.62	500.84	494.91	481.05	466.75	458.76	454.20
55000	558.38	550.93	544.40	529.16	513.42	504.63	499.62
60000	609.14	601.01	593.89	577.26	560.09	550.51	545.04
65000	659.90	651.10	643.38	625.37	606.77	596.38	590.46
70000	710.67	701.18	692.87	673.47	653.44	642.26	635.88
75000	761.43	751.26	742.36	721.57	700.12	688.13	681.30
80000	812.19	801.35	791.85	769.68	746.79	734.01	726.72
100000	1015.23	1001.68	989.81	962.10	933.49	917.51	908.40

MONTHLY PAYMENT
NECESSARY TO AMORTIZE A LOAN

TERM AMOUNT	1 YEAR	1½ YEARS	2 YEARS	2½ YEARS	3 YEARS	4 YEARS	5 YEARS
$ 25	2.21	1.52	1.17	.96	.82	.65	.55
50	4.42	3.03	2.34	1.92	1.64	1.30	1.09
75	6.63	4.54	3.50	2.88	2.46	1.94	1.64
100	8.84	6.06	4.67	3.83	3.23	2.59	2.18
200	17.68	12.11	9.33	7.66	6.55	5.17	4.35
300	26.52	18.16	13.99	11.49	9.83	7.76	6.53
400	35.36	24.21	18.65	15.32	13.10	10.34	8.70
500	44.20	30.26	23.31	19.14	16.37	12.93	10.88
600	53.03	36.32	27.97	22.97	19.65	15.51	13.05
700	61.87	42.37	32.63	26.80	22.92	18.10	15.22
800	70.71	48.42	37.29	30.63	26.20	20.68	17.40
900	79.55	54.47	41.95	34.46	29.47	23.27	19.57
1000	88.39	60.52	46.61	38.28	32.74	25.85	21.75
2000	176.77	121.04	93.22	76.56	65.48	51.70	43.49
3000	265.15	181.56	139.83	114.84	98.22	77.54	65.23
4000	353.53	242.08	186.44	153.12	130.96	103.39	86.97
5000	441.91	302.60	233.04	191.40	163.70	129.23	108.72
6000	530.29	363.12	279.65	229.67	196.44	155.08	130.46
7000	618.68	423.63	326.26	267.95	229.18	180.92	152.20
8000	707.06	484.15	372.87	306.23	261.91	206.77	173.94
9000	795.44	544.67	419.48	344.51	294.65	232.61	195.69
10000	883.82	605.19	466.08	382.79	327.39	258.46	217.43
11000	972.20	665.71	512.69	421.06	360.13	284.31	239.17
12000	1060.58	726.23	559.30	459.34	392.87	310.15	260.91
13000	1148.97	786.75	605.91	497.62	425.61	336.00	282.66
14000	1237.35	847.26	652.51	535.90	458.35	361.84	304.40
15000	1325.73	907.78	699.12	574.18	491.09	387.69	326.14
16000	1414.11	968.30	745.73	612.45	523.82	413.53	347.88
17000	1502.49	1028.82	792.34	650.73	556.56	439.38	369.63
18000	1590.87	1089.34	838.95	689.01	589.30	465.22	391.37
19000	1679.26	1149.86	885.55	727.29	622.04	491.07	413.11
20000	1767.64	1210.38	932.16	765.57	654.78	516.92	434.85
21000	1856.02	1270.89	978.77	803.84	687.52	542.76	456.60
22000	1944.40	1331.41	1025.38	842.12	720.26	568.61	478.34
23000	2032.78	1391.93	1071.99	880.40	753.00	594.45	500.08
24000	2121.16	1452.45	1118.59	918.68	785.73	620.30	521.82
25000	2209.55	1512.97	1165.20	956.96	818.47	646.14	543.57
26000	2297.93	1573.49	1211.81	995.23	851.21	671.99	565.31
27000	2386.31	1634.01	1258.42	1033.51	883.95	697.83	587.05
28000	2474.69	1694.52	1305.02	1071.79	916.69	723.68	608.79
29000	2563.07	1755.04	1351.63	1110.07	949.43	749.53	630.54
30000	2651.45	1815.56	1398.24	1148.35	982.17	775.37	652.28
31000	2739.84	1876.08	1444.85	1186.62	1014.91	801.22	674.02
32000	2828.22	1936.60	1491.46	1224.90	1047.64	827.06	695.76
33000	2916.60	1997.12	1538.06	1263.18	1080.38	852.91	717.50
34000	3004.98	2057.64	1584.67	1301.46	1113.12	878.75	739.25
35000	3093.36	2118.15	1631.28	1339.74	1145.86	904.60	760.99
40000	3535.27	2420.75	1864.32	1531.13	1309.55	1033.83	869.70
45000	3977.18	2723.34	2097.36	1722.52	1473.25	1163.05	978.41
50000	4419.09	3025.93	2330.40	1913.91	1636.94	1292.28	1087.13
55000	4861.00	3328.52	2563.44	2105.30	1800.63	1421.51	1195.84
60000	5302.90	3631.12	2796.48	2296.69	1964.33	1550.74	1304.55
65000	5744.81	3933.71	3029.51	2488.08	2128.02	1679.96	1413.26
70000	6186.72	4236.30	3262.55	2679.47	2291.72	1809.19	1521.97
75000	6628.63	4538.90	3495.59	2870.86	2455.41	1938.42	1630.69
80000	7070.54	4841.49	3728.63	3062.25	2619.10	2067.65	1739.40
100000	8838.17	6051.86	4660.79	3827.81	3273.88	2584.56	2174.25

TERM AMOUNT	6 YEARS	7 YEARS	8 YEARS	9 YEARS	10 YEARS	11 YEARS	12 YEARS
$ 25	.48	.43	.40	.37	.35	.33	.32
50	.96	.86	.79	.74	.69	.66	.63
75	1.43	1.29	1.18	1.10	1.04	.99	.95
100	1.91	1.72	1.58	1.47	1.38	1.31	1.26
200	3.81	3.43	3.15	2.93	2.76	2.62	2.51
300	5.72	5.14	4.72	4.39	4.14	3.93	3.77
400	7.62	6.85	6.29	5.86	5.52	5.24	5.02
500	9.52	8.57	7.86	7.32	6.89	6.55	6.27
600	11.43	10.28	9.43	8.78	8.27	7.86	7.53
700	13.33	11.99	11.00	10.24	9.65	9.17	8.78
800	15.23	13.70	12.57	11.71	11.03	10.48	10.03
900	17.14	15.42	14.14	13.17	12.40	11.79	11.29
1000	19.04	17.13	15.71	14.63	13.78	13.10	12.54
2000	38.07	34.25	31.42	29.26	27.56	26.19	25.08
3000	57.11	51.37	47.13	43.88	41.33	39.28	37.61
4000	76.14	68.49	62.84	58.51	55.11	52.37	50.15
5000	95.18	85.62	78.55	73.13	68.88	65.47	62.68
6000	114.21	102.74	94.26	87.76	82.66	78.56	75.22
7000	133.24	119.86	109.96	102.39	96.43	91.65	87.75
8000	152.28	136.98	125.67	117.01	110.21	104.74	100.29
9000	171.31	154.11	141.38	131.64	123.98	117.84	112.82
10000	190.35	171.23	157.09	146.26	137.76	130.93	125.36
11000	209.38	188.35	172.80	160.89	151.53	144.02	137.90
12000	228.41	205.47	188.51	175.52	165.31	157.11	150.43
13000	247.45	222.60	204.21	190.14	179.08	170.21	162.97
14000	266.48	239.72	219.92	204.77	192.86	183.30	175.50
15000	285.52	256.84	235.63	219.39	206.63	196.39	188.04
16000	304.55	273.96	251.34	234.02	220.41	209.48	200.57
17000	323.58	291.09	267.05	248.64	234.18	222.57	213.11
18000	342.62	308.21	282.76	263.27	247.96	235.67	225.64
19000	361.65	325.33	298.47	277.90	261.73	248.76	238.18
20000	380.69	342.45	314.17	292.52	275.51	261.85	250.72
21000	399.72	359.58	329.88	307.15	289.28	274.94	263.25
22000	418.75	376.70	345.59	321.77	303.06	288.04	275.79
23000	437.79	393.82	361.30	336.40	316.83	301.13	288.32
24000	456.82	410.94	377.01	351.03	330.61	314.22	300.86
25000	475.86	428.07	392.72	365.65	344.38	327.31	313.39
26000	494.89	445.19	408.42	380.28	358.16	340.41	325.93
27000	513.93	462.31	424.13	394.90	371.93	353.50	338.46
28000	532.96	479.43	439.84	409.53	385.71	366.59	351.00
29000	551.99	496.56	455.55	424.15	399.48	379.68	363.54
30000	571.03	513.68	471.26	438.78	413.26	392.78	376.07
31000	590.06	530.80	486.97	453.41	427.03	405.87	388.61
32000	609.10	547.92	502.67	468.03	440.81	418.96	401.14
33000	628.13	565.05	518.38	482.66	454.58	432.05	413.68
34000	647.16	582.17	534.09	497.28	468.36	445.14	426.21
35000	666.20	599.29	549.80	511.91	482.13	458.24	438.75
40000	761.37	684.90	628.34	585.04	551.01	523.70	501.43
45000	856.54	770.51	706.88	658.17	619.88	589.16	564.10
50000	951.71	856.13	785.43	731.30	688.76	654.62	626.78
55000	1046.88	941.74	863.97	804.43	757.63	720.08	689.46
60000	1142.05	1027.35	942.51	877.56	826.51	785.55	752.14
65000	1237.22	1112.96	1021.05	950.69	895.38	851.01	814.82
70000	1332.39	1198.58	1099.59	1023.82	964.26	916.47	877.49
75000	1427.56	1284.19	1178.14	1096.94	1033.13	981.93	940.17
80000	1522.73	1369.80	1256.68	1170.07	1102.01	1047.39	1002.85
100000	1903.41	1712.25	1570.85	1462.59	1377.51	1309.24	1253.56

MONTHLY PAYMENT
NECESSARY TO AMORTIZE A LOAN

TERM AMOUNT	13 YEARS	14 YEARS	15 YEARS	16 YEARS	17 YEARS	18 YEARS	19 YEARS
$ 25	.31	.30	.29	.28	.28	.27	.27
50	.61	.59	.57	.56	.55	.54	.53
75	.91	.88	.86	.84	.82	.80	.79
100	1.21	1.17	1.14	1.11	1.09	1.07	1.05
200	2.42	2.34	2.28	2.22	2.18	2.14	2.10
300	3.63	3.51	3.41	3.33	3.26	3.20	3.15
400	4.84	4.68	4.55	4.44	4.35	4.27	4.19
500	6.04	5.85	5.69	5.55	5.43	5.33	5.24
600	7.25	7.02	6.82	6.66	6.52	6.40	6.29
700	8.46	8.19	7.96	7.77	7.60	7.46	7.34
800	9.67	9.36	9.10	8.88	8.69	8.53	8.38
900	10.87	10.53	10.23	9.99	9.77	9.59	9.43
1000	12.08	11.70	11.37	11.10	10.86	10.66	10.48
2000	24.16	23.39	22.74	22.19	21.71	21.31	20.95
3000	36.23	35.08	34.10	33.28	32.57	31.96	31.43
4000	48.31	46.77	45.47	44.37	43.42	42.61	41.90
5000	60.38	58.46	56.83	55.46	54.27	53.26	52.38
6000	72.46	70.15	68.20	66.55	65.13	63.91	62.85
7000	84.53	81.84	79.57	77.64	75.98	74.56	73.33
8000	96.61	93.53	90.93	88.73	86.84	85.21	83.80
9000	108.68	105.22	102.30	99.82	97.69	95.86	94.28
10000	120.76	116.91	113.66	110.91	108.54	106.51	104.75
11000	132.83	128.60	125.03	122.00	119.40	117.16	115.23
12000	144.91	140.29	136.40	133.09	130.25	127.81	125.70
13000	156.98	151.98	147.76	144.18	141.10	138.46	136.18
14000	169.06	163.67	159.13	155.27	151.96	149.11	146.65
15000	181.13	175.36	170.49	166.36	162.81	159.76	157.12
16000	193.21	187.05	181.86	177.45	173.67	170.41	167.60
17000	205.28	198.74	193.23	188.54	184.52	181.06	178.07
18000	217.36	210.43	204.59	199.63	195.37	191.71	188.55
19000	229.44	222.13	215.96	210.72	206.23	202.36	199.02
20000	241.51	233.82	227.32	221.81	217.08	213.01	209.50
21000	253.59	245.51	238.69	232.90	227.93	223.67	219.97
22000	265.66	257.20	250.06	243.99	238.79	234.32	230.45
23000	277.74	268.89	261.42	255.08	249.64	244.97	240.92
24000	289.81	280.58	272.79	266.17	260.50	255.62	251.40
25000	301.89	292.27	284.15	277.26	271.35	266.27	261.87
26000	313.96	303.96	295.52	288.35	282.20	276.92	272.35
27000	326.04	315.65	306.89	299.44	293.06	287.57	282.82
28000	338.11	327.34	318.25	310.53	303.91	298.22	293.29
29000	350.19	339.03	329.62	321.62	314.77	308.87	303.77
30000	362.26	350.72	340.98	332.71	325.62	319.52	314.24
31000	374.34	362.41	352.35	343.80	336.47	330.17	324.72
32000	386.41	374.10	363.72	354.89	347.33	340.82	335.19
33000	398.49	385.79	375.08	365.98	358.18	351.47	345.67
34000	410.56	397.48	386.45	377.07	369.03	362.12	356.14
35000	422.64	409.17	397.81	388.10	379.89	372.77	366.62
40000	483.02	467.63	454.64	443.61	434.16	426.02	418.99
45000	543.39	526.08	511.47	499.06	488.43	479.28	471.36
50000	603.77	584.53	568.30	554.51	542.70	532.53	523.74
55000	664.15	642.98	625.13	609.96	596.96	585.78	576.11
60000	724.52	701.44	681.96	665.41	651.23	639.05	628.48
65000	784.90	759.89	738.79	720.86	705.50	692.29	680.86
70000	845.27	818.34	795.62	776.31	759.77	745.54	733.23
75000	905.65	876.80	852.45	831.76	814.04	798.79	785.60
80000	966.03	935.25	909.28	887.21	868.31	852.04	837.98
100000	1207.53	1169.06	1136.60	1109.01	1085.39	1065.05	1047.47

TERM AMOUNT	20 YEARS	21 YEARS	22 YEARS	25 YEARS	30 YEARS	35 YEARS	40 YEARS
$ 25	.26	.26	.26	.25	.24	.24	.24
50	.52	.51	.51	.50	.48	.47	.47
75	.78	.77	.76	.74	.72	.71	.70
100	1.04	1.02	1.01	.99	.96	.94	.93
200	2.07	2.04	2.02	1.97	1.91	1.88	1.86
300	3.10	3.06	3.03	2.95	2.86	2.82	2.79
400	4.13	4.08	4.03	3.93	3.81	3.75	3.72
500	5.17	5.10	5.04	4.91	4.77	4.69	4.65
600	6.20	6.12	6.05	5.89	5.72	5.63	5.57
700	7.23	7.14	7.06	6.87	6.67	6.56	6.50
800	8.26	8.16	8.06	7.85	7.62	7.50	7.43
900	9.29	9.17	9.07	8.83	8.58	8.44	8.36
1000	10.33	10.19	10.08	9.81	9.53	9.37	9.29
2000	20.65	20.38	20.15	19.61	19.05	18.74	18.57
3000	30.97	30.57	30.22	29.41	28.57	28.11	27.85
4000	41.29	40.76	40.29	39.21	38.10	37.48	37.14
5000	51.61	50.95	50.37	49.01	47.62	46.85	46.42
6000	61.94	61.14	60.44	58.81	57.14	56.22	55.70
7000	72.26	71.33	70.51	68.61	66.67	65.59	64.99
8000	82.58	81.51	80.58	78.41	76.19	74.96	74.27
9000	92.90	91.70	90.66	88.22	85.71	84.33	83.55
10000	103.22	101.89	100.73	98.02	95.24	93.70	92.83
11000	113.55	112.08	110.80	107.82	104.76	103.07	102.12
12000	123.87	122.27	120.87	117.62	114.28	112.44	111.40
13000	134.19	132.46	130.94	127.42	123.81	121.81	120.68
14000	144.51	142.65	141.02	137.22	133.33	131.18	129.97
15000	154.83	152.84	151.09	147.02	142.85	140.55	139.25
16000	165.16	163.02	161.16	156.82	152.38	149.92	148.53
17000	175.48	173.21	171.23	166.62	161.90	159.29	157.82
18000	185.80	183.40	181.31	176.43	171.42	168.66	167.10
19000	196.12	193.59	191.38	186.23	180.95	178.03	176.38
20000	206.44	203.78	201.45	196.13	190.47	187.40	185.66
21000	216.76	213.97	211.52	205.83	199.99	196.77	194.95
22000	227.09	224.16	221.59	215.63	209.52	206.14	204.23
23000	237.41	234.35	231.67	225.43	219.04	215.51	213.51
24000	247.73	244.53	241.74	235.23	228.56	224.87	222.80
25000	258.05	254.72	251.81	245.03	238.09	234.24	232.08
26000	268.37	264.91	261.88	254.83	247.61	243.61	241.36
27000	278.70	275.10	271.96	264.64	257.13	252.98	250.64
28000	289.02	285.29	282.03	274.44	266.66	262.35	259.93
29000	299.34	295.48	292.10	284.24	276.18	271.72	269.21
30000	309.66	305.67	302.17	294.04	285.70	281.09	278.49
31000	319.98	315.85	312.24	303.84	295.23	290.46	287.78
32000	330.31	326.04	322.32	313.64	304.75	299.83	297.06
33000	340.63	336.23	332.39	323.44	314.27	309.20	306.34
34000	350.95	346.42	342.46	333.24	323.79	318.57	315.63
35000	361.27	356.61	352.53	343.04	333.32	327.94	324.91
40000	412.88	407.55	402.89	392.05	380.93	374.79	371.32
45000	464.49	458.50	453.26	441.06	428.55	421.64	417.74
50000	516.10	509.44	503.62	490.06	476.17	468.48	464.15
55000	567.71	560.38	553.98	539.07	523.78	515.33	510.57
60000	619.32	611.33	604.34	588.07	571.40	562.18	556.98
65000	670.93	662.27	654.70	637.08	619.02	609.03	603.40
70000	722.54	713.21	705.06	686.08	666.63	655.88	649.81
75000	774.15	764.16	755.42	735.09	714.25	702.72	696.23
80000	825.76	815.10	805.78	784.10	761.86	749.57	742.64
100000	1032.19	1018.88	1007.23	980.12	952.33	936.96	928.30

73

11¼%

TERM AMOUNT	1 YEAR	1½ YEARS	2 YEARS	2½ YEARS	3 YEARS	4 YEARS	5 YEARS
$ 25	2.22	1.52	1.17	.96	.83	.65	.55
50	4.43	3.04	2.34	1.92	1.65	1.30	1.10
75	6.64	4.55	3.51	2.88	2.47	1.95	1.65
100	8.85	6.07	4.68	3.84	3.29	2.60	2.19
200	17.70	12.13	9.35	7.68	6.58	5.20	4.38
300	26.55	18.20	14.02	11.52	9.86	7.80	6.57
400	35.40	24.26	18.69	15.36	13.15	10.39	8.75
500	44.25	30.32	23.37	19.20	16.43	12.99	10.94
600	53.10	36.39	28.04	23.04	19.72	15.59	13.13
700	61.95	42.45	32.71	26.88	23.01	18.18	15.31
800	70.80	48.51	37.38	30.72	26.29	20.78	17.50
900	79.65	54.58	42.06	34.56	29.58	23.38	19.69
1000	88.50	60.64	46.73	38.40	32.86	25.97	21.87
2000	177.00	121.27	93.45	76.80	65.72	51.94	43.74
3000	265.50	181.91	140.18	115.19	98.58	77.91	65.61
4000	354.00	242.54	186.90	153.59	131.43	103.87	87.47
5000	442.50	303.18	233.62	191.98	164.29	129.84	109.34
6000	530.99	363.81	280.35	230.38	197.15	155.81	131.21
7000	619.49	424.44	327.07	268.77	230.01	181.77	153.08
8000	707.99	485.08	373.80	307.17	262.86	207.74	174.94
9000	796.49	545.71	420.52	345.56	295.72	233.71	196.81
10000	884.99	606.35	467.24	383.96	328.58	259.68	218.68
11000	973.49	666.98	513.97	422.35	361.43	285.64	240.55
12000	1061.98	727.62	560.69	460.75	394.29	311.61	262.41
13000	1150.48	788.25	607.42	499.14	427.15	337.58	284.28
14000	1238.98	848.88	654.14	537.54	460.01	363.54	306.15
15000	1327.48	909.52	700.86	575.93	492.86	389.51	328.01
16000	1415.98	970.15	747.59	614.33	525.72	415.48	349.88
17000	1504.48	1030.79	794.31	652.72	558.58	441.45	371.75
18000	1592.97	1091.42	841.04	691.12	591.44	467.41	393.62
19000	1681.47	1152.06	887.76	729.51	624.29	493.38	415.48
20000	1769.97	1212.69	934.48	767.91	657.15	519.35	437.35
21000	1858.47	1273.32	981.21	806.31	690.01	545.31	459.22
22000	1946.97	1333.96	1027.93	844.70	722.86	571.28	481.09
23000	2035.47	1394.59	1074.66	883.10	755.72	597.25	502.95
24000	2123.96	1455.23	1121.38	921.49	788.58	623.22	524.82
25000	2212.46	1515.86	1168.10	959.89	821.44	649.18	546.69
26000	2300.96	1576.49	1214.83	998.28	854.29	675.15	568.56
27000	2389.46	1637.13	1261.55	1036.68	887.15	701.12	590.42
28000	2477.96	1697.76	1308.28	1075.07	920.01	727.08	612.29
29000	2566.46	1758.40	1355.00	1113.47	952.86	753.05	634.16
30000	2654.95	1819.03	1401.72	1151.86	985.72	779.02	656.02
31000	2743.45	1879.67	1448.45	1190.26	1018.58	804.99	677.89
32000	2831.95	1940.30	1495.17	1228.65	1051.44	830.95	699.76
33000	2920.95	2000.93	1541.90	1267.05	1084.29	856.92	721.63
34000	3008.95	2061.57	1588.62	1305.44	1117.15	882.89	743.49
35000	3097.45	2122.20	1635.34	1343.84	1150.01	908.85	765.36
40000	3539.94	2425.37	1868.96	1535.82	1314.29	1038.69	874.70
45000	3982.43	2728.55	2102.58	1727.79	1478.58	1168.52	984.03
50000	4424.92	3031.72	2336.20	1919.79	1642.87	1298.36	1093.37
55000	4867.41	3334.89	2569.82	2111.74	1807.15	1428.20	1202.71
60000	5309.90	3638.06	2803.44	2303.72	1971.44	1558.03	1312.04
65000	5752.40	3941.23	3037.06	2495.70	2135.73	1687.87	1421.38
70000	6194.89	4244.40	3270.68	2687.67	2300.01	1817.70	1530.72
75000	6637.38	4547.57	3504.30	2879.65	2464.30	1947.54	1640.05
80000	7079.87	4850.74	3737.92	3071.63	2628.58	2077.37	1749.39
100000	8849.84	6063.43	4672.40	3839.53	3285.73	2596.71	2186.74

74

TERM AMOUNT	6 YEARS	7 YEARS	8 YEARS	9 YEARS	10 YEARS	11 YEARS	12 YEARS
$ 25	.48	.44	.40	.37	.35	.34	.32
50	.96	.87	.80	.74	.70	.67	.64
75	1.44	1.30	1.19	1.11	1.05	1.00	.96
100	1.92	1.73	1.59	1.48	1.40	1.33	1.27
200	3.84	3.46	3.17	2.96	2.79	2.65	2.54
300	5.75	5.18	4.76	4.43	4.18	3.98	3.81
400	7.67	6.91	6.34	5.91	5.57	5.30	5.08
500	9.59	8.63	7.93	7.39	6.96	6.62	6.35
600	11.50	10.36	9.51	8.86	8.36	7.95	7.62
700	13.42	12.08	11.10	10.34	9.75	9.27	8.88
800	15.33	13.81	12.68	11.82	11.14	10.60	10.15
900	17.25	15.53	14.26	13.29	12.53	11.92	11.42
1000	19.17	17.26	15.85	14.77	13.92	13.24	12.69
2000	38.33	34.51	31.69	29.53	27.84	26.48	25.37
3000	57.49	51.77	47.54	44.30	41.76	39.72	38.06
4000	76.65	69.02	63.38	59.06	55.67	52.96	50.74
5000	95.82	86.28	79.22	73.83	69.59	66.19	63.42
6000	114.98	103.53	95.07	88.59	83.51	79.43	76.11
7000	134.14	120.78	110.91	103.36	97.42	92.67	88.79
8000	153.30	138.04	126.75	118.12	111.34	105.91	101.48
9000	172.47	155.29	142.60	132.88	125.26	119.14	114.16
10000	191.63	172.55	158.44	147.65	139.17	132.38	126.84
11000	210.79	189.80	174.28	162.41	153.09	145.62	139.53
12000	229.95	207.06	190.13	177.18	167.01	158.86	152.21
13000	249.12	224.31	205.97	191.94	180.92	172.09	164.90
14000	268.28	241.56	221.82	206.71	194.84	185.33	177.58
15000	287.44	258.82	237.66	221.47	208.76	198.57	190.26
16000	306.60	276.07	253.50	236.24	222.68	211.81	202.95
17000	325.77	293.33	269.35	251.00	236.59	225.04	215.63
18000	344.93	310.58	285.19	265.76	250.51	238.28	228.32
19000	364.09	327.83	301.03	280.53	264.43	251.52	241.00
20000	383.25	345.09	316.88	295.29	278.34	264.76	253.68
21000	402.41	362.34	332.72	310.06	292.26	277.99	266.37
22000	421.58	379.60	348.56	324.82	306.18	291.23	279.05
23000	440.74	396.85	364.41	339.59	320.09	304.47	291.74
24000	459.90	414.11	380.25	354.35	334.01	317.71	304.42
25000	479.06	431.36	396.09	369.12	347.93	330.94	317.10
26000	498.23	448.61	411.94	383.88	361.84	344.18	329.79
27000	517.39	465.87	427.78	398.64	375.76	357.42	342.47
28000	536.55	483.12	443.63	413.41	389.68	370.66	355.16
29000	555.71	500.38	459.47	428.17	403.59	383.89	367.84
30000	574.88	517.63	475.31	442.94	417.51	397.13	380.52
31000	594.04	534.88	491.16	457.70	431.43	410.37	393.21
32000	613.20	552.14	507.00	472.47	445.35	423.61	405.89
33000	632.36	569.39	522.84	487.23	459.26	436.84	418.57
34000	651.53	586.65	538.69	502.00	473.18	450.08	431.26
35000	670.69	603.90	554.53	516.76	487.10	463.32	443.94
40000	766.50	690.17	633.75	590.58	556.68	529.51	507.36
45000	862.31	776.44	712.97	664.40	626.27	595.69	570.78
50000	958.12	862.71	792.18	738.23	695.85	661.88	634.20
55000	1053.94	948.98	871.40	812.05	765.43	728.07	697.62
60000	1149.75	1035.26	950.62	885.87	835.02	794.26	761.04
65000	1245.56	1121.53	1029.84	959.69	904.60	860.44	824.46
70000	1341.37	1207.80	1109.06	1033.51	974.19	926.63	887.88
75000	1437.18	1294.07	1188.27	1107.34	1043.77	992.82	951.30
80000	1532.99	1380.34	1267.49	1181.16	1113.36	1059.01	1014.72
100000	1916.24	1725.42	1584.36	1476.45	1391.69	1323.75	1268.40

MONTHLY PAYMENT
NECESSARY TO AMORTIZE A LOAN

TERM AMOUNT	13 YEARS	14 YEARS	15 YEARS	16 YEARS	17 YEARS	18 YEARS	19 YEARS
$ 25	.31	.30	.29	.29	.28	.28	.27
50	.62	.60	.58	.57	.56	.55	.54
75	.92	.89	.87	.85	.83	.82	.80
100	1.23	1.19	1.16	1.13	1.11	1.09	1.07
200	2.45	2.37	2.31	2.26	2.21	2.17	2.13
300	3.67	3.56	3.46	3.38	3.31	3.25	3.20
400	4.90	4.74	4.61	4.51	4.41	4.33	4.26
500	6.12	5.93	5.77	5.63	5.51	5.41	5.33
600	7.34	7.11	6.92	6.76	6.62	6.49	6.39
700	8.56	8.30	8.07	7.88	7.72	7.58	7.46
800	9.79	9.48	9.22	9.01	8.82	8.66	8.52
900	11.01	10.67	10.38	10.13	9.92	9.74	9.58
1000	12.23	11.85	11.53	11.26	11.02	10.82	10.65
2000	24.46	23.70	23.05	22.51	22.04	21.64	21.29
3000	36.69	35.54	34.58	33.76	33.06	32.45	31.93
4000	48.91	47.39	46.10	45.01	44.07	43.27	42.58
5000	61.14	59.23	57.62	56.26	55.09	54.09	53.22
6000	73.37	71.08	69.15	67.51	66.11	64.90	63.86
7000	85.59	82.92	80.67	78.76	77.12	75.72	74.51
8000	97.82	94.77	92.19	90.01	88.14	86.53	85.15
9000	110.05	106.61	103.72	101.26	99.16	97.35	95.79
10000	122.27	118.46	115.24	112.51	110.17	108.17	106.43
11000	134.50	130.30	126.76	123.76	121.19	118.98	117.08
12000	146.73	142.15	138.29	135.01	132.21	129.80	127.72
13000	158.95	153.99	149.81	146.26	143.22	140.62	138.36
14000	171.18	165.84	161.33	157.51	154.24	151.43	149.01
15000	183.41	177.68	172.86	168.76	165.26	162.25	159.65
16000	195.63	189.53	184.38	180.01	176.27	173.06	170.29
17000	207.86	201.37	195.90	191.26	187.29	183.88	180.93
18000	220.09	213.22	207.43	202.51	198.31	194.70	191.58
19000	232.31	225.06	218.95	213.76	209.33	205.51	202.22
20000	244.54	236.91	230.47	225.01	220.34	216.33	212.86
21000	256.77	248.75	242.00	236.26	231.36	227.15	223.51
22000	268.99	260.60	253.52	247.51	242.38	237.96	234.15
23000	281.22	272.44	265.04	258.76	253.39	248.78	244.79
24000	293.45	284.29	276.57	270.01	264.41	259.59	255.43
25000	305.67	296.13	288.09	281.26	275.43	270.41	266.08
26000	317.90	307.98	299.61	292.51	286.44	281.23	276.72
27000	330.13	319.82	311.14	303.76	297.46	292.04	287.36
28000	342.35	331.67	322.66	315.01	308.48	302.86	298.01
29000	354.58	343.51	334.18	326.26	319.49	313.67	308.65
30000	366.81	355.36	345.71	337.51	330.51	324.49	319.29
31000	379.03	367.20	357.23	348.77	341.53	335.31	329.93
32000	391.26	379.05	368.76	360.02	352.54	346.12	340.58
33000	403.49	390.89	380.28	371.27	363.56	356.94	351.22
34000	415.72	402.74	391.80	382.52	374.58	367.76	361.86
35000	427.94	414.58	403.33	393.77	385.60	378.57	372.51
40000	489.08	473.81	460.94	450.02	440.68	432.65	425.72
45000	550.21	533.03	518.56	506.27	495.76	486.73	478.93
50000	611.34	592.26	576.18	562.52	550.85	540.82	532.15
55000	672.48	651.48	633.79	618.77	605.93	594.90	585.36
60000	733.61	710.71	691.41	675.02	661.02	648.98	638.58
65000	794.75	769.94	749.03	731.28	716.10	703.06	691.79
70000	855.88	829.16	806.65	787.53	771.19	757.14	745.01
75000	917.01	888.39	864.26	843.78	826.27	811.22	798.22
80000	978.15	947.61	921.88	900.03	881.35	865.30	851.44
100000	1222.68	1184.51	1152.35	1125.04	1101.69	1081.63	1064.29

76

TERM AMOUNT	20 YEARS	21 YEARS	22 YEARS	25 YEARS	30 YEARS	35 YEARS	40 YEARS
$ 25	.27	.26	.26	.25	.25	.24	.24
50	.53	.52	.52	.50	.49	.48	.48
75	.79	.78	.77	.75	.73	.72	.72
100	1.05	1.04	1.03	1.00	.98	.96	.95
200	2.10	2.08	2.05	2.00	1.95	1.92	1.90
300	3.15	3.11	3.08	3.00	2.92	2.87	2.85
400	4.20	4.15	4.10	4.00	3.89	3.83	3.80
500	5.25	5.19	5.13	5.00	4.86	4.79	4.75
600	6.30	6.22	6.15	5.99	5.83	5.74	5.69
700	7.35	7.26	7.18	6.99	6.80	6.70	6.64
800	8.40	8.29	8.20	7.99	7.78	7.66	7.59
900	9.45	9.33	9.23	8.99	8.75	8.61	8.54
1000	10.50	10.37	10.25	9.99	9.72	9.57	9.49
2000	20.99	20.73	20.50	19.97	19.43	19.13	18.97
3000	31.48	31.09	30.75	29.95	29.14	28.70	28.45
4000	41.98	41.45	40.99	39.93	38.86	38.26	37.94
5000	52.47	51.81	51.24	49.92	48.57	47.83	47.42
6000	62.96	62.18	61.49	59.90	58.28	57.39	56.90
7000	73.45	72.54	71.74	69.88	67.99	66.96	66.38
8000	83.95	82.90	81.98	79.86	77.71	76.52	75.87
9000	94.44	93.26	92.23	89.85	87.42	86.09	85.35
10000	104.93	103.62	102.48	99.83	97.13	95.65	94.83
11000	115.42	113.98	112.73	109.81	106.84	105.22	104.31
12000	125.92	124.35	122.97	119.79	116.56	114.78	113.80
13000	136.41	134.71	133.22	129.78	126.27	124.35	123.28
14000	146.90	145.07	143.47	139.76	135.98	133.91	132.76
15000	157.39	155.43	153.72	149.74	145.69	143.48	142.24
16000	167.89	165.79	163.96	159.72	155.41	153.04	151.73
17000	178.38	176.15	174.21	169.71	165.12	162.61	161.21
18000	188.87	186.52	184.46	179.69	174.83	172.17	170.69
19000	199.36	196.88	194.71	189.67	184.54	181.74	180.17
20000	209.86	207.24	204.95	199.65	194.26	191.30	189.66
21000	220.35	217.60	215.20	209.64	203.97	200.87	199.14
22000	230.84	227.96	225.45	219.62	213.68	210.43	208.62
23000	241.33	238.32	235.70	229.60	223.40	220.00	218.10
24000	251.83	248.69	245.94	239.58	233.11	229.56	227.59
25000	262.32	259.05	256.19	249.56	242.82	239.13	237.07
26000	272.81	269.41	266.44	259.55	252.53	248.69	246.55
27000	283.30	279.77	276.69	269.53	262.25	258.26	256.03
28000	293.80	290.13	286.93	279.51	271.96	267.82	265.52
29000	304.29	300.49	297.18	289.49	281.67	277.39	275.00
30000	314.78	310.86	307.43	299.48	291.38	286.95	284.48
31000	325.27	321.22	317.68	309.46	301.10	296.52	293.96
32000	335.77	331.58	327.92	319.44	310.81	306.08	303.45
33000	346.26	341.94	338.17	329.42	320.52	315.65	312.93
34000	356.75	352.30	348.42	339.41	330.23	325.21	322.41
35000	367.24	362.66	358.67	349.39	339.95	334.78	331.90
40000	419.71	414.47	409.90	399.30	388.51	382.60	379.31
45000	472.17	466.28	461.14	449.21	437.07	430.43	426.72
50000	524.63	518.09	512.38	499.12	485.64	478.25	474.13
55000	577.10	569.90	563.62	549.04	534.20	526.08	521.55
60000	629.56	621.71	614.85	598.95	582.76	573.90	568.96
65000	682.02	673.52	666.09	648.86	631.32	621.73	616.37
70000	734.48	725.32	717.33	698.77	679.89	669.55	663.79
75000	786.95	777.13	768.56	748.68	728.45	717.38	711.20
80000	839.41	828.94	819.80	798.60	777.01	765.20	758.61
100000	1049.26	1036.18	1024.75	998.24	971.27	956.50	948.26

77

11½%

TERM AMOUNT	1 YEAR	1½ YEARS	2 YEARS	2½ YEARS	3 YEARS	4 YEARS	5 YEARS
$ 25	2.22	1.52	1.18	.97	.83	.66	.55
50	4.44	3.04	2.35	1.93	1.65	1.31	1.10
75	6.65	4.56	3.52	2.89	2.48	1.96	1.65
100	8.87	6.08	4.69	3.86	3.30	2.61	2.20
200	17.73	12.16	9.37	7.71	6.60	5.22	4.40
300	26.59	18.23	14.06	11.56	9.90	7.83	6.60
400	35.45	24.31	18.74	15.41	13.20	10.44	8.80
500	44.31	30.38	23.43	19.26	16.49	13.05	11.00
600	53.17	36.46	28.11	23.11	19.79	15.66	13.20
700	62.04	42.53	32.79	26.96	23.09	18.27	15.40
800	70.90	48.61	37.48	30.82	26.39	20.88	17.60
900	79.76	54.68	42.16	34.67	29.68	23.49	19.80
1000	88.62	60.76	46.85	38.52	32.98	26.09	22.00
2000	177.24	121.51	93.69	77.03	65.96	52.18	43.99
3000	265.85	182.26	140.53	115.54	98.93	78.27	65.98
4000	354.47	243.01	187.37	154.06	131.91	104.36	87.98
5000	443.08	303.76	234.21	192.57	164.89	130.45	109.97
6000	531.70	364.51	281.05	231.08	197.86	156.54	131.96
7000	620.31	425.26	327.89	269.59	230.84	182.63	153.95
8000	708.93	486.01	374.73	308.11	263.81	208.72	175.95
9000	797.54	546.76	421.57	346.62	296.79	234.81	197.94
10000	886.16	607.51	468.41	385.13	329.77	260.90	219.93
11000	974.77	668.26	515.25	423.64	362.74	286.98	241.92
12000	1063.39	729.01	562.09	462.16	395.72	313.07	263.92
13000	1152.00	789.76	608.93	500.67	428.69	339.16	285.91
14000	1240.62	850.51	655.77	539.18	461.67	365.25	307.90
15000	1329.23	911.26	702.61	577.69	494.64	391.34	329.89
16000	1417.85	972.01	749.45	616.21	527.62	417.43	351.89
17000	1506.46	1032.76	796.29	654.72	560.60	443.52	373.88
18000	1595.08	1093.51	843.13	693.23	593.57	469.61	395.87
19000	1683.69	1154.26	889.97	731.75	626.55	495.70	417.86
20000	1772.31	1215.01	936.81	770.26	659.53	521.79	439.86
21000	1860.92	1275.76	983.65	808.77	692.50	547.87	461.85
22000	1949.54	1336.51	1030.49	847.28	725.48	573.96	483.84
23000	2038.15	1397.26	1077.33	885.80	758.45	600.05	505.83
24000	2126.77	1458.01	1124.17	924.31	791.43	626.14	527.83
25000	2215.38	1518.76	1171.01	962.82	824.41	652.23	549.82
26000	2304.00	1579.51	1217.85	1001.33	857.38	678.32	571.81
27000	2392.61	1640.26	1264.69	1039.85	890.36	704.41	593.81
28000	2481.23	1701.01	1311.53	1078.36	923.33	730.50	615.80
29000	2569.84	1761.76	1358.37	1116.87	956.31	756.59	637.79
30000	2658.46	1822.51	1405.21	1155.38	989.29	782.68	659.78
31000	2747.07	1883.26	1452.05	1193.90	1022.26	808.76	681.78
32000	2835.69	1944.01	1498.90	1232.41	1055.24	834.85	703.77
33000	2924.30	2004.76	1545.74	1270.92	1088.21	860.94	725.76
34000	3012.92	2065.51	1592.58	1309.44	1121.19	887.03	747.75
35000	3101.53	2126.26	1639.42	1347.95	1154.17	913.12	769.75
40000	3544.61	2430.01	1873.62	1540.51	1319.05	1043.57	879.71
45000	3987.68	2733.76	2107.82	1733.07	1483.93	1174.01	989.67
50000	4430.76	3037.51	2342.02	1925.64	1648.81	1304.46	1099.64
55000	4873.83	3341.26	2576.22	2118.20	1813.69	1434.90	1209.60
60000	5316.91	3645.01	2810.42	2310.76	1978.57	1565.35	1319.56
65000	5759.98	3948.76	3044.63	2503.33	2143.45	1695.79	1429.52
70000	6203.06	4252.51	3278.83	2695.89	2308.33	1826.24	1539.49
75000	6646.13	4556.26	3513.03	2888.45	2473.21	1956.68	1649.45
80000	7089.21	4860.01	3747.23	3081.02	2638.09	2087.13	1759.41
100000	8861.51	6075.01	4684.04	3851.27	3297.61	2608.91	2199.26

TERM AMOUNT	6 YEARS	7 YEARS	8 YEARS	9 YEARS	10 YEARS	11 YEARS	12 YEARS
$ 25	.49	.44	.40	.38	.36	.34	.33
50	.97	.87	.80	.75	.71	.67	.65
75	1.45	1.31	1.20	1.12	1.06	1.01	.97
100	1.93	1.74	1.60	1.50	1.41	1.34	1.29
200	3.86	3.48	3.20	2.99	2.82	2.68	2.57
300	5.79	5.22	4.80	4.48	4.22	4.02	3.85
400	7.72	6.96	6.40	5.97	5.63	5.36	5.14
500	9.65	8.70	7.99	7.46	7.03	6.70	6.42
600	11.58	10.44	9.59	8.95	8.44	8.04	7.70
700	13.51	12.18	11.19	10.44	9.85	9.37	8.99
800	15.44	13.91	12.79	11.93	11.25	10.71	10.27
900	17.37	15.65	14.39	13.42	12.66	12.05	11.55
1000	19.30	17.39	15.98	14.91	14.06	13.39	12.84
2000	38.59	34.78	31.96	29.81	28.12	26.77	25.67
3000	57.88	52.16	47.94	44.72	42.18	40.16	38.50
4000	77.17	69.55	63.92	59.62	56.24	53.54	51.34
5000	96.46	86.94	79.90	74.52	70.30	66.92	64.17
6000	115.75	104.32	95.88	89.43	84.36	80.31	77.00
7000	135.04	121.71	111.86	104.33	98.42	93.69	89.84
8000	154.33	139.10	127.84	119.23	112.48	107.07	102.67
9000	173.63	156.48	143.82	134.14	126.54	120.46	115.50
10000	192.92	173.87	159.80	149.04	140.60	133.84	128.34
11000	212.21	191.26	175.78	163.95	154.69	147.22	141.17
12000	231.50	208.64	191.76	178.85	168.72	160.61	154.00
13000	250.79	226.03	207.74	193.75	182.78	173.99	166.84
14000	270.08	243.42	223.72	208.66	196.84	187.37	179.67
15000	289.37	260.80	239.70	223.56	210.90	200.76	192.50
16000	308.66	278.19	255.67	238.46	224.95	214.14	205.34
17000	327.95	295.57	271.65	253.37	239.02	227.52	218.17
18000	347.25	312.96	287.63	268.27	253.08	240.91	231.00
19000	366.54	330.35	303.61	283.17	267.14	254.29	243.84
20000	385.83	347.73	319.59	298.08	281.20	267.68	256.67
21000	405.12	365.12	335.57	312.98	295.26	281.06	269.50
22000	424.41	382.51	351.55	327.89	309.31	294.44	282.33
23000	443.70	399.89	367.53	342.79	323.37	307.83	295.17
24000	462.99	417.28	383.51	357.69	337.43	321.21	308.00
25000	482.28	434.67	399.49	372.60	351.49	334.59	320.83
26000	501.58	452.05	415.47	387.50	365.55	347.98	333.67
27000	520.87	469.44	431.45	402.40	379.61	361.36	346.50
28000	540.16	486.83	447.43	417.31	393.67	374.74	359.33
29000	559.45	504.21	463.41	432.21	407.73	388.13	372.17
30000	578.74	521.60	479.39	447.11	421.79	401.51	385.00
31000	598.03	538.99	495.37	462.02	435.85	414.89	397.84
32000	617.32	556.37	511.34	476.92	449.91	428.28	410.67
33000	636.61	573.76	527.32	491.83	463.97	441.66	423.50
34000	655.90	591.14	543.30	506.73	478.03	455.04	436.33
35000	675.20	608.53	559.28	521.63	492.09	468.43	449.17
40000	771.65	695.46	639.18	596.15	562.39	535.35	513.33
45000	868.11	782.40	719.08	670.67	632.68	602.26	577.50
50000	964.56	869.33	798.97	745.19	702.98	669.18	641.66
55000	1061.02	956.26	878.87	819.71	773.28	736.10	705.83
60000	1157.47	1043.19	958.77	894.22	843.58	803.02	769.99
65000	1253.93	1130.12	1038.66	968.74	913.88	869.93	834.16
70000	1350.39	1217.06	1118.56	1043.26	984.17	936.85	898.33
75000	1446.84	1303.99	1198.46	1117.78	1054.47	1003.77	962.49
80000	1543.30	1390.92	1278.35	1192.30	1124.77	1070.69	1026.66
100000	1929.12	1738.65	1597.94	1490.37	1405.96	1338.36	1283.32

MONTHLY PAYMENT
NECESSARY TO AMORTIZE A LOAN

TERM AMOUNT	13 YEARS	14 YEARS	15 YEARS	16 YEARS	17 YEARS	18 YEARS	19 YEARS
$ 25	.31	.31	.30	.29	.28	.28	.28
50	.62	.61	.59	.58	.56	.55	.55
75	.93	.91	.88	.86	.84	.83	.82
100	1.24	1.21	1.17	1.15	1.12	1.10	1.09
200	2.48	2.41	2.34	2.29	2.24	2.20	2.17
300	3.72	3.61	3.51	3.43	3.36	3.30	3.25
400	4.96	4.81	4.68	4.57	4.48	4.40	4.33
500	6.19	6.01	5.85	5.71	5.60	5.50	5.41
600	7.43	7.21	7.01	6.85	6.71	6.59	6.49
700	8.67	8.41	8.18	7.99	7.83	7.69	7.57
800	9.91	9.61	9.35	9.13	8.95	8.79	8.65
900	11.15	10.81	10.52	1C.28	10.07	9.89	9.74
1000	12.38	12.01	11.69	11.42	11.19	10.99	10.82
2000	24.76	24.01	23.37	22.83	22.37	21.97	21.63
3000	37.14	36.01	35.05	34.24	33.55	32.95	32.44
4000	49.52	48.01	46.73	45.65	44.73	43.94	43.25
5000	61.90	60.01	58.41	57.06	55.91	54.92	54.07
6000	74.28	72.01	70.10	68.47	67.09	65.90	64.88
7000	86.66	84.01	81.78	79.89	78.27	76.89	75.69
8000	99.04	96.01	93.46	91.30	89.45	87.87	86.50
9000	111.42	108.01	105.14	102.71	100.63	98.85	97.31
10000	123.80	120.01	116.82	114.12	111.81	109.83	108.13
11000	136.18	132.01	128.51	125.53	123.00	120.82	118.94
12000	148.56	144.01	140.19	136.94	134.18	131.80	129.75
13000	160.93	156.01	151.87	148.36	145.36	142.78	140.56
14000	173.31	168.01	163.55	159.77	156.54	153.77	151.38
15000	185.69	180.01	175.23	171.18	167.72	164.75	162.19
16000	198.07	192.01	186.92	182.59	178.90	175.73	173.00
17000	210.45	204.01	198.60	194.00	190.08	186.72	183.81
18000	222.83	216.01	210.28	205.41	201.26	197.70	194.62
19000	235.21	228.02	221.96	216.83	212.44	208.68	205.44
20000	247.58	240.02	233.64	228.24	223.62	219.66	216.25
21000	259.97	252.02	245.32	239.65	234.81	230.65	227.06
22000	272.35	264.02	257.01	251.06	245.99	241.63	237.87
23000	284.73	276.02	268.69	262.47	257.17	252.61	248.69
24000	297.11	288.02	280.37	273.88	268.35	263.60	259.50
25000	309.48	300.02	292.05	285.30	279.53	274.58	270.31
26000	321.86	312.02	303.73	296.71	290.71	285.56	281.12
27000	334.24	324.02	315.42	308.12	301.89	296.54	291.93
28000	346.62	336.02	327.10	319.53	313.07	307.53	302.75
29000	359.00	348.02	338.78	330.94	324.25	318.51	313.56
30000	371.38	360.02	350.46	342.35	335.43	329.49	324.37
31000	383.76	372.02	362.14	353.77	346.61	340.48	335.18
32000	396.14	384.02	373.83	365.18	357.80	351.46	345.99
33000	408.52	396.02	385.51	376.59	368.98	362.44	356.81
34000	420.90	408.02	397.19	388.00	380.16	373.43	367.62
35000	433.28	420.02	408.87	399.41	391.34	384.41	378.43
40000	495.17	480.03	467.28	456.47	447.24	439.32	432.49
45000	557.07	540.03	525.69	513.53	503.15	494.24	486.55
50000	618.96	600.03	584.10	570.59	559.05	549.15	540.61
55000	680.86	660.04	642.51	627.65	614.96	604.07	594.67
60000	742.76	720.04	700.92	684.70	670.86	658.98	648.74
65000	804.65	780.04	759.33	741.76	726.77	713.90	702.80
70000	866.55	840.04	817.74	798.82	782.67	768.81	756.86
75000	928.44	900.05	876.15	855.88	838.58	823.73	810.92
80000	990.34	960.05	934.56	912.94	894.48	878.64	864.98
100000	1237.92	1200.06	1168.19	1141.17	1118.10	1098.30	1081.22

TERM AMOUNT	20 YEARS	21 YEARS	22 YEARS	25 YEARS	30 YEARS	35 YEARS	40 YEARS
$ 25	.27	.27	.27	.26	.25	.25	.25
50	.54	.53	.53	.51	.50	.49	.49
75	.80	.80	.79	.77	.75	.74	.73
100	1.07	1.06	1.05	1.02	1.00	.98	.97
200	2.14	2.11	2.09	2.04	1.99	1.96	1.94
300	3.20	3.17	3.13	3.05	2.98	2.93	2.91
400	4.27	4.22	4.17	4.07	3.97	3.91	3.88
500	5.34	5.27	5.22	5.09	4.96	4.89	4.85
600	6.40	6.33	6.26	6.10	5.95	5.86	5.81
700	7.47	7.38	7.30	7.12	6.94	6.84	6.78
800	8.54	8.43	8.34	8.14	7.93	7.81	7.75
900	9.60	9.49	9.39	9.15	8.92	8.79	8.72
1000	10.67	10.54	10.43	10.17	9.91	9.77	9.69
2000	21.33	21.08	20.85	20.33	19.81	19.53	19.37
3000	32.00	31.61	31.28	30.50	29.71	29.29	29.05
4000	42.66	42.15	41.70	40.66	39.62	39.05	38.74
5000	53.33	52.68	52.12	50.83	49.52	48.81	48.42
6000	63.99	63.22	62.55	60.99	59.42	58.57	58.10
7000	74.66	73.76	72.97	71.16	69.33	68.33	67.78
8000	85.32	84.29	83.39	81.32	79.23	78.09	77.47
9000	95.98	94.83	93.82	91.49	89.13	87.85	87.15
10000	106.65	105.36	104.24	101.65	99.03	97.62	96.83
11000	117.31	115.90	114.67	111.82	108.94	107.38	106.52
12000	127.98	126.43	125.09	121.98	118.84	117.14	116.20
13000	138.64	136.97	135.51	132.15	128.74	126.90	125.88
14000	149.31	147.51	145.94	142.31	138.65	136.66	135.56
15000	159.97	158.04	156.36	152.48	148.55	146.42	145.25
16000	170.63	168.58	166.78	162.64	158.45	156.18	154.93
17000	181.30	179.11	177.21	172.80	168.35	165.94	164.61
18000	191.96	189.65	187.63	182.97	178.26	175.70	174.30
19000	202.63	200.18	198.06	193.13	188.16	185.47	183.98
20000	213.29	210.72	208.48	203.30	198.06	195.23	193.66
21000	223.96	221.26	218.90	213.46	207.97	204.99	203.34
22000	234.62	231.79	229.33	223.63	217.87	214.75	213.03
23000	245.28	242.33	239.75	233.79	227.77	224.51	222.71
24000	255.95	252.86	250.17	243.96	237.67	234.27	232.39
25000	266.61	263.40	260.60	254.12	247.58	244.03	242.08
26000	277.28	273.94	271.02	264.29	257.48	253.79	251.76
27000	287.94	284.47	281.45	274.45	267.38	263.55	261.44
28000	298.61	295.01	291.87	284.62	277.29	273.32	271.12
29000	309.27	305.54	302.29	294.78	287.19	283.08	280.81
30000	319.93	316.08	312.72	304.95	297.09	292.84	290.49
31000	330.60	326.61	323.14	315.11	307.00	302.60	300.17
32000	341.26	337.15	333.56	325.28	316.90	312.36	309.86
33000	351.93	347.69	343.99	335.44	326.80	322.12	319.54
34000	362.59	358.22	354.41	345.60	336.70	331.88	329.22
35000	373.26	368.76	364.84	355.77	346.61	341.64	338.90
40000	426.58	421.44	416.95	406.59	396.12	390.45	387.32
45000	479.90	474.11	469.07	457.42	445.64	439.25	435.73
50000	533.22	526.79	521.19	508.24	495.15	488.06	484.15
55000	586.54	579.47	573.31	559.06	544.67	536.86	532.56
60000	639.86	632.15	625.43	609.89	594.18	585.67	580.97
65000	693.18	684.83	677.55	660.71	643.69	634.47	629.39
70000	746.51	737.51	729.67	711.53	693.21	683.28	677.80
75000	799.83	790.19	781.79	762.36	742.72	732.09	726.22
80000	853.15	842.87	833.90	813.18	792.24	780.89	774.63
100000	1066.43	1053.58	1042.38	1016.47	990.30	976.11	968.29

81

11¾%

MONTHLY PAYMENT
NECESSARY TO AMORTIZE A LOAN

TERM AMOUNT	1 YEAR	1½ YEARS	2 YEARS	2½ YEARS	3 YEARS	4 YEARS	5 YEARS
$ 25	2.22	1.53	1.18	.97	.83	.66	.56
50	4.44	3.05	2.35	1.94	1.66	1.32	1.11
75	6.66	4.57	3.53	2.90	2.49	1.97	1.66
100	8.88	6.09	4.70	3.87	3.31	2.63	2.22
200	17.75	12.18	9.40	7.73	6.62	5.25	4.43
300	26.62	18.26	14.09	11.59	9.93	7.87	6.64
400	35.50	24.35	18.79	15.46	13.24	10.49	8.85
500	44.37	30.44	23.48	19.32	16.55	13.11	11.06
600	53.24	36.52	28.18	23.18	19.86	15.73	13.28
700	62.12	42.61	32.87	27.05	23.17	18.35	15.49
800	70.99	48.70	37.57	30.91	26.48	20.97	17.70
900	79.86	54.78	42.27	34.77	29.79	23.60	19.91
1000	88.74	60.87	46.96	38.64	33.10	26.22	22.12
2000	177.47	121.74	93.92	77.27	66.20	52.43	44.24
3000	266.20	182.60	140.88	115.90	99.29	78.64	66.36
4000	354.93	243.47	187.83	154.53	132.39	104.85	88.48
5000	443.66	304.33	234.79	193.16	165.48	131.06	110.60
6000	532.40	365.20	281.75	231.79	198.58	157.27	132.71
7000	621.13	426.07	328.70	270.42	231.67	183.48	154.83
8000	709.86	486.93	375.66	309.05	264.77	209.70	176.95
9000	798.59	547.80	422.62	347.68	297.86	235.91	199.07
10000	887.32	608.66	469.57	386.31	330.96	262.12	221.19
11000	976.06	669.53	516.53	424.94	364.05	288.33	243.31
12000	1064.79	730.40	563.49	463.57	397.15	314.54	265.42
13000	1153.52	791.26	610.44	502.20	430.24	340.75	287.54
14000	1242.25	852.13	657.40	540.83	463.34	366.96	309.66
15000	1330.98	912.99	704.36	579.46	496.43	393.17	331.78
16000	1419.72	973.86	751.31	618.09	529.53	419.39	353.90
17000	1508.45	1034.73	798.27	656.72	562.62	445.60	376.02
18000	1597.18	1095.59	845.23	695.35	595.72	471.81	398.13
19000	1685.91	1156.46	892.18	733.98	628.81	498.02	420.25
20000	1774.64	1217.32	939.14	772.61	661.91	524.23	442.37
21000	1863.37	1278.19	986.10	811.24	695.00	550.44	464.49
22000	1952.11	1339.06	1033.05	849.87	728.10	576.65	486.61
23000	2040.84	1399.92	1080.01	888.50	761.19	602.86	508.73
24000	2129.57	1460.79	1126.97	927.13	794.29	629.08	530.84
25000	2218.30	1521.65	1173.93	965.76	827.38	655.29	552.96
26000	2307.03	1582.52	1220.88	1004.39	860.48	681.50	575.08
27000	2395.77	1643.39	1267.84	1043.02	893.57	707.71	597.20
28000	2484.50	1704.25	1314.80	1081.65	926.67	733.92	619.32
29000	2573.23	1765.12	1361.75	1120.28	959.76	760.13	641.44
30000	2661.96	1825.98	1408.71	1158.91	992.86	786.34	663.55
31000	2750.69	1886.85	1455.67	1197.54	1025.95	812.55	685.67
32000	2839.43	1947.72	1502.62	1236.17	1059.05	838.77	707.79
33000	2928.16	2008.58	1549.58	1274.80	1092.14	864.98	729.91
34000	3016.89	2069.45	1596.54	1313.43	1125.24	891.19	752.03
35000	3105.62	2130.31	1643.49	1352.06	1158.33	917.40	774.15
40000	3549.28	2434.64	1878.28	1545.22	1323.81	1048.46	884.74
45000	3992.94	2738.97	2113.06	1738.37	1489.28	1179.51	995.33
50000	4436.60	3043.30	2347.85	1931.52	1654.76	1310.57	1105.92
55000	4880.26	3347.63	2582.63	2124.67	1820.23	1441.62	1216.51
60000	5323.92	3651.96	2817.44	2317.82	1985.71	1572.68	1327.10
65000	5767.58	3956.29	3052.20	2510.97	2151.18	1703.74	1437.70
70000	6211.24	4260.62	3286.98	2704.12	2316.66	1834.79	1548.29
75000	6654.90	4564.95	3521.77	2897.28	2482.13	1965.85	1658.88
80000	7098.56	4869.28	3756.55	3090.43	2647.61	2096.91	1769.47
100000	8873.19	6086.60	4695.69	3863.03	3309.51	2621.13	2211.84

TERM AMOUNT	6 YEARS	7 YEARS	8 YEARS	9 YEARS	10 YEARS	11 YEARS	12 YEARS
$ 25	.49	.44	.41	.38	.36	.34	.33
50	.98	.88	.81	.76	.72	.68	.65
75	1.46	1.32	1.21	1.13	1.07	1.02	.98
100	1.95	1.76	1.62	1.51	1.43	1.36	1.30
200	3.89	3.51	3.23	3.01	2.85	2.71	2.60
300	5.83	5.26	4.84	4.52	4.27	4.06	3.90
400	7.77	7.01	6.45	6.02	5.69	5.42	5.20
500	9.72	8.76	8.06	7.53	7.11	6.77	6.50
600	11.66	10.52	9.67	9.03	8.53	8.12	7.79
700	13.60	12.27	11.29	10.54	9.95	9.48	9.09
800	15.54	14.02	12.90	12.04	11.37	10.83	10.39
900	17.48	15.77	14.51	13.54	12.79	12.18	11.69
1000	19.43	17.52	16.12	15.05	14.21	13.54	12.99
2000	38.85	35.04	32.24	30.09	28.41	27.07	25.97
3000	58.27	52.56	48.35	45.14	42.61	40.60	38.95
4000	77.69	70.08	64.47	60.18	56.82	54.13	51.94
5000	97.11	87.60	80.58	75.22	71.02	67.66	64.92
6000	116.53	105.12	96.70	90.27	85.22	81.19	77.90
7000	135.95	122.64	112.82	105.31	99.43	94.72	90.89
8000	155.37	140.16	128.93	120.35	113.63	108.25	103.87
9000	174.79	157.68	145.05	135.40	127.83	121.78	116.85
10000	194.21	175.20	161.16	150.44	142.03	135.31	129.84
11000	213.63	192.72	177.28	165.48	156.24	148.84	142.82
12000	233.05	210.24	193.39	180.53	170.44	162.37	155.80
13000	252.47	227.76	209.51	195.57	184.64	175.90	168.79
14000	271.89	245.28	225.63	210.62	198.85	189.43	181.77
15000	291.31	262.79	241.74	225.66	213.05	202.96	194.75
16000	310.73	280.31	257.86	240.70	227.25	216.49	207.74
17000	330.15	297.83	273.97	255.75	241.46	230.02	220.72
18000	349.57	315.35	290.09	270.79	255.66	243.55	233.70
19000	368.99	332.87	306.21	285.83	269.86	257.08	246.69
20000	388.41	350.39	322.32	300.88	284.06	270.61	259.67
21000	407.83	367.91	338.44	315.92	298.27	284.14	272.65
22000	427.25	385.43	354.55	330.96	312.47	297.67	285.64
23000	446.67	402.95	370.67	346.01	326.67	311.20	298.62
24000	466.10	420.47	386.78	361.05	340.88	324.73	311.60
25000	485.52	437.99	402.90	376.10	355.08	338.26	324.59
26000	504.94	455.51	419.02	391.14	369.28	351.79	337.57
27000	524.36	473.03	435.13	406.18	383.48	365.32	350.55
28000	543.78	490.55	451.25	421.23	397.69	378.85	363.54
29000	563.20	508.07	467.36	436.27	411.89	392.38	376.52
30000	582.62	525.58	483.48	451.31	426.09	405.91	389.50
31000	602.04	543.10	499.59	466.36	440.30	419.44	402.49
32000	621.46	560.62	515.71	481.40	454.50	432.97	415.47
33000	640.88	578.14	531.83	496.44	468.70	446.50	428.45
34000	660.30	595.66	547.94	511.49	482.91	460.03	441.44
35000	679.72	613.18	564.06	526.53	497.11	473.57	454.42
40000	776.82	700.78	644.64	601.75	568.12	541.22	519.34
45000	873.92	788.37	725.22	676.97	639.14	608.87	584.25
50000	971.03	875.97	805.79	752.19	710.15	676.52	649.17
55000	1068.13	963.57	886.37	827.41	781.17	744.17	714.08
60000	1165.23	1051.16	966.95	902.62	852.18	811.82	779.00
65000	1262.33	1138.76	1047.53	977.84	923.20	879.47	843.92
70000	1359.44	1226.36	1128.11	1053.06	994.21	947.13	908.83
75000	1456.54	1313.95	1208.69	1128.28	1065.23	1014.78	973.75
80000	1553.64	1401.55	1289.27	1203.49	1136.24	1082.43	1038.67
100000	1942.05	1751.94	1611.58	1504.37	1420.30	1353.03	1298.33

11¾%

MONTHLY PAYMENT
NECESSARY TO AMORTIZE A LOAN

TERM AMOUNT	13 YEARS	14 YEARS	15 YEARS	16 YEARS	17 YEARS	18 YEARS	19 YEARS
$ 25	.32	.31	.30	.29	.29	.28	.28
50	.63	.61	.60	.58	.57	.56	.55
75	.94	.92	.89	.87	.86	.84	.83
100	1.26	1.22	1.19	1.16	1.14	1.12	1.10
200	2.51	2.44	2.37	2.32	2.27	2.24	2.20
300	3.76	3.65	3.56	3.48	3.41	3.35	3.30
400	5.02	4.87	4.74	4.63	4.54	4.47	4.40
500	6.27	6.08	5.93	5.79	5.68	5.58	5.50
600	7.52	7.30	7.11	6.95	6.81	6.70	6.59
700	8.78	8.51	8.29	8.11	7.95	7.81	7.69
800	10.03	9.73	9.48	9.26	9.08	8.93	8.79
900	11.28	10.95	10.66	10.42	10.22	10.04	9.89
1000	12.54	12.16	11.85	11.58	11.35	11.16	10.99
2000	25.07	24.32	23.69	23.15	22.70	22.31	21.97
3000	37.60	36.48	35.53	34.73	34.04	33.46	32.95
4000	50.13	48.63	47.37	46.30	45.39	44.61	43.94
5000	62.67	60.79	59.21	57.87	56.74	55.76	54.92
6000	75.20	72.95	71.05	69.45	68.08	66.91	65.90
7000	87.73	85.10	82.89	81.02	79.43	78.06	76.88
8000	100.26	97.26	94.74	92.60	90.77	89.21	87.87
9000	112.80	109.42	106.58	104.17	102.12	100.36	98.85
10000	125.33	121.57	118.42	115.74	113.47	111.51	109.83
11000	137.86	133.73	130.26	127.32	124.81	122.66	120.81
12000	150.39	145.89	142.10	138.89	136.16	133.81	131.80
13000	162.93	158.05	153.94	150.47	147.50	144.96	142.78
14000	175.46	170.20	165.78	162.04	158.85	156.12	153.76
15000	187.99	182.36	177.62	173.61	170.20	167.27	164.74
16000	200.52	194.52	189.47	185.19	181.54	178.42	175.73
17000	213.06	206.67	201.31	196.76	192.89	189.57	186.71
18000	225.59	218.83	213.15	208.34	204.23	200.72	197.69
19000	238.12	230.99	224.99	219.91	215.58	211.87	208.67
20000	250.65	243.14	236.83	231.48	226.93	223.02	219.66
21000	263.19	255.30	248.67	243.06	238.27	234.17	230.64
22000	275.72	267.46	260.51	254.63	249.62	245.32	241.62
23000	288.25	279.62	272.36	266.21	260.96	256.47	252.60
24000	300.78	291.77	284.20	277.78	272.31	267.62	263.59
25000	313.32	303.93	296.04	289.35	283.66	278.77	274.57
26000	325.85	316.09	307.88	300.93	295.00	289.92	285.55
27000	338.38	328.24	319.72	312.50	306.35	301.07	296.53
28000	350.91	340.40	331.56	324.08	317.69	312.23	307.52
29000	363.45	352.56	343.40	335.65	329.04	323.38	318.50
30000	375.98	364.71	355.24	347.22	340.39	334.53	329.48
31000	388.51	376.87	367.09	358.80	351.73	345.68	340.46
32000	401.04	389.03	378.93	370.37	363.08	356.83	351.45
33000	413.58	401.18	390.77	381.95	374.43	367.98	362.43
34000	426.11	413.34	402.61	393.52	385.77	379.13	373.41
35000	438.64	425.50	414.45	405.09	397.12	390.28	384.39
40000	501.30	486.28	473.66	462.96	453.85	446.03	439.31
45000	563.97	547.07	532.86	520.83	510.58	501.79	494.22
50000	626.63	607.85	592.07	578.70	567.31	557.54	549.13
55000	689.29	668.64	651.28	636.57	624.04	613.29	604.04
60000	751.95	729.42	710.48	694.44	680.77	669.05	658.96
65000	814.62	790.21	769.69	752.31	737.50	724.80	713.87
70000	877.28	850.99	828.90	810.18	794.23	780.56	768.78
75000	939.94	911.78	888.10	868.05	850.96	836.31	823.69
80000	1002.60	972.56	947.31	925.92	907.69	892.06	878.61
100000	1253.25	1215.70	1184.14	1157.40	1134.61	1115.08	1098.26

TERM AMOUNT	20 YEARS	21 YEARS	22 YEARS	25 YEARS	30 YEARS	35 YEARS	40 YEARS
$ 25	.28	.27	.27	.26	.26	.25	.25
50	.55	.54	.54	.52	.51	.50	.50
75	.82	.81	.80	.78	.76	.75	.75
100	1.09	1.08	1.07	1.04	1.01	1.00	.99
200	2.17	2.15	2.13	2.07	2.02	2.00	1.98
300	3.26	3.22	3.19	3.11	3.03	2.99	2.97
400	4.34	4.29	4.25	4.14	4.04	3.99	3.96
500	5.42	5.36	5.31	5.18	5.05	4.98	4.95
600	6.51	6.43	6.37	6.21	6.06	5.98	5.94
700	7.59	7.50	7.43	7.25	7.07	6.98	6.92
800	8.67	8.57	8.49	8.28	8.08	7.97	7.91
900	9.76	9.64	9.55	9.32	9.09	8.97	8.90
1000	10.84	10.72	10.61	10.35	10.10	9.96	9.89
2000	21.68	21.43	21.21	20.70	20.19	19.92	19.77
3000	32.52	32.14	31.81	31.05	30.29	29.88	29.66
4000	43.35	42.85	42.41	41.40	40.38	39.84	39.54
5000	54.19	53.56	53.01	51.74	50.48	49.79	49.42
6000	65.03	64.27	63.61	62.09	60.57	59.75	59.31
7000	75.86	74.98	74.21	72.44	70.66	69.71	69.19
8000	86.70	85.69	84.81	82.79	80.76	79.67	79.07
9000	97.54	96.40	95.41	93.14	90.85	89.63	88.95
10000	108.38	107.11	106.02	103.48	100.95	99.58	98.84
11000	119.21	117.82	116.62	113.83	111.04	109.54	108.73
12000	130.05	128.54	127.22	124.18	121.13	119.50	118.61
13000	140.89	139.25	137.82	134.53	131.23	129.46	128.49
14000	151.72	149.96	148.42	144.88	141.32	139.42	138.38
15000	162.56	160.67	159.02	155.22	151.42	149.37	148.26
16000	173.40	171.38	169.62	165.57	161.51	159.33	158.15
17000	184.24	182.09	180.22	175.92	171.60	169.29	168.03
18000	195.07	192.80	190.82	186.27	181.70	179.25	177.91
19000	205.91	203.51	201.43	196.62	191.79	189.21	187.79
20000	216.75	214.22	212.03	206.96	201.89	199.16	197.68
21000	227.58	224.93	222.63	217.31	211.98	209.12	207.56
22000	238.42	235.64	233.23	227.66	222.08	219.08	217.45
23000	249.26	246.36	243.83	238.01	232.17	229.04	227.33
24000	260.09	257.07	254.43	248.36	242.26	239.00	237.21
25000	270.93	267.78	265.03	258.70	252.36	248.95	247.10
26000	281.77	278.49	275.63	269.05	262.45	258.91	256.98
27000	292.61	289.20	286.23	279.40	272.55	268.87	266.86
28000	303.44	299.91	296.83	289.75	282.64	278.83	276.75
29000	314.28	310.62	307.44	300.10	292.73	288.79	286.63
30000	325.12	321.33	318.04	310.44	302.83	298.74	296.51
31000	335.95	332.05	328.64	320.79	312.92	308.70	306.40
32000	346.79	342.75	339.24	331.14	323.02	318.66	316.28
33000	357.63	353.46	349.84	341.49	333.11	328.62	326.17
34000	368.47	364.17	360.44	351.84	343.20	338.57	336.05
35000	379.30	374.89	371.04	362.18	353.30	348.53	345.93
40000	433.49	428.44	424.05	413.92	403.77	398.32	395.35
45000	487.67	481.99	477.05	465.66	454.24	448.11	444.77
50000	541.86	535.55	530.06	517.40	504.71	497.90	494.19
55000	596.04	589.10	583.06	569.14	555.18	547.69	543.61
60000	650.23	642.66	636.07	620.88	605.65	597.48	593.02
65000	704.41	696.21	689.07	672.62	656.12	647.27	642.44
70000	758.60	749.77	742.08	724.36	706.59	697.06	691.86
75000	812.79	803.32	795.08	776.10	757.06	746.85	741.28
80000	866.97	856.88	848.09	827.84	807.53	796.64	790.70
100000	1083.71	1071.09	1060.11	1034.80	1009.41	995.80	988.37

12%

TERM AMOUNT	1 YEAR	1½ YEARS	2 YEARS	2½ YEARS	3 YEARS	4 YEARS	5 YEARS
$ 25	2.23	1.53	1.18	.97	.84	.66	.56
50	4.45	3.05	2.36	1.94	1.67	1.32	1.12
75	6.67	4.58	3.54	2.91	2.50	1.98	1.67
100	8.89	6.10	4.71	3.88	3.33	2.64	2.23
200	17.77	12.20	9.42	7.75	6.65	5.27	4.45
300	26.66	18.30	14.13	11.63	9.97	7.91	6.68
400	35.54	24.40	18.83	15.50	13.29	10.54	8.90
500	44.43	30.50	23.54	19.38	16.61	13.17	11.13
600	53.31	36.59	28.25	23.25	19.93	15.81	13.35
700	62.20	42.69	32.96	27.13	23.26	18.44	15.58
800	71.08	48.79	37.66	31.00	26.58	21.07	17.80
900	79.97	54.89	42.37	34.88	29.90	23.71	20.03
1000	88.85	60.99	47.08	38.75	33.22	26.34	22.25
2000	177.70	121.99	94.15	77.50	66.43	52.67	44.49
3000	266.55	182.95	141.23	116.25	99.65	79.01	66.74
4000	355.40	243.93	188.30	155.00	132.86	105.34	88.98
5000	444.25	304.92	235.37	193.75	166.08	131.67	111.23
6000	533.10	365.90	282.45	232.49	199.29	158.01	133.47
7000	621.95	426.88	329.52	271.24	232.51	184.34	155.72
8000	710.80	487.86	376.59	309.99	265.72	210.68	177.96
9000	799.64	548.84	423.67	348.74	298.93	237.01	200.21
10000	888.49	609.83	470.74	387.49	332.15	263.34	222.45
11000	977.34	670.81	517.81	426.23	365.36	289.68	244.69
12000	1066.19	731.79	564.89	464.98	398.58	316.01	266.94
13000	1155.04	792.77	611.96	503.73	431.79	342.34	289.18
14000	1243.89	853.75	659.03	542.48	465.01	368.68	311.43
15000	1332.74	914.74	706.11	581.23	498.22	395.01	333.67
16000	1421.59	975.72	753.18	619.97	531.43	421.35	355.92
17000	1510.43	1036.70	800.25	658.72	564.65	447.68	378.16
18000	1599.28	1097.68	847.33	697.47	597.86	474.01	400.41
19000	1688.13	1158.66	894.40	736.22	631.08	500.35	422.65
20000	1776.98	1219.65	941.47	774.96	664.29	526.68	444.89
21000	1865.83	1280.63	988.55	813.72	697.51	553.02	467.14
22000	1954.68	1341.61	1035.62	852.46	730.72	579.35	489.38
23000	2043.53	1402.59	1082.69	891.21	763.93	605.68	511.63
24000	2132.38	1463.57	1129.77	929.96	797.15	632.02	533.87
25000	2221.22	1524.56	1176.84	968.71	830.36	658.35	556.12
26000	2310.07	1585.54	1223.92	1007.46	863.58	684.68	578.36
27000	2398.92	1646.52	1270.99	1046.20	896.79	711.02	600.61
28000	2487.77	1707.50	1318.06	1084.95	930.01	737.35	622.85
29000	2576.62	1768.48	1365.14	1123.70	963.22	763.69	645.09
30000	2665.47	1829.47	1412.21	1162.45	996.43	790.02	667.34
31000	2754.32	1890.45	1459.28	1201.20	1029.65	816.35	689.58
32000	2843.17	1951.43	1506.36	1239.94	1062.86	842.69	711.83
33000	2932.02	2012.41	1553.43	1278.69	1096.08	869.02	734.07
34000	3020.86	2073.39	1600.50	1317.44	1129.29	895.36	756.32
35000	3109.71	2134.38	1647.58	1356.19	1162.51	921.69	778.56
40000	3553.96	2439.29	1882.94	1549.93	1328.58	1053.36	889.78
45000	3998.20	2744.20	2118.31	1743.67	1494.65	1185.03	1001.01
50000	4442.44	3049.11	2353.68	1937.41	1660.72	1316.70	1112.23
55000	4886.69	3354.02	2589.05	2131.15	1826.79	1448.37	1223.45
60000	5330.93	3658.93	2824.41	2324.89	1992.86	1580.04	1334.67
65000	5775.18	3963.84	3059.78	2518.63	2158.94	1711.70	1445.89
70000	6219.42	4268.75	3295.15	2712.37	2325.01	1843.37	1557.12
75000	6663.66	4573.66	3530.52	2906.11	2491.08	1975.04	1668.34
80000	7107.91	4878.57	3765.88	3099.85	2657.15	2106.71	1779.56
100000	8884.88	6098.21	4707.35	3874.82	3321.44	2633.39	2224.45

86

TERM AMOUNT	6 YEARS	7 YEARS	8 YEARS	9 YEARS	10 YEARS	11 YEARS	12 YEARS
$ 25	.49	.45	.41	.38	.36	.35	.33
50	.98	.89	.82	.76	.72	.69	.66
75	1.47	1.33	1.22	1.14	1.08	1.03	.99
100	1.96	1.77	1.63	1.52	1.44	1.37	1.32
200	3.92	3.54	3.26	3.04	2.87	2.74	2.63
300	5.87	5.30	4.88	4.56	4.31	4.11	3.95
400	7.83	7.07	6.51	6.08	5.74	5.48	5.26
500	9.78	8.83	8.13	7.60	7.18	6.84	6.57
600	11.74	10.60	9.76	9.12	8.61	8.21	7.89
700	13.69	12.36	11.38	10.63	10.05	9.58	9.20
800	15.65	14.13	13.01	12.15	11.48	10.95	10.51
900	17.60	15.89	14.63	13.67	12.92	12.32	11.83
1000	19.56	17.66	16.26	15.19	14.35	13.68	13.14
2000	39.11	35.31	32.51	30.37	28.70	27.36	26.27
3000	58.66	52.96	48.76	45.56	43.05	41.04	39.41
4000	78.21	70.62	65.02	60.74	57.39	54.72	52.54
5000	97.76	88.27	81.27	75.93	71.74	68.39	65.68
6000	117.31	105.92	97.52	91.11	86.09	82.07	78.81
7000	136.86	123.57	113.77	106.29	100.43	95.75	91.94
8000	156.41	141.23	130.03	121.48	114.78	109.43	105.08
9000	175.96	158.88	146.28	136.66	129.13	123.11	118.21
10000	195.51	176.53	162.53	151.85	143.48	136.78	131.35
11000	215.06	194.19	178.79	167.03	157.82	150.46	144.48
12000	234.61	211.84	195.04	182.22	172.17	164.14	157.62
13000	254.16	229.49	211.29	197.40	186.52	177.82	170.75
14000	273.71	247.14	227.54	212.58	200.86	191.50	183.88
15000	293.26	264.80	243.80	227.77	215.21	205.17	197.02
16000	312.81	282.45	260.05	242.95	229.56	218.85	210.15
17000	332.36	300.10	276.30	258.14	243.91	232.53	223.29
18000	351.91	317.75	292.56	273.32	258.25	246.21	236.42
19000	371.46	335.41	308.81	288.51	272.60	259.88	249.55
20000	391.01	353.06	325.06	303.69	286.95	273.56	262.69
21000	410.56	370.71	341.31	318.87	301.29	287.24	275.82
22000	430.11	388.37	357.57	334.06	315.64	300.92	288.96
23000	449.66	406.02	373.82	349.24	329.99	314.60	302.09
24000	469.21	423.67	390.07	364.43	344.34	328.27	315.23
25000	488.76	441.32	406.33	379.61	358.68	341.95	328.36
26000	508.31	458.98	422.58	394.80	373.03	355.63	341.49
27000	527.86	476.63	438.83	409.98	387.38	369.31	354.63
28000	547.41	494.28	455.08	425.16	401.72	382.99	367.76
29000	566.96	511.93	471.34	440.35	416.07	396.66	380.90
30000	586.51	529.59	487.59	455.53	430.42	410.34	394.03
31000	606.06	547.24	503.84	470.72	444.77	424.02	407.16
32000	625.61	564.89	520.10	485.90	459.11	437.70	420.30
33000	645.16	582.55	536.35	501.08	473.46	451.37	433.43
34000	664.71	600.20	552.60	516.27	487.81	465.05	446.57
35000	684.26	617.85	568.85	531.45	502.15	478.73	459.70
40000	782.01	706.11	650.12	607.37	573.89	547.12	525.37
45000	879.76	794.38	731.38	683.30	645.62	615.51	591.04
50000	977.51	882.64	812.65	759.22	717.36	683.90	656.71
55000	1075.27	970.91	893.91	835.14	789.10	752.29	722.39
60000	1173.02	1059.17	975.18	911.06	860.83	820.68	788.06
65000	1270.77	1147.43	1056.44	986.98	932.57	889.07	853.73
70000	1368.52	1235.70	1137.70	1062.90	1004.30	957.46	919.40
75000	1466.27	1323.96	1218.97	1138.82	1076.04	1025.85	985.07
80000	1564.02	1412.22	1300.23	1214.74	1147.77	1094.24	1050.74
100000	1955.02	1765.28	1625.29	1518.43	1434.71	1367.79	1313.42

12%

MONTHLY PAYMENT
NECESSARY TO AMORTIZE A LOAN

TERM AMOUNT	13 YEARS	14 YEARS	15 YEARS	16 YEARS	17 YEARS	18 YEARS	19 YEARS
$ 25	.32	.31	.31	.30	.29	.29	.28
50	.64	.62	.61	.59	.58	.57	.56
75	.96	.93	.91	.89	.87	.85	.84
100	1.27	1.24	1.21	1.18	1.16	1.14	1.12
200	2.54	2.47	2.41	2.35	2.31	2.27	2.24
300	3.81	3.70	3.61	3.53	3.46	3.40	3.35
400	5.08	4.93	4.81	4.70	4.61	4.53	4.47
500	6.35	6.16	6.01	5.87	5.76	5.66	5.58
600	7.62	7.39	7.21	7.05	6.91	6.80	6.70
700	8.89	8.63	8.41	8.22	8.06	7.93	7.81
800	10.15	9.86	9.61	9.39	9.21	9.06	8.93
900	11.42	11.09	10.81	10.57	10.37	10.19	10.04
1000	12.69	12.32	12.01	11.74	11.52	11.32	11.16
2000	25.38	24.63	24.01	23.48	23.03	22.64	22.31
3000	38.06	36.95	36.01	35.22	34.54	33.96	33.47
4000	50.75	49.26	48.01	46.95	46.05	45.28	44.62
5000	63.44	61.58	60.01	58.69	57.57	56.60	55.77
6000	76.12	73.89	72.02	70.43	69.08	67.92	66.93
7000	88.81	86.21	84.02	82.17	80.59	79.24	78.08
8000	101.50	98.52	96.02	93.90	92.10	90.56	89.24
9000	114.18	110.83	108.02	105.64	103.61	101.88	100.39
10000	126.87	123.15	120.02	117.38	115.13	113.20	111.54
11000	139.56	135.46	132.02	129.11	126.64	124.52	122.70
12000	152.24	147.78	144.03	140.85	138.15	135.84	133.85
13000	164.93	160.09	156.03	152.59	149.66	147.16	145.01
14000	177.62	172.41	168.03	164.33	161.18	158.48	156.16
15000	190.30	184.72	180.03	176.06	172.69	169.80	167.31
16000	202.99	197.03	192.03	187.80	184.20	181.12	178.47
17000	215.68	209.35	204.03	199.54	195.71	192.44	189.62
18000	228.36	221.66	216.04	211.28	207.22	203.76	200.77
19000	241.05	233.98	228.04	223.01	218.74	215.06	211.93
20000	253.74	246.29	240.04	234.75	230.25	226.40	223.08
21000	266.42	258.61	252.04	246.49	241.76	237.71	234.24
22000	279.11	270.92	264.04	258.22	253.27	249.03	245.39
23000	291.80	283.23	276.04	269.96	264.78	260.35	256.54
24000	304.48	295.55	288.05	281.70	276.30	271.67	267.70
25000	317.17	307.86	300.05	293.44	287.81	282.99	278.85
26000	329.86	320.18	312.05	305.17	299.32	294.31	290.01
27000	342.54	332.49	324.05	316.91	310.83	305.63	301.16
28000	355.23	344.81	336.05	328.65	322.35	316.95	312.31
29000	367.92	357.12	348.05	340.39	333.86	328.27	323.47
30000	380.60	369.43	360.06	352.12	345.37	339.59	334.62
31000	393.29	381.75	372.06	363.86	356.88	350.91	345.77
32000	405.98	394.06	384.06	375.60	368.39	362.23	356.93
33000	418.66	406.38	396.06	387.33	379.91	373.55	368.08
34000	431.35	418.69	408.06	399.07	391.42	384.87	379.24
35000	444.04	431.01	420.06	410.81	402.93	396.19	390.39
40000	507.47	492.58	480.07	469.50	460.49	452.79	446.16
45000	570.90	554.15	540.08	528.18	518.05	509.38	501.93
50000	634.34	615.72	600.09	586.87	575.61	565.98	557.70
55000	697.77	677.29	660.10	645.55	633.17	622.58	613.47
60000	761.20	738.86	720.11	704.24	690.73	679.12	669.24
65000	824.64	800.43	780.11	762.93	748.30	735.77	725.01
70000	888.07	862.01	840.12	821.61	805.86	792.37	780.78
75000	951.50	923.58	900.13	880.30	863.42	848.97	836.54
80000	1014.94	985.15	960.14	938.99	920.98	905.57	892.31
100000	1268.67	1231.43	1200.18	1173.73	1151.22	1131.96	1115.39

TERM AMOUNT	20 YEARS	21 YEARS	22 YEARS	25 YEARS	30 YEARS	35 YEARS	40 YEARS
$ 25	.28	.28	.27	.27	.26	.26	.26
50	.56	.55	.54	.53	.52	.51	.51
75	.83	.82	.81	.79	.78	.77	.76
100	1.11	1.09	1.08	1.06	1.03	1.02	1.01
200	2.21	2.18	2.16	2.11	2.06	2.04	2.02
300	3.31	3.27	3.24	3.16	3.09	3.05	3.03
400	4.41	4.36	4.32	4.22	4.12	4.07	4.04
500	5.51	5.45	5.39	5.27	5.15	5.08	5.05
600	6.61	6.54	6.47	6.32	6.18	6.10	6.06
700	7.71	7.63	7.55	7.38	7.21	7.11	7.06
800	8.81	8.71	8.63	8.43	8.23	8.13	8.07
900	9.91	9.80	9.71	9.48	9.26	9.14	9.08
1000	11.02	10.89	10.78	10.54	10.29	10.16	10.09
2000	22.03	21.78	21.56	21.07	20.58	20.32	20.17
3000	33.04	32.67	32.34	31.60	30.86	30.47	30.26
4000	44.05	43.55	43.12	42.13	41.15	40.63	40.34
5000	55.06	54.44	53.90	52.67	51.44	50.78	50.43
6000	66.07	65.33	64.68	63.20	61.72	60.94	60.51
7000	77.08	76.21	75.46	73.73	72.01	71.09	70.60
8000	88.09	87.10	86.24	84.26	82.29	81.25	80.68
9000	99.10	97.99	97.02	94.80	92.58	91.40	90.77
10000	110.11	108.87	107.80	105.33	102.87	101.56	100.85
11000	121.12	119.76	118.58	115.86	113.15	111.72	110.94
12000	132.14	130.65	129.36	126.39	123.44	121.87	121.02
13000	143.15	141.54	140.14	136.92	133.72	132.03	131.11
14000	154.16	152.42	150.92	147.46	144.01	142.18	141.19
15000	165.17	163.31	161.70	157.99	154.30	152.34	151.28
16000	176.18	174.20	172.48	168.52	164.58	162.49	161.36
17000	187.19	185.08	183.25	179.05	174.87	172.65	171.45
18000	198.20	195.97	194.03	189.59	185.16	182.80	181.53
19000	209.21	206.86	204.81	200.12	195.44	192.96	191.62
20000	220.22	217.74	215.59	210.65	205.73	203.11	201.70
21000	231.23	228.63	226.37	221.18	216.01	213.27	211.79
22000	242.24	239.52	237.15	231.71	226.30	223.43	221.87
23000	253.25	250.41	247.93	242.25	236.59	233.58	231.96
24000	264.27	261.29	258.71	252.78	246.87	243.74	242.04
25000	275.28	272.18	269.49	263.31	257.16	253.89	252.13
26000	286.29	283.07	280.27	273.84	267.45	264.05	262.21
27000	297.30	293.95	291.05	284.38	277.73	274.20	272.30
28000	308.31	304.84	301.83	294.91	288.02	284.36	282.38
29000	319.32	315.73	312.61	305.44	298.30	294.51	292.47
30000	330.33	326.61	323.39	315.97	308.59	304.67	302.55
31000	341.34	337.50	334.17	326.50	318.87	314.83	312.64
32000	352.35	348.39	344.95	337.04	329.16	324.98	322.72
33000	363.36	359.28	355.72	347.57	339.45	335.14	332.81
34000	374.37	370.16	366.50	358.10	349.73	345.29	342.89
35000	385.39	381.05	377.28	368.63	360.02	355.45	352.98
40000	440.44	435.48	431.18	421.29	411.45	406.22	403.40
45000	495.49	489.92	485.08	473.96	462.88	457.00	453.83
50000	550.55	544.35	538.97	526.62	514.31	507.78	504.25
55000	605.60	598.79	592.87	579.28	565.74	558.56	554.68
60000	660.66	653.22	646.77	631.94	617.17	609.33	605.10
65000	715.71	707.66	700.66	684.60	668.60	660.11	655.53
70000	770.77	762.09	754.56	737.26	720.03	710.89	705.95
75000	825.82	816.53	808.46	789.92	771.46	761.67	756.38
80000	880.87	870.96	862.36	842.58	822.90	812.44	806.80
100000	1101.09	1088.70	1077.94	1053.23	1028.62	1015.55	1008.50

12¼%

MONTHLY PAYMENT
NECESSARY TO AMORTIZE A LOAN

TERM AMOUNT	1 YEAR	1½ YEARS	2 YEARS	2½ YEARS	3 YEARS	4 YEARS	5 YEARS
$ 25	2.23	1.53	1.18	.98	.84	.67	.56
50	4.45	3.06	2.36	1.95	1.67	1.33	1.12
75	6.68	4.59	3.54	2.92	2.51	1.99	1.68
100	8.90	6.11	4.72	3.89	3.34	2.65	2.24
200	17.80	12.22	9.44	7.78	6.67	5.30	4.48
300	26.69	18.33	14.16	11.66	10.01	7.94	6.72
400	35.59	24.44	18.88	15.55	13.34	10.59	8.95
500	44.49	30.55	23.60	19.44	16.67	13.23	11.19
600	53.38	36.66	28.32	23.32	20.01	15.88	13.43
700	62.28	42.77	33.04	27.21	23.34	18.52	15.66
800	71.18	48.88	37.76	31.10	26.67	21.17	17.90
900	80.07	54.99	42.48	34.98	30.01	23.82	20.14
1000	88.97	61.10	47.20	38.87	33.34	26.46	22.38
2000	177.94	122.20	94.39	77.74	66.67	52.92	44.75
3000	266.90	183.30	141.58	116.60	100.01	79.38	67.12
4000	355.87	244.40	188.77	155.47	133.34	105.83	89.49
5000	444.83	305.50	235.96	194.34	166.67	132.29	111.86
6000	533.80	366.59	283.15	233.20	200.01	158.75	134.23
7000	622.77	427.69	330.34	272.07	233.34	185.20	156.60
8000	711.73	488.79	377.53	310.93	266.68	211.66	178.97
9000	800.70	549.89	424.72	349.80	300.01	238.12	201.34
10000	889.66	610.99	471.91	388.67	333.34	264.57	223.71
11000	978.63	672.09	519.10	427.53	366.68	291.03	246.09
12000	1067.59	733.18	566.29	466.40	400.01	317.49	268.46
13000	1156.56	794.28	613.48	505.27	433.34	343.94	290.83
14000	1245.53	855.38	660.67	544.13	466.68	370.40	313.20
15000	1334.49	916.48	707.86	583.00	500.01	396.86	335.57
16000	1423.46	977.58	755.05	621.86	533.34	423.31	357.94
17000	1512.42	1038.68	802.24	660.73	566.68	449.77	380.31
18000	1601.39	1099.77	849.43	699.60	600.01	476.23	402.68
19000	1690.35	1160.87	896.62	738.46	633.35	502.68	425.05
20000	1779.32	1221.97	943.81	777.33	666.68	529.14	447.42
21000	1868.29	1283.07	991.00	816.19	700.02	555.60	469.80
22000	1957.25	1344.17	1038.19	855.06	733.35	582.05	492.17
23000	2046.22	1405.26	1085.38	893.93	766.68	608.51	514.54
24000	2135.18	1466.36	1132.57	932.79	800.02	634.97	536.91
25000	2224.15	1527.46	1179.76	971.66	833.35	661.42	559.28
26000	2313.12	1588.56	1226.95	1010.53	866.68	687.88	581.65
27000	2402.08	1649.66	1274.14	1049.39	900.02	714.34	604.02
28000	2491.05	1710.76	1321.33	1088.26	933.35	740.79	626.39
29000	2580.01	1771.85	1368.52	1127.12	966.69	767.25	648.76
30000	2668.98	1832.95	1415.71	1165.99	1000.02	793.71	671.13
31000	2757.94	1894.05	1462.90	1204.86	1033.35	820.16	693.51
32000	2846.91	1955.15	1510.09	1243.72	1066.69	846.62	715.88
33000	2935.88	2016.25	1557.29	1282.59	1100.02	873.08	738.25
34000	3024.84	2077.35	1604.48	1321.45	1133.36	899.53	760.62
35000	3113.81	2138.44	1651.68	1360.32	1166.69	925.99	782.99
40000	3558.64	2443.93	1887.62	1554.65	1333.36	1058.28	894.84
45000	4003.47	2749.43	2123.57	1748.98	1500.03	1190.56	1006.70
50000	4448.30	3054.92	2359.52	1943.31	1666.70	1322.84	1118.55
55000	4893.12	3360.41	2595.47	2137.64	1833.37	1455.13	1230.41
60000	5337.95	3665.90	2831.42	2331.97	2000.04	1587.41	1342.26
65000	5782.78	3971.39	3067.37	2526.31	2166.70	1719.69	1454.12
70000	6227.61	4276.88	3303.33	2720.64	2333.37	1851.98	1565.97
75000	6672.44	4582.37	3539.28	2914.97	2500.04	1984.26	1677.83
80000	7117.27	4887.86	3775.23	3109.30	2666.71	2116.55	1789.68
100000	8896.58	6109.83	4719.04	3886.63	3333.38	2645.68	2237.10

90

TERM AMOUNT	6 YEARS	7 YEARS	8 YEARS	9 YEARS	10 YEARS	11 YEARS	12 YEARS
$ 25	.50	.45	.41	.39	.37	.35	.34
50	.99	.89	.82	.77	.73	.70	.67
75	1.48	1.34	1.23	1.15	1.09	1.04	1.00
100	1.97	1.78	1.64	1.54	1.45	1.39	1.33
200	3.94	3.56	3.28	3.07	2.90	2.77	2.66
300	5.91	5.34	4.92	4.60	4.35	4.15	3.99
400	7.88	7.12	6.56	6.14	5.80	5.54	5.32
500	9.85	8.90	8.20	7.67	7.25	6.92	6.65
600	11.81	10.68	9.84	9.20	8.70	8.30	7.98
700	13.78	12.46	11.48	10.73	10.15	9.68	9.31
800	15.75	14.23	13.12	12.27	11.60	11.07	10.63
900	17.72	16.01	14.76	13.80	13.05	12.45	11.96
1000	19.69	17.79	16.40	15.33	14.50	13.83	13.29
2000	39.37	35.58	32.79	30.66	28.99	27.66	26.58
3000	59.05	53.37	49.18	45.98	43.48	41.48	39.86
4000	78.73	71.15	65.57	61.31	57.97	55.31	53.15
5000	98.41	88.94	81.96	76.63	72.46	69.14	66.43
6000	118.09	106.73	98.35	91.96	86.96	82.96	79.72
7000	137.77	124.51	114.74	107.28	101.45	96.79	93.01
8000	157.45	142.30	131.13	122.61	115.94	110.62	106.29
9000	177.13	160.09	147.52	137.93	130.43	124.44	119.58
10000	196.81	177.87	163.91	153.26	144.92	138.27	132.86
11000	216.49	195.66	180.30	168.59	159.42	152.09	146.15
12000	236.17	213.45	196.69	183.91	173.91	165.92	159.44
13000	255.85	231.23	213.08	199.24	188.40	179.75	172.72
14000	275.53	249.02	229.47	214.56	202.89	193.57	186.01
15000	295.21	266.81	245.86	229.89	217.38	207.40	199.29
16000	314.89	284.59	262.25	245.21	231.88	221.23	212.58
17000	334.57	302.38	278.64	260.54	246.37	235.05	225.87
18000	354.25	320.17	295.03	275.86	260.86	248.88	239.15
19000	373.93	337.95	311.42	291.19	275.35	262.70	252.44
20000	393.61	355.74	327.83	306.52	289.84	276.53	265.72
21000	413.29	373.53	344.21	321.84	304.34	290.36	279.01
22000	432.97	391.31	360.60	337.17	318.83	304.18	292.30
23000	452.66	409.10	376.99	352.49	333.32	318.01	305.58
24000	472.34	426.89	393.38	367.82	347.81	331.84	318.87
25000	492.02	444.67	409.77	383.14	362.30	345.66	332.15
26000	511.70	462.46	426.16	398.47	376.80	359.49	345.44
27000	531.38	480.25	442.55	413.79	391.29	373.31	358.73
28000	551.06	498.03	458.94	429.12	405.78	387.14	372.01
29000	570.74	515.82	475.33	444.45	420.27	400.97	385.30
30000	590.42	533.61	491.72	459.77	434.76	414.79	398.58
31000	610.10	551.39	508.11	475.10	449.26	428.62	411.87
32000	629.78	569.18	524.50	490.42	463.75	442.45	425.16
33000	649.46	586.97	540.89	505.75	478.24	456.27	438.44
34000	669.14	604.75	557.28	521.07	492.73	470.10	451.73
35000	688.82	622.54	573.67	536.40	507.22	483.92	465.01
40000	787.22	711.47	655.63	613.03	579.68	553.06	531.44
45000	885.62	800.41	737.58	689.65	652.14	622.19	597.87
50000	984.03	889.34	819.53	766.28	724.60	691.32	664.30
55000	1082.43	978.27	901.48	842.91	797.06	760.45	730.73
60000	1180.83	1067.21	983.44	919.54	869.52	829.58	797.16
65000	1279.23	1156.14	1065.39	996.17	941.98	898.71	863.59
70000	1377.64	1245.07	1147.34	1072.79	1014.44	967.84	930.02
75000	1476.04	1334.01	1229.29	1149.42	1086.90	1036.97	996.45
80000	1574.44	1422.94	1311.25	1226.05	1159.36	1106.11	1062.88
100000	1968.05	1778.68	1639.06	1532.56	1449.20	1382.63	1328.60

12¼%

TERM AMOUNT	13 YEARS	14 YEARS	15 YEARS	16 YEARS	17 YEARS	18 YEARS	19 YEARS
$ 25	.33	.32	.31	.30	.30	.29	.29
50	.65	.63	.61	.60	.59	.58	.57
75	.97	.94	.92	.90	.88	.87	.85
100	1.29	1.25	1.22	1.20	1.17	1.15	1.14
200	2.57	2.50	2.44	2.39	2.34	2.30	2.27
300	3.86	3.75	3.65	3.58	3.51	3.45	3.40
400	5.14	4.99	4.87	4.77	4.68	4.60	4.54
500	6.43	6.24	6.09	5.96	5.84	5.75	5.67
600	7.71	7.49	7.30	7.15	7.01	6.90	6.80
700	8.99	8.74	8.52	8.34	8.18	8.05	7.93
800	10.28	9.98	9.74	9.53	9.35	9.20	9.07
900	11.56	11.23	10.95	10.72	10.52	10.35	10.20
1000	12.85	12.48	12.17	11.91	11.68	11.49	11.33
2000	25.69	24.95	24.33	23.81	23.36	22.98	22.66
3000	38.53	37.42	36.49	35.71	35.04	34.47	33.98
4000	51.37	49.90	48.66	47.61	46.72	45.96	45.31
5000	64.21	62.37	60.82	59.51	58.40	57.45	56.64
6000	77.06	74.84	72.98	71.41	70.08	68.94	67.96
7000	89.90	87.31	85.15	83.32	81.76	80.43	79.29
8000	102.74	99.79	97.31	95.22	93.44	91.92	90.61
9000	115.58	112.26	109.47	107.12	105.12	103.41	101.94
10000	128.42	124.73	121.63	119.02	116.80	114.90	113.27
11000	141.26	137.20	133.80	130.92	128.48	126.39	124.59
12000	154.11	149.68	145.96	142.82	140.16	137.88	135.92
13000	166.95	162.15	158.12	154.72	151.83	149.37	147.25
14000	179.79	174.62	170.29	166.63	163.51	160.85	158.57
15000	192.63	187.10	182.45	178.53	175.19	172.34	169.90
16000	205.47	199.57	194.61	190.43	186.87	183.83	181.22
17000	218.31	212.04	206.78	202.33	198.55	195.32	192.55
18000	231.16	224.51	218.94	214.23	210.23	206.81	203.88
19000	244.00	236.98	231.10	226.13	221.91	218.30	215.20
20000	256.84	249.46	243.26	238.04	233.59	229.79	226.53
21000	269.68	261.93	255.43	249.94	245.27	241.28	237.86
22000	282.52	274.40	267.59	261.84	256.95	252.77	249.18
23000	295.36	286.87	279.75	273.74	268.63	264.26	260.51
24000	308.21	299.35	291.92	285.64	280.31	275.75	271.83
25000	321.05	311.82	304.08	297.54	291.99	287.24	283.16
26000	333.89	324.29	316.24	309.44	303.66	298.73	294.49
27000	346.73	336.76	328.41	321.35	315.34	310.22	305.81
28000	359.57	349.24	340.57	333.25	327.02	321.70	317.14
29000	372.42	361.71	352.73	345.15	338.70	333.19	328.46
30000	385.26	374.18	364.89	357.05	350.38	344.68	339.79
31000	398.10	386.65	377.06	368.95	362.06	356.17	351.12
32000	410.94	399.13	389.22	380.85	373.74	367.66	362.44
33000	423.78	411.60	401.38	392.75	385.42	379.15	373.77
34000	436.62	424.07	413.55	404.66	397.10	390.64	385.10
35000	449.47	436.54	425.71	416.56	408.78	402.13	396.42
40000	513.67	498.91	486.52	476.07	467.17	459.58	453.05
45000	577.88	561.27	547.34	535.57	525.57	517.02	509.68
50000	642.09	623.63	608.15	595.08	583.97	574.47	566.31
55000	706.30	685.99	668.97	654.59	642.36	631.91	622.95
60000	770.51	748.36	729.78	714.10	700.76	689.36	679.58
65000	834.72	810.72	790.60	773.60	759.15	746.81	736.21
70000	898.93	873.08	851.41	833.11	817.55	804.25	792.84
75000	963.13	935.45	912.23	892.62	875.95	861.70	849.47
80000	1027.34	997.81	973.04	952.13	934.34	919.15	906.10
100000	1284.18	1247.26	1216.30	1190.16	1167.93	1148.93	1132.62

TERM AMOUNT	20 YEARS	21 YEARS	22 YEARS	25 YEARS	30 YEARS	35 YEARS	40 YEARS
$ 25	.28	.28	.28	.27	.27	.26	.26
50	.56	.56	.55	.54	.53	.52	.52
75	.84	.83	.83	.81	.79	.78	.78
100	1.12	1.11	1.10	1.08	1.05	1.04	1.03
200	2.24	2.22	2.20	2.15	2.10	2.08	2.06
300	3.36	3.32	3.29	3.22	3.15	3.11	3.09
400	4.48	4.43	4.39	4.29	4.20	4.15	4.12
500	5.60	5.54	5.48	5.36	5.24	5.18	5.15
600	6.72	6.64	6.58	6.44	6.29	6.22	6.18
700	7.83	7.75	7.68	7.51	7.34	7.25	7.21
800	8.95	8.86	8.77	8.58	8.39	8.29	8.23
900	10.07	9.96	9.87	9.65	9.44	9.32	9.26
1000	11.19	11.07	10.96	10.72	10.48	10.36	10.29
2000	22.38	22.13	21.92	21.44	20.96	20.71	20.58
3000	33.56	33.20	32.88	32.16	31.44	31.07	30.87
4000	44.75	44.26	43.84	42.87	41.92	41.42	41.15
5000	55.93	55.33	54.80	53.59	52.40	51.77	51.44
6000	67.12	66.39	65.76	64.31	62.88	62.13	61.73
7000	78.30	77.45	76.72	75.03	73.36	72.48	72.01
8000	89.49	88.52	87.67	85.74	84.32	82.83	82.30
9000	100.68	99.58	98.63	96.46	94.32	93.19	92.59
10000	111.86	110.65	109.59	107.18	104.79	103.54	102.87
11000	123.05	121.71	120.55	117.90	115.27	113.90	113.16
12000	134.23	132.77	131.51	128.61	125.75	124.25	123.45
13000	145.42	143.84	142.47	139.33	136.23	134.60	133.73
14000	156.60	154.90	153.43	150.05	146.71	144.96	144.02
15000	167.79	165.97	164.39	160.77	157.19	155.31	154.31
16000	178.98	177.03	175.34	171.48	167.67	165.66	164.59
17000	190.16	188.09	186.30	182.20	178.15	176.02	174.88
18000	201.35	199.16	197.26	192.92	188.63	186.37	185.17
19000	212.53	210.22	208.22	203.64	199.11	196.73	195.46
20000	223.72	221.29	219.18	214.35	209.58	207.08	205.74
21000	234.90	232.35	230.14	225.07	220.06	217.43	216.03
22000	246.09	243.42	241.10	235.79	230.54	227.79	226.32
23000	257.27	254.48	252.05	246.51	241.02	238.14	236.60
24000	268.46	265.54	263.01	257.22	251.50	248.49	246.89
25000	279.65	276.61	273.97	267.94	261.98	258.85	257.18
26000	290.83	287.67	284.93	278.66	272.46	269.20	267.46
27000	302.02	298.74	295.89	289.38	282.94	279.56	277.75
28000	313.20	309.80	306.85	300.09	293.42	289.91	288.04
29000	324.39	320.86	317.81	310.81	303.89	300.26	298.32
30000	335.57	331.93	328.77	321.53	314.37	310.62	308.61
31000	346.76	342.99	339.72	332.25	324.85	320.97	318.90
32000	357.95	354.06	350.68	342.96	335.33	331.32	329.18
33000	369.13	365.12	361.64	353.68	345.81	341.68	339.47
34000	380.32	376.18	372.60	364.40	356.29	352.03	349.76
35000	391.50	387.25	383.56	375.12	366.77	362.38	360.05
40000	447.43	442.57	438.35	428.70	419.16	414.15	411.48
45000	503.36	497.89	493.15	482.29	471.56	465.92	462.91
50000	559.29	553.21	547.94	535.88	523.95	517.69	514.35
55000	615.22	608.53	602.73	589.46	576.35	569.46	565.78
60000	671.14	663.85	657.53	643.05	628.74	621.23	617.22
65000	727.07	719.17	712.32	696.64	681.14	673.00	668.65
70000	783.00	774.49	767.11	750.23	733.53	724.76	720.09
75000	838.93	829.81	821.91	803.81	785.93	776.53	771.52
80000	894.86	885.13	876.70	857.40	838.32	828.30	822.95
100000	1118.57	1106.42	1095.87	1071.75	1047.90	1035.38	1028.69

MONTHLY PAYMENT
NECESSARY TO AMORTIZE A LOAN

TERM AMOUNT	1 YEAR	1½ YEARS	2 YEARS	2½ YEARS	3 YEARS	4 YEARS	5 YEARS
$ 25	2.23	1.54	1.19	.98	.84	.67	.57
50	4.46	3.07	2.37	1.95	1.68	1.33	1.13
75	6.69	4.60	3.55	2.93	2.51	2.00	1.69
100	8.91	6.13	4.74	3.90	3.35	2.66	2.25
200	17.82	12.25	9.47	7.80	6.70	5.32	4.50
300	26.73	18.37	14.20	11.70	10.04	7.98	6.75
400	35.64	24.49	18.93	15.60	13.39	10.64	9.00
500	44.55	30.61	23.66	19.50	16.73	13.29	11.25
600	53.45	36.73	28.39	23.40	20.08	15.95	13.50
700	62.36	42.86	33.12	27.29	23.42	18.61	15.75
800	71.27	48.98	37.85	31.19	26.77	21.27	18.00
900	80.18	55.10	42.58	35.09	30.11	23.93	20.25
1000	89.09	61.22	47.31	38.99	33.46	26.58	22.50
2000	178.17	122.43	94.62	77.97	66.91	53.16	45.00
3000	267.25	183.65	141.93	116.96	100.37	79.74	67.50
4000	356.34	244.86	189.23	155.94	133.82	106.32	90.00
5000	445.42	306.08	236.54	194.93	167.27	132.90	112.49
6000	534.50	367.29	283.85	233.91	200.73	159.48	134.99
7000	623.59	428.51	331.16	272.90	234.18	186.06	157.49
8000	712.67	489.72	378.46	311.88	267.63	212.64	179.99
9000	801.75	550.94	425.77	350.86	301.09	239.22	202.49
10000	890.83	612.15	473.08	389.85	334.54	265.80	224.98
11000	979.92	673.37	520.39	428.83	367.99	292.38	247.48
12000	1069.00	734.58	567.69	467.82	401.45	318.96	269.98
13000	1158.08	795.79	615.00	506.80	434.90	345.54	292.48
14000	1247.17	857.01	662.31	545.79	468.36	372.12	314.98
15000	1336.25	918.22	709.61	584.77	501.81	398.70	337.47
16000	1425.33	979.44	756.92	623.76	535.26	425.28	359.97
17000	1514.41	1040.65	804.23	662.74	568.72	451.86	382.47
18000	1603.50	1101.87	851.54	701.72	602.17	478.44	404.97
19000	1692.58	1163.08	898.84	740.71	635.62	505.02	427.47
20000	1781.66	1224.30	946.15	779.69	669.08	531.60	449.96
21000	1870.75	1285.51	993.46	818.68	702.53	558.18	472.46
22000	1959.83	1346.73	1040.77	857.66	735.98	584.76	494.96
23000	2048.91	1407.94	1088.07	896.65	769.44	611.34	517.46
24000	2137.99	1469.15	1135.38	935.63	802.89	637.92	539.96
25000	2227.08	1530.37	1182.69	974.62	836.35	664.50	562.45
26000	2316.16	1591.58	1230.00	1013.60	869.80	691.08	584.95
27000	2405.24	1652.80	1277.30	1052.58	903.25	717.66	607.45
28000	2494.33	1714.01	1324.61	1091.57	936.71	744.24	629.95
29000	2583.41	1775.23	1371.92	1130.55	970.16	770.82	652.45
30000	2672.49	1836.44	1419.22	1169.54	1003.61	797.40	674.94
31000	2761.57	1897.66	1466.53	1208.52	1037.07	823.98	697.44
32000	2850.66	1958.87	1513.84	1247.51	1070.52	850.56	719.94
33000	2939.74	2020.09	1561.15	1286.49	1103.97	877.14	742.44
34000	3028.82	2081.30	1608.45	1325.47	1137.43	903.72	764.93
35000	3117.91	2142.51	1655.76	1364.46	1170.88	930.30	787.43
40000	3563.32	2448.59	1892.30	1559.38	1338.15	1063.20	899.92
45000	4008.73	2754.66	2128.83	1754.30	1505.42	1196.10	1012.41
50000	4454.15	3060.73	2365.37	1949.23	1672.69	1329.00	1124.90
55000	4899.56	3366.81	2601.91	2144.15	1839.95	1461.90	1237.39
60000	5344.98	3672.88	2838.44	2339.07	2007.22	1594.80	1349.88
65000	5790.39	3978.95	3074.98	2533.99	2174.49	1727.70	1462.37
70000	6235.81	4285.02	3311.52	2728.91	2341.76	1860.60	1574.86
75000	6681.22	4591.10	3548.05	2923.84	2509.03	1993.50	1687.35
80000	7126.63	4897.17	3784.59	3118.76	2676.30	2126.40	1799.84
100000	8908.29	6121.46	4730.74	3898.45	3345.37	2658.00	2249.80

TERM AMOUNT	6 YEARS	7 YEARS	8 YEARS	9 YEARS	10 YEARS	11 YEARS	12 YEARS
$ 25	.50	.45	.42	.39	.37	.35	.34
50	1.00	.90	.83	.78	.74	.70	.68
75	1.49	1.35	1.24	1.17	1.10	1.05	1.01
100	1.99	1.80	1.66	1.55	1.47	1.40	1.35
200	3.97	3.59	3.31	3.10	2.93	2.80	2.69
300	5.95	5.38	4.96	4.65	4.40	4.20	4.04
400	7.93	7.17	6.62	6.19	5.86	5.60	5.38
500	9.91	8.97	8.27	7.74	7.32	6.99	6.72
600	11.89	10.76	9.92	9.29	8.79	8.39	8.07
700	13.87	12.55	11.58	10.83	10.25	9.79	9.41
800	15.85	14.34	13.23	12.38	11.72	11.19	10.76
900	17.84	16.13	14.88	13.93	13.18	12.58	12.10
1000	19.82	17.93	16.53	15.47	14.64	13.98	13.44
2000	39.63	35.85	33.06	30.94	29.28	27.96	26.88
3000	59.44	53.77	49.59	46.41	43.92	41.93	40.32
4000	79.25	71.69	66.12	61.88	58.56	55.91	53.76
5000	99.06	89.61	82.65	77.34	73.19	69.88	67.20
6000	118.87	107.53	99.18	92.81	87.83	83.86	80.64
7000	138.68	125.45	115.71	108.28	102.47	97.83	94.08
8000	158.49	143.37	132.24	123.75	117.11	111.81	107.51
9000	178.31	161.30	148.76	139.21	131.74	125.78	120.95
10000	198.12	179.22	165.29	154.68	146.38	139.76	134.39
11000	217.93	197.14	181.82	170.15	161.02	153.73	147.83
12000	237.74	215.06	198.35	185.62	175.66	167.71	161.27
13000	257.55	232.98	214.88	201.08	190.29	181.69	174.71
14000	277.36	250.90	231.41	216.55	204.93	195.66	188.15
15000	297.17	268.82	247.94	232.02	219.57	209.64	201.58
16000	316.98	286.74	264.47	247.49	234.21	223.61	215.02
17000	336.80	304.67	280.99	262.95	248.84	237.59	228.46
18000	356.61	322.59	297.52	278.42	263.48	251.56	241.90
19000	376.42	340.51	314.05	293.89	278.12	265.54	255.34
20000	396.23	358.43	330.58	309.36	292.76	279.51	268.78
21000	416.04	376.35	347.11	324.82	307.39	293.49	282.22
22000	435.85	394.27	363.64	340.29	322.03	307.46	295.65
23000	455.66	412.19	380.17	355.76	336.67	321.44	309.09
24000	475.47	430.11	396.70	371.23	351.31	335.42	322.53
25000	495.28	448.04	413.23	386.69	365.95	349.39	335.97
26000	515.10	465.96	429.75	402.16	380.58	363.37	349.41
27000	534.91	483.88	446.28	417.63	395.22	377.34	362.85
28000	554.72	501.80	462.81	433.10	409.86	391.32	376.29
29000	574.53	519.72	479.34	448.56	424.50	405.29	389.72
30000	594.34	537.64	495.87	464.03	439.13	419.27	403.16
31000	614.15	555.56	512.40	479.50	453.77	433.24	416.60
32000	633.96	573.48	528.93	494.97	468.41	447.22	430.04
33000	653.77	591.41	545.46	510.43	483.05	461.19	443.48
34000	673.59	609.33	561.98	525.90	497.68	475.17	456.92
35000	693.40	627.25	578.51	541.37	512.32	489.15	470.36
40000	792.45	716.85	661.16	618.71	585.51	559.02	537.55
45000	891.51	806.46	743.80	696.04	658.70	628.90	604.74
50000	990.56	896.07	826.45	773.38	731.89	698.78	671.93
55000	1089.62	985.67	909.09	850.72	805.07	768.65	739.13
60000	1188.68	1075.28	991.73	928.06	878.26	838.53	806.32
65000	1287.73	1164.89	1074.38	1005.40	951.45	908.41	873.51
70000	1386.79	1254.49	1157.02	1082.73	1024.64	978.29	940.71
75000	1485.84	1344.10	1239.67	1160.07	1097.83	1048.16	1007.90
80000	1584.90	1433.70	1322.31	1237.41	1171.01	1118.04	1075.09
100000	1981.12	1792.13	1652.89	1546.76	1463.77	1397.55	1343.86

12½%

TERM AMOUNT	13 YEARS	14 YEARS	15 YEARS	16 YEARS	17 YEARS	18 YEARS	19 YEARS
$ 25	.33	.32	.31	.31	.30	.30	.29
50	.65	.64	.62	.61	.60	.59	.58
75	.98	.95	.93	.91	.89	.88	.87
100	1.30	1.27	1.24	1.21	1.19	1.17	1.15
200	2.60	2.53	2.47	2.42	2.37	2.34	2.30
300	3.90	3.79	3.70	3.63	3.56	3.50	3.45
400	5.20	5.06	4.94	4.83	4.74	4.67	4.60
500	6.50	6.32	6.17	6.04	5.93	5.84	5.75
600	7.80	7.58	7.40	7.25	7.11	7.00	6.90
700	9.10	8.85	8.63	8.45	8.30	8.17	8.05
800	10.40	10.11	9.87	9.66	9.48	9.33	9.20
900	11.70	11.37	11.10	10.87	10.67	10.50	10.35
1000	13.00	12.64	12.33	12.07	11.85	11.67	11.50
2000	26.00	25.27	24.66	24.14	23.70	23.33	23.00
3000	39.00	37.90	36.98	36.21	35.55	34.99	34.50
4000	52.00	50.53	49.31	48.27	47.39	46.65	46.00
5000	64.99	63.16	61.63	60.34	59.24	58.31	57.50
6000	77.99	75.80	73.96	72.41	71.09	69.97	69.00
7000	90.99	88.43	86.28	84.47	82.94	81.63	80.50
8000	103.99	101.06	98.61	96.54	94.78	93.29	92.00
9000	116.98	113.69	110.93	108.61	106.63	104.95	103.50
10000	129.98	126.32	123.26	120.67	118.48	116.61	115.00
11000	142.98	138.95	135.58	132.74	130.32	128.27	126.50
12000	155.98	151.59	147.91	144.81	142.17	139.93	138.00
13000	168.97	164.22	160.23	156.87	154.02	151.59	149.50
14000	181.97	176.85	172.56	168.94	165.87	163.25	161.00
15000	194.97	189.48	184.88	181.01	177.71	174.91	172.50
16000	207.97	202.11	197.21	193.07	189.56	186.57	184.00
17000	220.97	214.74	209.53	205.14	201.41	198.23	195.50
18000	233.96	227.38	221.86	217.21	213.26	209.89	207.00
19000	246.96	240.01	234.18	229.27	225.10	221.55	218.50
20000	259.96	252.64	246.51	241.34	236.95	233.21	230.00
21000	272.96	265.27	258.83	253.41	248.80	244.87	241.49
22000	285.95	277.90	271.16	265.47	260.64	256.53	252.99
23000	298.95	290.53	283.49	277.54	272.49	268.19	264.49
24000	311.95	303.17	295.81	289.61	284.34	279.85	275.99
25000	324.95	315.80	308.14	301.67	296.19	291.51	287.49
26000	337.94	328.43	320.46	313.74	308.03	303.17	298.99
27000	350.94	341.06	332.79	325.81	319.88	314.83	310.49
28000	363.94	353.69	345.11	337.87	331.73	326.49	321.99
29000	376.94	366.32	357.44	349.94	343.58	338.15	333.49
30000	389.93	378.96	369.76	362.01	355.42	349.81	344.99
31000	402.93	391.59	382.09	374.07	367.27	361.47	356.49
32000	415.93	404.22	394.41	386.14	379.12	373.13	367.99
33000	428.93	416.85	406.74	398.21	390.96	384.79	379.49
34000	441.93	429.48	419.06	410.27	402.81	396.45	390.99
35000	454.92	442.11	431.39	422.34	414.66	408.11	402.49
40000	519.91	505.27	493.01	482.67	473.90	466.41	459.99
45000	584.90	568.43	554.64	543.01	533.13	524.71	517.48
50000	649.89	631.59	616.27	603.34	592.37	583.01	574.98
55000	714.88	694.75	677.89	663.67	651.60	641.31	632.48
60000	779.86	757.91	739.52	724.01	710.84	699.61	689.98
65000	844.85	821.06	801.14	784.34	770.08	757.91	747.47
70000	909.84	884.22	862.77	844.67	829.31	816.21	804.97
75000	974.83	947.38	924.40	905.01	888.55	874.51	862.47
80000	1039.82	1010.54	986.02	965.34	947.79	932.81	919.97
100000	1299.77	1263.17	1232.53	1206.67	1184.73	1166.01	1149.96

MONTHLY PAYMENT
NECESSARY TO AMORTIZE A LOAN   12½%

TERM / AMOUNT	20 YEARS	21 YEARS	22 YEARS	25 YEARS	30 YEARS	35 YEARS	40 YEARS
$ 25	.29	.29	.28	.28	.27	.27	.27
50	.57	.57	.56	.55	.54	.53	.53
75	.86	.85	.84	.82	.81	.80	.79
100	1.14	1.13	1.12	1.10	1.07	1.06	1.05
200	2.28	2.25	2.23	2.19	2.14	2.12	2.10
300	3.41	3.38	3.35	3.28	3.21	3.17	3.15
400	4.55	4.50	4.46	4.37	4.27	4.23	4.20
500	5.69	5.63	5.57	5.46	5.34	5.28	5.25
600	6.82	6.75	6.69	6.55	6.41	6.34	6.30
700	7.96	7.87	7.80	7.64	7.48	7.39	7.35
800	9.09	9.00	8.92	8.73	8.54	8.45	8.40
900	10.23	10.12	10.03	9.82	9.61	9.50	9.45
1000	11.37	11.25	11.14	10.91	10.68	10.56	10.49
2000	22.73	22.49	22.28	21.81	21.35	21.11	20.98
3000	34.09	33.73	33.42	32.72	32.02	31.66	31.47
4000	45.45	44.97	44.56	43.62	42.70	42.22	41.96
5000	56.81	56.22	55.70	54.52	53.37	52.77	52.45
6000	68.17	67.46	66.84	65.43	64.04	63.32	62.94
7000	79.53	78.70	77.98	76.33	74.71	73.87	73.43
8000	90.90	89.94	89.12	87.23	85.39	84.43	83.92
9000	102.26	101.18	100.26	98.14	96.06	94.98	94.41
10000	113.62	112.43	111.39	109.04	106.73	105.53	104.90
11000	124.98	123.67	122.53	119.94	117.40	116.08	115.39
12000	136.34	134.91	133.67	130.85	128.08	126.64	125.88
13000	147.70	146.15	144.81	141.75	138.75	137.19	136.36
14000	159.06	157.40	155.95	152.65	149.42	147.74	146.85
15000	170.43	168.64	167.09	163.56	160.09	158.29	157.34
16000	181.79	179.88	178.23	174.46	170.77	168.85	167.83
17000	193.15	191.12	189.37	185.37	181.44	179.40	178.32
18000	204.51	202.36	200.51	196.27	192.11	189.95	188.81
19000	215.87	213.61	211.65	207.17	202.78	200.50	199.30
20000	227.23	224.85	222.78	218.08	213.46	211.06	209.79
21000	238.59	236.09	233.92	228.98	224.13	221.61	220.28
22000	249.96	247.33	245.06	239.88	234.80	232.16	230.77
23000	261.32	258.58	256.20	250.79	245.47	242.71	241.26
24000	272.68	269.82	267.34	261.69	256.15	253.27	251.75
25000	284.04	281.06	278.48	272.59	266.82	263.82	262.23
26000	295.40	292.30	289.62	283.50	277.49	274.37	272.72
27000	306.76	303.54	300.76	294.40	288.16	284.92	283.21
28000	318.12	314.79	311.90	305.30	298.84	295.48	293.70
29000	329.49	326.03	323.03	316.21	309.51	306.03	304.19
30000	340.85	337.27	334.17	327.11	320.18	316.58	314.68
31000	352.21	348.51	345.31	338.01	330.85	327.13	325.17
32000	363.57	359.75	356.45	348.92	341.53	337.69	335.66
33000	374.93	371.00	367.59	359.82	352.20	348.24	346.15
34000	386.29	382.24	378.73	370.73	362.87	358.79	356.64
35000	397.65	393.48	389.87	381.63	373.55	369.34	367.13
40000	454.46	449.69	445.56	436.15	426.91	422.11	419.57
45000	511.27	505.90	501.26	490.66	480.27	474.87	472.02
50000	568.08	562.11	556.95	545.18	533.63	527.63	524.46
55000	624.88	618.32	612.65	599.70	587.00	580.39	576.91
60000	681.69	674.54	668.34	654.22	640.36	633.16	629.36
65000	738.50	730.75	724.04	708.74	693.72	685.92	681.80
70000	795.30	786.96	779.73	763.25	747.09	738.68	734.25
75000	852.11	843.17	835.43	817.77	800.45	791.45	786.69
80000	908.92	899.38	891.12	872.29	853.81	844.21	839.14
100000	1136.15	1124.22	1113.90	1090.36	1067.26	1055.26	1048.92

12¾%

MONTHLY PAYMENT
NECESSARY TO AMORTIZE A LOAN

TERM AMOUNT	1 YEAR	1½ YEARS	2 YEARS	2½ YEARS	3 YEARS	4 YEARS	5 YEARS
$ 25	2.24	1.54	1.19	.98	.84	.67	.57
50	4.47	3.07	2.38	1.96	1.68	1.34	1.14
75	6.70	4.60	3.56	2.94	2.52	2.01	1.70
100	8.93	6.14	4.75	3.92	3.36	2.68	2.27
200	17.85	12.27	9.49	7.83	6.72	5.35	4.53
300	26.77	18.40	14.23	11.74	10.08	8.02	6.79
400	35.69	24.54	18.97	15.65	13.43	10.69	9.06
500	44.61	30.67	23.72	19.56	16.79	13.36	11.32
600	53.53	36.80	28.46	23.47	20.15	16.03	13.58
700	62.45	42.94	33.20	27.38	23.51	18.70	15.84
800	71.37	49.07	37.94	31.29	26.86	21.37	18.11
900	80.29	55.20	42.69	35.20	30.22	24.04	20.37
1000	89.21	61.34	47.43	39.11	33.58	26.71	22.63
2000	178.41	122.67	94.85	78.21	67.15	53.41	45.26
3000	267.61	184.00	142.28	117.31	100.73	80.12	67.88
4000	356.81	245.33	189.70	156.42	134.30	106.82	90.51
5000	446.01	306.66	237.13	195.52	167.87	133.52	113.13
6000	535.21	367.99	284.55	234.62	201.45	160.23	135.76
7000	624.41	429.32	331.98	273.73	235.02	186.93	158.38
8000	713.61	490.65	379.40	312.83	268.59	213.63	181.01
9000	802.81	551.98	426.83	351.93	302.17	240.34	203.63
10000	892.01	613.32	474.25	391.03	335.74	267.04	226.26
11000	981.21	674.65	521.67	430.14	369.32	293.74	248.88
12000	1070.41	735.98	569.10	469.24	402.89	320.45	271.51
13000	1159.61	797.31	616.52	508.34	436.46	347.15	294.13
14000	1248.81	858.64	663.95	547.45	470.04	373.86	316.76
15000	1338.01	919.97	711.37	586.55	503.61	400.56	339.38
16000	1427.21	981.30	758.80	625.65	537.18	427.26	362.01
17000	1516.41	1042.63	806.22	664.75	570.76	453.97	384.64
18000	1605.61	1103.96	853.65	703.86	604.33	480.67	407.26
19000	1694.81	1165.29	901.07	742.96	637.90	507.37	429.89
20000	1784.01	1226.63	948.49	782.06	671.48	534.08	452.51
21000	1873.21	1287.96	995.92	821.17	705.05	560.78	475.14
22000	1962.41	1349.29	1043.34	860.27	738.63	587.48	497.76
23000	2051.61	1410.62	1090.77	899.37	772.20	614.19	520.39
24000	2140.81	1471.95	1138.19	938.47	805.77	640.89	543.01
25000	2230.01	1533.28	1185.62	977.58	839.35	667.59	565.64
26000	2319.21	1594.61	1233.04	1016.68	872.92	694.30	588.26
27000	2408.41	1655.94	1280.47	1055.78	906.49	721.00	610.89
28000	2497.61	1717.27	1327.89	1094.89	940.07	747.71	633.51
29000	2586.81	1778.60	1375.31	1133.99	973.64	774.41	656.14
30000	2676.01	1839.94	1422.74	1173.09	1007.21	801.11	678.76
31000	2765.21	1901.27	1470.16	1212.19	1040.79	827.82	701.39
32000	2854.41	1962.60	1517.59	1251.30	1074.36	854.52	724.01
33000	2943.61	2023.93	1565.01	1290.40	1107.94	881.22	746.64
34000	3032.81	2085.26	1612.44	1329.50	1141.51	907.93	769.27
35000	3122.01	2146.59	1659.86	1368.61	1175.08	934.63	791.89
40000	3568.01	2453.25	1896.98	1564.68	1342.95	1068.15	905.02
45000	4014.01	2759.90	2134.11	1759.63	1510.82	1201.67	1018.14
50000	4460.01	3066.56	2371.23	1955.15	1678.69	1335.18	1131.27
55000	4906.01	3373.21	2608.35	2150.66	1846.56	1468.70	1244.40
60000	5352.01	3679.87	2845.47	2346.18	2014.42	1602.22	1357.52
65000	5798.01	3986.52	3082.60	2541.69	2182.29	1735.74	1470.65
70000	6244.01	4293.18	3319.72	2737.21	2350.16	1869.26	1583.78
75000	6690.01	4599.83	3556.84	2932.72	2518.03	2002.77	1696.90
80000	7136.01	4906.49	3793.96	3128.23	2685.90	2136.29	1810.03
100000	8920.01	6133.11	4742.45	3910.29	3357.37	2670.36	2262.54

98

TERM AMOUNT	6 YEARS	7 YEARS	8 YEARS	9 YEARS	10 YEARS	11 YEARS	12 YEARS
$ 25	.50	.46	.42	.40	.37	.36	.34
50	1.00	.91	.84	.79	.74	.71	.68
75	1.50	1.36	1.26	1.18	1.11	1.06	1.02
100	2.00	1.81	1.67	1.57	1.48	1.42	1.36
200	3.99	3.62	3.34	3.13	2.96	2.83	2.72
300	5.99	5.42	5.01	4.69	4.44	4.24	4.08
400	7.98	7.23	6.67	6.25	5.92	5.66	5.44
500	9.98	9.03	8.34	7.81	7.40	7.07	6.80
600	11.97	10.84	10.01	9.37	8.88	8.48	8.16
700	13.96	12.64	11.67	10.93	10.35	9.89	9.52
800	15.96	14.45	13.34	12.49	11.83	11.31	10.88
900	17.95	16.26	15.01	14.05	13.31	12.72	12.24
1000	19.95	18.06	16.67	15.62	14.79	14.13	13.60
2000	39.89	36.12	33.34	31.23	29.57	28.26	27.19
3000	59.83	54.17	50.01	46.84	44.36	42.38	40.78
4000	79.77	72.23	66.68	62.45	59.14	56.51	54.37
5000	99.72	90.29	83.34	78.06	73.92	70.63	67.97
6000	119.66	108.34	100.01	93.67	88.71	84.76	81.56
7000	139.60	126.40	116.68	109.28	103.49	98.88	95.15
8000	159.54	144.46	133.35	124.89	118.28	113.01	108.74
9000	179.49	162.51	150.01	140.50	133.06	127.13	122.33
10000	199.43	180.57	166.68	156.11	147.84	141.26	135.93
11000	219.37	198.62	183.35	171.72	162.63	155.38	149.52
12000	239.31	216.68	200.02	187.33	177.41	169.51	163.11
13000	259.26	234.74	216.69	202.94	192.20	183.63	176.70
14000	279.20	252.79	233.35	218.55	206.98	197.76	190.29
15000	299.14	270.85	250.02	234.16	221.76	211.89	203.89
16000	319.08	288.91	266.69	249.77	236.55	226.01	217.48
17000	339.03	306.96	283.36	265.38	251.33	240.14	231.07
18000	358.97	325.02	300.02	280.99	266.12	254.26	244.66
19000	378.91	343.08	316.69	296.60	280.90	268.39	258.25
20000	398.85	361.13	333.36	312.21	295.68	282.51	271.85
21000	418.80	379.19	350.03	327.82	310.47	296.64	285.44
22000	438.74	397.24	366.69	343.43	325.25	310.76	299.03
23000	458.68	415.30	383.36	359.04	340.04	324.89	312.62
24000	478.62	433.36	400.03	374.65	354.82	339.01	326.21
25000	498.57	451.41	416.70	390.26	369.60	353.14	339.81
26000	518.51	469.47	433.37	405.87	384.39	367.26	353.40
27000	538.45	487.53	450.03	421.48	399.17	381.39	366.99
28000	558.39	505.58	466.70	437.09	413.96	395.52	380.58
29000	578.33	523.64	483.37	452.70	428.74	409.64	394.17
30000	598.28	541.69	500.04	468.31	443.52	423.77	407.77
31000	618.22	559.75	516.70	483.92	458.31	437.89	421.36
32000	638.16	577.81	533.37	499.53	473.09	452.02	434.95
33000	658.10	595.86	550.04	515.14	487.88	466.14	448.54
34000	678.05	613.92	566.71	530.75	502.66	480.27	462.13
35000	697.99	631.98	583.38	546.36	517.44	494.39	475.73
40000	797.70	722.26	666.71	624.41	591.36	565.02	543.69
45000	897.41	812.54	750.05	702.47	665.28	635.65	611.65
50000	997.13	902.82	833.39	780.52	739.20	706.27	679.61
55000	1096.84	993.10	916.73	858.57	813.12	776.90	747.57
60000	1196.55	1083.38	1000.07	936.62	887.04	847.53	815.53
65000	1296.26	1173.67	1083.41	1014.67	960.96	918.15	883.49
70000	1395.97	1263.95	1166.75	1092.72	1034.88	988.78	951.45
75000	1495.69	1354.23	1250.08	1170.77	1108.80	1059.41	1019.41
80000	1595.40	1444.51	1333.42	1248.82	1182.72	1130.04	1087.37
100000	1994.25	1805.64	1666.78	1561.03	1478.40	1412.54	1359.21

12¾%

MONTHLY PAYMENT
NECESSARY TO AMORTIZE A LOAN

TERM AMOUNT	13 YEARS	14 YEARS	15 YEARS	16 YEARS	17 YEARS	18 YEARS	19 YEARS
$ 25	.33	.32	.32	.31	.31	.30	.30
50	.66	.64	.63	.62	.61	.60	.59
75	.99	.96	.94	.92	.91	.89	.88
100	1.32	1.28	1.25	1.23	1.21	1.19	1.17
200	2.64	2.56	2.50	2.45	2.41	2.37	2.34
300	3.95	3.84	3.75	3.67	3.61	3.55	3.51
400	5.27	5.12	5.00	4.90	4.81	4.74	4.67
500	6.58	6.40	6.25	6.12	6.01	5.92	5.84
600	7.90	7.68	7.50	7.34	7.21	7.10	7.01
700	9.21	8.96	8.75	8.57	8.42	8.29	8.18
800	10.53	10.24	10.00	9.79	9.62	9.47	9.34
900	11.84	11.52	11.24	11.01	10.82	10.65	10.51
1000	13.16	12.80	12.49	12.24	12.02	11.84	11.68
2000	26.31	25.59	24.98	24.47	24.04	23.67	23.35
3000	39.47	38.38	37.47	36.70	36.05	35.50	35.03
4000	52.62	51.17	49.96	48.94	48.07	47.33	46.70
5000	65.78	63.96	62.45	61.17	60.09	59.16	58.37
6000	78.93	76.76	74.94	73.40	72.10	71.00	70.05
7000	92.09	89.55	87.42	85.63	84.12	82.83	81.72
8000	105.24	102.34	99.91	97.87	96.13	94.66	93.40
9000	118.40	115.13	112.40	110.10	108.15	106.49	105.07
10000	131.55	127.92	124.89	122.33	120.17	118.32	116.74
11000	144.70	140.71	137.38	134.57	132.18	130.15	128.42
12000	157.86	153.51	149.87	146.80	144.20	141.99	140.09
13000	171.01	166.30	162.35	159.03	156.22	153.82	151.76
14000	184.17	179.09	174.84	171.26	168.23	165.65	163.44
15000	197.32	191.88	187.33	183.50	180.25	177.48	175.11
16000	210.48	204.67	199.82	195.73	192.26	189.31	186.79
17000	223.63	217.46	212.31	207.96	204.28	201.14	198.46
18000	236.79	230.26	224.80	220.20	216.30	212.98	210.13
19000	249.94	243.05	237.28	232.43	228.31	224.81	221.81
20000	263.09	255.84	249.77	244.66	240.33	236.64	233.48
21000	276.25	268.63	262.26	256.89	252.35	248.47	245.15
22000	289.40	281.42	274.75	269.13	264.36	260.30	256.83
23000	302.56	294.21	287.24	281.36	276.38	272.13	268.50
24000	315.71	307.01	299.73	293.59	288.39	283.97	280.18
25000	328.87	319.80	312.21	305.83	300.41	295.80	291.85
26000	342.02	332.59	324.70	318.06	312.43	307.63	303.52
27000	355.18	345.38	337.19	330.29	324.44	319.46	315.20
28000	368.33	358.17	349.68	342.52	336.46	331.29	326.87
29000	381.48	370.96	362.17	354.76	348.48	343.12	338.54
30000	394.64	383.76	374.66	366.99	360.49	354.96	350.22
31000	407.79	396.55	387.14	379.22	372.51	366.79	361.89
32000	420.95	409.34	399.63	391.46	384.52	378.62	373.57
33000	434.10	422.13	412.12	403.69	396.54	390.45	385.24
34000	447.26	434.92	424.61	415.92	408.56	402.28	396.91
35000	460.41	447.72	437.10	428.15	420.57	414.11	408.59
40000	526.18	511.67	499.54	489.32	480.65	473.27	466.90
45000	591.96	575.63	561.98	550.48	540.74	532.43	525.32
50000	657.73	639.59	624.42	611.65	600.82	591.59	583.69
55000	723.50	703.55	686.87	672.81	660.90	650.75	642.06
60000	789.27	767.51	749.31	733.97	720.98	709.91	700.43
65000	855.04	831.47	811.75	795.14	781.06	769.07	758.80
70000	920.82	895.43	874.19	856.30	841.14	829.22	817.17
75000	986.59	959.38	936.63	917.47	901.22	887.33	875.54
80000	1052.36	1023.34	999.07	978.63	961.30	946.54	933.91
100000	1315.45	1279.18	1248.84	1223.29	1201.63	1183.17	1167.38

TERM AMOUNT	20 YEARS	21 YEARS	22 YEARS	25 YEARS	30 YEARS	35 YEARS	40 YEARS
$ 25	.29	.29	.29	.28	.28	.27	.27
50	.58	.58	.57	.56	.55	.54	.54
75	.87	.86	.85	.84	.82	.81	.81
100	1.16	1.15	1.14	1.11	1.09	1.08	1.07
200	2.31	2.29	2.27	2.22	2.18	2.16	2.14
300	3.47	3.43	3.40	3.33	3.27	3.23	3.21
400	4.62	4.57	4.53	4.44	4.35	4.31	4.28
500	5.77	5.72	5.67	5.55	5.44	5.38	5.35
600	6.93	6.86	6.80	6.66	6.53	6.46	6.42
700	8.08	8.00	7.93	7.77	7.61	7.53	7.49
800	9.24	9.14	9.06	8.88	8.70	8.61	8.56
900	10.39	10.28	10.19	9.99	9.79	9.68	9.63
1000	11.54	11.43	11.33	11.10	10.87	10.76	10.70
2000	23.08	22.85	22.65	22.19	21.74	21.51	21.39
3000	34.62	34.27	33.97	33.28	32.61	32.26	32.08
4000	46.16	45.69	45.29	44.37	43.47	43.01	42.77
5000	57.70	57.11	56.61	55.46	54.34	53.76	53.46
6000	69.23	68.53	67.93	66.55	65.21	64.52	64.16
7000	80.77	79.95	79.25	77.64	76.07	75.27	74.85
8000	92.31	91.37	90.57	88.73	86.94	86.02	85.54
9000	103.85	102.80	101.89	99.82	97.81	96.77	96.23
10000	115.39	114.22	113.21	110.91	108.67	107.52	106.92
11000	126.92	125.64	124.53	122.00	119.54	118.28	117.62
12000	138.46	137.06	135.85	133.09	130.41	129.03	128.31
13000	150.00	148.48	147.17	144.18	141.28	139.78	139.00
14000	161.54	159.90	158.49	155.27	152.14	150.53	149.69
15000	173.08	171.32	169.81	166.36	163.01	161.28	160.38
16000	184.61	182.74	181.13	177.45	173.88	172.04	171.08
17000	196.15	194.17	192.45	188.54	184.74	182.79	181.77
18000	207.69	205.59	203.77	199.63	195.61	193.54	192.46
19000	219.23	217.01	215.09	210.72	206.48	204.29	203.15
20000	230.77	228.43	226.41	221.82	217.34	215.04	213.84
21000	242.31	239.85	237.73	232.91	228.21	225.80	224.54
22000	253.84	251.27	249.05	244.00	239.08	236.55	235.23
23000	265.38	262.69	260.37	255.09	249.94	247.30	245.92
24000	276.92	274.11	271.69	266.18	260.81	258.05	256.61
25000	288.46	285.54	283.01	277.27	271.68	268.80	267.30
26000	300.00	296.96	294.33	288.36	282.55	279.56	278.00
27000	311.53	308.38	305.65	299.45	293.41	290.31	288.69
28000	323.07	319.80	316.97	310.54	304.28	301.06	299.38
29000	334.61	331.22	328.29	321.63	315.15	311.81	310.07
30000	346.15	342.64	339.61	332.72	326.01	322.56	320.76
31000	357.69	354.06	350.93	343.81	336.88	333.32	331.46
32000	369.22	365.48	362.25	354.90	347.75	344.07	342.15
33000	380.76	376.90	373.57	365.99	358.61	354.82	352.84
34000	392.30	388.33	384.89	377.08	369.48	365.57	363.53
35000	403.84	399.75	396.21	388.17	380.35	376.32	374.22
40000	461.53	456.85	452.81	443.63	434.68	430.08	427.68
45000	519.22	513.96	509.41	499.08	489.02	483.84	481.14
50000	576.91	571.07	566.01	554.53	543.35	537.60	534.60
55000	634.60	628.17	622.61	609.98	597.69	591.36	588.06
60000	692.29	685.28	679.21	665.44	652.02	645.12	641.52
65000	749.98	742.38	735.82	720.89	706.36	698.88	694.98
70000	807.67	799.49	792.42	776.34	760.69	752.64	748.44
75000	865.36	856.60	849.02	831.79	815.02	806.40	801.90
80000	923.05	913.70	905.62	887.25	869.36	860.16	855.36
100000	1153.82	1142.13	1132.02	1109.06	1086.70	1075.20	1069.20

TERM AMOUNT	1 YEAR	1½ YEARS	2 YEARS	2½ YEARS	3 YEARS	4 YEARS	5 YEARS
$ 25	2.24	1.54	1.19	.99	.85	.68	.57
50	4.47	3.08	2.38	1.97	1.69	1.35	1.14
75	6.70	4.61	3.57	2.95	2.53	2.02	1.71
100	8.94	6.15	4.76	3.93	3.37	2.69	2.28
200	17.87	12.29	9.51	7.85	6.74	5.37	4.56
300	26.80	18.44	14.27	11.77	10.11	8.05	6.83
400	35.73	24.58	19.02	15.69	13.48	10.74	9.11
500	44.66	30.73	23.78	19.62	16.85	13.42	11.38
600	53.60	36.87	28.53	23.54	20.22	16.10	13.66
700	62.53	43.02	33.28	27.46	23.59	18.78	15.93
800	71.46	49.16	38.04	31.38	26.96	21.47	18.21
900	80.39	55.31	42.79	35.30	30.33	24.15	20.48
1000	89.32	61.45	47.55	39.23	33.70	26.83	22.76
2000	178.64	122.90	95.09	78.45	67.39	53.66	45.51
3000	267.96	184.35	142.63	117.67	101.09	80.49	68.26
4000	357.27	245.80	190.17	156.89	134.78	107.31	91.02
5000	446.59	307.24	237.71	196.11	168.47	134.14	113.77
6000	535.91	368.69	285.26	235.33	202.17	160.97	136.52
7000	625.23	430.14	332.80	274.56	235.86	187.80	159.28
8000	714.54	491.59	380.34	313.78	269.56	214.62	182.03
9000	803.86	553.03	427.88	353.00	303.25	241.45	204.78
10000	893.18	614.48	475.42	392.22	336.94	268.28	227.54
11000	982.50	675.93	522.97	431.44	370.64	295.11	250.29
12000	1071.81	737.38	570.51	470.66	404.33	321.93	273.04
13000	1161.13	798.82	618.05	509.89	438.03	348.76	295.79
14000	1250.45	860.27	665.59	549.11	471.72	375.59	318.55
15000	1339.76	921.72	713.13	588.33	505.41	402.42	341.30
16000	1429.08	983.17	760.67	627.55	539.11	429.24	364.05
17000	1518.40	1044.61	808.22	666.77	572.80	456.07	386.81
18000	1607.72	1106.06	855.76	705.99	606.50	482.90	409.56
19000	1697.03	1167.51	903.30	745.21	640.19	509.73	432.31
20000	1786.35	1228.96	950.84	784.44	673.88	536.55	455.07
21000	1875.67	1290.40	998.38	823.66	707.58	563.33	477.82
22000	1964.99	1351.85	1045.93	862.88	741.27	590.21	500.57
23000	2054.30	1413.30	1093.47	902.10	774.97	617.04	523.33
24000	2143.62	1474.75	1141.01	941.32	808.66	643.86	546.08
25000	2232.94	1536.19	1188.55	980.54	842.35	670.69	568.83
26000	2322.25	1597.64	1236.09	1019.77	876.05	697.52	591.58
27000	2411.57	1659.09	1283.63	1058.99	909.74	724.35	614.34
28000	2500.89	1720.54	1331.18	1098.21	943.44	751.17	637.09
29000	2590.21	1781.99	1378.72	1137.43	977.13	778.00	659.84
30000	2679.52	1843.43	1426.26	1176.65	1010.82	804.83	682.60
31000	2768.84	1904.88	1473.80	1215.87	1044.52	831.66	705.35
32000	2858.16	1966.33	1521.34	1255.09	1078.21	858.48	728.10
33000	2947.48	2027.78	1568.89	1294.32	1111.91	885.31	750.86
34000	3036.79	2089.22	1616.43	1333.54	1145.60	912.14	773.61
35000	3126.11	2150.67	1663.97	1372.76	1179.29	938.97	796.36
40000	3572.70	2457.91	1901.68	1568.87	1347.76	1073.10	910.13
45000	4019.28	2765.15	2139.39	1764.97	1516.23	1207.24	1023.89
50000	4465.87	3072.38	2377.10	1961.08	1684.70	1341.38	1137.66
55000	4912.46	3379.62	2614.81	2157.19	1853.17	1475.52	1251.42
60000	5359.04	3686.86	2852.51	2353.30	2021.64	1609.65	1365.19
65000	5805.63	3994.10	3090.22	2549.41	2190.11	1743.79	1478.95
70000	6252.21	4301.34	3327.93	2745.51	2358.58	1877.93	1592.72
75000	6698.80	4608.57	3565.64	2941.62	2527.05	2012.07	1706.49
80000	7145.39	4915.81	3803.35	3137.73	2695.52	2146.20	1820.25
100000	8931.73	6144.76	4754.19	3922.16	3369.40	2682.75	2275.31

TERM AMOUNT	6 YEARS	7 YEARS	8 YEARS	9 YEARS	10 YEARS	11 YEARS	12 YEARS
$ 25	.51	.46	.43	.40	.38	.36	.35
50	1.01	.91	.85	.79	.75	.72	.69
75	1.51	1.37	1.27	1.19	1.12	1.08	1.04
100	2.01	1.82	1.69	1.58	1.50	1.43	1.38
200	4.02	3.64	3.37	3.16	2.99	2.86	2.75
300	6.03	5.46	5.05	4.73	4.48	4.29	4.13
400	8.03	7.28	6.73	6.31	5.98	5.72	5.50
500	10.04	9.10	8.41	7.88	7.47	7.14	6.88
600	12.05	10.92	10.09	9.46	8.96	8.57	8.25
700	14.06	12.74	11.77	11.03	10.46	10.00	9.63
800	16.06	14.56	13.45	12.61	11.95	11.43	11.00
900	18.07	16.38	15.13	14.18	13.44	12.85	12.38
1000	20.08	18.20	16.81	15.76	14.94	14.28	13.75
2000	40.15	36.39	33.62	31.51	29.87	28.56	27.50
3000	60.23	54.58	50.43	47.27	44.80	42.83	41.24
4000	80.30	72.77	67.23	63.02	59.73	57.11	54.99
5000	100.38	90.96	84.04	78.77	74.66	71.39	68.74
6000	120.45	109.16	100.85	94.53	89.59	85.66	82.48
7000	140.52	127.35	117.66	110.28	104.52	99.94	96.23
8000	160.60	145.54	134.46	126.03	119.45	114.21	109.98
9000	180.67	163.73	151.27	141.79	134.38	128.49	123.72
10000	200.75	181.92	168.08	157.54	149.32	142.77	137.47
11000	220.82	200.12	184.88	173.29	164.25	157.04	151.21
12000	240.89	218.31	201.69	189.05	179.18	171.32	164.96
13000	260.97	236.50	218.50	204.80	194.11	185.59	178.71
14000	281.04	254.69	235.31	220.56	209.04	199.87	192.45
15000	301.12	272.88	252.11	236.31	223.97	214.15	206.20
16000	321.19	291.08	268.92	252.06	238.90	228.42	219.95
17000	341.26	309.27	285.73	267.82	253.83	242.70	233.69
18000	361.34	327.46	302.54	283.57	268.76	256.97	247.44
19000	381.41	345.65	319.34	299.32	283.70	271.25	261.18
20000	401.49	363.84	336.15	315.08	298.63	285.53	274.93
21000	421.56	382.04	352.96	330.83	313.56	299.80	288.68
22000	441.64	400.23	369.76	346.58	328.49	314.08	302.42
23000	461.71	418.42	386.57	362.34	343.42	328.36	316.17
24000	481.78	436.61	403.38	378.09	356.35	342.63	329.92
25000	501.86	454.80	420.19	393.84	373.28	356.91	343.66
26000	521.93	473.00	436.99	409.60	388.21	371.18	357.41
27000	542.01	491.19	453.80	425.35	403.14	385.46	371.15
28000	562.08	509.38	470.61	441.11	418.08	399.74	384.90
29000	582.15	527.57	487.42	456.86	433.01	414.01	398.65
30000	602.23	545.76	504.22	472.61	447.94	428.29	412.39
31000	622.30	563.96	521.03	488.37	462.87	442.56	426.14
32000	642.38	582.15	537.84	504.12	477.80	456.84	439.89
33000	662.45	600.34	554.64	519.87	492.73	471.12	453.63
34000	682.52	618.53	571.45	535.63	507.66	485.39	467.38
35000	702.60	636.72	588.26	551.38	522.59	499.67	481.12
40000	802.97	727.68	672.30	630.15	597.25	571.05	549.86
45000	903.34	818.64	756.33	708.92	671.90	642.43	618.59
50000	1003.71	909.60	840.37	787.68	746.56	713.81	687.32
55000	1104.08	1000.56	924.40	866.45	821.21	785.19	756.05
60000	1204.45	1091.52	1008.44	945.22	895.87	856.57	824.78
65000	1304.82	1182.48	1092.48	1023.99	970.52	927.95	893.51
70000	1405.19	1273.44	1176.51	1102.76	1045.18	999.33	962.24
75000	1505.56	1364.40	1260.55	1181.52	1119.84	1070.71	1030.97
80000	1605.93	1455.36	1344.59	1260.29	1194.49	1142.09	1099.71
100000	2007.42	1819.20	1680.73	1575.36	1493.11	1427.62	1374.63

MONTHLY PAYMENT
NECESSARY TO AMORTIZE A LOAN

TERM AMOUNT	13 YEARS	14 YEARS	15 YEARS	16 YEARS	17 YEARS	18 YEARS	19 YEARS
$ 25	.34	.33	.32	.31	.31	.31	.30
50	.67	.65	.64	.62	.61	.61	.60
75	1.00	.98	.95	.93	.92	.91	.89
100	1.34	1.30	1.27	1.24	1.22	1.21	1.19
200	2.67	2.60	2.54	2.48	2.44	2.41	2.37
300	4.00	3.89	3.80	3.72	3.66	3.61	3.56
400	5.33	5.19	5.07	4.96	4.88	4.81	4.74
500	6.66	6.48	6.33	6.20	6.10	6.01	5.93
600	7.99	7.78	7.60	7.44	7.32	7.21	7.11
700	9.32	9.07	8.86	8.68	8.54	8.41	8.30
800	10.65	10.37	10.13	9.92	9.75	9.61	9.48
900	11.99	11.66	11.39	11.16	10.97	10.81	10.67
1000	13.32	12.96	12.66	12.40	12.19	12.01	11.85
2000	26.63	25.91	25.31	24.80	24.38	24.01	23.70
3000	39.94	38.86	37.96	37.20	36.56	36.02	35.55
4000	53.25	51.82	50.61	49.60	48.75	48.02	47.40
5000	66.57	64.77	63.27	62.00	60.93	60.03	59.25
6000	79.88	77.72	75.92	74.40	73.12	72.03	71.10
7000	93.19	90.67	88.57	86.80	85.31	84.04	82.95
8000	106.50	103.63	101.22	99.20	97.49	96.04	94.80
9000	119.81	116.58	113.88	111.60	109.68	108.04	106.65
10000	133.13	129.53	126.53	124.00	121.87	120.05	118.49
11000	146.44	142.48	139.18	136.40	134.05	132.05	130.34
12000	159.75	155.44	151.83	148.80	146.24	144.06	142.19
13000	173.06	168.39	164.49	161.20	158.42	156.06	154.04
14000	186.37	181.34	177.14	173.60	170.61	168.07	165.89
15000	199.69	194.29	189.79	186.00	182.80	180.07	177.74
16000	213.00	207.25	202.44	198.40	194.98	192.07	189.59
17000	226.31	220.20	215.10	210.80	207.17	204.08	201.44
18000	239.62	233.15	227.75	223.20	219.36	216.08	213.29
19000	252.93	246.11	240.40	235.60	231.54	228.09	225.14
20000	266.25	259.06	253.05	248.00	243.73	240.09	236.98
21000	279.56	272.01	265.71	260.40	255.91	252.10	248.83
22000	292.87	284.96	278.36	272.80	268.10	264.10	260.68
23000	306.18	297.92	291.01	285.20	280.29	276.10	272.53
24000	319.50	310.87	303.66	297.60	292.47	288.11	284.38
25000	332.81	323.82	316.32	310.00	304.66	300.11	296.23
26000	346.12	336.77	328.97	322.40	316.84	312.12	308.08
27000	359.43	349.73	341.62	334.80	329.03	324.12	319.93
28000	372.74	362.68	354.27	347.20	341.22	336.13	331.78
29000	386.06	375.63	366.93	359.60	353.40	348.13	343.63
30000	399.37	388.58	379.58	372.00	365.59	360.13	355.47
31000	412.68	401.54	392.23	384.40	377.78	372.14	367.32
32000	425.99	414.49	404.88	396.80	389.96	384.14	379.17
33000	439.30	427.44	417.53	409.20	402.15	396.15	391.02
34000	452.62	440.39	430.19	421.60	414.33	408.15	402.87
35000	465.93	453.35	442.84	434.00	426.52	420.16	414.72
40000	532.49	518.11	506.06	496.00	487.45	480.18	473.96
45000	599.05	582.87	569.36	558.00	548.38	540.20	533.21
50000	665.61	647.64	632.63	620.00	609.31	600.22	592.45
55000	732.17	712.40	695.89	682.00	670.24	660.24	651.70
60000	798.73	777.16	759.15	744.00	731.17	720.26	710.94
65000	865.29	841.93	822.41	806.00	792.10	780.29	770.19
70000	931.85	906.69	885.67	868.00	853.04	840.31	829.43
75000	998.41	971.45	948.94	930.00	913.97	900.33	888.68
80000	1064.97	1036.22	1012.20	992.00	974.90	960.35	947.92
100000	1331.22	1295.27	1265.25	1239.99	1218.62	1200.44	1184.90

TERM AMOUNT	20 YEARS	21 YEARS	22 YEARS	25 YEARS	30 YEARS	35 YEARS	40 YEARS
$ 25	.30	.30	.29	.29	.28	.28	.28
50	.59	.59	.58	.57	.56	.55	.55
75	.88	.88	.87	.85	.83	.83	.82
100	1.18	1.17	1.16	1.13	1.11	1.10	1.09
200	2.35	2.33	2.31	2.26	2.22	2.20	2.18
300	3.52	3.49	3.46	3.39	3.32	3.29	3.27
400	4.69	4.65	4.61	4.52	4.43	4.39	4.36
500	5.86	5.81	5.76	5.64	5.54	5.48	5.45
600	7.03	6.97	6.91	6.77	6.64	6.58	6.54
700	8.21	8.13	8.06	7.90	7.75	7.67	7.63
800	9.38	9.29	9.21	9.03	8.85	8.77	8.72
900	10.55	10.45	10.36	10.16	9.96	9.86	9.81
1000	11.72	11.61	11.51	11.28	11.07	10.96	10.90
2000	23.44	23.21	23.01	22.56	22.13	21.91	21.80
3000	35.15	34.81	34.51	33.84	33.19	32.86	32.69
4000	46.87	46.41	46.01	45.12	44.25	43.81	43.59
5000	58.58	58.01	57.52	56.40	55.31	54.76	54.48
6000	70.30	69.61	69.02	67.68	66.38	65.72	65.38
7000	82.02	81.21	80.52	78.95	77.44	76.67	76.27
8000	93.73	92.81	92.02	90.23	88.50	87.62	87.17
9000	105.45	104.42	103.53	101.51	99.56	98.57	98.06
10000	117.16	116.02	115.03	112.79	110.62	109.52	108.96
11000	128.88	127.62	126.53	124.07	121.69	120.48	119.85
12000	140.59	139.22	138.03	135.35	132.75	131.43	130.75
13000	152.31	150.82	149.53	146.62	143.81	142.38	141.64
14000	164.03	162.42	161.04	157.90	154.87	153.33	152.54
15000	175.74	174.02	172.54	169.18	165.93	164.28	163.43
16000	187.46	185.62	184.04	180.46	177.00	175.24	174.33
17000	199.17	197.22	195.54	191.74	188.06	186.19	185.22
18000	210.89	208.83	207.05	203.02	199.12	197.14	196.12
19000	222.60	220.43	218.55	214.29	210.18	208.09	207.01
20000	234.32	232.03	230.05	225.57	221.24	219.04	217.91
21000	246.04	243.63	241.55	236.85	232.31	230.00	228.80
22000	257.75	255.23	253.05	248.13	243.37	240.95	239.70
23000	269.47	266.83	264.56	259.41	254.43	251.90	250.59
24000	281.18	278.43	276.06	270.69	265.49	262.85	261.49
25000	292.90	290.03	287.56	281.96	276.55	273.80	272.38
26000	304.61	301.63	299.06	293.24	287.62	284.76	283.28
27000	316.33	313.24	310.57	304.52	298.68	295.71	294.17
28000	328.05	324.84	322.07	315.80	309.74	306.66	305.07
29000	339.76	336.44	333.57	327.08	320.80	317.61	315.96
30000	351.48	348.04	345.07	338.36	331.86	328.56	326.86
31000	363.19	359.64	356.58	349.63	342.93	339.51	337.75
32000	374.91	371.24	368.08	360.91	353.99	350.47	348.65
33000	386.62	382.84	379.58	372.19	365.05	361.42	359.54
34000	398.34	394.44	391.08	383.47	376.11	372.37	370.44
35000	410.06	406.04	402.58	394.75	387.17	383.32	381.33
40000	468.64	464.05	460.10	451.14	442.48	438.08	435.81
45000	527.21	522.06	517.61	507.53	497.79	492.84	490.29
50000	585.79	580.06	575.12	563.92	553.10	547.60	544.76
55000	644.37	638.07	632.63	620.31	608.41	602.36	599.24
60000	702.95	696.07	690.14	676.71	663.72	657.12	653.71
65000	761.53	754.08	747.65	733.10	719.03	711.88	708.19
70000	820.11	812.08	805.16	789.49	774.34	766.64	762.66
75000	878.69	870.09	862.67	845.88	829.65	821.40	817.14
80000	937.27	928.10	920.19	902.27	884.96	876.16	871.62
100000	1171.58	1160.12	1150.23	1127.84	1106.20	1095.20	1089.52

13¼%
MONTHLY PAYMENT
NECESSARY TO AMORTIZE A LOAN

TERM AMOUNT	1 YEAR	1½ YEARS	2 YEARS	2½ YEARS	3 YEARS	4 YEARS	5 YEARS
$ 25	2.24	1.54	1.20	.99	.85	.68	.58
50	4.48	3.08	2.39	1.97	1.70	1.35	1.15
75	6.71	4.62	3.58	2.96	2.54	2.03	1.72
100	8.95	6.16	4.77	3.94	3.39	2.70	2.29
200	17.89	12.32	9.54	7.87	6.77	5.40	4.58
300	26.84	18.47	14.30	11.81	10.15	8.09	6.87
400	35.78	24.63	19.07	15.74	13.53	10.79	9.16
500	44.72	30.79	23.83	19.68	16.91	13.48	11.45
600	53.67	36.94	28.60	23.61	20.29	16.18	13.73
700	62.61	43.10	33.37	27.54	23.68	18.87	16.02
800	71.55	49.26	38.13	31.48	27.06	21.57	18.31
900	80.50	55.41	42.90	35.41	30.44	24.26	20.60
1000	89.44	61.57	47.66	39.35	33.82	26.96	22.89
2000	178.87	123.13	95.32	78.69	67.63	53.91	45.77
3000	268.31	184.70	142.98	118.03	101.45	80.86	68.65
4000	357.74	246.26	190.64	157.37	135.26	107.81	91.53
5000	447.18	307.83	238.30	196.71	169.08	134.76	114.41
6000	536.61	369.39	286.05	236.05	202.89	161.72	137.29
7000	626.05	430.96	333.62	275.39	236.71	188.67	160.17
8000	715.48	492.52	381.28	314.73	270.52	215.62	183.06
9000	804.92	554.08	428.94	354.07	304.34	242.57	205.94
10000	894.35	615.65	476.60	393.41	338.15	269.52	228.82
11000	983.79	677.21	524.26	432.75	371.96	296.47	251.70
12000	1073.22	738.78	571.92	472.09	405.78	323.43	274.58
13000	1162.65	800.34	619.58	511.43	439.59	350.38	297.46
14000	1252.09	861.91	667.24	550.77	473.41	377.33	320.34
15000	1341.52	923.47	714.90	590.11	507.22	404.28	343.22
16000	1430.96	985.03	762.55	629.45	541.04	431.23	366.11
17000	1520.39	1046.60	810.21	668.79	574.85	458.18	388.99
18000	1609.83	1108.16	857.87	708.13	608.67	485.14	411.87
19000	1699.26	1169.73	905.53	747.47	642.48	512.09	434.75
20000	1788.70	1231.29	953.19	786.81	676.29	539.04	457.63
21000	1878.13	1292.86	1000.85	826.15	710.11	565.99	480.51
22000	1967.57	1354.42	1048.51	865.49	743.92	592.94	503.39
23000	2057.00	1415.98	1096.17	904.84	777.74	619.90	526.27
24000	2146.44	1477.55	1143.83	944.18	811.55	646.85	549.16
25000	2235.87	1539.11	1191.49	983.52	845.37	673.80	572.04
26000	2325.30	1600.68	1239.15	1022.86	879.18	700.75	594.92
27000	2414.74	1662.24	1286.81	1062.20	913.00	727.70	617.80
28000	2504.17	1723.81	1334.47	1101.54	946.81	754.65	640.68
29000	2593.61	1785.37	1382.13	1140.88	980.63	781.61	663.56
30000	2683.04	1846.93	1429.79	1180.22	1014.44	808.56	686.44
31000	2772.48	1908.50	1477.44	1219.56	1048.25	835.51	709.32
32000	2861.91	1970.06	1525.10	1258.90	1082.07	862.46	732.21
33000	2951.35	2031.63	1572.76	1298.24	1115.88	889.41	755.09
34000	3040.78	2093.19	1620.42	1337.58	1149.70	916.36	777.97
35000	3130.22	2154.76	1668.08	1376.92	1183.51	943.32	800.85
40000	3577.39	2462.58	1906.40	1573.62	1352.58	1078.09	915.26
45000	4024.56	2770.40	2144.68	1770.32	1521.66	1212.83	1029.66
50000	4471.74	3078.22	2382.97	1967.03	1690.73	1347.59	1144.07
55000	4918.91	3386.04	2621.27	2163.73	1859.80	1482.35	1258.47
60000	5366.08	3693.86	2859.57	2360.43	2028.87	1617.11	1372.88
65000	5813.25	4001.68	3097.86	2557.13	2197.95	1751.87	1487.29
70000	6260.43	4309.51	3336.16	2753.84	2367.02	1886.63	1601.69
75000	6707.60	4617.33	3574.46	2950.54	2536.09	2021.39	1716.10
80000	7154.77	4925.15	3812.75	3147.24	2705.16	2156.14	1830.51
100000	8943.47	6156.43	4765.94	3934.05	3381.45	2695.18	2288.13

TERM AMOUNT	6 YEARS	7 YEARS	8 YEARS	9 YEARS	10 YEARS	11 YEARS	12 YEARS
$ 25	.51	.46	.43	.40	.38	.37	.35
50	1.02	.92	.85	.80	.76	.73	.70
75	1.52	1.38	1.28	1.20	1.14	1.09	1.05
100	2.03	1.84	1.70	1.59	1.51	1.45	1.40
200	4.05	3.67	3.39	3.18	3.02	2.89	2.79
300	6.07	5.50	5.09	4.77	4.53	4.33	4.18
400	8.09	7.34	6.78	6.36	6.04	5.78	5.57
500	10.11	9.17	8.48	7.95	7.54	7.22	6.96
600	12.13	11.00	10.17	9.54	9.05	8.66	8.35
700	14.15	12.83	11.87	11.13	10.56	10.10	9.74
800	16.17	14.67	13.56	12.72	12.07	11.55	11.13
900	18.19	16.50	15.26	14.31	13.58	12.99	12.52
1000	20.21	18.33	16.95	15.90	15.08	14.43	13.91
2000	40.42	36.66	33.90	31.80	30.16	28.86	27.81
3000	60.62	54.99	50.85	47.70	45.24	43.29	41.71
4000	80.83	73.32	67.79	63.60	60.32	57.72	55.61
5000	101.04	91.65	84.74	79.49	75.40	72.14	69.51
6000	121.24	109.97	101.69	95.39	90.48	86.57	83.41
7000	141.45	128.30	118.64	111.29	105.56	101.00	97.31
8000	161.66	146.63	135.58	127.19	120.64	115.43	111.22
9000	181.86	164.96	152.53	143.08	135.72	129.85	125.12
10000	202.07	183.29	169.48	158.98	150.79	144.28	139.02
11000	222.27	201.61	186.43	174.88	165.87	158.71	152.92
12000	242.48	219.94	203.37	190.78	180.95	173.14	166.82
13000	262.69	238.27	220.32	206.67	196.03	187.56	180.72
14000	282.89	256.60	237.27	222.57	211.11	201.99	194.62
15000	303.10	274.93	254.22	238.47	226.19	216.42	208.52
16000	323.31	293.26	271.16	254.37	241.27	230.85	222.43
17000	343.51	311.58	288.11	270.26	256.35	245.27	236.33
18000	363.72	329.91	305.06	286.16	271.43	259.70	250.23
19000	383.92	348.24	322.01	302.06	286.50	274.13	264.13
20000	404.13	366.57	338.95	317.96	301.58	288.56	278.03
21000	424.34	384.90	355.90	333.85	316.66	302.98	291.93
22000	444.54	403.22	372.85	349.75	331.74	317.41	305.83
23000	464.75	421.55	389.80	365.65	346.82	331.84	319.74
24000	484.96	439.88	406.74	381.55	361.90	346.27	333.64
25000	505.16	458.21	423.69	397.45	376.98	360.70	347.54
26000	525.37	476.54	440.64	413.34	392.06	375.12	361.44
27000	545.57	494.87	457.58	429.24	407.14	389.55	375.34
28000	565.78	513.19	474.53	445.14	422.21	403.98	389.24
29000	585.99	531.52	491.48	461.04	437.29	418.41	403.14
30000	606.19	549.85	508.43	476.93	452.37	432.83	417.04
31000	626.40	568.18	525.37	492.83	467.45	447.26	430.95
32000	646.61	586.51	542.32	508.73	482.53	461.69	444.85
33000	666.81	604.83	559.27	524.63	497.61	476.12	458.75
34000	687.02	623.16	576.22	540.52	512.69	490.54	472.65
35000	707.23	641.49	593.16	556.42	527.77	504.97	486.55
40000	808.26	733.13	677.90	635.91	603.16	577.11	556.06
45000	909.29	824.77	762.64	715.40	678.56	649.25	625.56
50000	1010.32	916.41	847.38	794.89	753.95	721.39	695.07
55000	1111.35	1008.05	932.11	874.37	829.34	793.52	764.58
60000	1212.38	1099.69	1016.85	953.86	904.74	865.66	834.08
65000	1313.41	1191.33	1101.59	1033.35	980.13	937.80	903.59
70000	1414.45	1282.98	1186.32	1112.84	1055.53	1009.94	973.10
75000	1515.48	1374.62	1271.06	1192.33	1130.92	1082.08	1042.60
80000	1616.51	1466.26	1355.80	1271.81	1206.32	1154.21	1112.11
100000	2020.63	1832.82	1694.75	1589.77	1507.89	1442.77	1390.14

13¼%

MONTHLY PAYMENT
NECESSARY TO AMORTIZE A LOAN

TERM AMOUNT	13 YEARS	14 YEARS	15 YEARS	16 YEARS	17 YEARS	18 YEARS	19 YEARS
$ 25	.34	.33	.33	.32	.31	.31	.31
50	.68	.66	.65	.63	.62	.61	.61
75	1.02	.99	.97	.95	.93	.92	.91
100	1.35	1.32	1.29	1.26	1.24	1.22	1.21
200	2.70	2.63	2.57	2.52	2.48	2.44	2.41
300	4.05	3.94	3.85	3.78	3.71	3.66	3.61
400	5.39	5.25	5.13	5.03	4.95	4.88	4.82
500	6.74	6.56	6.41	6.29	6.18	6.09	6.02
600	8.09	7.87	7.70	7.55	7.42	7.31	7.22
700	9.43	9.19	8.98	8.80	8.65	8.53	8.42
800	10.78	10.50	10.26	10.06	9.89	9.75	9.63
900	12.13	11.81	11.54	11.32	11.13	10.97	10.83
1000	13.48	13.12	12.82	12.57	12.36	12.18	12.03
2000	26.95	26.23	25.64	25.14	24.72	24.36	24.06
3000	40.42	39.35	38.46	37.71	37.08	36.54	36.08
4000	53.89	52.46	51.27	50.28	49.43	48.72	48.11
5000	67.36	65.58	64.09	62.84	61.79	60.89	60.13
6000	80.83	78.69	76.91	75.41	74.15	73.07	72.16
7000	94.30	91.81	89.73	87.98	86.50	85.25	84.18
8000	107.77	104.92	102.54	100.55	98.86	97.43	96.21
9000	121.24	118.03	115.36	113.12	111.22	109.61	108.23
10000	134.71	131.15	128.18	125.68	123.57	121.78	120.26
11000	148.18	144.26	141.00	138.25	135.93	133.96	132.28
12000	161.65	157.38	153.81	150.82	148.29	146.14	144.31
13000	175.12	170.49	166.63	163.39	160.65	158.32	156.33
14000	188.59	183.61	179.45	175.95	173.00	170.50	168.36
15000	202.06	196.72	192.27	188.52	185.36	182.67	180.38
16000	215.53	209.84	205.08	201.09	197.72	194.85	192.41
17000	229.01	222.95	217.90	213.66	210.07	207.03	204.43
18000	242.48	236.06	230.72	226.23	222.43	219.21	216.46
19000	255.95	249.18	243.53	238.79	234.79	231.38	228.48
20000	269.42	262.29	256.35	251.36	247.14	243.56	240.51
21000	282.89	275.41	269.17	263.93	259.50	255.74	252.53
22000	296.36	288.52	281.99	276.50	271.86	267.92	264.56
23000	309.83	301.64	294.80	289.07	284.22	280.10	276.58
24000	323.30	314.75	307.62	301.63	296.57	292.27	288.61
25000	336.77	327.87	320.44	314.20	308.93	304.45	300.63
26000	350.24	340.98	333.26	326.77	321.29	316.63	312.66
27000	363.71	354.09	346.07	339.34	333.64	328.81	324.68
28000	377.18	367.21	358.89	351.90	346.00	340.99	336.71
29000	390.65	380.32	371.71	364.47	358.36	353.16	348.73
30000	404.12	393.44	384.53	377.04	370.71	365.34	360.76
31000	417.59	406.55	397.34	389.61	383.07	377.52	372.78
32000	431.06	419.67	410.16	402.18	395.43	389.70	384.81
33000	444.53	432.78	422.98	414.74	407.78	401.87	396.83
34000	458.01	445.90	435.80	427.31	420.14	414.05	408.86
35000	471.48	459.01	448.61	439.88	432.50	426.23	420.88
40000	538.83	524.58	512.70	502.72	494.28	487.12	481.01
45000	606.18	590.15	576.79	565.56	556.07	548.01	541.13
50000	673.53	655.73	640.87	628.40	617.85	608.90	601.26
55000	740.89	721.30	704.96	691.24	679.64	669.79	661.39
60000	808.24	786.87	769.05	754.08	741.42	730.68	721.51
65000	875.59	852.44	833.13	816.91	803.21	791.57	781.64
70000	942.95	918.01	897.22	879.75	864.99	852.46	841.76
75000	1010.30	983.59	961.31	942.59	926.78	913.35	901.89
80000	1077.65	1049.16	1025.39	1005.43	988.56	974.23	962.01
100000	1347.06	1311.45	1281.74	1256.79	1235.70	1217.79	1202.51

108

TERM AMOUNT	20 YEARS	21 YEARS	22 YEARS	25 YEARS	30 YEARS	35 YEARS	40 YEARS
$ 25	.30	.30	.30	.29	.29	.28	.28
50	.60	.59	.59	.58	.57	.56	.56
75	.90	.89	.88	.87	.85	.84	.84
100	1.19	1.18	1.17	1.15	1.13	1.12	1.11
200	2.38	2.36	2.34	2.30	2.26	2.24	2.22
300	3.57	3.54	3.51	3.45	3.38	3.35	3.33
400	4.76	4.72	4.68	4.59	4.51	4.47	4.44
500	5.95	5.90	5.85	5.74	5.63	5.58	5.55
600	7.14	7.07	7.02	6.89	6.76	6.70	6.66
700	8.33	8.25	8.18	8.03	7.89	7.81	7.77
800	9.52	9.43	9.35	9.18	9.01	8.93	8.88
900	10.71	10.61	10.52	10.33	10.14	10.04	9.99
1000	11.90	11.79	11.69	11.47	11.26	11.16	11.10
2000	23.79	23.57	23.38	22.94	22.52	22.31	22.20
3000	35.69	35.35	35.06	34.41	33.78	33.46	33.30
4000	47.58	47.13	46.75	45.87	45.04	44.61	44.40
5000	59.48	58.91	58.43	57.34	56.29	55.77	55.50
6000	71.37	70.70	70.12	68.81	67.55	66.92	66.60
7000	83.27	82.48	81.80	80.27	78.81	78.07	77.70
8000	95.16	94.26	93.49	91.74	90.07	89.22	88.79
9000	107.05	106.04	105.17	103.21	101.32	100.38	99.89
10000	118.95	117.82	116.86	114.68	112.58	111.53	110.99
11000	130.84	129.61	128.54	126.14	123.84	122.68	122.09
12000	142.74	141.39	140.23	137.61	135.10	133.83	133.19
13000	154.63	153.17	151.91	149.08	146.36	144.99	144.29
14000	166.53	164.95	163.60	160.54	157.61	156.14	155.39
15000	178.42	176.73	175.28	172.01	168.87	167.29	166.49
16000	190.31	188.52	186.97	183.48	180.13	178.44	177.58
17000	202.21	200.30	198.65	194.94	191.39	189.60	188.68
18000	214.10	212.08	210.34	206.41	202.64	200.75	199.78
19000	226.00	223.86	222.02	217.88	213.90	211.90	210.88
20000	237.89	235.64	233.71	229.35	225.16	223.05	221.98
21000	249.79	247.43	245.40	240.81	236.42	234.21	233.08
22000	261.68	259.21	257.08	252.28	247.68	245.36	244.18
23000	273.57	270.99	268.77	263.75	258.93	256.51	255.28
24000	285.47	282.77	280.45	275.21	270.19	267.66	266.37
25000	297.36	294.55	292.14	286.68	281.45	278.82	277.47
26000	309.26	306.34	303.82	298.15	292.71	289.97	288.57
27000	321.15	318.12	315.51	309.61	303.96	301.12	299.67
28000	333.05	329.90	327.19	321.08	315.22	312.27	310.77
29000	344.94	341.68	338.88	332.55	326.48	323.43	321.87
30000	356.83	353.46	350.56	344.02	337.74	334.58	332.97
31000	368.73	365.25	362.25	355.48	348.99	345.73	344.06
32000	380.62	377.03	373.93	366.95	360.25	356.88	355.16
33000	392.52	388.81	385.62	378.42	371.51	368.03	366.26
34000	404.41	400.59	397.30	389.88	382.77	379.19	377.36
35000	416.31	412.37	408.99	401.35	394.03	390.34	388.46
40000	475.78	471.28	467.42	458.69	450.31	446.10	443.95
45000	535.25	530.19	525.84	516.02	506.60	501.86	499.45
50000	594.72	589.10	584.27	573.36	562.89	557.63	554.94
55000	654.19	648.01	642.69	630.69	619.18	613.39	610.43
60000	713.66	706.92	701.12	688.03	675.47	669.15	665.93
65000	773.13	765.83	759.55	745.36	731.76	724.91	721.42
70000	832.61	824.74	817.97	802.70	788.05	780.67	776.91
75000	892.08	883.65	876.40	860.03	844.34	836.44	832.41
80000	951.55	942.56	934.83	917.37	900.62	892.20	887.90
100000	1189.44	1178.20	1168.53	1146.71	1125.78	1115.25	1109.87

13½%

TERM AMOUNT	1 YEAR	1½ YEARS	2 YEARS	2½ YEARS	3 YEARS	4 YEARS	5 YEARS
$ 25	2.24	1.55	1.20	.99	.85	.68	.58
50	4.48	3.09	2.39	1.98	1.70	1.36	1.16
75	6.72	4.63	3.59	2.96	2.55	2.04	1.73
100	8.96	6.17	4.78	3.95	3.40	2.71	2.31
200	17.92	12.34	9.56	7.90	6.79	5.42	4.61
300	26.87	18.51	14.34	11.84	10.19	8.13	6.91
400	35.83	24.68	19.12	15.79	13.58	10.84	9.21
500	44.78	30.85	23.89	19.73	16.97	13.54	11.51
600	53.74	37.01	28.67	23.68	20.37	16.25	13.81
700	62.69	43.18	33.45	27.63	23.76	18.96	16.11
800	71.65	49.35	38.23	31.57	27.15	21.67	18.41
900	80.60	55.52	43.00	35.52	30.55	24.37	20.71
1000	89.56	61.69	47.78	39.46	33.94	27.08	23.01
2000	179.11	123.37	95.56	78.92	67.88	54.16	46.02
3000	268.66	185.05	143.34	118.38	101.81	81.23	69.03
4000	358.22	246.73	191.11	157.84	135.75	108.31	92.04
5000	447.77	308.41	238.89	197.30	169.68	135.39	115.05
6000	537.32	370.09	286.67	236.76	203.62	162.46	138.06
7000	626.87	431.77	334.44	276.22	237.55	189.54	161.07
8000	716.42	493.45	382.22	315.68	271.49	216.62	184.08
9000	805.97	555.14	430.00	355.14	305.42	243.69	207.09
10000	895.53	616.82	477.78	394.60	339.36	270.77	230.10
11000	985.08	678.50	525.55	434.06	373.29	297.84	253.11
12000	1074.63	740.18	573.33	473.52	407.23	324.92	276.12
13000	1164.18	801.86	621.11	512.98	441.16	352.00	299.13
14000	1253.73	863.54	668.88	552.44	475.10	379.07	322.14
15000	1343.29	925.22	716.66	591.90	509.03	406.15	345.15
16000	1432.84	986.90	764.44	631.36	542.97	433.23	368.16
17000	1522.39	1048.58	812.21	670.82	576.90	460.30	391.17
18000	1611.94	1110.27	859.99	710.28	610.84	487.38	414.18
19000	1701.49	1171.95	907.77	749.74	644.78	514.46	437.19
20000	1791.05	1233.63	955.55	789.20	678.71	541.53	460.20
21000	1880.60	1295.31	1003.32	828.66	712.65	568.61	483.21
22000	1970.15	1356.99	1051.10	868.11	746.58	595.68	506.22
23000	2059.70	1418.67	1098.88	907.57	780.52	622.76	529.23
24000	2149.25	1480.35	1146.65	947.03	814.45	649.84	552.24
25000	2238.81	1542.03	1194.43	986.49	848.39	676.91	575.25
26000	2328.36	1603.71	1242.21	1025.95	882.32	703.99	598.26
27000	2417.91	1665.40	1289.98	1065.41	916.26	731.07	621.27
28000	2507.46	1727.08	1337.76	1104.87	950.19	758.14	644.28
29000	2597.01	1788.76	1385.54	1144.33	984.13	785.22	667.29
30000	2686.57	1850.44	1433.32	1183.79	1018.06	812.29	690.30
31000	2776.12	1912.12	1481.09	1223.25	1052.00	839.37	713.31
32000	2865.67	1973.80	1528.87	1262.71	1085.93	866.45	736.32
33000	2955.22	2035.48	1576.65	1302.17	1119.87	893.52	759.33
34000	3044.77	2097.16	1624.42	1341.63	1153.80	920.60	782.34
35000	3134.33	2158.84	1672.20	1381.09	1187.74	947.68	805.35
40000	3582.09	2467.06	1911.09	1578.39	1357.42	1083.06	920.40
45000	4029.85	2775.66	2149.97	1775.68	1527.09	1218.44	1035.45
50000	4477.61	3084.06	2388.86	1972.98	1696.77	1353.82	1150.50
55000	4925.37	3392.47	2627.74	2170.28	1866.45	1489.20	1265.55
60000	5373.13	3700.87	2866.63	2367.58	2036.12	1624.58	1380.60
65000	5820.89	4009.28	3105.51	2564.87	2205.80	1759.97	1495.64
70000	6268.65	4317.68	3344.40	2762.17	2375.48	1895.35	1610.69
75000	6716.41	4626.09	3583.28	2959.47	2545.15	2030.73	1725.74
80000	7164.17	4934.50	3822.17	3156.77	2714.83	2166.11	1840.79
100000	8955.21	6168.12	4777.71	3945.96	3393.53	2707.64	2300.99

TERM AMOUNT	6 YEARS	7 YEARS	8 YEARS	9 YEARS	10 YEARS	11 YEARS	12 YEARS
$ 25	.51	.47	.43	.41	.39	.37	.36
50	1.02	.93	.86	.81	.77	.73	.71
75	1.53	1.39	1.29	1.21	1.15	1.10	1.06
100	2.04	1.85	1.71	1.61	1.53	1.46	1.41
200	4.07	3.70	3.42	3.21	3.05	2.92	2.82
300	6.11	5.54	5.13	4.82	4.57	4.38	4.22
400	8.14	7.39	6.84	6.42	6.10	5.84	5.63
500	10.17	9.24	8.55	8.03	7.62	7.29	7.03
600	12.21	11.08	10.26	9.63	9.14	8.75	8.44
700	14.24	12.93	11.97	11.23	10.66	10.21	9.85
800	16.28	14.78	13.68	12.84	12.19	11.67	11.25
900	18.31	16.62	15.38	14.44	13.71	13.13	12.66
1000	20.34	18.47	17.09	16.05	15.23	14.58	14.06
2000	40.68	36.93	34.18	32.09	30.46	29.16	28.12
3000	61.02	55.40	51.27	48.13	45.69	43.74	42.18
4000	81.36	73.86	68.36	64.17	60.91	58.32	56.23
5000	101.70	92.33	85.45	80.22	76.14	72.90	70.29
6000	122.04	110.79	102.53	96.26	91.37	87.48	84.35
7000	142.38	129.26	119.62	112.30	106.60	102.06	98.41
8000	162.72	147.72	136.71	128.34	121.82	116.64	112.46
9000	183.06	166.19	153.80	144.39	137.05	131.22	126.52
10000	203.39	184.65	170.89	160.43	152.28	145.80	140.58
11000	223.73	203.12	187.97	176.47	167.51	160.38	154.63
12000	244.07	221.58	205.06	192.51	182.73	174.96	168.69
13000	264.41	240.05	222.15	208.56	197.96	189.54	182.75
14000	284.75	258.51	239.24	224.60	213.19	204.12	196.81
15000	305.09	276.98	256.33	240.64	228.42	218.70	210.86
16000	325.43	295.44	273.42	256.68	243.64	233.28	224.92
17000	345.77	313.91	290.50	272.72	258.87	247.86	238.98
18000	366.11	332.37	307.59	288.77	274.10	262.44	253.03
19000	386.45	350.84	324.68	304.81	289.33	277.02	267.09
20000	406.78	369.30	341.77	320.85	304.55	291.60	281.15
21000	427.12	387.77	358.86	336.89	319.78	306.18	295.21
22000	447.46	406.23	375.94	352.94	335.01	320.76	309.26
23000	467.80	424.70	393.03	368.98	350.24	335.34	323.32
24000	488.14	443.16	410.12	385.02	365.46	349.92	337.38
25000	508.48	461.63	427.21	401.06	380.69	364.50	351.43
26000	528.82	480.09	444.30	417.11	395.92	379.08	365.49
27000	549.16	498.56	461.39	433.15	411.15	393.66	379.55
28000	569.50	517.02	478.47	449.19	426.37	408.24	393.61
29000	589.83	535.49	495.56	465.23	441.60	422.82	407.66
30000	610.17	553.95	512.65	481.27	456.83	437.40	421.72
31000	630.51	572.42	529.74	497.32	472.06	451.98	435.78
32000	650.85	590.88	546.83	513.36	487.28	466.56	449.83
33000	671.19	609.35	563.91	529.40	502.51	481.14	463.89
34000	691.53	627.81	581.00	545.44	517.74	495.72	477.95
35000	711.87	646.28	598.09	561.49	532.97	510.30	492.01
40000	813.56	738.60	683.53	641.70	609.10	583.20	562.29
45000	915.26	830.93	768.97	721.91	685.24	656.10	632.58
50000	1016.95	923.25	854.41	802.12	761.38	729.00	702.86
55000	1118.65	1015.57	939.85	882.33	837.51	801.90	773.15
60000	1220.34	1107.90	1025.29	962.54	913.65	874.80	843.44
65000	1322.04	1200.22	1110.74	1042.76	989.79	947.70	913.72
70000	1423.73	1292.55	1196.18	1122.97	1065.93	1020.60	984.01
75000	1525.43	1384.87	1281.62	1203.18	1142.06	1093.50	1054.29
80000	1627.12	1477.20	1367.06	1283.39	1218.20	1166.39	1124.58
100000	2033.90	1846.49	1708.82	1604.24	1522.75	1457.99	1405.72

13½%

TERM AMOUNT	13 YEARS	14 YEARS	15 YEARS	16 YEARS	17 YEARS	18 YEARS	19 YEARS
$ 25	.35	.34	.33	.32	.32	.31	.31
50	.69	.67	.65	.64	.63	.62	.62
75	1.03	1.00	.98	.96	.94	.93	.92
100	1.37	1.33	1.30	1.28	1.26	1.24	1.23
200	2.73	2.66	2.60	2.55	2.51	2.48	2.45
300	4.09	3.99	3.90	3.83	3.76	3.71	3.67
400	5.46	5.32	5.20	5.10	5.02	4.95	4.89
500	6.82	6.64	6.50	6.37	6.27	6.18	6.11
600	8.18	7.97	7.79	7.65	7.52	7.42	7.33
700	9.55	9.30	9.09	8.92	8.78	8.65	8.55
800	10.91	10.63	10.39	10.19	10.03	9.89	9.77
900	12.27	11.95	11.69	11.47	11.28	11.12	10.99
1000	13.63	13.28	12.99	12.74	12.53	12.36	12.21
2000	27.26	26.56	25.97	25.48	25.06	24.71	24.41
3000	40.89	39.84	38.95	38.22	37.59	37.06	36.61
4000	54.52	53.11	51.94	50.95	50.12	49.41	48.81
5000	68.15	66.39	64.92	63.69	62.65	61.77	61.02
6000	81.78	79.67	77.90	76.43	75.18	74.12	73.22
7000	95.41	92.94	90.89	89.16	87.71	86.47	85.42
8000	109.04	106.22	103.87	101.90	100.23	98.82	97.62
9000	122.67	119.50	116.85	114.64	112.76	111.18	109.82
10000	136.30	132.78	129.84	127.37	125.29	123.53	122.03
11000	149.93	146.05	142.82	140.11	137.82	135.88	134.23
12000	163.56	159.33	155.80	152.85	150.35	148.23	146.43
13000	177.19	172.61	168.79	165.58	162.88	160.59	158.63
14000	190.82	185.88	181.77	178.32	175.41	172.94	170.83
15000	204.45	199.16	194.75	191.06	187.94	185.29	183.04
16000	218.08	212.44	207.74	203.79	200.46	197.64	195.24
17000	231.71	225.72	220.72	216.53	212.99	209.99	207.44
18000	245.34	238.99	233.70	229.27	225.52	222.35	219.64
19000	258.97	252.27	246.69	242.00	238.05	234.70	231.85
20000	272.60	265.55	259.67	254.74	250.58	247.05	244.05
21000	286.23	278.82	272.65	267.48	263.11	259.40	256.25
22000	299.86	292.10	285.64	280.21	275.64	271.76	268.45
23000	313.49	305.38	298.62	292.95	288.16	284.11	280.65
24000	327.12	318.65	311.60	305.69	300.69	296.46	292.86
25000	340.75	331.93	324.58	318.42	313.22	308.81	305.06
26000	354.38	345.21	337.57	331.16	325.75	321.17	317.26
27000	368.01	358.49	350.55	343.90	338.28	333.52	329.46
28000	381.64	371.76	363.53	356.63	350.81	345.87	341.66
29000	395.27	385.04	376.52	369.37	363.34	358.22	353.87
30000	408.90	398.32	389.50	382.11	375.87	370.57	366.07
31000	422.53	411.59	402.48	394.84	388.39	382.93	378.27
32000	436.16	424.87	415.47	407.58	400.92	395.28	390.47
33000	449.79	438.15	428.45	420.32	413.45	407.63	402.67
34000	463.42	451.43	441.43	433.05	425.98	419.98	414.88
35000	477.05	464.70	454.42	445.79	438.51	432.34	427.08
40000	545.20	531.09	519.33	509.47	501.15	494.10	488.09
45000	613.35	597.47*	584.25	573.16	563.80	555.86	549.10
50000	681.50	663.86	649.16	636.84	626.44	617.62	610.11
55000	749.65	730.24	714.08	700.52	689.08	679.38	671.12
60000	817.80	796.63	779.00	764.21	751.73	741.14	732.13
65000	885.95	863.01	843.91	827.89	814.37	802.91	793.14
70000	954.10	929.40	908.83	891.57	877.01	864.67	854.15
75000	1022.25	995.79	973.74	955.26	939.66	926.43	915.16
80000	1090.40	1062.17	1038.66	1018.94	1002.30	988.19	976.17
100000	1363.00	1327.71	1298.32	1273.67	1252.87	1235.24	1220.22

TERM AMOUNT	20 YEARS	21 YEARS	22 YEARS	25 YEARS	30 YEARS	35 YEARS	40 YEARS
$ 25	.31	.30	.30	.30	.29	.29	.29
50	.61	.60	.60	.59	.58	.57	.57
75	.91	.90	.90	.88	.86	.86	.85
100	1.21	1.20	1.19	1.17	1.15	1.14	1.14
200	2.42	2.40	2.38	2.34	2.30	2.28	2.27
300	3.63	3.59	3.57	3.50	3.44	3.41	3.40
400	4.83	4.79	4.75	4.67	4.59	4.55	4.53
500	6.04	5.99	5.94	5.83	5.73	5.68	5.66
600	7.25	7.18	7.13	7.00	6.88	6.82	6.79
700	8.46	8.38	8.31	8.16	8.02	7.95	7.92
800	9.66	9.58	9.50	9.33	9.17	9.09	9.05
900	10.87	10.77	10.69	1C.50	10.31	10.22	10.18
1000	12.08	11.97	11.87	11.66	11.46	11.36	11.31
2000	24.15	23.93	23.74	23.31	22.91	22.71	22.61
3000	36.23	35.90	35.61	34.97	34.37	34.07	33.91
4000	48.30	47.86	47.48	46.63	45.82	45.42	45.22
5000	60.37	59.82	59.35	58.29	57.28	56.77	56.52
6000	72.45	71.79	71.22	69.94	68.73	68.13	67.82
7000	84.52	83.75	83.09	81.60	80.18	79.48	79.12
8000	96.59	95.71	94.96	93.26	91.64	90.83	90.43
9000	108.67	107.68	106.83	104.91	103.09	102.19	101.73
10000	120.74	119.64	118.70	116.57	114.55	113.54	113.03
11000	132.82	131.61	130.57	128.23	126.00	124.89	124.33
12000	144.89	143.57	142.43	139.88	137.45	136.25	135.64
13000	156.96	155.53	154.30	151.54	148.91	147.60	146.94
14000	169.04	167.50	166.17	163.20	160.36	158.95	158.24
15000	181.11	179.46	178.04	174.85	171.82	170.31	169.54
16000	193.18	191.42	189.91	186.51	183.27	181.66	180.85
17000	205.26	203.39	201.78	198.16	194.73	193.01	192.15
18000	217.33	215.35	213.65	209.82	206.18	204.37	203.45
19000	229.41	227.32	225.52	221.48	217.63	215.72	214.75
20000	241.48	239.28	237.39	233.13	229.09	227.07	226.06
21000	253.55	251.24	249.26	244.79	240.54	238.43	237.36
22000	265.63	263.21	261.13	256.45	252.00	249.78	248.66
23000	277.70	275.17	272.99	268.10	263.45	261.13	259.97
24000	289.77	287.13	284.86	279.76	274.90	272.49	271.27
25000	3C1.85	299.10	296.73	291.42	286.36	2B3.84	282.57
26000	313.92	311.06	308.60	303.07	297.81	295.19	293.87
27000	326.00	323.02	320.47	314.73	309.27	306.55	305.18
28000	338.07	334.99	332.34	326.39	320.72	317.90	316.48
29000	350.14	346.95	344.21	338.04	332.17	329.25	327.78
30000	362.22	358.92	356.08	349.70	343.63	340.61	339.08
31000	374.29	370.88	367.95	361.35	355.08	351.96	350.39
32000	386.36	382.84	379.82	373.01	366.54	363.31	361.69
33000	398.44	394.81	391.69	384.67	377.99	374.67	372.99
34000	410.51	406.77	403.55	396.32	389.45	386.02	384.29
35000	422.59	418.73	415.42	407.98	400.90	397.37	395.60
40000	482.95	478.55	474.77	466.26	458.07	454.64	452.11
45000	543.32	538.37	534.11	524.55	515.44	510.91	508.62
50000	603.69	598.19	593.46	582.83	572.71	567.68	565.14
55000	664.06	658.01	652.81	641.11	629.98	624.44	621.65
60000	724.43	717.83	712.15	699.39	687.25	681.21	678.16
65000	784.80	777.65	771.50	757.67	744.52	737.98	734.67
70000	845.17	837.46	830.84	815.96	801.79	794.74	791.19
75000	905.54	897.28	890.19	874.24	859.06	851.51	847.70
80000	965.90	957.10	949.53	932.52	916.33	908.28	904.21
100000	1207.38	1196.37	1186.92	1165.65	1145.42	1135.35	1130.27

MONTHLY PAYMENT
NECESSARY TO AMORTIZE A LOAN

TERM AMOUNT	1 YEAR	1½ YEARS	2 YEARS	2½ YEARS	3 YEARS	4 YEARS	5 YEARS
$ 25	2.25	1.55	1.20	.99	.86	.69	.58
50	4.49	3.09	2.40	1.98	1.71	1.37	1.16
75	6.73	4.64	3.60	2.97	2.56	2.05	1.74
100	8.97	6.18	4.79	3.96	3.41	2.73	2.32
200	17.94	12.36	9.58	7.92	6.82	5.45	4.63
300	26.91	18.54	14.37	11.89	10.22	8.17	6.95
400	35.87	24.72	19.16	15.84	13.63	10.89	9.26
500	44.84	30.90	23.95	19.79	17.03	13.61	11.57
600	53.81	37.08	28.74	23.75	20.44	16.33	13.89
700	62.77	43.26	33.53	27.71	23.84	19.05	16.20
800	71.74	49.44	38.32	31.67	27.25	21.77	18.52
900	80.71	55.62	43.11	35.63	30.66	24.49	20.83
1000	89.67	61.80	47.90	39.58	34.06	27.21	23.14
2000	179.34	123.60	95.79	79.16	68.12	54.41	46.28
3000	269.01	185.40	143.69	118.74	102.17	81.61	69.42
4000	358.68	247.20	191.58	158.32	136.23	108.81	92.56
5000	448.35	309.00	239.48	197.90	170.29	136.01	115.70
6000	538.02	370.79	287.37	237.48	204.34	163.21	138.84
7000	627.69	432.59	335.27	277.06	238.40	190.41	161.98
8000	717.36	494.39	383.16	316.64	272.46	217.61	185.12
9000	807.03	556.19	431.06	356.21	306.51	244.82	208.25
10000	896.70	617.99	478.95	395.79	340.57	272.02	231.39
11000	986.37	679.78	526.85	435.37	374.62	299.22	254.53
12000	1076.04	741.58	574.74	474.95	408.68	326.42	277.67
13000	1165.71	803.38	622.64	514.53	442.74	353.62	300.81
14000	1255.38	865.18	670.53	554.11	476.79	380.82	323.95
15000	1345.05	926.98	718.43	593.69	510.85	408.02	347.09
16000	1434.72	988.77	766.32	633.27	544.91	435.22	370.23
17000	1524.39	1050.57	814.22	672.85	578.96	462.43	393.37
18000	1614.06	1112.37	862.11	712.42	613.02	489.63	416.50
19000	1703.73	1174.17	910.01	752.00	647.08	516.83	439.64
20000	1793.40	1235.97	957.90	791.58	681.13	544.03	462.78
21000	1883.07	1297.76	1005.80	831.16	715.19	571.23	485.92
22000	1972.73	1359.56	1053.69	870.74	749.24	598.43	509.06
23000	2062.40	1421.36	1101.59	910.32	783.30	625.63	532.20
24000	2152.07	1483.16	1149.48	949.90	817.36	652.83	555.34
25000	2241.74	1544.96	1197.38	989.48	851.41	680.04	578.48
26000	2331.41	1606.76	1245.27	1029.05	885.47	707.24	601.61
27000	2421.08	1668.55	1293.17	1068.63	919.53	734.44	624.75
28000	2510.75	1730.35	1341.06	1108.21	953.58	761.64	647.89
29000	2600.42	1792.15	1388.96	1147.79	987.64	788.84	671.03
30000	2690.09	1853.95	1436.85	1187.37	1021.69	816.04	694.17
31000	2779.76	1915.75	1484.75	1226.95	1055.75	843.24	717.31
32000	2869.43	1977.54	1532.64	1266.53	1089.81	870.44	740.45
33000	2959.10	2039.34	1580.54	1306.11	1123.86	897.65	763.59
34000	3048.77	2101.14	1628.43	1345.69	1157.92	924.85	786.73
35000	3138.44	2162.94	1676.33	1385.26	1191.98	952.05	809.86
40000	3586.79	2471.93	1915.80	1583.16	1362.26	1088.05	925.56
45000	4035.13	2780.92	2155.27	1781.05	1532.54	1224.06	1041.25
50000	4483.48	3089.91	2394.75	1978.95	1702.82	1360.07	1156.95
55000	4931.83	3398.90	2634.22	2176.84	1873.10	1496.07	1272.64
60000	5380.18	3707.89	2873.70	2374.74	2043.38	1632.08	1388.34
65000	5828.52	4016.88	3113.17	2572.63	2213.67	1768.09	1504.03
70000	6276.87	4325.87	3352.65	2770.52	2383.95	1904.09	1619.72
75000	6725.22	4634.86	3592.12	2968.42	2554.23	2040.10	1735.42
80000	7173.57	4943.85	3831.59	3166.31	2724.51	2176.10	1851.11
100000	8966.96	6179.81	4789.49	3957.89	3405.64	2720.13	2313.89

114

TERM AMOUNT	6 YEARS	7 YEARS	8 YEARS	9 YEARS	10 YEARS	11 YEARS	12 YEARS
$ 25	.52	.47	.44	.41	.39	.37	.36
50	1.03	.94	.87	.81	.77	.74	.72
75	1.54	1.40	1.30	1.22	1.16	1.11	1.07
100	2.05	1.87	1.73	1.62	1.54	1.48	1.43
200	4.10	3.73	3.45	3.24	3.08	2.95	2.85
300	6.15	5.59	5.17	4.86	4.62	4.42	4.27
400	8.19	7.45	6.90	6.48	6.16	5.90	5.69
500	10.24	9.31	8.62	8.10	7.69	7.37	7.11
600	12.29	11.17	10.34	9.72	9.23	8.84	8.53
700	14.34	13.03	12.07	11.34	10.77	10.32	9.95
800	16.38	14.89	13.79	12.96	12.31	11.79	11.38
900	18.43	16.75	15.51	14.57	13.84	13.26	12.80
1000	20.48	18.61	17.23	16.19	15.38	14.74	14.22
2000	40.95	37.21	34.46	32.38	30.76	29.47	28.43
3000	61.42	55.81	51.69	48.57	46.14	44.20	42.65
4000	81.89	74.41	68.92	64.76	61.51	58.94	56.86
5000	102.37	93.02	86.15	80.94	76.89	73.67	71.07
6000	122.84	111.62	103.38	97.13	92.27	88.40	85.29
7000	143.31	130.22	120.61	113.32	107.64	103.14	99.50
8000	163.78	148.82	137.84	129.51	123.02	117.87	113.72
9000	184.25	167.42	155.07	145.69	138.40	132.60	127.93
10000	204.73	186.03	172.30	161.88	153.77	147.33	142.14
11000	225.20	204.63	189.53	178.07	169.15	162.07	156.36
12000	245.67	223.23	206.76	194.26	184.53	176.80	170.57
13000	266.14	241.83	223.99	210.44	199.90	191.53	184.78
14000	286.61	260.44	241.22	226.63	215.28	206.27	199.00
15000	307.09	279.04	258.45	242.82	230.66	221.00	213.21
16000	327.56	297.64	275.68	259.01	246.03	235.73	227.43
17000	348.03	316.24	292.91	275.20	261.41	250.46	241.64
18000	368.50	334.84	310.14	291.38	276.79	265.20	255.85
19000	388.98	353.45	327.37	307.57	292.16	279.93	270.07
20000	409.45	372.05	344.60	323.76	307.54	294.66	284.28
21000	429.92	390.65	361.83	339.95	322.92	309.40	298.50
22000	450.39	409.25	379.05	356.13	338.29	324.13	312.71
23000	470.86	427.86	396.28	372.32	353.67	338.86	326.92
24000	491.34	446.46	413.51	388.51	369.05	353.59	341.14
25000	511.81	465.06	430.74	404.70	384.42	368.33	355.35
26000	532.28	483.66	447.97	420.88	399.80	383.06	369.56
27000	552.75	502.26	465.20	437.07	415.18	397.79	383.78
28000	573.22	520.87	482.43	453.26	430.55	412.53	397.99
29000	593.70	539.47	499.66	469.45	445.93	427.26	412.21
30000	614.17	558.07	516.89	485.64	461.31	441.99	426.42
1000	634.64	576.67	534.12	501.82	476.68	456.72	440.63
○○○	655.11	595.27	551.35	518.01	492.06	471.46	454.85
○○○	675.58	613.88	568.58	534.20	507.44	486.19	469.06
○○○	696.06	632.48	585.81	550.39	522.81	500.92	483.28
○○○	716.53	651.08	603.04	566.57	538.19	515.66	497.49
○○○	818.89	744.09	689.19	647.51	615.07	589.32	568.56
	921.25	837.10	775.33	728.45	691.96	662.98	639.63
	1023.61	930.11	861.48	809.39	768.84	736.65	710.70
	1125.97	1023.12	947.63	890.33	845.72	810.31	781.77
	1228.33	1116.14	1033.78	971.27	922.61	883.98	852.83
○330.69	1209.15	1119.92	1052.20	999.49	957.64	923.90
7○33.05	1302.16	1206.07	1133.14	1076.37	1031.31	994.97
7○35.41	1395.17	1292.22	1214.08	1153.26	1104.97	1066.04
8○37.77	1488.18	1378.37	1295.02	1230.14	1178.64	1137.11
100○7.22	1860.22	1722.96	1618.77	1537.67	1473.29	1421.39

115

13¾%

MONTHLY PAYMENT
NECESSARY TO AMORTIZE A LOAN

TERM AMOUNT	13 YEARS	14 YEARS	15 YEARS	16 YEARS	17 YEARS	18 YEARS	19 YEARS
$ 25	.35	.34	.33	.33	.32	.32	.31
50	.69	.68	.66	.65	.64	.63	.62
75	1.04	1.01	.99	.97	.96	.94	.93
100	1.38	1.35	1.32	1.30	1.28	1.26	1.24
200	2.76	2.69	2.63	2.59	2.55	2.51	2.48
300	4.14	4.04	3.95	3.88	3.82	3.76	3.72
400	5.52	5.38	5.26	5.17	5.09	5.02	4.96
500	6.90	6.73	6.58	6.46	6.36	6.27	6.20
600	8.28	8.07	7.89	7.75	7.63	7.52	7.43
700	9.66	9.41	9.21	9.04	8.90	8.77	8.67
800	11.04	10.76	10.52	10.33	10.17	10.03	9.91
900	12.42	12.10	11.84	11.62	11.44	11.28	11.15
1000	13.80	13.45	13.15	12.91	12.71	12.53	12.39
2000	27.59	26.89	26.30	25.82	25.41	25.06	24.77
3000	41.38	40.33	39.45	38.72	38.11	37.59	37.15
4000	55.17	53.77	52.60	51.63	50.81	50.12	49.53
5000	68.96	67.21	65.75	64.54	63.51	62.64	61.91
6000	82.75	80.65	78.90	77.44	76.21	75.17	74.29
7000	96.54	94.09	92.05	90.35	88.91	87.70	86.67
8000	110.33	107.53	105.20	103.26	101.62	100.23	99.05
9000	124.12	120.97	118.35	116.16	114.32	112.75	111.43
10000	137.91	134.41	131.50	129.07	127.02	125.28	123.81
11000	151.70	147.85	144.65	141.98	139.72	137.81	136.19
12000	165.49	161.29	157.80	154.88	152.42	150.34	148.57
13000	179.28	174.73	170.95	167.79	165.12	162.86	160.95
14000	193.07	188.17	184.10	180.69	177.82	175.39	173.33
15000	206.86	201.61	197.25	193.60	190.52	187.92	185.71
16000	220.65	215.05	210.40	206.51	203.23	200.45	198.09
17000	234.44	228.49	223.55	219.41	215.93	212.97	210.47
18000	248.23	241.94	236.70	232.32	228.63	225.50	222.85
19000	262.02	255.38	249.85	245.23	241.33	238.03	235.23
20000	275.81	268.82	263.00	258.13	254.03	250.56	247.61
21000	289.60	282.26	276.15	271.04	266.73	263.09	259.99
22000	303.39	295.70	289.30	283.95	279.43	275.61	272.37
23000	317.18	309.14	302.45	296.85	292.13	288.14	284.75
24000	330.97	322.58	315.60	309.76	304.84	300.67	297.13
25000	344.76	336.02	328.75	322.67	317.54	313.20	309.51
26000	358.55	349.46	341.90	335.57	330.24	325.72	321.89
27000	372.34	362.90	355.05	348.48	342.94	338.25	334.27
28000	386.13	376.34	368.20	361.38	355.64	350.78	346.65
29000	399.92	389.78	381.35	374.29	368.34	363.31	359.03
30000	413.71	403.22	394.50	387.20	381.05	375.83	371.41
31000	427.50	416.66	407.65	400.10	393.75	388.36	383.79
32000	441.29	430.10	420.80	413.01	406.45	400.89	396.17
33000	455.08	443.54	433.95	425.92	419.15	413.42	408.55
34000	468.87	456.98	447.10	438.82	431.85	425.94	420.93
35000	482.66	470.42	460.25	451.73	444.55	438.47	433.31
40000	551.61	537.49	526.00	516.26	508.06	501.11	495.21
45000	620.56	604.83	591.75	580.79	571.56	563.75	557.11
50000	689.51	672.03	657.50	645.33	635.07	626.39	619.01
55000	758.46	739.24	723.25	709.86	698.58	689.03	680.91
60000	827.41	806.44	789.00	774.39	762.08	751.66	742.81
65000	896.36	873.64	854.75	838.92	825.59	814.30	804.71
70000	965.31	940.84	920.50	903.45	889.10	876.94	866.61
75000	1034.26	1008.05	986.25	967.99	952.60	939.58	928.51
80000	1103.21	1075.25	1051.99	1032.52	1016.11	1002.22	990.41
100000	1379.01	1344.06	1314.99	1290.65	1270.13	1252.77	1238.01

116

TERM AMOUNT	20 YEARS	21 YEARS	22 YEARS	25 YEARS	30 YEARS	35 YEARS	40 YEARS
$ 25	.31	.31	.31	.30	.30	.29	.29
50	.62	.61	.61	.60	.59	.58	.58
75	.92	.92	.91	.89	.88	.87	.87
100	1.23	1.22	1.21	1.19	1.17	1.16	1.16
200	2.46	2.43	2.42	2.37	2.34	2.32	2.31
300	3.68	3.65	3.62	3.56	3.50	3.47	3.46
400	4.91	4.86	4.83	4.74	4.67	4.63	4.61
500	6.13	6.08	6.03	5.93	5.83	5.78	5.76
600	7.36	7.29	7.24	7.11	7.00	6.94	6.91
700	8.58	8.51	8.44	8.30	8.16	8.09	8.06
800	9.81	9.72	9.65	9.48	9.33	9.25	9.21
900	11.03	10.94	10.85	1C.67	10.49	10.40	10.36
1000	12.26	12.15	12.06	11.85	11.66	11.56	11.51
2000	24.51	24.30	24.11	23.70	23.31	23.11	23.02
3000	36.77	36.44	36.17	35.54	34.96	34.67	34.53
4000	49.02	48.59	48.22	47.39	46.61	46.22	46.03
5000	61.28	60.74	60.27	59.24	58.26	57.78	57.54
6000	73.53	72.88	72.33	71.08	69.91	69.33	69.05
7000	85.78	85.03	84.38	82.93	81.56	80.89	80.55
8000	98.04	97.18	96.44	94.78	93.21	92.44	92.06
9000	110.29	109.32	108.49	106.62	104.87	104.00	103.57
10000	122.55	121.47	120.54	118.47	116.52	115.55	115.07
11000	134.80	133.61	132.60	130.32	128.17	127.11	126.58
12000	147.05	145.76	144.65	142.16	139.82	138.66	138.09
13000	159.31	157.91	156.70	154.01	151.47	150.22	149.59
14000	171.56	170.05	168.76	165.86	163.12	161.77	161.10
15000	183.82	182.20	180.81	177.70	174.77	173.33	172.61
16000	196.07	194.35	192.87	189.55	186.42	184.88	184.11
17000	208.32	206.49	204.92	201.40	198.07	196.44	195.62
18000	220.58	218.64	216.97	213.24	209.73	207.99	207.13
19000	232.83	230.78	229.03	225.09	221.38	219.55	218.64
20000	245.09	242.93	241.08	236.94	233.03	231.10	230.14
21000	257.34	255.08	253.13	248.78	244.68	242.66	241.65
22000	269.59	267.22	265.19	260.63	256.33	254.21	253.16
23000	281.85	279.37	277.24	272.48	267.98	265.77	264.66
24000	294.10	291.52	289.30	284.32	279.63	277.32	276.17
25000	306.36	303.66	301.35	296.17	291.28	288.88	287.68
26000	318.61	315.81	313.40	308.02	302.93	300.43	299.18
27000	330.86	327.95	325.46	319.86	314.59	311.99	310.69
28000	343.12	340.10	337.51	331.71	326.24	323.54	322.20
29000	355.37	352.25	349.57	343.56	337.89	335.10	333.70
30000	367.63	364.39	361.62	355.40	349.54	346.65	345.21
31000	379.88	376.54	373.67	367.25	361.19	358.21	356.72
32000	392.13	388.69	385.73	379.10	372.84	369.76	368.22
33000	404.39	400.83	397.78	39C.94	384.49	381.32	379.73
34000	416.64	412.98	409.83	402.79	396.14	392.87	391.24
35000	428.90	425.12	421.89	414.64	407.79	404.42	402.74
40000	490.17	485.86	482.16	473.87	466.05	462.20	460.28
45000	551.44	546.59	542.43	533.1C	524.31	519.97	517.81
50000	612.71	607.32	602.69	592.34	582.56	577.75	575.35
55000	673.98	668.05	662.96	651.57	640.82	635.52	632.88
60000	735.25	728.78	723.23	71C.80	699.07	693.30	690.42
65000	796.52	789.51	783.50	770.04	757.33	751.07	747.95
70000	857.79	850.24	843.77	829.27	815.58	808.84	805.48
75000	919.06	910.98	904.04	888.50	873.84	866.62	863.02
80000	980.33	971.71	964.31	947.74	932.1C	924.39	920.55
100000	1225.41	1214.63	1205.38	1184.67	1165.12	1155.49	1150.69

MONTHLY PAYMENT
NECESSARY TO AMORTIZE A LOAN

TERM AMOUNT	1 YEAR	1½ YEARS	2 YEARS	2½ YEARS	3 YEARS	4 YEARS	5 YEARS
$ 25	2.25	1.55	1.21	1.00	.86	.69	.59
50	4.49	3.10	2.41	1.99	1.71	1.37	1.17
75	6.74	4.65	3.61	2.98	2.57	2.05	1.75
100	8.98	6.20	4.81	3.97	3.42	2.74	2.33
200	17.96	12.39	9.61	7.94	6.84	5.47	4.66
300	26.94	18.58	14.41	11.91	10.26	8.20	6.99
400	35.92	24.77	19.21	15.88	13.68	10.94	9.31
500	44.90	30.96	24.01	19.85	17.09	13.67	11.64
600	53.88	37.15	28.81	23.82	20.51	16.40	13.97
700	62.86	43.35	33.61	27.79	23.93	19.13	16.29
800	71.83	49.54	38.42	31.76	27.35	21.87	18.62
900	80.81	55.73	43.22	35.73	30.76	24.60	20.95
1000	89.79	61.92	48.02	39.70	34.18	27.33	23.27
2000	179.58	123.84	96.03	79.40	68.36	54.66	46.54
3000	269.37	185.75	144.04	119.10	102.54	81.98	69.81
4000	359.15	247.67	192.06	158.80	136.72	109.31	93.08
5000	448.94	309.58	240.07	198.50	170.89	136.64	116.35
6000	538.73	371.50	288.08	238.20	205.07	163.96	139.61
7000	628.51	433.41	336.10	277.89	239.25	191.29	162.88
8000	718.30	495.33	384.11	317.59	273.43	218.62	186.15
9000	808.09	557.24	432.12	357.29	307.60	245.94	209.42
10000	897.88	619.16	480.13	396.99	341.78	273.27	232.69
11000	987.66	681.07	528.15	436.69	375.96	300.60	255.96
12000	1077.45	742.99	576.16	476.39	410.14	327.92	279.22
13000	1167.24	804.90	624.17	516.08	444.31	355.25	302.49
14000	1257.02	866.82	672.19	555.78	478.49	382.58	325.76
15000	1346.81	928.73	720.20	595.48	512.67	409.90	349.03
16000	1436.60	990.65	768.21	635.18	546.85	437.23	372.30
17000	1526.39	1052.56	816.22	674.88	581.02	464.56	395.57
18000	1616.17	1114.48	864.24	714.58	615.20	491.88	418.83
19000	1705.96	1176.39	912.25	754.27	649.38	519.21	442.10
20000	1795.75	1238.31	960.26	793.97	683.56	546.53	465.37
21000	1885.53	1300.22	1008.28	833.67	717.74	573.86	488.64
22000	1975.32	1362.14	1056.29	873.37	751.91	601.19	511.91
23000	2065.11	1424.05	1104.30	913.07	786.09	628.51	535.17
24000	2154.90	1485.97	1152.31	952.77	820.27	655.84	558.44
25000	2244.68	1547.88	1200.33	992.46	854.45	683.17	581.71
26000	2334.47	1609.80	1248.34	1032.16	888.62	710.49	604.98
27000	2424.26	1671.71	1296.35	1071.86	922.80	737.82	628.25
28000	2514.04	1733.63	1344.37	1111.56	956.98	765.15	651.52
29000	2603.83	1795.55	1392.38	1151.26	991.16	792.47	674.78
30000	2693.62	1857.46	1440.39	1190.96	1025.33	819.80	698.05
31000	2783.41	1919.38	1488.40	1230.65	1059.51	847.13	721.32
32000	2873.19	1981.29	1536.42	1270.35	1093.69	874.45	744.59
33000	2962.98	2043.21	1584.43	1310.05	1127.87	901.78	767.86
34000	3052.77	2105.12	1632.44	1349.75	1162.04	929.11	791.13
35000	3142.55	2167.04	1680.46	1389.45	1196.22	956.43	814.39
40000	3591.49	2476.61	1920.52	1587.94	1367.11	1093.06	930.74
45000	4040.43	2786.19	2160.58	1786.43	1538.00	1229.70	1047.08
50000	4489.36	3095.76	2400.65	1984.92	1708.89	1366.33	1163.42
55000	4938.30	3405.34	2640.71	2183.41	1879.77	1502.96	1279.76
60000	5387.23	3714.92	2880.78	2381.91	2050.66	1639.59	1396.10
65000	5836.17	4024.49	3120.84	2580.40	2221.55	1776.23	1512.44
70000	6285.10	4334.07	3360.91	2778.89	2392.44	1912.86	1628.78
75000	6734.04	4643.64	3600.97	2977.38	2563.33	2049.49	1745.12
80000	7182.97	4953.22	3841.04	3175.87	2734.22	2186.12	1861.47
100000	8978.72	6191.52	4801.29	3969.84	3417.77	2732.65	2326.83

TERM AMOUNT	6 YEARS	7 YEARS	8 YEARS	9 YEARS	10 YEARS	11 YEARS	12 YEARS
$ 25	.52	.47	.44	.41	.39	.38	.36
50	1.04	.94	.87	.82	.78	.75	.72
75	1.55	1.41	1.31	1.23	1.17	1.12	1.08
100	2.07	1.88	1.74	1.64	1.56	1.49	1.44
200	4.13	3.75	3.48	3.27	3.11	2.98	2.88
300	6.19	5.63	5.22	4.91	4.66	4.47	4.32
400	8.25	7.50	6.95	6.54	6.22	5.96	5.75
500	10.31	9.38	8.69	8.17	7.77	7.45	7.19
600	12.37	11.25	10.43	9.81	9.32	8.94	8.63
700	14.43	13.12	12.17	11.44	10.87	10.43	10.06
800	16.49	15.00	13.90	13.07	12.43	11.91	11.50
900	18.55	16.87	15.64	14.71	13.98	13.40	12.94
1000	20.61	18.75	17.38	16.34	15.53	14.89	14.38
2000	41.22	37.49	34.75	32.67	31.06	29.78	28.75
3000	61.82	56.23	52.12	49.01	46.58	44.66	43.12
4000	82.43	74.97	69.49	65.34	62.11	59.55	57.49
5000	103.03	93.71	86.86	81.67	77.64	74.44	71.86
6000	123.64	112.45	104.23	98.01	93.16	89.32	86.23
7000	144.25	131.19	121.61	114.34	108.69	104.21	100.60
8000	164.85	149.93	138.98	130.67	124.22	119.10	114.98
9000	185.46	168.67	156.35	147.01	139.74	133.98	129.35
10000	206.06	187.41	173.72	163.34	155.27	148.87	143.72
11000	226.67	206.15	191.09	179.68	170.80	163.76	158.09
12000	247.27	224.89	208.46	196.01	186.32	178.64	172.46
13000	267.88	243.63	225.83	212.34	201.85	193.53	186.83
14000	288.49	262.37	243.21	228.68	217.38	208.42	201.20
15000	309.09	281.11	260.58	245.01	232.90	223.30	215.57
16000	329.70	299.85	277.95	261.34	248.45	238.19	229.95
17000	350.30	318.59	295.32	277.68	263.96	253.08	244.32
18000	370.91	337.33	312.69	294.01	279.48	267.96	258.69
19000	391.51	356.07	330.06	310.35	295.01	282.85	273.06
20000	412.12	374.81	347.44	326.68	310.54	297.74	287.43
21000	432.73	393.55	364.81	343.01	326.06	312.62	301.80
22000	453.33	412.29	382.18	359.35	341.59	327.51	316.17
23000	473.94	431.03	399.55	375.68	357.12	342.40	330.54
24000	494.54	449.77	416.92	392.01	372.64	357.28	344.92
25000	515.15	468.51	434.29	408.35	388.17	372.17	359.29
26000	535.75	487.25	451.66	424.68	403.70	387.06	373.66
27000	556.36	505.99	469.04	441.01	419.22	401.94	388.03
28000	576.97	524.73	486.41	457.35	434.75	416.83	402.40
29000	597.57	543.47	503.78	473.68	450.28	431.72	416.77
30000	618.18	562.21	521.15	490.02	465.80	446.60	431.14
31000	638.78	580.95	538.52	506.35	481.33	461.49	445.51
32000	659.39	599.69	555.89	522.68	496.86	476.38	459.89
33000	679.99	618.43	573.26	539.02	512.38	491.26	474.26
34000	700.60	637.17	590.64	555.35	527.91	506.15	488.63
35000	721.21	655.91	608.01	571.68	543.44	521.04	503.00
40000	824.23	749.61	694.87	653.35	621.05	595.47	574.86
45000	927.26	843.31	781.72	735.02	698.70	669.90	646.71
50000	1030.29	937.01	868.58	816.69	776.34	744.34	718.57
55000	1133.32	1030.71	955.44	898.36	853.97	818.77	790.42
60000	1236.35	1124.41	1042.30	980.03	931.60	893.20	862.28
65000	1339.38	1218.11	1129.15	1061.70	1009.24	967.64	934.14
70000	1442.41	1311.81	1216.01	1143.36	1086.87	1042.07	1005.99
75000	1545.44	1405.51	1302.87	1225.03	1164.50	1116.50	1077.85
80000	1648.46	1499.21	1389.73	1306.70	1242.14	1190.94	1149.71
100000	2060.58	1874.01	1737.16	1633.38	1552.67	1488.67	1437.13

MONTHLY PAYMENT
NECESSARY TO AMORTIZE A LOAN

TERM AMOUNT	13 YEARS	14 YEARS	15 YEARS	16 YEARS	17 YEARS	18 YEARS	19 YEARS
$ 25	.35	.35	.34	.33	.33	.32	.32
50	.70	.69	.67	.66	.65	.64	.63
75	1.05	1.03	1.00	.99	.97	.96	.95
100	1.40	1.37	1.34	1.31	1.29	1.28	1.26
200	2.80	2.73	2.67	2.62	2.58	2.55	2.52
300	4.19	4.09	4.00	3.93	3.87	3.82	3.77
400	5.59	5.45	5.33	5.24	5.15	5.09	5.03
500	6.98	6.81	6.66	6.54	6.44	6.36	6.28
600	8.38	8.17	8.00	7.85	7.73	7.63	7.54
700	9.77	9.53	9.33	9.16	9.02	8.90	8.80
800	11.17	10.89	10.66	1C.47	10.30	10.17	10.05
900	12.56	12.25	11.99	11.77	11.59	11.44	11.31
1000	13.96	13.61	13.32	13.08	12.88	12.71	12.56
2000	27.91	27.21	26.64	26.16	25.75	25.41	25.12
3000	41.86	40.82	39.96	39.24	38.63	38.12	37.68
4000	55.81	54.42	53.27	52.31	51.50	50.82	50.24
5000	69.76	68.03	66.59	65.39	64.38	63.52	62.80
6000	83.71	81.63	79.91	78.47	77.25	76.23	75.36
7000	97.66	95.24	93.23	91.54	90.13	88.93	87.92
8000	111.61	108.84	106.54	104.62	103.00	101.64	100.48
9000	125.56	122.45	119.86	117.70	115.88	114.34	113.03
10000	139.52	136.05	133.18	130.77	128.75	127.04	125.59
11000	153.47	149.66	146.50	143.85	141.63	139.75	138.15
12000	167.42	163.26	159.81	156.93	154.50	152.45	150.71
13000	181.37	176.87	173.13	170.C1	167.38	165.15	163.27
14000	195.32	190.47	186.45	183.08	180.25	177.86	175.83
15000	209.27	204.08	199.77	196.16	193.13	190.56	188.39
16000	223.22	217.68	213.08	209.24	206.00	203.27	200.95
17000	237.17	231.29	226.40	222.31	218.88	215.97	213.50
18000	251.12	244.89	239.72	235.39	231.75	228.67	226.06
19000	265.07	258.50	253.04	248.47	244.63	241.38	238.62
20000	279.03	272.10	266.35	261.54	257.50	254.08	251.18
21000	292.98	285.71	279.67	274.62	270.38	266.79	263.74
22000	306.93	299.31	292.99	287.70	283.25	279.49	276.30
23000	320.88	312.92	306.31	30C.78	296.12	292.19	288.86
24000	334.83	326.52	319.62	313.85	309.00	304.90	301.42
25000	348.78	340.13	332.94	326.93	321.87	317.60	313.97
26000	362.73	353.73	346.26	34C.01	334.75	330.30	326.53
27000	376.68	367.34	359.58	353.08	347.62	343.01	339.09
28000	390.63	380.94	372.89	366.16	360.50	355.71	351.65
29000	404.58	394.55	386.21	379.24	373.37	368.42	364.21
30000	418.54	408.15	399.53	392.31	386.25	381.12	376.77
31000	432.49	421.76	412.84	405.39	399.12	393.82	389.33
32000	446.44	435.36	426.16	418.47	412.00	406.53	401.89
33000	460.39	448.97	439.48	431.55	424.87	419.23	414.44
34000	474.34	462.57	452.80	444.62	437.75	431.94	427.00
35000	488.29	476.18	466.11	457.70	450.62	444.64	439.56
40000	558.05	544.20	532.70	523.08	515.00	508.16	502.36
45000	627.80	612.23	599.29	588.47	579.37	571.68	565.15
50000	697.56	680.25	665.88	653.85	643.74	635.20	627.94
55000	767.31	748.27	732.46	719.24	708.12	698.72	690.74
60000	837.07	816.30	799.05	784.62	772.49	762.23	753.53
65000	906.82	884.32	865.64	850.01	836.86	825.75	816.32
70000	976.58	952.35	932.22	915.39	901.24	889.27	879.12
75000	1046.33	1020.37	998.81	980.78	965.61	952.79	941.91
80000	1116.09	1088.40	1065.40	1046.16	1029.99	1016.31	1004.71
100000	1395.11	1360.49	1331.75	1307.70	1287.48	1270.39	1255.88

TERM AMOUNT	20 YEARS	21 YEARS	22 YEARS	25 YEARS	30 YEARS	35 YEARS	40 YEARS
$ 25	.32	.31	.31	.31	.30	.30	.30
50	.63	.62	.62	.61	.60	.59	.59
75	.94	.93	.92	.91	.89	.89	.88
100	1.25	1.24	1.23	1.21	1.19	1.18	1.18
200	2.49	2.47	2.45	2.41	2.37	2.36	2.35
300	3.74	3.70	3.68	3.62	3.56	3.53	3.52
400	4.98	4.94	4.90	4.82	4.74	4.71	4.69
500	6.22	6.17	6.12	6.02	5.93	5.88	5.86
600	7.47	7.40	7.35	7.23	7.11	7.06	7.03
700	8.71	8.64	8.57	8.43	8.30	8.23	8.20
800	9.95	9.87	9.80	9.64	9.48	9.41	9.37
900	11.20	11.10	11.02	1C.84	1C.67	10.59	10.55
1000	12.44	12.33	12.24	12.04	11.85	11.76	11.72
2000	24.88	24.66	24.48	24.08	23.70	23.52	23.43
3000	37.31	36.99	36.72	36.13	35.55	35.28	35.14
4000	49.75	49.32	48.96	48.16	47.40	47.03	46.85
5000	62.18	61.65	61.20	6C.19	59.25	58.79	58.56
6000	74.62	73.98	73.44	72.23	71.10	70.55	70.27
7000	87.05	86.31	85.68	84.27	82.95	82.30	81.98
8000	99.49	98.64	97.92	96.31	94.79	94.06	93.70
9000	111.92	110.97	110.16	108.34	106.64	105.82	105.41
10000	124.36	123.30	122.40	12C.38	118.49	117.57	117.12
11000	136.79	135.63	134.64	132.42	130.34	129.33	128.83
12000	149.23	147.96	146.88	144.46	142.19	141.09	140.54
13000	161.66	160.29	159.12	156.49	154.04	152.84	152.25
14000	174.10	172.62	171.36	168.53	165.89	164.60	163.96
15000	186.53	184.95	183.59	180.57	177.74	176.36	175.68
16000	198.97	197.28	195.83	192.61	189.58	188.11	187.39
17000	211.40	209.61	208.07	204.64	201.43	199.87	199.10
18000	223.84	221.94	220.31	216.68	213.28	211.63	210.81
19000	236.27	234.27	232.55	228.72	225.13	223.38	222.52
20000	248.71	246.60	244.79	24C.76	236.98	235.14	234.23
21000	261.14	258.93	257.03	252.79	248.83	246.90	245.94
22000	273.58	271.26	269.27	264.83	260.68	258.65	257.66
23000	286.01	233.59	281.51	276.87	272.53	270.41	269.37
24000	298.45	295.92	293.75	288.91	284.37	282.17	281.08
25000	310.89	308.25	305.99	300.95	296.22	293.92	292.79
26000	323.32	320.58	318.23	312.98	308.07	305.68	304.50
27000	335.76	332.91	330.47	325.02	319.92	317.44	316.21
28000	348.19	345.24	342.71	337.06	331.77	329.19	327.92
29000	360.63	357.57	354.94	349.10	343.62	340.95	339.64
30000	373.06	369.90	367.18	361.13	355.47	352.71	351.35
31000	385.50	382.22	379.42	373.17	367.32	364.46	363.06
32000	397.93	394.55	391.66	385.21	379.16	376.22	374.77
33000	410.37	406.88	403.90	397.25	391.01	387.98	386.48
34000	422.80	419.21	416.14	409.28	402.86	399.73	398.19
35000	435.24	431.54	428.38	421.32	414.71	411.49	409.90
40000	497.41	493.19	489.58	481.51	473.95	470.27	468.46
45000	559.59	554.84	550.77	541.70	533.20	529.06	527.02
50000	621.77	616.49	611.97	601.89	592.44	587.84	585.58
55000	683.94	678.14	673.17	662.07	651.68	646.63	644.13
60000	746.12	739.79	734.36	722.26	710.93	705.41	702.69
65000	808.29	801.43	795.56	782.45	770.17	764.19	761.25
70000	870.47	863.08	856.76	842.64	829.42	822.98	819.80
75000	932.65	924.73	917.95	902.83	888.66	881.76	878.36
80000	994.82	986.38	979.15	963.C1	947.90	940.54	936.92
100000	1243.53	1232.97	1223.93	1203.77	1184.88	1175.68	1171.15

14¼%

MONTHLY PAYMENT
NECESSARY TO AMORTIZE A LOAN

TERM AMOUNT	1 YEAR	1½ YEARS	2 YEARS	2½ YEARS	3 YEARS	4 YEARS	5 YEARS
$ 25	2.25	1.56	1.21	1.00	.86	.69	.59
50	4.50	3.11	2.41	2.00	1.72	1.38	1.17
75	6.75	4.66	3.61	2.99	2.58	2.06	1.76
100	9.00	6.21	4.82	3.99	3.43	2.75	2.34
200	17.99	12.41	9.63	7.97	6.86	5.50	4.68
300	26.98	18.61	14.44	11.95	10.29	8.24	7.02
400	35.97	24.82	19.26	15.93	13.72	10.99	9.36
500	44.96	31.02	24.07	19.91	17.15	13.73	11.70
600	53.95	37.22	28.88	23.90	20.58	16.48	14.04
700	62.94	43.43	33.70	27.88	24.01	19.22	16.38
800	71.93	49.63	38.51	31.86	27.44	21.97	18.72
900	80.92	55.83	43.32	35.84	30.87	24.71	21.06
1000	89.91	62.04	48.14	39.82	34.30	27.46	23.40
2000	179.81	124.07	96.27	79.64	68.60	54.91	46.80
3000	269.72	186.10	144.40	119.46	102.90	82.36	70.20
4000	359.62	248.13	192.53	159.28	137.20	109.81	93.60
5000	449.53	310.17	240.66	199.10	171.50	137.27	117.00
6000	539.43	372.20	288.79	238.91	205.80	164.72	140.39
7000	629.34	434.23	336.92	278.73	240.10	192.17	163.79
8000	719.24	496.26	385.05	318.55	274.40	219.62	187.19
9000	809.15	558.30	433.18	358.37	308.70	247.07	210.59
10000	899.05	620.33	481.32	398.19	343.00	274.53	233.99
11000	988.96	682.36	529.45	438.00	377.30	301.98	257.38
12000	1078.86	744.39	577.58	477.82	411.60	329.43	280.78
13000	1168.77	806.43	625.71	517.64	445.89	356.88	304.18
14000	1258.67	868.46	673.84	557.46	480.19	384.33	327.58
15000	1348.58	930.49	721.97	597.28	514.49	411.79	350.98
16000	1438.48	992.52	770.10	637.10	548.79	439.24	374.37
17000	1528.39	1054.56	818.23	676.91	583.09	466.69	397.77
18000	1618.29	1116.59	866.36	716.73	617.39	494.14	421.17
19000	1708.20	1178.62	914.50	756.55	651.69	521.59	444.57
20000	1798.10	1240.65	962.63	796.37	685.99	549.05	467.97
21000	1888.01	1302.69	1010.76	836.18	720.29	576.50	491.36
22000	1977.91	1364.72	1058.89	876.00	754.59	603.95	514.76
23000	2067.82	1426.75	1107.02	915.82	788.89	631.40	538.16
24000	2157.72	1488.78	1155.15	955.64	823.19	658.85	561.56
25000	2247.62	1550.81	1203.28	995.46	857.48	686.31	584.96
26000	2337.53	1612.85	1251.41	1035.28	891.78	713.76	608.35
27000	2427.43	1674.88	1299.54	1075.09	926.08	741.21	631.75
28000	2517.34	1736.91	1347.67	1114.91	960.38	768.66	655.15
29000	2607.24	1798.94	1395.81	1154.73	994.68	796.11	678.55
30000	2697.15	1860.98	1443.94	1194.55	1028.98	823.57	701.95
31000	2787.05	1923.01	1492.07	1234.37	1063.28	851.02	725.34
32000	2876.96	1985.04	1540.20	1274.18	1097.58	878.47	748.74
33000	2966.86	2047.07	1588.33	1314.00	1131.88	905.92	772.14
34000	3056.77	2109.11	1636.46	1353.82	1166.18	933.37	795.54
35000	3146.67	2171.14	1684.59	1393.64	1200.48	960.83	818.94
40000	3596.02	2481.30	1925.25	1592.73	1371.97	1098.09	935.93
45000	4045.72	2791.46	2165.90	1791.82	1543.47	1235.35	1052.92
50000	4495.24	3101.62	2406.56	1990.91	1714.96	1372.61	1169.91
55000	4944.77	3411.79	2647.21	2190.00	1886.46	1509.87	1286.90
60000	5394.29	3721.95	2887.87	2389.09	2057.96	1647.13	1403.89
65000	5843.82	4032.11	3128.52	2588.18	2229.45	1784.39	1520.88
70000	6293.34	4342.27	3369.18	2787.27	2400.95	1921.65	1637.87
75000	6742.86	4652.43	3609.84	2986.36	2572.44	2058.91	1754.86
80000	7192.39	4962.60	3850.49	3185.45	2743.94	2196.17	1871.85
100000	8990.48	6203.24	4813.11	3981.81	3429.92	2745.21	2339.81

TERM AMOUNT	6 YEARS	7 YEARS	8 YEARS	9 YEARS	10 YEARS	11 YEARS	12 YEARS
$ 25	.52	.48	.44	.42	.40	.38	.37
50	1.04	.95	.88	.83	.79	.76	.73
75	1.56	1.42	1.32	1.24	1.18	1.13	1.09
100	2.08	1.89	1.76	1.65	1.57	1.51	1.46
200	4.15	3.78	3.51	3.30	3.14	3.01	2.91
300	6.23	5.67	5.26	4.95	4.71	4.52	4.36
400	8.30	7.56	7.01	6.60	6.28	6.02	5.82
500	10.37	9.44	8.76	8.25	7.84	7.53	7.27
600	12.45	11.33	10.51	9.89	9.41	9.03	8.72
700	14.52	13.22	12.26	11.54	10.98	10.53	10.18
800	16.60	15.11	14.02	13.19	12.55	12.04	11.63
900	18.67	17.00	15.77	14.84	14.11	13.54	13.08
1000	20.74	18.88	17.52	16.49	15.68	15.05	14.53
2000	41.48	37.76	35.03	32.97	31.36	30.09	29.06
3000	62.22	56.64	52.55	49.45	47.04	45.13	43.59
4000	82.96	75.52	70.06	65.93	62.71	60.17	58.12
5000	103.70	94.40	87.58	82.41	78.39	75.21	72.65
6000	124.44	113.28	105.09	98.89	94.07	90.25	87.18
7000	145.18	132.15	122.60	115.37	109.75	105.29	101.71
8000	165.92	151.03	140.12	131.85	125.42	120.33	116.24
9000	186.66	169.91	157.63	148.33	141.10	135.38	130.77
10000	207.40	188.79	175.15	164.81	156.78	150.42	145.30
11000	228.14	207.67	192.66	181.29	172.46	165.46	159.83
12000	248.88	226.55	210.17	197.77	188.13	180.50	174.36
13000	269.62	245.42	227.69	214.25	203.81	195.54	188.89
14000	290.36	264.30	245.20	230.73	219.49	210.58	203.42
15000	311.10	283.18	262.72	247.21	235.16	225.62	217.95
16000	331.84	302.06	280.23	263.69	250.84	240.66	232.48
17000	352.58	320.94	297.74	280.17	266.52	255.71	247.01
18000	373.32	339.82	315.26	296.65	282.20	270.75	261.54
19000	394.06	358.69	332.77	313.13	297.87	285.79	276.07
20000	414.80	377.57	350.29	329.61	313.55	300.83	290.59
21000	435.54	396.45	367.80	346.09	329.23	315.87	305.12
22000	456.28	415.33	385.31	362.57	344.91	330.91	319.65
23000	477.02	434.21	402.83	375.05	360.58	345.95	334.18
24000	497.76	453.09	420.34	395.53	376.26	360.99	348.71
25000	518.50	471.96	437.86	412.01	391.94	376.03	363.24
26000	539.24	490.84	455.37	428.49	407.62	391.08	377.77
27000	559.98	509.72	472.89	444.98	423.29	406.12	392.30
28000	580.72	528.60	490.40	461.46	438.97	421.16	406.83
29000	601.46	547.48	507.91	477.94	454.65	436.20	421.36
30000	622.20	566.36	525.43	494.42	470.32	451.24	435.89
31000	642.94	585.24	542.94	510.90	486.00	466.28	450.42
32000	663.68	604.11	560.46	527.38	501.68	481.32	464.95
33000	684.42	622.99	577.97	543.86	517.36	496.36	479.48
34000	705.16	641.87	595.48	560.34	533.03	511.41	494.01
35000	725.90	660.75	613.00	576.82	548.71	526.45	508.54
40000	829.60	755.14	700.57	659.22	627.10	601.65	581.18
45000	933.30	849.53	788.14	741.62	705.48	676.86	653.83
50000	1037.00	943.92	875.71	824.02	783.87	752.06	726.48
55000	1140.70	1038.32	963.28	906.43	862.26	827.27	799.13
60000	1244.40	1132.71	1050.85	988.83	940.64	902.48	871.77
65000	1348.09	1227.10	1138.42	1071.23	1019.03	977.68	944.42
70000	1451.79	1321.49	1225.99	1153.63	1097.42	1052.89	1017.07
75000	1555.49	1415.88	1313.56	1236.03	1175.80	1128.09	1089.72
80000	1659.19	1510.28	1401.13	1318.44	1254.19	1203.30	1162.36
100000	2073.99	1887.84	1751.41	1648.04	1567.74	1504.12	1452.95

TERM AMOUNT	13 YEARS	14 YEARS	15 YEARS	16 YEARS	17 YEARS	18 YEARS	19 YEARS
$ 25	.36	.35	.34	.34	.33	.33	.32
50	.71	.69	.68	.67	.66	.65	.64
75	1.06	1.04	1.02	1.00	.98	.97	.96
100	1.42	1.38	1.35	1.33	1.31	1.29	1.28
200	2.83	2.76	2.70	2.65	2.61	2.58	2.55
300	4.24	4.14	4.05	3.98	3.92	3.87	3.83
400	5.65	5.51	5.40	5.30	5.22	5.16	5.10
500	7.06	6.89	6.75	6.63	6.53	6.45	6.37
600	8.47	8.27	8.10	7.95	7.83	7.73	7.65
700	9.88	9.64	9.45	9.28	9.14	9.02	8.92
800	11.30	11.02	10.79	1C.60	10.44	10.31	10.20
900	12.71	12.40	12.14	11.93	11.75	11.60	11.47
1000	14.12	13.78	13.49	13.25	13.05	12.89	12.74
2000	28.23	27.55	26.98	26.50	26.10	25.77	25.48
3000	42.34	41.32	40.46	39.75	39.15	38.65	38.22
4000	56.46	55.09	53.95	53.00	52.20	51.53	50.96
5000	70.57	68.86	67.43	66.25	65.25	64.41	63.70
6000	84.68	82.63	80.92	79.50	78.30	77.29	76.44
7000	98.79	96.40	94.41	92.74	91.35	90.17	89.19
8000	112.91	110.17	107.89	105.99	104.40	103.05	101.91
9000	127.02	123.94	121.38	119.24	117.45	115.93	114.65
10000	141.13	137.71	134.86	132.49	130.50	128.81	127.39
11000	155.25	151.48	148.35	145.74	143.54	141.69	140.13
12000	169.36	165.25	161.83	158.99	156.59	154.58	152.87
13000	183.47	179.02	175.32	172.23	169.64	167.46	165.60
14000	197.58	192.79	188.81	185.48	182.69	180.34	178.34
15000	211.70	206.56	202.29	198.73	195.74	193.22	191.08
16000	225.81	220.33	215.78	211.98	208.79	206.10	203.82
17000	239.92	234.10	229.26	225.23	221.84	218.98	216.56
18000	254.04	247.87	242.75	238.48	234.89	231.86	229.30
19000	268.15	261.64	256.24	251.73	247.94	244.74	242.03
20000	282.26	275.41	269.72	264.97	260.99	257.62	254.77
21000	296.37	289.18	283.21	278.22	274.04	270.50	267.51
22000	310.49	302.95	296.69	291.47	287.08	283.38	280.25
23000	324.60	316.72	310.18	304.72	300.13	296.27	292.99
24000	338.71	330.49	323.66	317.97	313.18	309.15	305.73
25000	352.83	344.26	337.15	331.22	326.23	322.03	318.46
26000	366.94	358.03	350.64	344.46	339.28	334.91	331.20
27000	381.05	371.80	364.12	357.71	352.33	347.79	343.94
28000	395.16	385.57	377.61	37C.96	365.38	360.67	356.68
29000	409.28	399.34	391.09	384.21	378.43	373.55	369.42
30000	423.39	413.11	404.58	397.46	391.48	386.43	382.16
31000	437.50	426.88	418.06	41C.71	404.53	399.31	394.89
32000	451.61	440.65	431.55	423.95	417.58	412.19	407.63
33000	465.73	454.42	445.04	437.20	430.62	425.07	420.37
34000	479.84	468.19	458.52	45C.45	443.67	437.95	433.11
35000	493.95	481.96	472.01	463.70	456.72	450.84	445.85
40000	564.52	550.81	539.44	529.94	521.97	515.24	509.54
45000	635.08	619.66	606.87	596.18	587.21	579.64	573.23
50000	705.65	688.51	674.29	662.43	652.46	644.05	636.92
55000	776.21	757.36	741.72	728.67	717.70	708.45	700.61
60000	846.77	826.21	809.15	794.91	782.95	772.86	764.31
65000	917.34	895.06	876.58	861.15	848.20	837.26	828.00
70000	987.90	963.91	944.01	927.39	913.44	901.67	891.69
75000	1058.47	1032.76	1011.44	993.64	978.69	966.07	955.38
80000	1129.03	1101.61	1078.87	1059.88	1043.93	1030.47	1019.07
100000	1411.29	1377.01	1348.58	1324.85	1304.91	1288.09	1273.84

MONTHLY PAYMENT
NECESSARY TO AMORTIZE A LOAN
14¼%

TERM AMOUNT	20 YEARS	21 YEARS	22 YEARS	25 YEARS	30 YEARS	35 YEARS	40 YEARS
$ 25	.32	.32	.32	.31	.31	.30	.30
50	.64	.63	.63	.62	.61	.60	.60
75	.95	.94	.94	.92	.91	.90	.90
100	1.27	1.26	1.25	1.23	1.21	1.20	1.20
200	2.53	2.51	2.49	2.45	2.41	2.40	2.39
300	3.79	3.76	3.73	3.67	3.62	3.59	3.58
400	5.05	5.01	4.98	4.90	4.82	4.79	4.77
500	6.31	6.26	6.22	6.12	6.03	5.98	5.96
600	7.58	7.51	7.46	7.34	7.23	7.18	7.15
700	8.84	8.76	8.70	8.57	8.44	8.38	8.35
800	10.10	10.02	9.95	9.79	9.64	9.57	9.54
900	11.36	11.27	11.19	11.01	10.85	10.77	10.73
1000	12.62	12.52	12.43	12.23	12.05	11.96	11.92
2000	25.24	25.03	24.86	24.46	24.10	23.92	23.84
3000	37.86	37.55	37.28	36.69	36.15	35.88	35.75
4000	50.47	50.06	49.71	48.91	48.19	47.84	47.67
5000	63.09	62.57	62.13	61.15	60.24	59.80	59.59
6000	75.71	75.09	74.56	73.38	72.29	71.76	71.50
7000	88.33	87.60	86.98	85.61	84.33	83.72	83.42
8000	100.94	100.12	99.41	97.84	96.38	95.68	95.33
9000	113.56	112.63	111.84	110.07	108.43	107.64	107.25
10000	126.18	125.14	124.26	122.30	120.47	119.60	119.17
11000	138.79	137.66	136.69	134.53	132.52	131.55	131.08
12000	151.41	150.17	149.11	146.76	144.57	143.51	143.00
13000	164.03	162.69	161.54	158.99	156.61	155.47	154.92
14000	176.65	175.20	173.96	171.21	168.66	167.43	166.83
15000	189.26	187.71	186.39	183.44	180.71	179.39	178.75
16000	201.88	200.23	198.81	195.67	192.75	191.35	190.66
17000	214.50	212.74	211.24	207.90	204.80	203.31	202.58
18000	227.11	225.25	223.67	220.13	216.85	215.27	214.50
19000	239.73	237.77	236.09	232.36	228.90	227.23	226.41
20000	252.35	250.28	248.52	244.59	240.94	239.19	238.33
21000	264.97	262.80	260.94	256.82	252.99	251.14	250.25
22000	277.58	275.31	273.37	269.05	265.04	263.10	262.16
23000	290.20	287.82	285.79	281.28	277.08	275.06	274.08
24000	302.82	300.34	298.22	293.51	289.13	287.02	285.99
25000	315.43	312.85	310.64	305.74	301.18	298.98	297.91
26000	328.05	325.37	323.07	317.97	313.22	310.94	309.83
27000	340.67	337.88	335.50	330.20	325.27	322.90	321.74
28000	353.29	350.39	347.92	342.42	337.32	334.86	333.66
29000	365.90	362.91	360.35	354.65	349.36	346.82	345.58
30000	378.52	375.42	372.77	366.88	361.41	358.78	357.49
31000	391.14	387.94	385.20	379.11	373.46	370.73	369.41
32000	403.76	400.45	397.62	391.34	385.50	382.69	381.32
33000	416.37	412.96	410.05	403.57	397.55	394.65	393.24
34000	428.99	425.48	422.47	415.80	409.60	406.61	405.16
35000	441.61	437.99	434.90	428.03	421.65	418.57	417.07
40000	504.69	500.56	497.05	489.18	481.88	478.37	476.65
45000	567.78	563.13	559.16	550.32	542.11	538.16	536.24
50000	630.86	625.70	621.28	611.47	602.35	597.96	595.82
55000	693.95	688.27	683.41	672.62	662.58	657.75	655.40
60000	757.04	750.84	745.54	733.76	722.82	717.55	714.98
65000	820.12	813.41	807.67	794.91	783.05	777.34	774.56
70000	883.21	875.98	869.80	856.05	843.29	837.14	834.14
75000	946.29	938.55	931.92	917.20	903.52	896.93	893.72
80000	1009.38	1001.12	994.05	978.35	963.75	956.73	953.30
100000	1261.72	1251.39	1242.56	1222.93	1204.69	1195.91	1191.63

125

14½%

TERM AMOUNT	1 YEAR	1½ YEARS	2 YEARS	2½ YEARS	3 YEARS	4 YEARS	5 YEARS
$ 25	2.26	1.56	1.21	1.00	.87	.69	.59
50	4.51	3.11	2.42	2.00	1.73	1.38	1.18
75	6.76	4.67	3.62	3.00	2.59	2.07	1.77
100	9.01	6.22	4.83	4.00	3.45	2.76	2.36
200	18.01	12.43	9.65	7.99	6.89	5.52	4.71
300	27.01	18.65	14.48	11.99	10.33	8.28	7.06
400	36.01	24.86	19.30	15.98	13.77	11.04	9.42
500	45.02	31.08	24.13	19.97	17.21	13.79	11.77
600	54.02	37.29	28.95	23.97	20.66	16.55	14.12
700	63.02	43.51	33.78	27.96	24.10	19.31	16.47
800	72.02	49.72	38.60	31.96	27.54	22.07	18.83
900	81.03	55.94	43.43	35.95	30.98	24.83	21.18
1000	90.03	62.15	48.25	39.94	34.43	27.58	23.53
2000	180.05	124.30	96.50	79.88	68.85	55.15	47.06
3000	270.07	186.45	144.75	119.82	103.27	82.74	70.59
4000	360.10	248.60	193.00	159.76	137.69	110.32	94.12
5000	450.12	310.75	241.25	199.70	172.11	137.89	117.65
6000	540.14	372.90	289.50	239.63	206.53	165.47	141.17
7000	630.16	435.05	337.75	279.57	240.95	193.05	164.70
8000	720.19	497.20	386.00	319.51	275.37	220.63	188.23
9000	810.21	559.35	434.25	359.45	309.79	248.21	211.76
10000	900.23	621.50	482.50	399.39	344.21	275.78	235.29
11000	990.25	683.65	530.75	439.32	378.64	303.36	258.82
12000	1080.28	745.80	579.00	479.26	413.06	330.94	282.34
13000	1170.30	807.95	627.25	519.20	447.48	358.52	305.87
14000	1260.32	870.10	675.50	559.14	481.90	386.10	329.40
15000	1350.34	932.25	723.75	599.08	516.32	413.67	352.93
16000	1440.37	994.40	772.00	639.01	550.74	441.25	376.46
17000	1530.39	1056.55	820.25	678.95	585.16	468.83	399.99
18000	1620.41	1118.70	868.49	718.89	619.58	496.41	423.51
19000	1710.43	1180.85	916.74	758.83	654.00	523.99	447.04
20000	1800.46	1243.00	964.99	798.77	688.42	551.56	470.57
21000	1890.48	1305.15	1013.24	838.70	722.85	579.14	494.10
22000	1980.50	1367.30	1061.49	878.64	757.27	606.72	517.63
23000	2070.52	1429.45	1109.74	918.58	791.69	634.30	541.16
24000	2160.55	1491.60	1157.99	958.52	826.11	661.88	564.68
25000	2250.57	1553.75	1206.24	998.46	860.53	689.45	588.21
26000	2340.59	1615.90	1254.49	1038.39	894.95	717.03	611.74
27000	2430.61	1678.05	1302.74	1078.33	929.37	744.61	635.27
28000	2520.64	1740.20	1350.99	1118.27	963.79	772.19	658.80
29000	2610.66	1802.35	1399.24	1158.21	998.21	799.77	682.33
30000	2700.68	1864.49	1447.49	1198.15	1032.63	827.34	705.85
31000	2790.70	1926.65	1495.74	1238.08	1067.06	854.92	729.38
32000	2880.73	1988.80	1543.99	1278.02	1101.48	882.50	752.91
33000	2970.75	2050.95	1592.24	1317.96	1135.90	910.08	776.44
34000	3060.77	2113.10	1640.49	1357.90	1170.32	937.66	799.97
35000	3150.79	2175.25	1688.73	1397.84	1204.74	965.23	823.49
40000	3600.91	2485.99	1929.98	1597.53	1376.84	1103.12	941.14
45000	4051.02	2796.74	2171.23	1797.22	1548.95	1241.01	1058.78
50000	4501.13	3107.49	2412.48	1996.91	1721.05	1378.90	1176.42
55000	4951.25	3418.24	2653.72	2196.60	1893.16	1516.79	1294.06
60000	5401.36	3728.99	2894.97	2396.29	2065.26	1654.68	1411.70
65000	5851.47	4039.74	3136.22	2595.98	2237.37	1792.57	1529.34
70000	630.58	4350.49	3377.46	2795.67	2409.47	1930.46	1646.98
75000	6751.70	4661.23	3618.71	2995.36	2581.58	2068.35	1764.63
80000	7201.81	4971.98	3859.96	3195.05	2753.68	2206.24	1882.27
100000	9002.26	6214.98	4824.95	3993.81	3442.10	2757.80	2352.83

TERM AMOUNT	6 YEARS	7 YEARS	8 YEARS	9 YEARS	10 YEARS	11 YEARS	12 YEARS
$ 25	.53	.48	.45	.42	.40	.38	.37
50	1.05	.96	.89	.84	.80	.75	.74
75	1.57	1.43	1.33	1.25	1.19	1.14	1.11
100	2.09	1.91	1.77	1.67	1.59	1.52	1.47
200	4.18	3.81	3.54	3.33	3.17	3.04	2.94
300	6.27	5.71	5.30	4.99	4.75	4.56	4.41
400	8.35	7.61	7.07	6.66	6.34	6.08	5.88
500	10.44	9.51	8.83	8.32	7.92	7.60	7.35
600	12.53	11.42	10.60	9.98	9.50	9.12	8.82
700	14.62	13.32	12.37	11.64	11.09	10.64	10.29
800	16.70	15.22	14.13	13.31	12.67	12.16	11.76
900	18.79	17.12	15.90	14.97	14.25	13.68	13.22
1000	20.88	19.02	17.66	16.63	15.83	15.20	14.69
2000	41.75	38.04	35.32	33.26	31.66	30.40	29.38
3000	62.63	57.06	52.98	49.89	47.49	45.59	44.07
4000	83.50	76.07	70.63	66.52	63.32	60.79	58.76
5000	104.38	95.09	88.29	83.14	79.15	75.99	73.45
6000	125.25	114.11	105.95	99.77	94.98	91.18	88.14
7000	146.13	133.13	123.61	116.40	110.81	106.38	102.82
8000	167.00	152.14	141.26	133.03	126.63	121.58	117.51
9000	187.87	171.16	158.92	149.65	142.46	136.77	132.20
10000	208.75	190.18	176.58	166.28	158.29	151.97	146.89
11000	229.62	209.20	194.23	182.91	174.12	167.17	161.58
12000	250.50	228.21	211.89	199.54	189.95	182.36	176.27
13000	271.37	247.23	229.55	216.17	205.78	197.56	190.96
14000	292.25	266.25	247.21	232.79	221.61	212.76	205.64
15000	313.12	285.26	264.86	249.42	237.44	227.95	220.33
16000	334.00	304.28	282.52	266.05	253.26	243.15	235.02
17000	354.87	323.30	300.18	282.68	269.09	258.34	249.71
18000	375.74	342.32	317.84	299.30	284.92	273.54	264.40
19000	396.62	361.33	335.49	315.93	300.75	288.74	279.09
20000	417.49	380.35	353.15	332.56	316.58	303.93	293.77
21000	438.37	399.37	370.81	349.19	332.41	319.13	308.46
22000	459.24	418.39	388.46	365.81	348.24	334.33	323.15
23000	480.12	437.40	406.12	382.44	364.06	349.52	337.84
24000	500.99	456.42	423.78	399.07	379.89	364.72	352.53
25000	521.87	475.44	441.44	415.70	395.72	379.92	367.22
26000	542.74	494.45	459.09	432.33	411.55	395.11	381.91
27000	563.61	513.47	476.75	448.95	427.38	410.31	396.59
28000	584.49	532.49	494.41	465.58	443.21	425.51	411.28
29000	605.36	551.51	512.07	482.21	459.04	440.70	425.97
30000	626.24	570.52	529.72	498.84	474.87	455.90	440.66
31000	647.11	589.54	547.38	515.46	490.69	471.09	455.35
32000	667.99	608.56	565.04	532.09	506.52	486.29	470.04
33000	688.86	627.58	582.69	548.72	522.35	501.49	484.73
34000	709.74	646.59	600.35	565.35	538.18	516.68	499.41
35000	730.61	665.61	618.01	581.98	554.01	531.88	514.10
40000	834.98	760.70	706.30	665.11	633.15	607.86	587.54
45000	939.35	855.78	794.58	748.25	712.30	683.84	660.99
50000	1043.73	950.87	882.87	831.39	791.44	759.83	734.43
55000	1148.10	1045.96	971.15	914.53	870.58	835.81	807.87
60000	1252.47	1141.04	1059.44	997.67	949.73	911.79	881.31
65000	1356.84	1236.13	1147.73	1080.81	1028.87	987.77	954.76
70000	1461.21	1331.22	1236.01	1163.95	1108.01	1063.76	1028.20
75000	1565.59	1426.30	1324.30	1247.08	1187.16	1139.74	1101.64
80000	1669.96	1521.39	1412.59	1330.22	1266.30	1215.72	1175.08
100000	2087.45	1901.74	1765.73	1662.78	1582.87	1519.65	1468.85

MONTHLY PAYMENT
NECESSARY TO AMORTIZE A LOAN

TERM AMOUNT	13 YEARS	14 YEARS	15 YEARS	16 YEARS	17 YEARS	18 YEARS	19 YEARS
$ 25	.36	.35	.35	.34	.34	.33	.33
50	.72	.70	.69	.68	.67	.66	.65
75	1.08	1.05	1.03	1.01	1.00	.98	.97
100	1.43	1.40	1.37	1.35	1.33	1.31	1.30
200	2.86	2.79	2.74	2.69	2.65	2.62	2.59
300	4.29	4.19	4.10	4.03	3.97	3.92	3.88
400	5.72	5.58	5.47	5.37	5.29	5.23	5.17
500	7.14	6.97	6.83	6.72	6.62	6.53	6.46
600	8.57	8.37	8.20	8.06	7.94	7.84	7.76
700	10.00	9.76	9.56	9.40	9.26	9.15	9.05
800	11.43	11.15	10.93	10.74	10.58	10.45	10.34
900	12.85	12.55	12.29	12.08	11.91	11.76	11.63
1000	14.28	13.94	13.66	13.43	13.23	13.06	12.92
2000	28.56	27.88	27.32	26.85	26.45	26.12	25.84
3000	42.83	41.81	40.97	40.27	39.68	39.18	38.76
4000	57.11	55.75	54.63	53.69	52.90	52.24	51.68
5000	71.38	69.69	68.28	67.11	66.13	65.30	64.60
6000	85.66	83.62	81.94	80.53	79.35	78.36	77.52
7000	99.93	97.56	95.59	93.95	92.57	91.42	90.44
8000	114.21	111.49	109.25	107.37	105.80	104.47	103.36
9000	128.48	125.43	122.90	120.79	119.02	117.53	116.27
10000	142.76	139.37	136.56	134.21	132.25	130.59	129.19
11000	157.03	153.30	150.21	147.63	145.47	143.65	142.11
12000	171.31	167.24	163.87	161.05	158.70	156.71	155.03
13000	185.58	181.17	177.52	174.47	171.92	169.77	167.95
14000	199.86	195.11	191.18	187.89	185.14	182.83	180.87
15000	214.14	209.05	204.83	201.32	198.37	195.89	193.79
16000	228.41	222.98	218.49	214.74	211.59	208.94	206.71
17000	242.69	236.92	232.14	228.16	224.82	222.00	219.62
18000	256.96	250.85	245.80	241.58	238.04	235.06	232.54
19000	271.24	264.79	259.45	255.00	251.27	248.12	245.46
20000	285.51	278.73	273.11	268.42	264.49	261.18	258.38
21000	299.79	292.66	286.76	281.84	277.71	274.24	271.30
22000	314.06	306.60	300.42	295.26	290.94	287.30	284.22
23000	328.34	320.53	314.07	308.68	304.16	300.36	297.14
24000	342.61	334.47	327.73	322.10	317.39	313.41	310.06
25000	356.89	348.41	341.38	335.52	330.61	326.47	322.97
26000	371.16	362.34	355.04	348.94	343.84	339.53	335.89
27000	385.44	376.28	368.69	362.36	357.06	352.59	348.81
28000	399.72	390.21	382.35	375.78	370.28	365.65	361.73
29000	413.99	404.15	396.00	389.21	383.51	378.71	374.65
30000	428.27	418.09	409.66	402.63	396.73	391.77	387.57
31000	442.54	432.02	423.31	416.05	409.96	404.83	400.49
32000	456.82	445.96	436.97	429.47	423.18	417.88	413.41
33000	471.09	459.89	450.62	442.89	436.41	430.94	426.32
34000	485.37	473.83	464.28	456.31	449.63	444.00	439.24
35000	499.64	487.77	477.93	469.73	462.85	457.06	452.16
40000	571.02	557.45	546.21	536.83	528.97	522.35	516.76
45000	642.40	627.13	614.48	603.94	595.10	587.65	581.35
50000	713.77	696.81	682.76	671.04	661.22	652.94	645.95
55000	785.15	766.49	751.03	738.14	727.34	718.24	710.54
60000	856.53	836.17	819.31	805.25	793.46	783.53	775.13
65000	927.90	905.85	887.58	872.35	859.58	848.82	839.72
70000	999.28	975.53	955.86	939.45	925.70	914.12	904.32
75000	1070.66	1045.21	1024.13	1006.56	991.82	979.41	968.91
80000	1142.04	1114.89	1092.41	1073.66	1057.94	1044.70	1033.51
100000	1427.54	1393.61	1365.51	1342.08	1322.43	1305.88	1291.88

14½%

TERM AMOUNT	20 YEARS	21 YEARS	22 YEARS	25 YEARS	30 YEARS	35 YEARS	40 YEARS
$ 25	.32	.32	.32	.32	.31	.31	.31
50	.64	.64	.64	.63	.62	.61	.61
75	.96	.96	.95	.94	.92	.92	.91
100	1.28	1.27	1.27	1.25	1.23	1.22	1.22
200	2.56	2.54	2.53	2.49	2.45	2.44	2.43
300	3.84	3.81	3.79	3.73	3.68	3.65	3.64
400	5.12	5.08	5.05	4.97	4.90	4.87	4.85
500	6.40	6.35	6.31	6.22	6.13	6.09	6.07
600	7.68	7.62	7.57	7.46	7.35	7.30	7.28
700	8.96	8.89	8.83	8.70	8.58	8.52	8.49
800	10.24	10.16	10.10	9.94	9.80	9.73	9.70
900	11.52	11.43	11.36	11.18	11.03	10.95	10.91
1000	12.80	12.70	12.62	12.43	12.25	12.17	12.13
2000	25.60	25.40	25.23	24.85	24.50	24.33	24.25
3000	38.40	38.10	37.84	37.27	36.74	36.49	36.37
4000	51.20	50.80	50.46	49.69	48.99	48.65	48.49
5000	64.00	63.50	63.07	62.11	61.23	60.81	60.61
6000	76.80	76.20	75.68	74.53	73.48	72.98	72.73
7000	89.60	88.90	88.29	86.96	85.72	85.14	84.85
8000	102.40	101.60	100.91	99.38	97.97	97.30	96.98
9000	115.20	114.29	113.52	111.80	110.22	109.46	109.10
10000	128.00	126.99	126.13	124.22	122.46	121.62	121.22
11000	140.80	139.69	138.74	136.64	134.71	133.78	133.34
12000	153.60	152.39	151.36	149.06	146.95	145.95	145.46
13000	166.40	165.09	163.97	161.49	159.20	158.11	157.58
14000	179.20	177.79	176.58	173.91	171.44	170.27	169.70
15000	192.00	190.49	189.19	186.33	183.69	182.43	181.82
16000	204.80	203.19	201.81	198.75	195.93	194.59	193.95
17000	217.60	215.89	214.42	211.17	208.18	206.75	206.07
18000	230.40	228.58	227.03	223.59	220.43	218.92	218.19
19000	243.20	241.28	239.65	236.02	232.67	231.08	230.31
20000	256.00	253.98	252.26	248.44	244.92	243.24	242.43
21000	268.80	266.68	264.87	260.86	257.16	255.40	254.55
22000	281.60	279.38	277.48	273.28	269.41	267.56	266.67
23000	294.40	292.08	290.10	285.70	281.65	279.72	278.80
24000	307.20	304.78	302.71	298.12	293.90	291.89	290.92
25000	320.00	317.48	315.32	310.55	306.14	304.05	303.04
26000	332.80	330.18	327.93	322.97	318.39	316.21	315.16
27000	345.60	342.87	340.55	335.39	330.64	328.37	327.28
28000	358.40	355.57	353.16	347.81	342.88	340.53	339.40
29000	371.20	368.27	365.77	360.23	355.13	352.69	351.52
30000	384.00	380.97	378.38	372.65	367.37	364.86	363.64
31000	396.80	393.67	391.00	385.08	379.62	377.02	375.77
32000	409.60	406.37	403.61	397.50	391.86	389.18	387.89
33000	422.40	419.07	416.22	409.92	404.11	401.34	400.01
34000	435.20	431.77	428.83	422.34	416.35	413.50	412.13
35000	448.00	444.47	441.45	434.76	428.60	425.66	424.25
40000	512.00	507.96	504.51	496.87	489.83	486.47	484.86
45000	576.00	571.45	567.57	558.98	551.06	547.28	545.46
50000	640.00	634.95	630.64	621.09	612.28	608.09	606.07
55000	704.00	698.44	693.70	683.19	673.51	668.90	666.68
60000	768.00	761.94	756.76	745.30	734.74	729.71	727.28
65000	832.00	825.43	819.83	807.41	795.97	790.52	787.89
70000	896.00	888.93	882.89	869.52	857.19	851.32	848.50
75000	960.00	952.42	945.95	931.63	918.42	912.13	909.10
80000	1024.00	1015.92	1009.02	993.74	979.65	972.94	969.71
100000	1280.00	1269.89	1261.27	1242.17	1224.56	1216.18	1212.14

MONTHLY PAYMENT
NECESSARY TO AMORTIZE A LOAN

TERM AMOUNT	1 YEAR	1½ YEARS	2 YEARS	2½ YEARS	3 YEARS	4 YEARS	5 YEARS
$ 25	2.26	1.56	1.21	1.01	.87	.70	.60
50	4.51	3.12	2.42	2.01	1.73	1.39	1.19
75	6.77	4.68	3.63	3.01	2.60	2.08	1.78
100	9.02	6.23	4.84	4.01	3.46	2.78	2.37
200	18.03	12.46	9.68	8.02	6.91	5.55	4.74
300	27.05	18.69	14.52	12.02	10.37	8.32	7.10
400	36.06	24.91	19.35	16.03	13.82	11.09	9.47
500	45.08	31.14	24.19	20.03	17.28	13.86	11.83
600	54.09	37.37	29.03	24.04	20.73	16.63	14.20
700	63.10	43.59	33.86	28.05	24.19	19.40	16.57
800	72.12	49.82	38.70	32.05	27.64	22.17	18.93
900	81.13	56.05	43.54	36.06	31.09	24.94	21.30
1000	90.15	62.27	48.37	40.06	34.55	27.71	23.66
2000	180.29	124.54	96.74	80.12	69.09	55.41	47.32
3000	270.43	186.81	145.11	120.18	103.63	83.12	70.98
4000	360.57	249.07	193.48	160.24	138.18	110.82	94.64
5000	450.71	311.34	241.84	200.30	172.72	138.53	118.30
6000	540.85	373.61	290.21	240.35	207.26	166.23	141.96
7000	630.99	435.88	338.58	280.41	241.81	193.93	165.62
8000	721.13	498.14	386.95	320.47	276.35	221.64	189.28
9000	811.27	560.41	435.32	360.53	310.89	249.34	212.94
10000	901.41	622.68	483.68	400.59	345.44	277.05	236.59
11000	991.55	684.94	532.05	440.65	379.98	304.75	260.25
12000	1081.69	747.21	580.42	480.70	414.52	332.46	283.91
13000	1171.83	809.48	628.79	520.76	449.06	360.16	307.57
14000	1261.97	871.75	677.16	560.82	483.61	387.86	331.23
15000	1352.11	934.01	725.52	600.88	518.15	415.57	354.89
16000	1442.25	996.28	773.89	640.94	552.69	443.27	378.55
17000	1532.39	1058.55	822.26	680.99	587.24	470.98	402.21
18000	1622.53	1120.81	870.63	721.05	621.78	498.68	425.87
19000	1712.67	1183.08	919.00	761.11	656.32	526.38	449.52
20000	1802.81	1245.35	967.36	801.17	690.87	554.09	473.18
21000	1892.95	1307.62	1015.73	841.23	725.41	581.79	496.84
22000	1983.09	1369.88	1064.10	881.29	759.95	609.50	520.50
23000	2073.23	1432.15	1112.47	921.34	794.49	637.20	544.16
24000	2163.37	1494.42	1160.84	961.40	829.04	664.91	567.82
25000	2253.51	1556.68	1209.20	1001.46	863.58	692.61	591.48
26000	2343.66	1618.95	1257.57	1041.52	898.12	720.31	615.14
27000	2433.80	1681.22	1305.94	1081.58	932.67	748.02	638.80
28000	2523.94	1743.49	1354.31	1121.63	967.21	775.72	662.45
29000	2614.08	1805.75	1402.68	1161.69	1001.75	803.43	686.11
30000	2704.22	1868.02	1451.04	1201.75	1036.30	831.13	709.77
31000	2794.36	1930.29	1499.41	1241.81	1070.84	858.83	733.43
32000	2884.50	1992.56	1547.78	1281.87	1105.38	886.54	757.09
33000	2974.64	2054.82	1596.15	1321.93	1139.92	914.24	780.75
34000	3064.78	2117.09	1644.52	1361.98	1174.47	941.95	804.41
35000	3154.92	2179.36	1692.88	1402.04	1209.01	969.65	828.07
40000	3605.62	2490.69	1934.72	1602.33	1381.73	1108.17	946.36
45000	4056.32	2802.03	2176.56	1802.62	1554.44	1246.69	1064.66
50000	4507.02	3113.36	2418.40	2002.91	1727.15	1385.21	1182.95
55000	4957.73	3424.70	2660.24	2203.21	1899.87	1523.74	1301.24
60000	5408.43	3736.04	2902.08	2403.50	2072.59	1662.26	1419.54
65000	5859.13	4047.37	3143.92	2603.79	2245.30	1800.78	1537.83
70000	6309.83	4358.71	3385.76	2804.08	2418.02	1939.30	1656.13
75000	6760.53	4670.04	3627.60	3004.37	2590.73	2077.82	1774.42
80000	7211.24	4981.38	3869.44	3204.66	2763.45	2216.34	1892.72
100000	9014.04	6226.72	4836.80	4005.82	3454.31	2770.42	2365.90

TERM AMOUNT	6 YEARS	7 YEARS	8 YEARS	9 YEARS	10 YEARS	11 YEARS	12 YEARS
$ 25	.53	.48	.45	.42	.40	.39	.38
50	1.06	.96	.90	.84	.80	.77	.75
75	1.58	1.44	1.34	1.26	1.20	1.16	1.12
100	2.11	1.92	1.79	1.68	1.60	1.54	1.49
200	4.21	3.84	3.57	3.36	3.20	3.08	2.97
300	6.31	5.75	5.35	5.04	4.80	4.61	4.46
400	8.41	7.67	7.13	6.72	6.40	6.15	5.94
500	10.51	9.58	8.91	8.39	8.00	7.68	7.43
600	12.61	11.50	10.69	10.07	9.59	9.22	8.91
700	14.71	13.41	12.47	11.75	11.19	10.75	10.40
800	16.81	15.33	14.25	13.43	12.79	12.29	11.88
900	18.91	17.25	16.03	15.10	14.39	13.82	13.37
1000	21.01	19.16	17.81	16.78	15.99	15.36	14.85
2000	42.02	38.32	35.61	33.56	31.97	30.71	29.70
3000	63.03	57.48	53.41	50.33	47.95	46.06	44.55
4000	84.04	76.63	71.21	67.11	63.93	61.41	59.40
5000	105.05	95.79	89.01	83.88	79.91	76.77	74.25
6000	126.06	114.95	106.81	100.66	95.89	92.12	89.09
7000	147.07	134.10	124.61	117.43	111.87	107.47	103.94
8000	168.08	153.26	142.41	134.21	127.85	122.82	118.79
9000	189.09	172.42	160.21	150.99	143.83	138.18	133.64
10000	210.10	191.57	178.02	167.76	159.81	153.53	148.49
11000	231.11	210.73	195.82	184.54	175.79	168.88	163.34
12000	252.12	229.89	213.62	201.31	191.77	184.23	178.18
13000	273.13	249.04	231.42	218.09	207.75	199.59	193.03
14000	294.14	268.20	249.22	234.86	223.74	214.94	207.88
15000	315.15	287.36	267.02	251.64	239.72	230.29	222.73
16000	336.16	306.51	284.82	268.42	255.70	245.64	237.58
17000	357.17	325.67	302.62	285.19	271.68	261.00	252.43
18000	378.18	344.83	320.42	301.97	287.66	276.35	267.27
19000	399.19	363.98	338.22	318.74	303.64	291.70	282.12
20000	420.19	383.14	356.03	335.52	319.62	307.05	296.97
21000	441.20	402.30	373.83	352.29	335.60	322.41	311.82
22000	462.21	421.45	391.63	369.07	351.58	337.76	326.67
23000	483.22	440.61	409.43	385.85	367.56	353.11	341.51
24000	504.23	459.77	427.23	402.62	383.54	368.46	356.36
25000	525.24	478.92	445.03	419.40	399.52	383.82	371.21
26000	546.25	498.08	462.83	436.17	415.50	399.17	386.06
27000	567.26	517.24	480.63	452.95	431.49	414.52	400.91
28000	588.27	536.39	498.43	469.72	447.47	429.87	415.76
29000	609.28	555.55	516.23	486.50	463.45	445.23	430.60
30000	630.29	574.71	534.04	503.28	479.43	460.58	445.45
31000	651.30	593.86	551.84	520.05	495.41	475.93	460.30
32000	672.31	613.02	569.64	536.83	511.39	491.28	475.15
33000	693.32	632.18	587.44	553.60	527.37	506.64	490.00
34000	714.33	651.33	605.24	570.38	543.35	521.99	504.85
35000	735.34	670.49	623.04	587.15	559.33	537.34	519.69
40000	840.38	766.28	712.05	671.03	639.23	614.10	593.94
45000	945.43	862.06	801.05	754.91	719.14	690.86	668.18
50000	1050.48	957.84	890.06	838.79	799.04	767.63	742.42
55000	1155.53	1053.63	979.06	922.67	878.95	844.39	816.66
60000	1260.57	1149.41	1068.07	1006.55	958.85	921.15	890.90
65000	1365.62	1245.19	1157.07	1090.43	1038.75	997.91	965.14
70000	1470.67	1340.98	1246.08	1174.30	1118.66	1074.68	1039.38
75000	1575.72	1436.76	1335.08	1258.18	1198.56	1151.44	1113.62
80000	1680.76	1532.55	1424.09	1342.06	1278.46	1228.20	1187.87
100000	2100.95	1915.68	1780.11	1677.58	1598.08	1535.25	1484.83

131

14¾%

MONTHLY PAYMENT
NECESSARY TO AMORTIZE A LOAN

TERM AMOUNT	13 YEARS	14 YEARS	15 YEARS	16 YEARS	17 YEARS	18 YEARS	19 YEARS
$ 25	.37	.36	.35	.34	.34	.34	.33
50	.73	.71	.70	.68	.68	.67	.66
75	1.09	1.06	1.04	1.02	1.01	1.00	.99
100	1.45	1.42	1.39	1.36	1.35	1.33	1.31
200	2.89	2.83	2.77	2.72	2.69	2.65	2.62
300	4.34	4.24	4.15	4.08	4.03	3.98	3.93
400	5.78	5.65	5.54	5.44	5.37	5.30	5.24
500	7.22	7.06	6.92	6.80	6.71	6.62	6.55
600	8.67	8.47	8.30	8.16	8.05	7.95	7.86
700	10.11	9.88	9.68	9.52	9.39	9.27	9.17
800	11.56	11.29	11.07	10.88	10.73	10.59	10.48
900	13.00	12.70	12.45	12.24	12.07	11.92	11.79
1000	14.44	14.11	13.83	13.60	13.41	13.24	13.10
2000	28.88	28.21	27.66	27.19	26.81	26.48	26.20
3000	43.32	42.31	41.48	40.79	40.21	39.72	39.30
4000	57.76	56.42	55.31	54.38	53.61	52.95	52.40
5000	72.20	70.52	69.13	67.97	67.01	66.19	65.50
6000	86.64	84.62	82.96	81.57	80.41	79.43	78.60
7000	101.08	98.72	96.78	95.16	93.81	92.67	91.70
8000	115.51	112.83	110.61	108.76	107.21	105.90	104.80
9000	129.95	126.93	124.43	122.35	120.61	119.14	117.90
10000	144.39	141.03	138.26	135.94	134.01	132.38	131.00
11000	158.83	155.14	152.08	149.54	147.41	145.62	144.10
12000	173.27	169.24	165.91	163.13	160.81	158.85	157.20
13000	187.71	183.34	179.73	176.72	174.21	172.09	170.30
14000	202.15	197.44	193.56	190.32	187.61	185.33	183.40
15000	216.59	211.55	207.38	203.91	201.01	198.57	196.50
16000	231.02	225.65	221.21	217.51	214.41	211.80	209.60
17000	245.46	239.75	235.03	231.10	227.81	225.04	222.70
18000	259.90	253.86	248.86	244.69	241.21	238.28	235.80
19000	274.34	267.96	262.68	258.29	254.61	251.52	248.90
20000	288.78	282.06	276.51	271.88	268.01	264.75	262.00
21000	303.22	296.16	290.33	285.47	281.41	277.99	275.10
22000	317.66	310.27	304.16	299.07	294.81	291.23	288.20
23000	332.10	324.37	317.98	312.66	308.21	304.47	301.30
24000	346.53	338.47	331.81	326.26	321.61	317.70	314.40
25000	360.97	352.58	345.63	339.85	335.01	330.94	327.50
26000	375.41	366.68	359.46	353.44	348.41	344.18	340.60
27000	389.85	380.78	373.28	367.04	361.81	357.42	353.70
28000	404.29	394.88	387.11	380.63	375.21	370.65	366.80
29000	418.73	408.99	400.93	394.23	388.61	383.89	379.90
30000	433.17	423.09	414.76	407.82	402.01	397.13	393.00
31000	447.61	437.19	428.58	421.41	415.41	410.37	406.10
32000	462.04	451.30	442.41	435.01	428.81	423.60	419.20
33000	476.48	465.40	456.23	448.60	442.21	436.84	432.30
34000	490.92	479.50	470.06	462.19	455.61	450.08	445.40
35000	505.36	493.60	483.88	475.79	469.01	463.31	458.50
40000	577.55	564.12	553.01	543.76	536.01	529.50	524.00
45000	649.75	634.63	622.13	611.73	603.01	595.69	589.50
50000	721.94	705.15	691.26	679.69	670.02	661.88	655.00
55000	794.14	775.66	760.38	747.66	737.02	728.06	720.50
60000	866.33	846.17	829.51	815.63	804.02	794.25	786.00
65000	938.52	916.69	898.63	883.60	871.02	860.44	851.50
70000	1010.72	987.20	967.76	951.57	938.02	926.62	917.00
75000	1082.91	1057.72	1036.88	1019.54	1005.02	992.81	982.50
80000	1155.10	1128.23	1106.01	1087.51	1072.02	1059.00	1048.00
100000	1443.88	1410.29	1382.51	1359.38	1340.03	1323.75	1310.00

132

TERM AMOUNT	20 YEARS	21 YEARS	22 YEARS	25 YEARS	30 YEARS	35 YEARS	40 YEARS
$ 25	.33	.33	.33	.32	.32	.31	.31
50	.65	.65	.65	.64	.63	.62	.62
75	.98	.97	.97	.95	.94	.93	.93
100	1.30	1.29	1.29	1.27	1.25	1.24	1.24
200	2.60	2.58	2.57	2.53	2.49	2.48	2.47
300	3.90	3.87	3.85	3.79	3.74	3.71	3.70
400	5.20	5.16	5.13	5.05	4.98	4.95	4.94
500	6.50	6.45	6.41	6.31	6.23	6.19	6.17
600	7.80	7.74	7.69	7.57	7.47	7.42	7.40
700	9.09	9.02	8.97	8.84	8.72	8.66	8.63
800	10.39	10.31	10.25	1C.10	9.96	9.90	9.87
900	11.69	11.60	11.53	11.36	11.21	11.13	11.10
1000	12.99	12.89	12.81	12.62	12.45	12.37	12.33
2000	25.97	25.77	25.61	25.23	24.89	24.73	24.66
3000	38.96	38.66	38.41	37.85	37.34	37.10	36.99
4000	51.94	51.54	51.21	5C.46	49.78	49.46	49.31
5000	64.92	64.43	64.01	63.08	62.23	61.83	61.64
6000	77.91	77.31	76.81	75.69	74.67	74.19	73.97
7000	90.89	90.20	89.61	88.31	87.12	86.56	86.29
8000	103.87	103.08	102.41	100.92	99.56	98.92	98.62
9000	116.86	115.97	115.21	113.54	112.01	111.29	110.95
10000	129.84	128.85	128.01	126.15	124.45	123.65	123.27
11000	142.82	141.74	140.81	138.77	136.90	136.02	135.60
12000	155.81	154.62	153.61	151.38	149.34	148.38	147.93
13000	168.79	167.51	166.41	164.00	161.79	160.75	160.25
14000	181.77	180.39	179.21	176.61	174.23	173.11	172.58
15000	194.76	193.27	192.01	189.22	186.68	185.48	184.91
16000	207.74	206.16	204.81	201.84	199.12	197.84	197.23
17000	220.73	219.04	217.61	214.45	211.57	210.21	209.56
18000	233.71	231.93	230.41	227.07	224.01	222.57	221.89
19000	246.69	244.81	243.21	239.68	236.46	234.94	234.21
20000	259.68	257.70	256.01	252.30	248.90	247.30	246.54
21000	272.66	270.58	268.81	264.91	261.35	259.66	258.87
22000	285.64	283.47	281.61	277.53	273.79	272.03	271.19
23000	298.63	296.35	294.42	290.14	286.23	284.39	283.52
24000	311.61	309.24	307.22	302.76	298.68	296.76	295.85
25000	324.59	322.12	320.02	315.37	311.12	309.12	308.17
26000	337.58	335.01	332.82	327.99	323.57	321.49	320.50
27000	350.56	347.89	345.62	34C.60	336.01	333.85	332.83
28000	363.54	360.78	358.42	353.22	348.46	346.22	345.15
29000	376.53	373.66	371.22	365.83	360.90	358.58	357.48
30000	389.51	386.54	384.02	378.44	373.35	370.95	369.81
31000	402.50	399.43	396.82	391.06	385.79	383.31	382.13
32000	415.48	412.31	409.62	403.67	398.24	395.68	394.46
33000	428.46	425.20	422.42	416.29	410.68	408.04	406.79
34000	441.45	438.08	435.22	428.90	423.13	420.41	419.11
35000	454.43	450.97	448.02	441.52	435.57	432.77	431.44
40000	519.35	515.39	512.02	504.59	497.80	494.59	493.07
45000	584.26	579.81	576.03	567.66	560.02	556.42	554.71
50000	649.18	644.24	640.03	630.74	622.24	618.24	616.34
55000	714.10	708.66	704.03	693.81	684.47	680.07	677.97
60000	779.02	773.08	768.03	756.88	746.69	741.89	739.61
65000	843.94	837.51	832.03	819.96	808.91	803.71	801.24
70000	908.85	901.93	896.04	883.03	871.14	865.54	862.87
75000	973.77	966.35	960.04	946.10	933.36	927.36	924.51
80000	1038.69	1030.78	1024.04	1009.18	995.59	989.18	986.14
100000	1298.36	1288.47	1280.05	1261.47	1244.48	1236.48	1232.67

MONTHLY PAYMENT
NECESSARY TO AMORTIZE A LOAN

TERM AMOUNT	1 YEAR	1½ YEARS	2 YEARS	2½ YEARS	3 YEARS	4 YEARS	5 YEARS
$ 25	2.26	1.56	1.22	1.01	.87	.70	.60
50	4.52	3.12	2.43	2.01	1.74	1.40	1.19
75	6.77	4.68	3.64	3.02	2.60	2.09	1.79
100	9.03	6.24	4.85	4.02	3.47	2.79	2.38
200	18.06	12.48	9.70	8.04	6.94	5.57	4.76
300	27.08	18.72	14.55	12.06	10.40	8.35	7.14
400	36.11	24.96	19.40	16.08	13.87	11.14	9.52
500	45.13	31.20	24.25	20.09	17.34	13.92	11.90
600	54.16	37.44	29.10	24.11	20.80	16.70	14.28
700	63.19	43.67	33.95	28.13	24.27	19.49	16.66
800	72.21	49.91	38.79	32.15	27.74	22.27	19.04
900	81.24	56.15	43.64	36.17	31.20	25.05	21.42
1000	90.26	62.39	48.49	40.18	34.67	27.84	23.79
2000	180.52	124.77	96.98	80.36	69.34	55.67	47.58
3000	270.78	187.16	145.46	120.54	104.00	83.50	71.37
4000	361.04	249.54	193.95	160.72	138.67	111.33	95.16
5000	451.30	311.93	242.44	200.90	173.33	139.16	118.95
6000	541.55	374.31	290.92	241.08	208.00	166.99	142.74
7000	631.81	436.70	339.41	281.25	242.66	194.82	166.53
8000	722.07	499.08	387.90	321.43	277.33	222.65	190.32
9000	812.33	561.47	436.38	361.61	311.99	250.48	214.11
10000	902.59	623.85	484.87	401.79	346.66	278.31	237.90
11000	992.85	686.24	533.36	441.97	381.32	306.14	261.69
12000	1083.10	748.62	581.84	482.15	415.99	333.97	285.48
13000	1173.36	811.01	630.33	522.33	450.65	361.80	309.27
14000	1263.62	873.39	678.82	562.50	485.32	389.64	333.06
15000	1353.88	935.78	727.30	602.68	519.98	417.47	356.85
16000	1444.14	998.16	775.79	642.86	554.65	445.30	380.64
17000	1534.40	1060.55	824.28	683.04	589.32	473.13	404.43
18000	1624.65	1122.93	872.76	723.22	623.98	500.96	428.22
19000	1714.91	1185.32	921.25	763.40	658.65	528.79	452.01
20000	1805.17	1247.70	969.74	803.58	693.31	556.62	475.80
21000	1895.43	1310.09	1018.22	843.75	727.98	584.45	499.59
22000	1985.69	1372.47	1066.71	883.93	762.64	612.28	523.38
23000	2075.95	1434.86	1115.20	924.11	797.31	640.11	547.17
24000	2166.20	1497.24	1163.68	964.29	831.97	667.94	570.96
25000	2256.46	1559.62	1212.17	1004.47	866.64	695.77	594.75
26000	2346.72	1622.01	1260.66	1044.65	901.30	723.60	618.54
27000	2436.98	1684.39	1309.14	1084.83	935.97	751.44	642.33
28000	2527.24	1746.78	1357.63	1125.00	970.63	779.27	666.12
29000	2617.50	1809.16	1406.12	1165.18	1005.30	807.10	689.91
30000	2707.75	1871.55	1454.60	1205.36	1039.96	834.93	713.70
31000	2798.01	1933.93	1503.09	1245.54	1074.63	862.76	737.49
32000	2888.27	1996.32	1551.58	1285.72	1109.30	890.59	761.28
33000	2978.53	2058.70	1600.06	1325.90	1143.96	918.42	785.07
34000	3068.79	2121.09	1648.55	1366.08	1178.63	946.25	808.86
35000	3159.05	2183.47	1697.04	1406.25	1213.29	974.08	832.65
40000	3610.34	2495.40	1939.47	1607.15	1386.62	1113.23	951.60
45000	4061.63	2807.32	2181.90	1808.04	1559.94	1252.39	1070.55
50000	4512.92	3119.24	2424.34	2008.93	1733.27	1391.54	1189.50
55000	4964.21	3431.17	2666.77	2209.82	1906.60	1530.70	1308.45
60000	5415.50	3743.09	2909.20	2410.72	2079.92	1669.85	1427.40
65000	5866.80	4055.02	3151.64	2611.61	2253.25	1809.00	1546.35
70000	6318.09	4366.94	3394.07	2812.50	2426.58	1948.16	1665.30
75000	6769.38	4678.86	3636.50	3013.40	2599.90	2087.31	1784.25
80000	7220.67	4990.79	3878.94	3214.29	2773.23	2226.46	1903.20
100000	9025.84	6238.48	4848.67	4017.86	3466.54	2783.08	2379.00

TERM AMOUNT	6 YEARS	7 YEARS	8 YEARS	9 YEARS	10 YEARS	11 YEARS	12 YEARS
$ 25	.53	.49	.45	.43	.41	.39	.38
50	1.06	.97	.90	.85	.81	.78	.76
75	1.59	1.45	1.35	1.27	1.22	1.17	1.13
100	2.12	1.93	1.80	1.70	1.62	1.56	1.51
200	4.23	3.86	3.59	3.39	3.23	3.11	3.01
300	6.35	5.79	5.39	5.08	4.85	4.66	4.51
400	8.46	7.72	7.18	6.77	6.46	6.21	6.01
500	10.58	9.65	8.98	8.47	8.07	7.76	7.51
600	12.69	11.58	10.77	1C.16	9.69	9.31	9.01
700	14.81	13.51	12.57	11.85	11.30	10.86	10.51
800	16.92	15.44	14.36	13.54	12.91	12.41	12.01
900	19.04	17.37	16.16	15.24	14.53	13.96	13.51
1000	21.15	19.30	17.95	16.93	16.14	15.51	15.01
2000	42.30	38.60	35.90	33.85	32.27	31.02	30.02
3000	63.44	57.90	53.84	50.78	48.41	46.53	45.03
4000	84.59	77.19	71.79	67.70	64.54	62.04	60.04
5000	105.73	96.49	89.73	84.63	80.67	77.55	75.05
6000	126.88	115.79	107.68	101.55	96.81	93.06	90.06
7000	148.02	135.08	125.62	118.48	112.94	108.57	105.07
8000	169.17	154.38	143.57	135.40	129.07	124.08	120.08
9000	190.31	173.68	161.51	152.32	145.21	139.59	135.08
10000	211.46	192.97	179.46	169.25	161.34	155.10	150.09
11000	232.60	212.27	197.40	186.17	177.47	170.61	165.10
12000	253.75	231.57	215.35	203.10	193.61	186.11	180.11
13000	274.89	250.86	233.30	220.02	209.74	201.62	195.12
14000	296.04	270.16	251.24	236.95	225.87	217.13	210.13
15000	317.18	289.46	269.19	253.87	242.01	232.64	225.14
16000	338.33	308.75	287.13	270.79	258.14	248.15	240.15
17000	359.47	328.05	305.08	287.72	274.27	263.66	255.15
18000	380.62	347.35	323.02	304.64	290.41	279.17	270.16
19000	401.76	366.64	340.97	321.57	306.54	294.68	285.17
20000	422.91	385.94	358.91	338.49	322.67	310.19	300.18
21000	444.05	405.24	376.86	355.42	338.81	325.70	315.19
22000	465.20	424.53	394.80	372.34	354.94	341.21	330.20
23000	486.34	443.83	412.75	389.26	371.08	356.72	345.21
24000	507.49	463.13	430.69	406.19	387.21	372.22	360.22
25000	528.63	482.42	448.64	423.11	403.34	387.73	375.22
26000	549.78	501.72	466.59	44C.04	419.48	403.24	390.23
27000	570.92	521.02	484.53	456.96	435.61	418.75	405.24
28000	592.07	540.31	502.48	473.89	451.74	434.26	420.25
29000	613.21	559.61	520.42	490.81	467.88	449.77	435.26
30000	634.36	578.91	538.37	507.74	484.01	465.28	450.27
31000	655.50	598.20	556.31	524.66	500.14	480.79	465.28
32000	676.65	617.50	574.26	541.58	516.28	496.30	480.29
33000	697.79	636.80	592.20	558.51	532.41	511.81	495.29
34000	718.94	656.09	610.15	575.43	548.54	527.32	510.30
35000	740.08	675.39	628.09	592.36	564.68	542.83	525.31
40000	845.81	771.88	717.82	676.98	645.34	620.37	600.36
45000	951.53	868.36	807.55	761.60	726.01	697.92	675.40
50000	1057.26	964.84	897.28	846.22	806.68	775.46	750.44
55000	1162.98	1061.33	987.00	93C.84	887.35	853.01	825.49
60000	1268.71	1157.81	1076.73	1015.47	968.01	930.55	900.53
65000	1374.43	1254.29	1166.46	1100.09	1048.68	1008.10	975.57
70000	1480.16	1350.78	1256.18	1184.71	1129.35	1085.65	1050.62
75000	1585.88	1447.26	1345.91	1269.33	1210.02	1163.19	1125.66
80000	1691.61	1543.75	1435.64	1353.95	1290.68	1240.74	1200.71
100000	2114.51	1929.68	1794.55	1692.44	1613.35	1550.92	1500.88

TERM AMOUNT	13 YEARS	14 YEARS	15 YEARS	16 YEARS	17 YEARS	18 YEARS	19 YEARS
$ 25	.37	.36	.35	.35	.34	.34	.34
50	.74	.72	.70	.69	.68	.68	.67
75	1.10	1.08	1.05	1.04	1.02	1.01	1.00
100	1.47	1.43	1.40	1.38	1.36	1.35	1.33
200	2.93	2.86	2.80	2.76	2.72	2.69	2.66
300	4.39	4.29	4.20	4.14	4.08	4.03	3.99
400	5.85	5.71	5.60	5.51	5.44	5.37	5.32
500	7.31	7.14	7.00	6.89	6.79	6.71	6.65
600	8.77	8.57	8.40	8.27	8.15	8.06	7.97
700	10.23	9.99	9.80	9.64	9.51	9.40	9.30
800	11.69	11.42	11.20	11.02	10.87	10.74	10.63
900	13.15	12.85	12.60	12.40	12.22	12.08	11.96
1000	14.61	14.28	14.00	13.77	13.58	13.42	13.29
2000	29.21	28.55	28.00	27.54	27.16	26.84	26.57
3000	43.81	42.82	41.99	41.31	40.74	40.26	39.85
4000	58.42	57.09	55.99	55.08	54.31	53.67	53.13
5000	73.02	71.36	69.98	68.84	67.89	67.09	66.41
6000	87.62	85.63	83.98	82.61	81.47	80.51	79.70
7000	102.23	99.90	97.98	96.38	95.04	93.92	92.98
8000	116.83	114.17	111.97	110.15	108.62	107.34	106.26
9000	131.43	128.44	125.97	123.91	122.20	120.76	119.54
10000	146.03	142.71	139.96	137.68	135.78	134.17	132.82
11000	160.64	156.98	153.96	151.45	149.35	147.59	146.11
12000	175.24	171.25	167.96	165.22	162.93	161.01	159.39
13000	189.84	185.52	181.95	178.99	176.51	174.42	172.67
14000	204.45	199.79	195.95	192.75	190.08	187.84	185.95
15000	219.05	214.06	209.94	206.52	203.66	201.26	199.23
16000	233.65	228.33	223.94	220.29	217.24	214.68	212.52
17000	248.25	242.60	237.93	234.06	230.81	228.09	225.80
18000	262.86	256.87	251.93	247.82	244.39	241.51	239.08
19000	277.46	271.14	265.93	261.59	257.97	254.93	252.36
20000	292.06	285.41	279.92	275.36	271.54	268.34	265.64
21000	306.67	299.68	293.92	289.13	285.12	281.76	278.93
22000	321.27	313.95	307.91	302.89	298.70	295.18	292.21
23000	335.87	328.22	321.91	316.66	312.28	308.59	305.49
24000	350.47	342.49	335.91	330.43	325.85	322.01	318.77
25000	365.08	356.76	349.90	344.20	339.43	335.43	332.05
26000	379.68	371.04	363.90	357.97	353.01	348.84	345.34
27000	394.28	385.31	377.89	371.73	366.58	362.26	358.62
28000	408.89	399.58	391.89	385.50	380.16	375.68	371.90
29000	423.49	413.85	405.89	399.27	393.74	389.10	385.18
30000	438.09	428.12	419.88	413.04	407.32	402.51	398.46
31000	452.69	442.39	433.88	426.80	420.89	415.93	411.75
32000	467.30	456.66	447.87	440.57	434.47	429.35	425.03
33000	481.90	470.93	461.87	454.34	448.05	442.76	438.31
34000	496.50	485.20	475.86	468.11	461.62	456.18	451.59
35000	511.11	499.47	489.86	481.87	475.20	469.60	464.87
40000	584.12	570.82	559.84	550.71	543.09	536.68	531.28
45000	657.13	642.17	629.82	619.55	610.97	603.77	597.69
50000	730.15	713.52	699.80	688.39	678.86	670.85	664.10
55000	803.16	784.88	769.78	757.23	746.74	737.93	730.51
60000	876.18	856.23	839.76	826.07	814.63	805.02	796.92
65000	949.19	927.58	909.74	894.91	882.51	872.10	863.33
70000	1022.21	998.93	979.72	963.74	950.40	939.19	929.74
75000	1095.22	1070.28	1049.70	1032.58	1018.28	1006.27	996.15
80000	1168.23	1141.64	1119.67	1101.42	1086.17	1073.36	1062.56
100000	1460.29	1427.04	1399.59	1376.77	1357.71	1341.70	1328.20

TERM AMOUNT	20 YEARS	21 YEARS	22 YEARS	25 YEARS	30 YEARS	35 YEARS	40 YEARS
$ 25	.33	.33	.33	.33	.32	.32	.32
50	.66	.66	.65	.65	.64	.63	.63
75	.99	.99	.98	.97	.95	.95	.94
100	1.32	1.31	1.30	1.29	1.27	1.26	1.26
200	2.64	2.62	2.60	2.57	2.53	2.52	2.51
300	3.96	3.93	3.90	3.85	3.80	3.78	3.76
400	5.27	5.23	5.20	5.13	5.06	5.03	5.02
500	6.59	6.54	6.50	6.41	6.33	6.29	6.27
600	7.91	7.85	7.80	7.69	7.59	7.55	7.52
700	9.22	9.15	9.10	8.97	8.86	8.80	8.78
800	10.54	10.46	10.40	10.25	10.12	10.06	10.03
900	11.86	11.77	11.70	11.53	11.38	11.32	11.28
1000	13.17	13.08	12.99	12.81	12.65	12.57	12.54
2000	26.34	26.15	25.98	25.62	25.29	25.14	25.07
3000	39.51	39.22	38.97	38.43	37.94	37.71	37.60
4000	52.68	52.29	51.96	51.24	50.58	50.28	50.13
5000	65.84	65.36	64.95	64.05	63.23	62.85	62.67
6000	79.01	78.43	77.94	76.85	75.87	75.41	75.20
7000	92.18	91.50	90.93	89.66	88.52	87.98	87.73
8000	105.35	104.57	103.92	102.47	101.16	100.55	100.26
9000	118.52	117.65	116.91	115.28	113.80	113.12	112.80
10000	131.68	130.72	129.89	128.09	126.45	125.69	125.33
11000	144.85	143.79	142.88	140.90	139.09	138.25	137.86
12000	158.02	156.86	155.87	153.70	151.74	150.82	150.39
13000	171.19	169.93	168.86	166.51	164.38	163.39	162.92
14000	184.36	183.00	181.85	179.32	177.03	175.96	175.46
15000	197.52	196.07	194.84	192.13	189.67	188.53	187.99
16000	210.69	209.14	207.83	204.94	202.32	201.10	200.52
17000	223.86	222.21	220.82	217.75	214.96	213.66	213.05
18000	237.03	235.29	233.81	230.55	227.60	226.23	225.59
19000	250.20	248.36	246.80	243.36	240.25	238.80	238.12
20000	263.36	261.43	259.78	256.17	252.89	251.37	250.65
21000	276.53	274.50	272.77	268.98	265.54	263.94	263.18
22000	289.70	287.57	285.76	281.79	278.18	276.50	275.71
23000	302.87	300.64	298.75	294.60	290.83	289.07	288.25
24000	316.03	313.71	311.74	307.40	303.47	301.64	300.78
25000	329.20	326.78	324.73	320.21	316.12	314.21	313.31
26000	342.37	339.86	337.72	333.02	328.76	326.78	325.84
27000	355.54	352.93	350.71	345.83	341.40	339.34	338.38
28000	368.71	366.00	363.70	358.64	354.05	351.91	350.91
29000	381.87	379.07	376.69	371.45	366.69	364.48	363.44
30000	395.04	392.14	389.67	384.25	379.34	377.05	375.97
31000	408.21	405.21	402.66	397.06	391.98	389.62	388.50
32000	421.38	418.28	415.65	409.87	404.63	402.19	401.04
33000	434.55	431.35	428.64	422.68	417.27	414.75	413.57
34000	447.71	444.42	441.63	435.49	429.92	427.32	426.10
35000	460.88	457.50	454.62	448.30	442.56	439.89	438.63
40000	526.72	522.85	519.56	512.34	505.78	502.73	501.29
45000	592.56	588.21	584.51	576.38	569.00	565.57	563.96
50000	658.40	653.56	649.45	640.42	632.23	628.41	626.62
55000	724.24	718.92	714.40	704.46	695.45	691.25	689.28
60000	790.08	784.28	779.34	768.50	758.67	754.09	751.94
65000	855.92	849.63	844.29	832.54	821.89	816.93	814.60
70000	921.76	914.99	909.23	896.59	885.12	879.77	877.26
75000	987.60	980.34	974.18	960.63	948.34	942.61	939.92
80000	1053.44	1045.70	1039.12	1024.67	1011.56	1005.46	1002.58
100000	1316.79	1307.12	1298.90	1280.84	1264.45	1256.82	1253.23

15½%

MONTHLY PAYMENT
NECESSARY TO AMORTIZE A LOAN

TERM AMOUNT	1 YEAR	1½ YEARS	2 YEARS	2½ YEARS	3 YEARS	4 YEARS	5 YEARS
$ 25	2.27	1.57	1.22	1.02	.88	.71	.61
50	4.53	3.14	2.44	2.03	1.75	1.41	1.21
75	6.79	4.70	3.66	3.04	2.62	2.11	1.81
100	9.05	6.27	4.88	4.05	3.50	2.81	2.41
200	18.10	12.53	9.75	8.09	6.99	5.62	4.82
300	27.15	18.79	14.62	12.13	10.48	8.43	7.22
400	36.20	25.05	19.49	16.17	13.97	11.24	9.63
500	45.25	31.32	24.37	20.21	17.46	14.05	12.03
600	54.30	37.58	29.24	24.26	20.95	16.86	14.44
700	63.35	43.84	34.11	28.30	24.44	19.66	16.84
800	72.40	50.10	38.98	32.34	27.93	22.47	19.25
900	81.45	56.36	43.86	36.38	31.42	25.28	21.65
1000	90.50	62.63	48.73	40.42	34.92	28.09	24.06
2000	180.99	125.25	97.45	80.84	69.83	56.17	48.11
3000	271.49	187.87	146.18	121.26	104.74	84.26	72.16
4000	361.98	250.49	194.90	161.68	139.65	112.34	96.22
5000	452.48	313.11	243.63	202.10	174.56	140.43	120.27
6000	542.97	375.73	292.35	242.52	209.47	168.51	144.32
7000	633.47	438.35	341.08	282.94	244.38	196.60	168.38
8000	723.96	500.97	389.80	323.36	279.29	224.68	192.43
9000	814.45	563.59	438.53	363.78	314.20	252.77	216.48
10000	904.95	626.21	487.25	404.20	349.11	280.85	240.54
11000	995.44	688.83	535.97	444.62	384.02	308.94	264.59
12000	1085.94	751.45	584.70	485.04	418.93	337.02	288.64
13000	1176.43	814.07	633.42	525.46	453.84	365.11	312.70
14000	1266.93	876.69	682.15	565.88	488.75	393.19	336.75
15000	1357.42	939.31	730.87	606.30	523.67	421.28	360.80
16000	1447.92	1001.93	779.60	646.72	558.58	449.36	384.86
17000	1538.41	1064.55	828.32	687.14	593.49	477.45	408.91
18000	1628.90	1127.17	877.05	727.56	628.40	505.53	432.96
19000	1719.40	1189.79	925.77	767.98	663.31	533.62	457.02
20000	1809.89	1252.41	974.50	808.40	698.22	561.70	481.07
21000	1900.39	1315.03	1023.22	848.82	733.13	589.79	505.12
22000	1990.88	1377.65	1071.94	889.24	768.04	617.87	529.18
23000	2081.38	1440.27	1120.67	929.66	802.95	645.96	553.23
24000	2171.87	1502.89	1169.39	970.08	837.86	674.04	577.28
25000	2262.37	1565.51	1218.12	1010.50	872.77	702.13	601.33
26000	2352.86	1628.13	1266.84	1050.92	907.68	730.21	625.39
27000	2443.35	1690.75	1315.57	1091.34	942.59	758.30	649.44
28000	2533.85	1753.37	1364.29	1131.76	977.50	786.38	673.49
29000	2624.34	1816.00	1413.02	1172.18	1012.41	814.47	697.55
30000	2714.84	1878.62	1461.74	1212.60	1047.33	842.55	721.60
31000	2805.33	1941.24	1510.47	1253.02	1082.24	870.64	745.65
32000	2895.83	2003.86	1559.19	1293.44	1117.15	898.72	769.71
33000	2986.32	2066.48	1607.91	1333.86	1152.06	926.81	793.76
34000	3076.82	2129.10	1656.64	1374.28	1186.97	954.89	817.81
35000	3167.31	2191.72	1705.36	1414.70	1221.88	982.98	841.87
40000	3619.78	2504.82	1948.99	1616.80	1396.43	1123.40	962.13
45000	4072.25	2817.92	2192.61	1818.90	1570.99	1263.82	1082.40
50000	4524.73	3131.02	2436.23	2021.00	1745.54	1404.25	1202.66
55000	4977.20	3444.12	2679.85	2223.10	1920.09	1544.67	1322.93
60000	5429.67	3757.23	2923.48	2425.20	2094.65	1685.10	1443.20
65000	5882.14	4070.33	3167.10	2627.30	2269.20	1825.52	1563.46
70000	6334.61	4383.43	3410.72	2829.40	2443.75	1965.95	1683.73
75000	6787.09	4696.53	3654.35	3031.50	2618.31	2106.37	1803.99
80000	7239.56	5009.63	3897.97	3233.60	2792.86	2246.79	1924.26
100000	9049.45	6262.04	4872.46	4041.99	3491.07	2808.49	2405.32

138

TERM AMOUNT	6 YEARS	7 YEARS	8 YEARS	9 YEARS	10 YEARS	11 YEARS	12 YEARS
$ 25	.54	.49	.46	.44	.42	.40	.39
50	1.08	.98	.92	.87	.83	.80	.77
75	1.61	1.47	1.37	1.30	1.24	1.19	1.15
100	2.15	1.96	1.83	1.73	1.65	1.59	1.54
200	4.29	3.92	3.65	3.45	3.29	3.17	3.07
300	6.43	5.88	5.48	5.17	4.94	4.75	4.60
400	8.57	7.84	7.30	6.89	6.58	6.33	6.14
500	10.71	9.79	9.12	8.62	8.23	7.92	7.67
600	12.86	11.75	10.95	10.34	9.87	9.50	9.20
700	15.00	13.71	12.77	12.06	11.51	11.08	10.74
800	17.14	15.67	14.59	13.78	13.16	12.66	12.27
900	19.28	17.63	16.42	15.51	14.80	14.25	13.80
1000	21.42	19.58	18.24	17.23	16.45	15.83	15.34
2000	42.84	39.16	36.48	34.45	32.89	31.65	30.67
3000	64.26	58.74	54.71	51.68	49.33	47.48	46.00
4000	85.67	78.32	72.95	68.90	65.77	63.30	61.33
5000	107.09	97.90	91.18	86.12	82.21	79.13	76.67
6000	128.51	117.48	109.42	103.35	98.65	94.95	92.00
7000	149.93	137.05	127.66	120.57	115.09	110.78	107.33
8000	171.34	156.63	145.89	137.79	131.53	126.60	122.66
9000	192.76	176.21	164.13	155.02	147.97	142.43	137.99
10000	214.18	195.79	182.36	172.24	164.42	158.25	153.33
11000	235.60	215.37	200.60	189.46	180.86	174.08	168.66
12000	257.01	234.95	218.84	206.69	197.30	189.90	183.99
13000	278.43	254.52	237.07	223.91	213.74	205.73	199.32
14000	299.85	274.10	255.31	241.13	230.18	221.55	214.65
15000	321.27	293.68	273.54	258.36	246.62	237.38	229.99
16000	342.68	313.26	291.78	275.58	263.06	253.20	245.32
17000	364.10	332.84	310.02	292.80	279.50	269.03	260.65
18000	385.52	352.42	328.25	310.03	295.94	284.85	275.98
19000	406.94	371.99	346.49	327.25	312.39	300.68	291.31
20000	428.35	391.57	364.72	344.48	328.83	316.50	306.65
21000	449.77	411.15	382.96	361.70	345.27	332.32	321.98
22000	471.19	430.73	401.20	378.92	361.71	348.15	337.31
23000	492.61	450.31	419.43	396.15	378.15	363.97	352.64
24000	514.02	469.89	437.67	413.37	394.59	379.80	367.97
25000	535.44	489.46	455.90	430.59	411.03	395.62	383.31
26000	556.86	509.04	474.14	447.82	427.47	411.45	398.64
27000	578.28	528.62	492.37	465.04	443.91	427.27	413.97
28000	599.69	548.20	510.61	482.26	460.35	443.10	429.30
29000	621.11	567.78	528.85	499.49	476.80	458.92	444.63
30000	642.53	587.36	547.08	516.71	493.24	474.75	459.97
31000	663.95	606.93	565.32	533.93	509.68	490.57	475.30
32000	685.36	626.51	583.55	551.16	526.12	506.40	490.63
33000	706.78	646.09	601.79	568.38	542.56	522.22	505.96
34000	728.20	665.67	620.03	585.60	559.00	538.05	521.29
35000	749.62	685.25	638.26	602.83	575.44	553.87	536.63
40000	856.70	783.14	729.44	688.95	657.65	632.99	613.29
45000	963.79	881.03	820.62	775.06	739.85	712.12	689.95
50000	1070.88	978.92	911.80	861.18	822.06	791.24	766.61
55000	1177.97	1076.81	1002.98	947.30	904.26	870.37	843.27
60000	1285.05	1174.71	1094.16	1033.42	986.47	949.49	919.93
65000	1392.14	1272.60	1185.34	1119.53	1068.67	1028.61	996.59
70000	1499.23	1370.49	1276.52	1205.65	1150.88	1107.74	1073.25
75000	1606.32	1468.38	1367.70	1291.77	1233.08	1186.86	1149.91
80000	1713.40	1566.27	1458.88	1377.89	1315.29	1265.98	1226.57
100000	2141.75	1957.84	1823.60	1722.36	1644.11	1582.48	1533.21

139

15½%

MONTHLY PAYMENT
NECESSARY TO AMORTIZE A LOAN

TERM AMOUNT	13 YEARS	14 YEARS	15 YEARS	16 YEARS	17 YEARS	18 YEARS	19 YEARS
$ 25	.38	.37	.36	.36	.35	.35	.35
50	.75	.74	.72	.71	.70	.69	.69
75	1.13	1.10	1.08	1.06	1.05	1.04	1.03
100	1.50	1.47	1.44	1.42	1.40	1.38	1.37
200	2.99	2.93	2.87	2.83	2.79	2.76	2.73
300	4.49	4.39	4.31	4.24	4.18	4.14	4.10
400	5.98	5.85	5.74	5.65	5.58	5.52	5.46
500	7.47	7.31	7.17	7.06	6.97	6.89	6.83
600	8.97	8.77	8.61	8.48	8.36	8.27	8.19
700	10.46	10.23	10.04	9.89	9.76	9.65	9.56
800	11.95	11.69	11.48	11.30	11.15	11.03	10.92
900	13.45	13.15	12.91	12.71	12.54	12.41	12.29
1000	14.94	14.61	14.34	14.12	13.94	13.78	13.65
2000	29.87	29.22	28.68	28.24	27.87	27.56	27.30
3000	44.81	43.83	43.02	42.36	41.80	41.34	40.95
4000	59.74	58.44	57.36	56.48	55.74	55.12	54.60
5000	74.67	73.04	71.70	70.59	69.67	68.90	68.25
6000	89.61	87.65	86.04	84.71	83.60	82.67	81.89
7000	104.54	102.26	100.38	98.83	97.54	96.45	95.54
8000	119.47	116.87	114.72	112.95	111.47	110.23	109.19
9000	134.41	131.48	129.06	127.07	125.40	124.01	122.84
10000	149.34	146.08	143.40	141.18	139.33	137.79	136.49
11000	164.27	160.69	157.74	155.30	153.27	151.57	150.14
12000	179.21	175.30	172.08	169.42	167.20	165.34	163.78
13000	194.14	189.91	186.42	183.54	181.13	179.12	177.43
14000	209.07	204.52	200.76	197.66	195.07	192.90	191.08
15000	224.01	219.12	215.10	211.77	209.00	206.68	204.73
16000	238.94	233.73	229.44	225.89	222.93	220.46	218.38
17000	253.87	248.34	243.78	240.01	236.86	234.23	232.03
18000	268.81	262.95	258.12	254.13	250.80	248.01	245.67
19000	283.74	277.56	272.46	268.24	264.73	261.79	259.32
20000	298.67	292.16	286.80	282.36	278.66	275.57	272.97
21000	313.61	306.77	301.14	296.48	292.60	289.35	286.62
22000	328.54	321.38	315.48	310.60	306.53	303.13	300.27
23000	343.47	335.99	329.82	324.72	320.46	316.90	313.91
24000	358.41	350.59	344.16	338.83	334.40	330.68	327.56
25000	373.34	365.20	358.50	352.95	348.33	344.46	341.21
26000	388.27	379.81	372.84	367.07	362.26	358.24	354.86
27000	403.21	394.42	387.18	381.19	376.19	372.02	368.51
28000	418.14	409.03	401.52	395.31	390.13	385.79	382.16
29000	433.08	423.63	415.86	409.42	404.06	399.57	395.80
30000	448.01	438.24	430.20	423.54	417.99	413.35	409.45
31000	462.94	452.85	444.54	437.66	431.93	427.13	423.10
32000	477.88	467.46	458.88	451.78	445.86	440.91	436.75
33000	492.81	482.07	473.22	465.89	459.79	454.69	450.40
34000	507.74	496.67	487.56	480.01	473.72	468.46	464.05
35000	522.68	511.28	501.90	494.13	487.66	482.24	477.69
40000	597.34	584.32	573.60	564.72	557.32	551.13	545.94
45000	672.01	657.36	645.30	635.31	626.99	620.02	614.18
50000	746.68	730.40	717.00	705.90	696.65	688.91	682.42
55000	821.35	803.44	788.70	776.49	766.32	757.81	750.66
60000	896.01	876.48	860.40	847.08	835.98	826.70	818.90
65000	970.68	949.52	932.10	917.67	905.65	895.59	887.14
70000	1045.35	1022.56	1003.80	988.26	975.31	964.48	955.38
75000	1120.01	1095.60	1075.50	1058.85	1044.97	1033.37	1023.62
80000	1194.68	1168.64	1147.20	1129.43	1114.64	1102.26	1091.87
100000	1493.35	1460.79	1434.00	1411.79	1393.30	1377.82	1364.83

140

TERM AMOUNT	20 YEARS	21 YEARS	22 YEARS	25 YEARS	30 YEARS	35 YEARS	40 YEARS
$ 25	.34	.34	.34	.33	.33	.33	.33
50	.68	.68	.67	.66	.66	.65	.65
75	1.02	1.01	1.01	.99	.98	.98	.98
100	1.36	1.35	1.34	1.32	1.31	1.30	1.30
200	2.71	2.69	2.68	2.64	2.61	2.60	2.59
300	4.07	4.04	4.02	3.96	3.92	3.90	3.89
400	5.42	5.38	5.35	5.28	5.22	5.20	5.18
500	6.77	6.73	6.69	6.60	6.53	6.49	6.48
600	8.13	8.07	8.03	7.92	7.83	7.79	7.77
700	9.48	9.42	9.36	9.24	9.14	9.09	9.07
800	10.84	10.76	10.70	10.56	10.44	10.39	10.36
900	12.19	12.11	12.04	11.88	11.75	11.68	11.65
1000	13.54	13.45	13.37	13.20	13.05	12.98	12.95
2000	27.08	26.90	26.74	26.40	26.10	25.96	25.89
3000	40.62	40.34	40.11	39.60	39.14	38.93	38.84
4000	54.16	53.79	53.48	52.79	52.19	51.91	51.78
5000	67.70	67.24	66.85	65.99	65.23	64.88	64.72
6000	81.24	80.68	80.21	79.19	78.28	77.86	77.67
7000	94.78	94.13	93.58	92.39	91.32	90.84	90.61
8000	108.32	107.58	106.95	105.58	104.37	103.81	103.56
9000	121.85	121.02	120.32	118.78	117.41	116.79	116.50
10000	135.39	134.47	133.69	131.98	130.46	129.76	129.44
11000	148.93	147.92	147.05	145.18	143.50	142.74	142.39
12000	162.47	161.36	160.42	158.37	156.55	155.72	155.33
13000	176.01	174.81	173.79	171.57	169.59	168.69	168.28
14000	189.55	188.25	187.16	184.77	182.64	181.67	181.22
15000	203.09	201.70	200.53	197.97	195.68	194.64	194.16
16000	216.63	215.15	213.89	211.16	208.73	207.62	207.11
17000	230.16	228.59	227.26	224.36	221.77	220.59	220.05
18000	243.70	242.04	240.63	237.56	234.82	233.57	233.00
19000	257.24	255.49	254.00	250.76	247.86	246.55	245.94
20000	270.78	268.93	267.37	263.95	260.91	259.52	258.88
21000	284.32	282.38	280.74	277.15	273.95	272.50	271.83
22000	297.86	295.83	294.10	290.35	287.00	285.47	284.77
23000	311.40	309.27	307.47	303.55	300.04	298.45	297.72
24000	324.94	322.72	320.84	316.74	313.09	311.43	310.66
25000	338.48	336.16	334.21	329.94	326.13	324.40	323.60
26000	352.01	349.61	347.58	343.14	339.18	337.38	336.55
27000	365.55	363.06	360.94	356.34	352.22	350.35	349.49
28000	379.09	376.50	374.31	369.53	365.27	363.33	362.44
29000	392.63	389.95	387.68	382.73	378.31	376.30	375.38
30000	406.17	403.40	401.05	395.93	391.36	389.28	388.32
31000	419.71	416.84	414.42	409.13	404.41	402.26	401.27
32000	433.25	430.29	427.78	422.32	417.45	415.23	414.21
33000	446.79	443.74	441.15	435.52	430.50	428.21	427.16
34000	460.32	457.18	454.52	448.72	443.54	441.18	440.10
35000	473.86	470.63	467.89	461.92	456.59	454.16	453.04
40000	541.56	537.86	534.73	527.90	521.81	519.04	517.76
45000	609.25	605.09	601.57	593.89	587.04	583.92	582.48
50000	676.95	672.32	668.41	659.88	652.26	648.80	647.20
55000	744.64	739.56	735.25	725.86	717.49	713.68	711.92
60000	812.33	806.79	802.09	791.85	782.72	778.56	776.64
65000	880.03	874.02	868.93	857.84	847.94	843.44	841.36
70000	947.72	941.25	935.77	923.83	913.17	908.31	906.08
75000	1015.42	1008.48	1002.61	985.81	978.39	973.19	970.80
80000	1083.11	1075.71	1069.45	1055.80	1043.62	1038.07	1035.52
100000	1353.89	1344.64	1336.82	1319.75	1304.52	1297.59	1294.40

MONTHLY PAYMENT
NECESSARY TO AMORTIZE A LOAN

TERM AMOUNT	1 YEAR	1½ YEARS	2 YEARS	2½ YEARS	3 YEARS	4 YEARS	5 YEARS
$ 25	2.27	1.58	1.23	1.02	.88	.71	.61
50	4.54	3.15	2.45	2.04	1.76	1.42	1.22
75	6.81	4.72	3.68	3.05	2.64	2.13	1.83
100	9.08	6.29	4.90	4.07	3.52	2.84	2.44
200	18.15	12.58	9.80	8.14	7.04	5.67	4.87
300	27.22	18.86	14.69	12.20	10.55	8.51	7.30
400	36.30	25.15	19.59	16.27	14.07	11.34	9.73
500	45.37	31.43	24.49	20.34	17.58	14.18	12.16
600	54.44	37.72	29.38	24.40	21.10	17.01	14.60
700	63.52	44.00	34.28	28.47	24.61	19.84	17.03
800	72.59	50.29	39.18	32.53	28.13	22.68	19.46
900	81.66	56.58	44.07	36.60	31.65	25.51	21.89
1000	90.74	62.86	48.97	40.67	35.16	28.35	24.32
2000	181.47	125.72	97.93	81.33	70.32	56.69	48.64
3000	272.20	188.57	146.89	121.99	105.48	85.03	72.96
4000	362.93	251.43	195.86	162.65	140.63	113.37	97.28
5000	453.66	314.29	244.82	203.32	175.79	141.71	121.60
6000	544.39	377.14	293.78	243.98	210.95	170.05	145.91
7000	635.12	440.00	342.75	284.64	246.10	198.39	170.23
8000	725.85	502.86	391.71	325.30	281.26	226.73	194.55
9000	816.58	565.71	440.67	365.96	316.42	255.07	218.87
10000	907.31	628.57	489.64	406.63	351.58	283.41	243.19
11000	998.04	691.43	538.60	447.29	386.73	311.75	267.50
12000	1088.78	754.28	587.56	487.95	421.89	340.09	291.82
13000	1179.51	817.14	636.53	528.61	457.05	368.43	316.14
14000	1270.24	880.00	685.49	569.27	492.20	396.77	340.46
15000	1360.97	942.85	734.45	609.94	527.36	425.11	364.78
16000	1451.70	1005.71	783.41	650.60	562.52	453.45	389.09
17000	1542.43	1068.56	832.38	691.26	597.67	481.79	413.41
18000	1633.16	1131.42	881.34	731.92	632.83	510.13	437.73
19000	1723.89	1194.28	930.30	772.58	667.99	538.47	462.05
20000	1814.62	1257.13	979.27	813.25	703.15	566.81	486.37
21000	1905.35	1319.99	1028.23	853.91	738.30	595.15	510.68
22000	1996.08	1382.85	1077.19	894.57	773.46	623.49	535.00
23000	2086.81	1445.70	1126.16	935.23	808.62	651.83	559.32
24000	2177.55	1508.56	1175.12	975.89	843.77	680.17	583.64
25000	2268.28	1571.42	1224.08	1016.56	878.93	708.51	607.96
26000	2359.01	1634.27	1273.05	1057.22	914.09	736.85	632.27
27000	2449.74	1697.13	1322.01	1097.88	949.24	765.19	656.59
28000	2540.47	1759.99	1370.97	1138.54	984.40	793.53	680.91
29000	2631.20	1822.84	1419.94	1179.21	1019.56	821.87	705.23
30000	2721.93	1885.70	1468.90	1219.87	1054.72	850.21	729.55
31000	2812.66	1948.55	1517.86	1260.53	1089.87	878.55	753.86
32000	2903.39	2011.41	1566.82	1301.19	1125.03	906.89	778.18
33000	2994.12	2074.27	1615.79	1341.85	1160.19	935.23	802.50
34000	3084.85	2137.12	1664.75	1382.52	1195.34	963.57	826.82
35000	3175.59	2199.98	1713.71	1423.18	1230.50	991.91	851.14
40000	3629.24	2514.98	1958.53	1626.49	1406.29	1133.62	972.73
45000	4082.89	2828.54	2203.34	1829.80	1582.07	1275.32	1094.32
50000	4536.55	3142.83	2448.16	2033.11	1757.86	1417.02	1215.91
55000	4990.20	3457.11	2692.98	2236.42	1933.64	1558.72	1337.50
60000	5443.86	3771.39	2937.79	2439.73	2109.43	1700.42	1459.09
65000	5897.51	4085.67	3182.61	2643.04	2285.21	1842.12	1580.68
70000	6351.17	4399.96	3427.42	2846.35	2461.00	1983.82	1702.27
75000	6804.82	4714.24	3672.24	3049.66	2636.78	2125.53	1823.86
80000	7258.47	5028.52	3917.05	3252.97	2812.57	2267.23	1945.45
100000	9073.09	6285.65	4896.32	4066.21	3515.71	2834.03	2431.81

TERM AMOUNT	6 YEARS	7 YEARS	8 YEARS	9 YEARS	10 YEARS	11 YEARS	12 YEARS
$ 25	.55	.50	.47	.44	.42	.41	.40
50	1.09	1.00	.93	.88	.84	.81	.79
75	1.63	1.49	1.39	1.32	1.26	1.22	1.18
100	2.17	1.99	1.86	1.76	1.68	1.62	1.57
200	4.34	3.98	3.71	3.51	3.36	3.23	3.14
300	6.51	5.96	5.56	5.26	5.03	4.85	4.70
400	8.68	7.95	7.42	7.02	6.71	6.46	6.27
500	10.85	9.94	9.27	8.77	8.38	8.08	7.83
600	13.02	11.92	11.12	10.52	10.06	9.69	9.40
700	15.19	13.91	12.98	12.27	11.73	11.31	10.97
800	17.36	15.89	14.83	14.03	13.41	12.92	12.53
900	19.53	17.88	16.68	15.78	15.08	14.53	14.10
1000	21.70	19.87	18.53	17.53	16.76	16.15	15.66
2000	43.39	39.73	37.06	35.06	33.51	32.29	31.32
3000	65.08	59.59	55.59	52.58	50.26	48.43	46.98
4000	86.77	79.45	74.12	70.11	67.01	64.58	62.64
5000	108.46	99.32	92.65	87.63	83.76	80.72	78.30
6000	130.16	119.18	111.18	105.16	100.51	96.86	93.95
7000	151.85	139.04	129.71	122.68	117.26	113.01	109.61
8000	173.54	158.90	148.24	140.21	134.02	129.15	125.27
9000	195.23	178.76	166.76	157.73	150.77	145.29	140.93
10000	216.92	198.63	185.29	175.26	167.52	161.44	156.59
11000	238.62	218.49	203.82	192.78	184.27	177.58	172.25
12000	260.31	238.35	222.35	210.31	201.02	193.72	187.90
13000	282.00	258.21	240.88	227.83	217.77	209.87	203.56
14000	303.69	278.07	259.41	245.36	234.52	226.01	219.22
15000	325.38	297.94	277.94	262.88	251.27	242.15	234.88
16000	347.07	317.80	296.47	280.41	268.05	258.30	250.54
17000	368.77	337.66	314.99	297.93	284.78	274.44	266.20
18000	390.46	357.52	333.52	315.46	301.53	290.58	281.85
19000	412.15	377.38	352.05	332.98	318.28	306.73	297.51
20000	433.84	397.25	370.58	350.51	335.03	322.87	313.17
21000	455.53	417.11	389.11	368.04	351.78	339.01	328.83
22000	477.23	436.97	407.64	385.56	368.53	355.15	344.49
23000	498.92	456.83	426.17	403.09	385.29	371.30	360.14
24000	520.61	476.69	444.70	420.61	402.04	387.44	375.80
25000	542.30	496.56	463.22	438.14	418.79	403.58	391.46
26000	563.99	516.42	481.75	455.66	435.54	419.73	407.12
27000	585.68	536.28	500.28	473.19	452.29	435.87	422.78
28000	607.38	556.14	518.81	490.71	469.04	452.01	438.44
29000	629.07	576.00	537.34	508.24	485.79	468.16	454.09
30000	650.76	595.87	555.87	525.76	502.54	484.30	469.75
31000	672.45	615.73	574.40	543.29	519.30	500.44	485.41
32000	694.14	635.59	592.93	560.81	536.05	516.59	501.07
33000	715.84	655.45	611.45	578.34	552.80	532.73	516.73
34000	737.53	675.32	629.98	595.86	569.55	548.87	532.39
35000	759.22	695.18	648.51	613.39	586.30	565.02	548.04
40000	867.68	794.49	741.16	701.02	670.06	645.74	626.34
45000	976.14	893.80	833.80	788.64	753.81	726.45	704.63
50000	1084.60	993.11	926.44	876.27	837.57	807.16	782.92
55000	1193.06	1092.42	1019.09	963.89	921.33	887.88	861.21
60000	1301.52	1191.73	1111.73	1051.52	1005.08	968.60	939.50
65000	1409.97	1291.04	1204.38	1139.15	1088.84	1049.31	1017.79
70000	1518.43	1390.35	1297.02	1226.77	1172.60	1130.03	1096.08
75000	1626.89	1489.66	1389.66	1314.40	1256.35	1210.74	1174.37
80000	1735.35	1588.97	1482.31	1402.03	1340.11	1291.46	1252.67
100000	2169.19	1986.21	1852.88	1752.53	1675.14	1614.32	1565.83

MONTHLY PAYMENT
NECESSARY TO AMORTIZE A LOAN

TERM AMOUNT	13 YEARS	14 YEARS	15 YEARS	16 YEARS	17 YEARS	18 YEARS	19 YEARS
$ 25	.39	.38	.37	.37	.36	.36	.36
50	.77	.75	.74	.73	.72	.71	.71
75	1.15	1.13	1.11	1.09	1.08	1.07	1.06
100	1.53	1.50	1.47	1.45	1.43	1.42	1.41
200	3.06	2.99	2.94	2.90	2.86	2.83	2.81
300	4.59	4.49	4.41	4.35	4.29	4.25	4.21
400	6.11	5.98	5.88	5.79	5.72	5.66	5.61
500	7.64	7.48	7.35	7.24	7.15	7.08	7.01
600	9.17	8.97	8.82	8.69	8.58	8.49	8.42
700	10.69	10.47	10.29	10.13	10.01	9.90	9.82
800	12.22	11.96	11.75	11.58	11.44	11.32	11.22
900	13.75	13.46	13.22	13.03	12.87	12.73	12.62
1000	15.27	14.95	14.69	14.48	14.30	14.15	14.02
2000	30.54	29.90	29.38	28.95	28.59	28.29	28.04
3000	45.81	44.85	44.07	43.42	42.88	42.43	42.06
4000	61.07	59.80	58.75	57.89	57.17	56.57	56.07
5000	76.34	74.75	73.44	72.36	71.46	70.72	70.09
6000	91.61	89.70	88.13	86.83	85.76	84.86	84.11
7000	106.87	104.64	102.81	101.30	100.05	99.00	98.13
8000	122.14	119.59	117.50	115.77	114.34	113.14	112.14
9000	137.41	134.54	132.19	130.24	128.63	127.29	126.16
10000	152.68	149.49	146.88	144.72	142.92	141.43	140.18
11000	167.94	164.44	161.56	159.19	157.22	155.57	154.20
12000	183.21	179.39	176.25	173.66	171.51	169.71	168.21
13000	198.48	194.33	190.94	188.13	185.80	183.86	182.23
14000	213.74	209.28	205.62	202.60	200.09	198.00	196.25
15000	229.01	224.23	220.31	217.07	214.38	212.14	210.27
16000	244.28	239.18	235.00	231.54	228.68	226.28	224.28
17000	259.54	254.13	249.68	246.01	242.97	240.43	238.30
18000	274.81	269.08	264.37	260.48	257.26	254.57	252.32
19000	290.08	284.03	279.06	274.96	271.55	268.71	266.34
20000	305.35	298.97	293.75	289.43	285.84	282.85	280.35
21000	320.61	313.92	308.43	303.90	300.13	297.00	294.37
22000	335.88	328.87	323.12	318.37	314.43	311.14	308.39
23000	351.15	343.82	337.81	332.84	328.72	325.28	322.41
24000	366.41	358.77	352.49	347.31	343.01	339.42	336.42
25000	381.68	373.72	367.18	361.78	357.30	353.57	350.44
26000	396.95	388.66	381.87	376.25	371.59	367.71	364.46
27000	412.22	403.61	396.55	390.72	385.89	381.85	378.48
28000	427.48	418.56	411.24	405.20	400.18	395.99	392.49
29000	442.75	433.51	425.93	419.67	414.47	410.14	406.51
30000	458.02	448.46	440.62	434.14	428.76	424.28	420.53
31000	473.28	463.41	455.30	448.61	443.05	438.42	434.55
32000	488.55	478.36	469.99	463.08	457.35	452.56	448.56
33000	503.82	493.30	484.68	477.55	471.64	466.71	462.58
34000	519.08	508.25	499.36	492.02	485.93	480.85	476.60
35000	534.35	523.20	514.05	506.49	500.22	494.99	490.62
40000	610.69	597.94	587.49	578.85	571.68	565.70	560.70
45000	687.02	672.69	660.92	651.20	643.14	636.42	630.79
50000	763.36	747.43	734.36	723.56	714.60	707.13	700.88
55000	839.69	822.17	807.79	795.92	786.06	777.84	770.97
60000	916.03	896.91	881.23	868.27	857.52	848.55	841.05
65000	992.36	971.65	954.66	940.63	928.98	919.27	911.14
70000	1068.70	1046.40	1028.10	1012.98	1000.44	989.98	981.23
75000	1145.03	1121.14	1101.53	1085.34	1071.90	1060.69	1051.31
80000	1221.37	1195.88	1174.97	1157.69	1143.36	1131.40	1121.40
100000	1526.71	1494.85	1468.71	1447.12	1429.19	1414.25	1401.75

TERM AMOUNT	20 YEARS	21 YEARS	22 YEARS	25 YEARS	30 YEARS	35 YEARS	40 YEARS
$ 25	.35	.35	.35	.34	.34	.34	.34
50	.70	.70	.69	.68	.68	.67	.67
75	1.05	1.04	1.04	1.02	1.01	1.01	1.01
100	1.40	1.39	1.38	1.36	1.35	1.34	1.34
200	2.79	2.77	2.75	2.72	2.69	2.68	2.68
300	4.18	4.15	4.13	4.08	4.04	4.02	4.01
400	5.57	5.53	5.50	5.44	5.38	5.36	5.35
500	6.96	6.92	6.88	6.80	6.73	6.70	6.68
600	8.35	8.30	8.25	8.16	8.07	8.04	8.02
700	9.74	9.68	9.63	9.52	9.42	9.37	9.35
800	11.14	11.06	11.00	1C.88	10.76	10.71	10.69
900	12.53	12.45	12.38	12.23	12.11	12.05	12.03
1000	13.92	13.83	13.75	13.59	13.45	13.39	13.36
2000	27.83	27.65	27.50	27.18	26.90	26.77	26.72
3000	41.74	41.48	41.25	40.77	40.35	40.16	40.07
4000	55.66	55.30	55.00	54.36	53.80	53.54	53.43
5000	69.57	69.13	68.75	67.95	67.24	66.93	66.79
6000	83.48	82.95	82.50	81.54	80.69	80.31	80.14
7000	97.39	96.78	96.25	95.13	94.14	93.70	93.50
8000	111.31	110.60	110.00	108.72	107.59	107.08	106.86
9000	125.22	124.42	123.75	122.30	121.03	120.47	120.21
10000	139.13	138.25	137.50	135.89	134.48	133.85	133.57
11000	153.04	152.07	151.25	149.48	147.93	147.24	146.93
12000	166.96	165.90	165.00	163.07	161.38	160.62	160.28
13000	180.87	179.72	178.75	176.66	174.82	174.01	173.64
14000	194.78	193.55	192.50	190.25	188.27	187.39	187.00
15000	208.69	207.37	206.25	203.84	201.72	200.78	200.35
16000	222.61	221.19	220.00	217.43	215.17	214.16	213.71
17000	236.52	235.02	233.75	231.02	228.61	227.54	227.07
18000	250.43	248.84	247.50	244.60	242.06	240.93	240.42
19000	264.34	262.67	261.25	258.19	255.51	254.31	253.78
20000	278.26	276.49	275.00	271.78	268.96	267.70	267.13
21000	292.17	290.32	288.75	285.37	282.40	281.08	280.49
22000	306.08	304.14	302.50	298.96	295.85	294.47	293.85
23000	319.99	317.96	316.25	312.55	309.30	307.85	307.20
24000	333.91	331.79	330.00	326.14	322.75	321.24	320.56
25000	347.82	345.61	343.75	339.73	336.19	334.62	333.92
26000	361.73	359.44	357.50	353.32	349.64	348.01	347.27
27000	375.64	373.26	371.25	366.90	363.09	361.39	360.63
28000	389.56	387.09	385.00	38C.49	376.54	374.78	373.99
29000	403.47	400.91	398.75	394.08	389.98	388.16	387.34
30000	417.38	414.73	412.50	407.67	403.43	401.55	400.70
31000	431.29	428.56	426.25	421.26	416.88	414.93	414.06
32000	445.21	442.38	440.00	434.85	430.33	428.32	427.41
33000	459.12	456.21	453.75	448.44	443.77	441.70	440.77
34000	473.03	470.03	467.50	462.03	457.22	455.08	454.13
35000	486.94	483.86	481.25	475.62	470.67	468.47	467.48
40000	556.51	552.98	550.00	543.56	537.91	535.39	534.26
45000	626.07	622.10	618.75	611.50	605.15	602.32	601.05
50000	695.63	691.22	687.50	679.45	672.38	669.24	667.83
55000	765.20	760.34	756.25	747.39	739.62	736.16	734.61
60000	834.76	829.46	825.00	815.34	806.86	803.09	801.39
65000	904.32	898.58	893.75	883.28	874.10	870.01	868.18
70000	973.88	967.71	962.50	951.23	941.33	936.93	934.96
75000	1043.45	1036.83	1031.25	1019.17	1008.57	1003.86	1001.74
80000	1113.01	1105.95	1100.00	1087.12	1075.81	1070.78	1068.52
100000	1391.26	1382.44	1375.00	1358.89	1344.76	1338.47	1335.65

17%

TERM AMOUNT	1 YEAR	1½ YEARS	2 YEARS	2½ YEARS	3 YEARS	4 YEARS	5 YEARS
$ 25	2.29	1.59	1.24	1.03	.90	.73	.63
50	4.57	3.17	2.48	2.06	1.79	1.45	1.25
75	6.85	4.75	3.71	3.09	2.68	2.17	1.87
100	9.13	6.34	4.95	4.12	3.57	2.89	2.49
200	18.25	12.67	9.89	8.23	7.14	5.78	4.98
300	27.37	19.00	14.84	12.35	10.70	8.67	7.46
400	36.49	25.34	19.78	16.46	14.27	11.55	9.95
500	45.61	31.67	24.73	20.58	17.83	14.43	12.43
600	54.73	38.00	29.67	24.69	21.40	17.32	14.92
700	63.85	44.34	34.61	28.81	24.96	20.20	17.40
800	72.97	50.67	39.56	32.92	28.53	23.09	19.89
900	82.09	57.00	44.50	37.04	32.09	25.97	22.37
1000	91.21	63.34	49.45	41.15	35.66	28.86	24.86
2000	182.41	126.67	98.89	82.30	71.31	57.72	49.71
3000	273.62	190.00	148.33	123.45	106.96	86.57	74.56
4000	364.82	253.33	197.77	164.60	142.62	115.43	99.42
5000	456.03	316.66	247.22	205.75	178.27	144.28	124.27
6000	547.23	379.99	296.66	246.90	213.92	173.14	149.12
7000	638.44	443.32	346.10	288.05	249.57	201.99	173.97
8000	729.64	506.65	395.54	329.20	285.23	230.85	198.83
9000	820.85	569.98	444.99	370.35	320.88	259.70	223.68
10000	912.05	633.31	494.43	411.49	356.53	288.56	248.53
11000	1003.26	696.64	543.87	452.64	392.19	317.41	273.38
12000	1094.46	759.97	593.31	493.79	427.84	346.27	298.24
13000	1185.67	823.30	642.75	534.94	463.49	375.12	323.09
14000	1276.87	886.63	692.20	576.09	499.14	403.98	347.94
15000	1368.08	949.96	741.64	617.24	534.80	432.83	372.79
16000	1459.28	1013.29	791.08	658.39	570.45	461.69	397.65
17000	1550.49	1076.62	840.52	699.54	606.10	490.54	422.50
18000	1641.69	1139.95	889.97	740.69	641.75	519.40	447.35
19000	1732.90	1203.28	939.41	781.84	677.41	548.25	472.20
20000	1824.10	1266.61	988.85	822.98	713.06	577.11	497.06
21000	1915.30	1329.94	1038.29	864.13	748.71	605.96	521.91
22000	2006.51	1393.27	1087.73	905.28	784.37	634.82	546.76
23000	2097.71	1456.60	1137.18	946.43	820.02	663.67	571.61
24000	2188.92	1519.93	1186.62	987.58	855.67	692.53	596.47
25000	2280.12	1583.26	1236.06	1028.73	891.32	721.38	621.32
26000	2371.33	1646.59	1285.50	1069.88	926.98	750.24	646.17
27000	2462.52	1709.92	1334.95	1111.03	962.63	779.09	671.02
28000	2553.74	1773.25	1384.39	1152.18	998.28	807.95	695.88
29000	2644.94	1836.58	1433.83	1193.33	1033.93	836.80	720.73
30000	2736.15	1899.91	1483.27	1234.47	1069.59	865.66	745.58
31000	2827.35	1963.24	1532.72	1275.62	1105.24	894.51	770.43
32000	2918.56	2026.57	1582.16	1316.77	1140.89	923.37	795.29
33000	3009.76	2089.90	1631.60	1357.92	1176.55	952.22	820.14
34000	3100.97	2153.23	1681.04	1399.07	1212.20	981.08	844.99
35000	3192.17	2216.56	1730.48	1440.22	1247.85	1009.93	869.85
40000	3648.20	2533.21	1977.70	1645.96	1426.11	1154.21	994.11
45000	4104.22	2849.86	2224.91	1851.71	1604.38	1298.48	1118.37
50000	4560.24	3166.51	2472.12	2057.45	1782.64	1442.76	1242.63
55000	5016.27	3483.16	2719.33	2263.20	1960.91	1587.03	1366.90
60000	5472.29	3799.81	2966.54	2468.94	2139.17	1731.31	1491.16
65000	5928.31	4116.46	3213.75	2674.69	2317.43	1875.58	1615.42
70000	6384.34	4433.11	3460.96	2880.43	2495.70	2019.86	1739.69
75000	6840.36	4749.76	3708.17	3086.18	2673.96	2164.13	1863.95
80000	7296.39	5066.41	3955.39	3291.92	2852.22	2308.41	1988.21
100000	9120.48	6333.01	4944.23	4114.90	3565.28	2885.51	2485.26

TERM AMOUNT	6 YEARS	7 YEARS	8 YEARS	9 YEARS	10 YEARS	11 YEARS	12 YEARS
$ 25	.56	.52	.48	.46	.44	.42	.41
50	1.12	1.03	.96	.91	.87	.84	.82
75	1.67	1.54	1.44	1.37	1.31	1.26	1.23
100	2.23	2.05	1.92	1.82	1.74	1.68	1.64
200	4.45	4.09	3.83	3.63	3.48	3.36	3.27
300	6.68	6.14	5.74	5.45	5.22	5.04	4.90
400	8.90	8.18	7.65	7.26	6.96	6.72	6.53
500	11.13	10.22	9.57	9.07	8.69	8.40	8.16
600	13.35	12.27	11.48	10.89	10.43	10.08	9.80
700	15.58	14.31	13.39	12.70	12.17	11.76	11.43
800	17.80	16.35	15.30	14.51	13.91	13.44	13.06
900	20.03	18.40	17.21	16.33	15.65	15.11	14.69
1000	22.25	20.44	19.13	18.14	17.38	16.79	16.32
2000	44.50	40.88	38.25	36.28	34.76	33.58	32.64
3000	66.74	61.31	57.37	54.41	52.14	50.37	48.96
4000	88.99	81.75	76.49	72.55	69.52	67.16	65.28
5000	111.24	102.18	95.61	90.69	86.90	83.95	81.60
6000	133.48	122.62	114.73	108.82	104.28	100.73	97.92
7000	155.73	143.06	133.86	126.96	121.66	117.52	114.24
8000	177.97	163.49	152.98	145.09	139.04	134.31	130.56
9000	200.22	183.93	172.10	163.23	156.42	151.10	146.88
10000	222.47	204.36	191.22	181.37	173.80	167.89	163.20
11000	244.71	224.80	210.34	199.50	191.18	184.68	179.52
12000	266.96	245.23	229.46	217.64	208.56	201.46	195.84
13000	289.20	265.67	248.58	235.78	225.94	218.25	212.15
14000	311.45	286.11	267.71	253.91	243.32	235.04	228.47
15000	333.70	306.54	286.83	272.05	260.70	251.83	244.79
16000	355.94	326.98	305.95	290.18	278.08	268.62	261.11
17000	378.19	347.41	325.07	308.32	295.46	285.41	277.43
18000	400.44	367.85	344.19	326.46	312.84	302.19	293.75
19000	422.68	388.29	363.31	344.59	330.22	318.98	310.07
20000	444.93	408.72	382.43	362.73	347.60	335.77	326.39
21000	467.17	429.16	401.56	380.86	364.98	352.56	342.71
22000	489.42	449.59	420.68	399.00	382.36	369.35	359.03
23000	511.67	470.03	439.80	417.14	399.74	386.14	375.35
24000	533.91	490.46	458.92	435.27	417.12	402.92	391.67
25000	556.16	510.90	478.04	453.41	434.50	419.71	407.99
26000	578.40	531.34	497.16	471.55	451.88	436.50	424.30
27000	600.65	551.77	516.28	489.68	469.26	453.29	440.62
28000	622.90	572.21	535.41	507.82	486.64	470.08	456.94
29000	645.14	592.64	554.53	525.95	504.02	486.87	473.26
30000	667.39	613.08	573.65	544.09	521.40	503.65	489.58
31000	689.64	633.51	592.77	562.23	538.78	520.44	505.90
32000	711.88	653.95	611.89	580.36	556.16	537.23	522.22
33000	734.13	674.39	631.01	598.50	573.54	554.02	538.54
34000	756.37	694.82	650.13	616.64	590.92	570.81	554.86
35000	778.62	715.26	669.26	634.77	608.30	587.60	571.18
40000	889.85	817.44	764.86	725.45	695.20	671.54	652.77
45000	1001.08	919.62	860.47	816.13	782.09	755.48	734.37
50000	1112.31	1021.80	956.08	906.81	868.99	839.42	815.97
55000	1223.54	1123.97	1051.68	997.50	955.89	923.36	897.56
60000	1334.77	1226.15	1147.29	1088.18	1042.79	1007.30	979.16
65000	1446.00	1328.33	1242.90	1178.86	1129.69	1091.25	1060.75
70000	1557.23	1430.51	1338.51	1269.54	1216.59	1175.19	1142.35
75000	1668.46	1532.69	1434.11	1360.22	1303.49	1259.13	1223.95
80000	1779.70	1634.87	1529.72	1450.90	1390.39	1343.07	1305.54
100000	2224.62	2043.59	1912.15	1813.62	1737.98	1678.84	1631.93

147

TERM AMOUNT	13 YEARS	14 YEARS	15 YEARS	16 YEARS	17 YEARS	18 YEARS	19 YEARS
$ 25	.40	.40	.39	.38	.38	.38	.37
50	.80	.79	.77	.76	.76	.75	.74
75	1.20	1.18	1.16	1.14	1.13	1.12	1.11
100	1.60	1.57	1.54	1.52	1.51	1.49	1.48
200	3.19	3.13	3.08	3.04	3.01	2.98	2.96
300	4.79	4.70	4.62	4.56	4.51	4.47	4.43
400	6.38	6.26	6.16	6.08	6.01	5.96	5.91
500	7.98	7.82	7.70	7.60	7.51	7.44	7.39
600	9.57	9.39	9.24	9.12	9.02	8.93	8.86
700	11.17	10.95	10.78	10.64	10.52	10.42	10.34
800	12.76	12.52	12.32	12.15	12.02	11.91	11.82
900	14.35	14.08	13.86	13.67	13.52	13.40	13.29
1000	15.95	15.64	15.40	15.19	15.02	14.88	14.77
2000	31.89	31.28	30.79	30.38	30.04	29.76	29.53
3000	47.83	46.92	46.18	45.56	45.06	44.64	44.30
4000	63.78	62.56	61.57	60.75	60.08	59.52	59.06
5000	79.72	78.20	76.96	75.94	75.10	74.40	73.83
6000	95.66	93.84	92.35	91.12	90.12	89.28	88.59
7000	111.61	109.47	107.74	106.31	105.13	104.16	103.35
8000	127.55	125.11	123.13	121.50	120.15	119.04	118.12
9000	143.49	140.75	138.52	136.68	135.17	133.92	132.88
10000	159.43	156.39	153.91	151.87	150.19	148.80	147.65
11000	175.38	172.03	169.30	167.05	165.21	163.68	162.41
12000	191.32	187.67	184.69	182.24	180.23	178.56	177.17
13000	207.26	203.30	200.08	197.43	195.24	193.44	191.94
14000	223.21	218.94	215.47	212.61	210.26	208.32	206.70
15000	239.15	234.58	230.86	227.80	225.28	223.20	221.47
16000	255.09	250.22	246.25	242.99	240.30	238.08	236.23
17000	271.04	265.86	261.64	258.17	255.32	252.96	250.99
18000	286.98	281.50	277.03	273.36	270.34	267.84	265.76
19000	302.92	297.13	292.42	288.55	285.36	282.71	280.52
20000	318.86	312.77	307.81	303.73	300.37	297.59	295.29
21000	334.81	328.41	323.20	318.92	315.39	312.47	310.05
22000	350.75	344.05	338.59	334.10	330.41	327.35	324.81
23000	366.69	359.69	353.98	349.29	345.43	342.23	339.58
24000	382.64	375.33	369.37	364.48	360.45	357.11	354.34
25000	398.58	390.96	384.76	379.66	375.47	371.99	369.11
26000	414.52	406.60	400.15	394.85	390.48	386.87	383.87
27000	430.46	422.24	415.54	410.04	405.50	401.75	398.64
28000	446.41	437.88	430.93	425.22	420.52	416.63	413.40
29000	462.35	453.52	446.32	440.41	435.54	431.51	428.16
30000	478.29	469.16	461.71	455.60	450.56	446.39	442.93
31000	494.24	484.79	477.10	470.78	465.58	461.27	457.69
32000	510.18	500.43	492.49	485.97	480.59	476.15	472.46
33000	526.12	516.07	507.88	501.15	495.61	491.03	487.22
34000	542.07	531.71	523.27	516.34	510.63	505.91	501.98
35000	558.01	547.35	538.66	531.53	525.65	520.79	516.75
40000	637.72	625.54	615.61	607.46	600.74	595.18	590.57
45000	717.44	703.73	692.56	683.39	675.83	669.58	664.39
50000	797.15	781.92	769.51	759.32	750.93	743.98	738.21
55000	876.87	860.12	846.46	835.25	826.02	818.38	812.03
60000	956.58	938.31	923.41	911.19	901.11	892.77	885.85
65000	1036.30	1016.50	1000.36	987.12	976.20	967.17	959.67
70000	1116.01	1094.69	1077.31	1063.05	1051.30	1041.57	1033.49
75000	1195.73	1172.88	1154.26	1138.98	1126.39	1115.97	1107.31
80000	1275.44	1251.08	1231.21	1214.91	1201.48	1190.36	1181.13
100000	1594.30	1563.84	1539.01	1518.64	1501.85	1487.95	1476.41

MONTHLY PAYMENT
NECESSARY TO AMORTIZE A LOAN
17%

TERM AMOUNT	20 YEARS	21 YEARS	22 YEARS	25 YEARS	30 YEARS	35 YEARS	40 YEARS
$ 25	.37	.37	.37	.36	.36	.36	.36
50	.74	.73	.73	.72	.72	.72	.71
75	1.11	1.10	1.09	1.08	1.07	1.07	1.07
100	1.47	1.46	1.46	1.44	1.43	1.43	1.42
200	2.94	2.92	2.91	2.88	2.86	2.85	2.84
300	4.41	4.38	4.36	4.32	4.28	4.27	4.26
400	5.87	5.84	5.81	5.76	5.71	5.69	5.68
500	7.34	7.30	7.27	7.19	7.13	7.11	7.10
600	8.81	8.76	8.72	8.63	8.56	8.53	8.51
700	10.27	10.22	10.17	1C.07	9.98	9.95	9.93
800	11.74	11.68	11.62	11.51	11.41	11.37	11.35
900	13.21	13.13	13.07	12.95	12.84	12.79	12.77
1000	14.67	14.59	14.53	14.38	14.26	14.21	14.19
2000	29.34	29.18	29.05	28.76	28.52	28.42	28.37
3000	44.01	43.77	43.57	43.14	42.78	42.62	42.55
4000	58.68	58.36	58.09	57.52	57.03	56.83	56.74
5000	73.35	72.94	72.61	71.89	71.29	71.03	70.92
6000	88.01	87.53	87.13	86.27	85.55	85.24	85.10
7000	102.68	102.12	101.65	1CC.65	99.80	99.44	99.29
8000	117.35	116.71	116.17	115.03	114.06	113.65	113.47
9000	132.02	131.30	130.69	129.41	128.32	127.85	127.65
10000	146.69	145.88	145.21	143.78	142.57	142.06	141.84
11000	161.35	160.47	159.73	158.16	156.83	156.26	156.02
12000	176.02	175.06	174.25	172.54	171.09	170.47	170.20
13000	190.69	189.65	188.77	186.92	185.34	184.67	184.39
14000	205.36	204.23	203.30	201.30	199.60	198.88	198.57
15000	220.03	218.82	217.82	215.67	213.86	213.08	212.75
16000	234.69	233.41	232.34	230.05	228.11	227.29	226.94
17000	249.36	248.00	246.86	244.43	242.37	241.49	241.12
18000	264.03	262.59	261.38	258.81	256.63	255.70	255.30
19000	278.70	277.17	275.90	273.19	270.88	269.90	269.49
20000	293.37	291.76	290.42	287.56	285.14	284.11	283.67
21000	308.03	306.35	304.94	301.94	299.40	298.32	297.85
22000	322.70	320.94	319.46	316.32	313.65	312.52	312.04
23000	337.37	335.52	333.98	330.70	327.91	326.73	326.22
24000	352.04	350.11	348.50	345.08	342.17	340.93	340.40
25000	366.71	364.70	363.02	359.45	356.42	355.14	354.59
26000	381.37	379.29	377.54	373.83	370.68	369.34	368.77
27000	396.04	393.88	392.07	388.21	384.94	383.55	382.95
28000	410.71	408.46	406.59	402.59	399.19	397.75	397.14
29000	425.38	423.05	421.11	416.97	413.45	411.96	411.32
30000	440.05	437.64	435.63	431.34	427.71	426.16	425.50
31000	454.71	452.23	450.15	445.72	441.96	440.37	439.69
32000	469.38	466.82	464.67	460.10	456.22	454.57	453.87
33000	484.05	481.40	479.19	474.48	470.48	468.78	468.05
34000	498.72	495.99	493.71	488.86	484.73	482.98	482.24
35000	513.39	510.58	508.23	503.23	498.99	497.19	496.42
40000	586.73	583.52	580.84	575.12	570.28	568.22	567.33
45000	660.07	656.46	653.44	647.01	641.56	639.24	638.25
50000	733.41	729.40	726.04	718.90	712.84	710.27	709.17
55000	806.75	802.34	798.65	79C.79	784.13	781.29	780.08
60000	880.09	875.27	871.25	862.68	855.41	852.32	851.00
65000	953.43	948.21	943.85	934.57	926.69	923.35	921.92
70000	1026.77	1021.15	1016.46	1006.46	997.98	994.37	992.83
75000	1100.11	1094.09	1089.06	1C78.35	1069.26	1065.40	1063.75
80000	1173.45	1167.03	1161.67	1150.24	1140.55	1136.43	1134.66
100000	1466.81	1458.79	1452.08	1437.80	1425.68	1420.53	1418.33

18%
MONTHLY PAYMENT
NECESSARY TO AMORTIZE A LOAN

TERM AMOUNT	1 YEAR	1½ YEARS	2 YEARS	2½ YEARS	3 YEARS	4 YEARS	5 YEARS
$ 25	2.30	1.60	1.25	1.05	.91	.74	.64
50	4.59	3.20	2.50	2.09	1.81	1.47	1.27
75	6.88	4.79	3.75	3.13	2.72	2.21	1.91
100	9.17	6.39	5.00	4.17	3.62	2.94	2.54
200	18.34	12.77	9.99	8.33	7.24	5.88	5.08
300	27.51	19.15	14.98	12.50	10.85	8.82	7.62
400	36.68	25.53	19.97	16.66	14.47	11.75	10.16
500	45.84	31.91	24.97	20.82	18.08	14.69	12.70
600	55.01	38.29	29.96	24.99	21.70	17.63	15.24
700	64.18	44.67	34.95	29.15	25.31	20.57	17.78
800	73.35	51.05	39.94	33.32	28.93	23.50	20.32
900	82.52	57.43	44.94	37.48	32.54	26.44	22.86
1000	91.68	63.81	49.93	41.64	36.16	29.38	25.40
2000	183.36	127.62	99.85	83.28	72.31	58.75	50.79
3000	275.00	191.42	149.78	124.92	108.46	88.13	76.19
4000	366.72	255.23	199.70	166.56	144.61	117.50	101.58
5000	458.40	319.03	249.63	208.20	180.77	146.88	126.97
6000	550.08	382.84	299.55	249.84	216.92	176.25	152.37
7000	641.76	446.65	349.47	291.48	253.07	205.63	177.76
8000	733.44	510.45	399.40	333.12	289.22	235.00	203.15
9000	825.12	574.26	449.32	374.76	325.38	264.38	228.55
10000	916.80	638.06	499.25	416.40	361.53	293.75	253.94
11000	1008.48	701.87	549.17	458.04	397.68	323.13	279.33
12000	1100.16	765.67	599.09	499.68	433.83	352.50	304.73
13000	1191.84	829.48	649.02	541.31	469.99	381.88	330.12
14000	1283.52	893.29	698.94	582.95	506.14	411.25	355.51
15000	1375.20	957.09	748.87	624.59	542.29	440.63	380.91
16000	1466.88	1020.90	798.79	666.23	578.44	470.00	406.30
17000	1558.56	1084.70	848.71	707.87	614.60	499.38	431.69
18000	1650.24	1148.51	898.64	749.51	650.75	528.75	457.09
19000	1741.92	1212.31	948.56	791.15	686.90	558.13	482.48
20000	1833.60	1276.12	998.49	832.79	723.05	587.50	507.87
21000	1925.28	1339.93	1048.41	874.43	759.21	616.88	533.27
22000	2016.96	1403.73	1098.34	916.07	795.36	646.25	558.66
23000	2108.64	1467.54	1148.26	957.71	831.51	675.63	584.05
24000	2200.32	1531.34	1198.18	999.35	867.66	705.00	609.45
25000	2292.00	1595.15	1248.11	1040.98	903.81	734.38	634.84
26000	2383.68	1658.96	1298.03	1082.62	939.97	763.75	660.23
27000	2475.36	1722.76	1347.96	1124.26	976.12	793.13	685.63
28000	2567.04	1786.57	1397.88	1165.90	1012.27	822.50	711.02
29000	2658.72	1850.37	1447.80	1207.54	1048.42	851.88	736.41
30000	2750.40	1914.18	1497.73	1249.18	1084.58	881.25	761.81
31000	2842.08	1977.98	1547.65	1290.82	1120.73	910.63	787.20
32000	2933.76	2041.79	1597.58	1332.46	1156.88	940.00	812.59
33000	3025.44	2105.60	1647.50	1374.10	1193.03	969.38	837.99
34000	3117.12	2169.40	1697.42	1415.74	1229.19	998.75	863.38
35000	3208.80	2233.21	1747.35	1457.38	1265.34	1028.13	888.77
40000	3667.20	2552.24	1996.97	1665.57	1446.10	1175.00	1015.74
45000	4125.60	2871.27	2246.59	1873.77	1626.86	1321.88	1142.71
50000	4584.00	3190.29	2496.21	2081.96	1807.62	1468.75	1269.68
55000	5042.40	3509.32	2745.83	2290.16	1988.39	1615.63	1396.64
60000	5500.80	3828.35	2995.45	2498.36	2169.15	1762.50	1523.61
65000	5959.20	4147.38	3245.07	2706.55	2349.91	1909.38	1650.58
70000	6417.60	4466.41	3494.69	2914.75	2530.67	2056.25	1777.54
75000	6876.00	4785.44	3744.31	3122.94	2711.43	2203.13	1904.51
80000	7334.40	5104.47	3993.93	3331.14	2892.20	2350.00	2031.48
100000	9168.00	6380.58	4992.42	4163.92	3615.24	2937.50	2539.35

150

TERM AMOUNT	6 YEARS	7 YEARS	8 YEARS	9 YEARS	10 YEARS	11 YEARS	12 YEARS
$ 25	.58	.53	.50	.47	.46	.44	.43
50	1.15	1.06	.99	.94	.91	.88	.85
75	1.72	1.58	1.48	1.41	1.36	1.31	1.28
100	2.29	2.11	1.98	1.88	1.81	1.75	1.70
200	4.57	4.21	3.95	3.76	3.61	3.49	3.40
300	6.85	6.31	5.92	5.63	5.41	5.24	5.10
400	9.13	8.41	7.89	7.51	7.21	6.98	6.80
500	11.41	10.51	9.87	9.38	9.01	8.73	8.50
600	13.69	12.62	11.84	11.26	10.82	10.47	10.20
700	15.97	14.72	13.81	13.13	12.62	12.22	11.90
800	18.25	16.82	15.78	15.01	14.42	13.96	13.60
900	20.53	18.92	17.76	16.89	16.22	15.70	15.30
1000	22.81	21.02	19.73	18.76	18.02	17.45	17.00
2000	45.62	42.04	39.45	37.52	36.04	34.89	33.99
3000	68.43	63.06	59.17	56.28	54.06	52.34	50.98
4000	91.24	84.08	78.90	75.03	72.08	69.78	67.97
5000	114.04	105.09	98.62	93.79	90.10	87.23	84.96
6000	136.85	126.11	118.34	112.55	108.12	104.67	101.95
7000	159.66	147.13	138.07	131.30	126.13	122.11	118.94
8000	182.47	168.15	157.79	150.06	144.15	139.56	135.93
9000	205.28	189.17	177.51	168.82	162.17	157.00	152.93
10000	228.08	210.18	197.24	187.57	180.19	174.45	169.92
11000	250.89	231.20	216.96	206.33	198.21	191.89	186.91
12000	273.70	252.22	236.68	225.09	216.23	209.34	203.90
13000	296.51	273.24	256.41	243.84	234.25	226.78	220.89
14000	319.31	294.25	276.13	262.60	252.26	244.22	237.88
15000	342.12	315.27	295.85	281.36	270.28	261.67	254.87
16000	364.93	336.29	315.58	300.12	288.30	279.11	271.86
17000	387.74	357.31	335.30	318.87	306.32	296.56	288.86
18000	410.55	378.33	355.02	337.63	324.34	314.00	305.85
19000	433.35	399.34	374.75	356.39	342.36	331.44	322.84
20000	456.16	420.36	394.47	375.14	360.38	348.89	339.83
21000	478.97	441.38	414.19	393.90	378.39	366.33	356.82
22000	501.78	462.40	433.92	412.66	396.41	383.78	373.81
23000	524.58	483.42	453.64	431.41	414.43	401.22	390.80
24000	547.39	504.43	473.36	450.17	432.45	418.67	407.79
25000	570.20	525.45	493.09	468.93	450.47	436.11	424.78
26000	593.01	546.47	512.81	487.68	468.49	453.55	441.78
27000	615.82	567.49	532.53	506.44	486.51	471.00	458.77
28000	638.62	588.50	552.25	525.20	504.52	488.44	475.76
29000	661.43	609.52	571.98	543.95	522.54	505.89	492.75
30000	684.24	630.54	591.70	562.71	540.56	523.33	509.74
31000	707.05	651.56	611.42	581.47	558.58	540.77	526.73
32000	729.85	672.58	631.15	600.23	576.60	558.22	543.72
33000	752.66	693.59	650.87	618.98	594.62	575.66	560.71
34000	775.47	714.61	670.59	637.74	612.63	593.11	577.71
35000	798.28	735.63	690.32	656.50	630.65	610.55	594.70
40000	912.32	840.72	788.93	750.28	720.75	697.77	679.65
45000	1026.36	945.81	887.55	844.06	810.84	784.99	764.61
50000	1140.39	1050.90	986.17	937.85	900.93	872.21	849.56
55000	1254.43	1155.99	1084.78	1031.63	991.02	959.43	934.52
60000	1368.47	1261.08	1183.40	1125.42	1081.11	1046.66	1019.48
65000	1482.51	1366.16	1282.01	1219.20	1171.21	1133.88	1104.43
70000	1596.55	1471.25	1380.63	1312.99	1261.30	1221.10	1189.39
75000	1710.59	1576.34	1479.25	1406.77	1351.39	1308.32	1274.34
80000	1824.63	1681.43	1577.86	1500.56	1441.49	1395.54	1359.30
100000	2280.78	2101.79	1972.33	1875.69	1801.86	1744.42	1699.12

151

18%

MONTHLY PAYMENT
NECESSARY TO AMORTIZE A LOAN

TERM AMOUNT	13 YEARS	14 YEARS	15 YEARS	16 YEARS	17 YEARS	18 YEARS	19 YEARS
$ 25	.42	.41	.41	.40	.40	.40	.39
50	.84	.82	.81	.80	.79	.79	.78
75	1.25	1.23	1.21	1.20	1.19	1.18	1.17
100	1.67	1.64	1.62	1.60	1.59	1.57	1.56
200	3.33	3.27	3.23	3.19	3.16	3.13	3.11
300	4.99	4.91	4.84	4.78	4.73	4.69	4.66
400	6.66	6.54	6.45	6.37	6.31	6.26	6.21
500	8.32	8.17	8.06	7.96	7.88	7.82	7.77
600	9.98	9.81	9.67	9.55	9.46	9.38	9.32
700	11.65	11.44	11.28	11.14	11.03	10.94	10.87
800	13.31	13.08	12.89	12.74	12.61	12.51	12.42
900	14.97	14.71	14.50	14.33	14.19	14.07	13.97
1000	16.64	16.34	16.11	15.92	15.76	15.63	15.53
2000	33.27	32.68	32.21	31.83	31.51	31.26	31.05
3000	49.90	49.02	48.32	47.74	47.27	46.89	46.57
4000	66.53	65.36	64.42	63.66	63.03	62.51	62.09
5000	83.16	81.70	80.53	79.57	78.78	78.14	77.61
6000	99.79	98.04	96.63	95.48	94.54	93.77	93.13
7000	116.42	114.38	112.73	111.39	110.30	109.39	108.65
8000	133.05	130.72	128.84	127.31	126.05	125.02	124.17
9000	149.68	147.06	144.94	143.22	141.81	140.65	139.69
10000	166.31	163.40	161.05	159.13	157.56	156.27	155.21
11000	182.94	179.74	177.15	175.04	173.32	171.90	170.73
12000	199.57	196.08	193.26	190.96	189.07	187.53	186.25
13000	216.20	212.42	209.36	206.87	204.83	203.15	201.78
14000	232.83	228.76	225.46	222.78	220.59	218.78	217.30
15000	249.46	245.10	241.57	238.69	236.34	234.41	232.82
16000	266.09	261.44	257.67	254.61	252.10	250.04	248.34
17000	282.72	277.78	273.78	270.52	267.85	265.66	263.86
18000	299.35	294.12	289.88	286.43	283.61	281.29	279.38
19000	315.98	310.46	305.98	302.34	299.36	296.92	294.90
20000	332.61	326.80	322.09	318.26	315.12	312.54	310.42
21000	349.24	343.13	338.19	334.17	330.88	328.17	325.94
22000	365.87	359.47	354.30	350.08	346.63	343.80	341.46
23000	382.50	375.81	370.40	365.99	362.39	359.42	356.98
24000	399.13	392.15	386.51	381.91	378.14	375.05	372.50
25000	415.76	408.49	402.61	397.82	393.90	390.68	388.02
26000	432.39	424.83	418.71	413.73	409.65	406.30	403.55
27000	449.02	441.17	434.82	429.64	425.41	421.93	419.07
28000	465.65	457.51	450.92	445.56	441.17	437.56	434.59
29000	482.28	473.85	467.03	461.47	456.92	453.19	450.11
30000	498.91	490.19	483.13	477.38	472.68	468.81	465.63
31000	515.54	506.53	499.24	493.29	488.43	484.44	481.15
32000	532.17	522.87	515.34	509.21	504.19	500.07	496.67
33000	548.80	539.21	531.44	525.12	519.94	515.69	512.19
34000	565.43	555.55	547.55	541.03	535.70	531.32	527.71
35000	582.06	571.89	563.65	556.94	551.46	546.95	543.23
40000	665.21	653.59	644.17	636.51	630.23	625.08	620.84
45000	748.36	735.28	724.69	716.07	709.01	703.22	698.44
50000	831.51	816.98	805.22	795.63	787.79	781.35	776.04
55000	914.66	898.68	885.74	875.20	866.57	859.49	853.65
60000	997.81	980.38	966.26	954.76	945.35	937.62	931.25
65000	1080.96	1062.07	1046.78	1034.32	1024.13	1015.75	1008.86
70000	1164.11	1143.77	1127.30	1113.88	1102.91	1093.89	1086.46
75000	1247.26	1225.47	1207.82	1193.45	1181.68	1172.02	1164.06
80000	1330.41	1307.17	1288.34	1273.01	1260.46	1250.16	1241.67
100000	1663.01	1633.96	1610.43	1591.26	1575.58	1562.70	1552.08

TERM AMOUNT	20 YEARS	21 YEARS	22 YEARS	25 YEARS	30 YEARS	35 YEARS	40 YEARS
$ 25	.39	.39	.39	.38	.38	.38	.38
50	.78	.77	.77	.76	.76	.76	.76
75	1.16	1.16	1.15	1.14	1.14	1.13	1.13
100	1.55	1.54	1.54	1.52	1.51	1.51	1.51
200	3.09	3.08	3.07	3.04	3.02	3.01	3.01
300	4.63	4.61	4.60	4.56	4.53	4.51	4.51
400	6.18	6.15	6.13	6.07	6.03	6.02	6.01
500	7.72	7.69	7.66	7.59	7.54	7.52	7.51
600	9.26	9.22	9.19	9.11	9.05	9.02	9.01
700	10.81	10.76	10.72	10.63	10.56	10.53	10.51
800	12.35	12.29	12.25	12.14	12.06	12.03	12.01
900	13.89	13.83	13.78	13.66	13.57	13.53	13.52
1000	15.44	15.37	15.31	15.18	15.08	15.03	15.02
2000	30.87	30.73	30.61	30.35	30.15	30.06	30.03
3000	46.30	46.09	45.91	45.53	45.22	45.09	45.04
4000	61.74	61.45	61.21	60.70	60.29	60.12	60.05
5000	77.17	76.81	76.51	75.88	75.36	75.15	75.06
6000	92.60	92.17	91.81	91.05	90.43	90.18	90.08
7000	108.04	107.53	107.11	106.23	105.50	105.21	105.09
8000	123.47	122.89	122.41	121.40	120.57	120.24	120.10
9000	138.90	138.25	137.71	136.57	135.64	135.27	135.11
10000	154.34	153.61	153.01	151.75	150.71	150.29	150.12
11000	169.77	168.97	168.31	166.92	165.78	165.32	165.14
12000	185.20	184.33	183.61	182.10	180.86	180.35	180.15
13000	200.64	199.69	198.91	197.27	195.93	195.38	195.16
14000	216.07	215.05	214.21	212.45	211.00	210.41	210.17
15000	231.50	230.41	229.51	227.62	226.07	225.44	225.18
16000	246.93	245.77	244.81	242.79	241.14	240.47	240.19
17000	262.37	261.13	260.11	257.97	256.21	255.50	255.21
18000	277.80	276.49	275.41	273.14	271.28	270.53	270.22
19000	293.23	291.86	290.71	288.32	286.35	285.55	285.23
20000	308.67	307.22	306.01	303.49	301.42	300.58	300.24
21000	324.10	322.58	321.31	318.67	316.49	315.61	315.25
22000	339.53	337.94	336.61	333.84	331.56	330.64	330.27
23000	354.97	353.30	351.91	349.01	346.63	345.67	345.28
24000	370.40	368.66	367.21	364.19	361.71	360.70	360.29
25000	385.83	384.02	382.51	379.36	376.78	375.73	375.30
26000	401.27	399.38	397.81	394.54	391.85	390.76	390.31
27000	416.70	414.74	413.12	409.71	406.92	405.79	405.32
28000	432.13	430.10	428.42	424.89	421.99	420.81	420.34
29000	447.57	445.46	443.72	440.06	437.06	435.84	435.35
30000	463.00	460.82	459.02	455.23	452.13	450.87	450.36
31000	478.43	476.18	474.32	470.41	467.20	465.90	465.37
32000	493.86	491.54	489.62	485.58	482.27	480.93	480.38
33000	509.30	506.90	504.92	500.76	497.34	495.96	495.40
34000	524.73	522.26	520.22	515.93	512.41	510.99	510.41
35000	540.16	537.62	535.52	531.11	527.48	526.02	525.42
40000	617.33	614.43	612.02	606.98	602.84	601.16	600.48
45000	694.50	691.23	688.52	682.85	678.19	676.31	675.54
50000	771.66	768.03	765.02	758.72	753.55	751.45	750.60
55000	848.83	844.84	841.53	834.59	828.90	826.60	825.66
60000	925.99	921.64	918.03	910.46	904.26	901.74	900.71
65000	1003.16	998.44	994.53	986.33	979.61	976.88	975.77
70000	1080.32	1075.24	1071.03	1062.21	1054.96	1052.03	1050.83
75000	1157.49	1152.05	1147.53	1138.08	1130.32	1127.17	1125.89
80000	1234.65	1228.85	1224.04	1213.95	1205.67	1202.32	1200.95
100000	1543.32	1536.06	1530.04	1517.43	1507.09	1502.90	1501.19

LOAN PROGRESS
CHARTS

LOAN PROGRESS CHART
Showing dollar balance remaining on a $1,000 loan **7%**

Age of Loan	ORIGINAL TERM IN YEARS											Age of Loan
	5	10	11	12	13	14	15	16	17	18	19	
1	827	928	937	945	951	956	961	965	968	971	974	1
2	641	852	870	886	899	910	919	927	934	940	946	2
3	442	769	798	822	642	859	874	887	898	907	916	3
4	229	681	721	754	782	806	826	843	858	872	884	4
5		586	638	681	717	748	774	797	816	834	849	5
6		485	550	603	648	686	719	747	771	793	812	6
7		376	455	519	574	620	659	693	723	749	772	7
8		259	352	429	494	549	596	636	671	702	730	8
9		134	243	333	408	472	527	575	616	652	684	9
10			126	230	317	391	454	509	556	598	635	10
11				119	218	303	375	438	492	540	583	11
12					113	209	291	362	424	478	526	12
13						108	201	281	351	412	466	13
14							104	194	272	341	401	14
15								100	188	264	332	15
16									97	182	257	16
17										94	177	17
18											92	18

Age of Loan	ORIGINAL TERM IN YEARS											Age of Loan
	20	21	22	23	24	25	27	29	30	35	40	
1	976	978	980	982	983	985	987	989	990	993	995	1
2	951	955	959	962	965	968	973	977	979	986	990	2
3	923	930	936	941	946	951	958	965	967	978	985	3
4	894	903	912	919	926	932	942	951	955	969	979	4
5	863	875	885	895	904	912	925	936	941	960	973	5
6	829	844	857	869	880	890	907	921	927	950	966	6
7	793	811	827	842	855	867	887	904	911	940	959	7
8	754	775	795	812	828	842	866	886	895	929	951	8
9	712	738	760	780	799	815	843	867	877	917	943	9
10	668	697	723	746	767	786	819	846	858	904	934	10
11	620	653	683	710	734	756	793	824	838	890	925	11
12	569	606	640	671	698	723	765	800	816	875	914	12
13	514	556	594	629	659	687	735	775	792	859	903	13
14	455	503	545	584	618	649	703	748	767	842	892	14
15	392	449	493	535	574	609	669	719	740	824	879	15
16	324	383	436	484	526	565	632	687	711	804	866	16
17	251	317	375	428	476	518	592	654	680	783	851	17
18	173	246	310	369	421	468	550	618	647	761	836	18
19	90	169	241	305	362	415	504	579	611	737	819	19
20		88	166	236	300	357	456	537	573	711	802	20
21			86	163	232	295	403	493	532	683	782	21
22				84	160	229	347	445	488	653	762	22
23					83	158	287	394	441	621	740	23
24						82	223	339	390	587	717	24
25							154	281	336	550	691	25
26							79	218	278	511	664	26
27								150	215	469	635	27
28								78	149	423	604	28
29									77	375	571	29
30										323	535	30
31										267	497	31
32										207	456	32
33										143	412	33
34										74	364	34
35											314	35

LOAN PROGRESS CHART
Showing dollar balance remaining on a $1,000 loan

Age of Loan	5	10	11	12	13	14	15	16	17	18	19	Age of Loan
							ORIGINAL TERM IN YEARS					
1	828	929	938	946	952	957	962	966	969	972	975	1
2	643	853	872	887	900	911	921	929	936	942	947	2
3	444	772	801	825	845	862	876	889	900	909	918	3
4	230	684	724	757	785	809	829	846	861	875	886	4
5		589	642	685	721	751	778	800	820	837	852	5
6		488	553	607	652	690	723	751	775	797	816	6
7		379	458	523	578	624	663	698	728	754	777	7
8		262	355	433	498	553	600	641	676	707	734	8
9		136	245	336	412	477	532	579	621	657	689	9
10			127	232	320	394	458	513	561	603	640	10
11				120	221	306	379	443	497	546	588	11
12					114	211	295	366	429	484	532	12
13						110	203	284	355	417	471	13
14							105	196	276	345	406	14
15								102	190	268	336	15
16									99	185	261	16
17										96	180	17
18											93	18

Age of Loan	20	21	22	23	24	25	27	29	30	35	40	Age of Loan
						ORIGINAL TERM IN YEARS						
1	977	979	981	982	984	985	988	989	990	994	996	1
2	956	960	964	967	969	972	976	980	987	991	992	2
3	925	932	938	943	948	952	960	966	969	979	986	3
4	897	906	914	922	928	934	944	953	957	971	980	4
5	866	878	889	898	907	915	928	939	944	962	974	5
6	833	848	861	873	884	893	910	924	930	953	968	6
7	797	815	830	846	859	871	891	908	915	943	961	7
8	759	780	799	817	832	846	870	890	899	932	954	8
9	718	743	765	785	804	820	848	872	882	921	946	9
10	673	702	728	752	773	792	824	851	862	908	938	10
11	626	659	689	716	740	761	799	830	843	895	929	11
12	574	612	646	677	704	729	771	806	822	880	919	12
13	519	562	601	635	666	694	742	781	799	865	908	13
14	460	509	552	590	625	656	710	755	774	848	897	14
15	397	451	499	542	581	616	676	726	749	831	885	15
16	328	388	442	490	533	572	639	695	719	811	872	16
17	255	322	381	434	482	525	600	661	688	791	858	17
18	176	250	315	374	427	475	557	625	655	769	843	18
19	91	172	245	310	368	421	512	587	619	745	827	19
20		89	169	241	305	363	463	545	581	719	809	20
21			88	166	237	300	410	501	540	692	791	21
22				86	163	233	354	453	496	662	771	22
23					85	161	293	401	448	630	749	23
24						83	227	346	397	596	726	24
25							157	286	342	559	701	25
26							81	222	284	520	674	26
27								153	220	477	645	27
28								80	152	431	614	28
29									79	382	589	29
30										330	545	30
31										273	506	31
32										212	471	32
33										146	420	33
34										76	373	34
35											321	35

LOAN PROGRESS CHART

Showing dollar balance remaining on a $1,000 loan **7½%**

Age of Loan	ORIGINAL TERM IN YEARS											Age of Loan
	5	**10**	**11**	**12**	**13**	**14**	**15**	**16**	**17**	**18**	**19**	
1	829	930	939	947	953	958	962	966	970	973	975	1
2	644	855	874	889	902	913	922	930	937	943	949	2
3	445	774	803	827	847	864	878	891	902	912	920	3
4	231	687	727	760	788	811	832	849	864	877	889	4
5		592	645	688	724	755	781	804	823	840	856	5
6		491	556	610	655	694	726	755	779	801	820	6
7		382	461	527	581	628	668	702	732	758	781	7
8		264	358	436	502	557	604	645	681	712	739	8
9		137	248	339	416	481	536	584	626	662	694	9
10			128	234	323	398	463	518	566	609	646	10
11				122	223	310	383	447	502	551	594	11
12					116	214	298	370	434	489	537	12
13						111	206	288	359	422	477	13
14							107	199	279	349	411	14
15								103	193	272	341	15
16									100	188	265	16
17										97	183	17
18											95	18

Age of Loan	ORIGINAL TERM IN YEARS											Age of Loan
	20	**21**	**22**	**23**	**24**	**25**	**27**	**29**	**30**	**35**	**40**	
1	978	980	981	983	985	986	988	990	990	994	996	1
2	953	958	961	965	968	971	975	979	981	987	991	2
3	927	934	940	945	950	954	961	968	970	980	987	3
4	899	908	917	924	931	936	947	955	959	973	982	4
5	869	881	892	901	910	917	931	941	946	964	976	5
6	836	851	865	876	887	897	913	927	933	955	970	6
7	801	819	835	850	863	875	895	911	918	946	964	7
8	763	785	804	821	837	851	875	894	903	935	957	8
9	723	748	770	791	809	825	853	876	886	924	949	9
10	679	708	734	757	778	797	830	856	868	912	941	10
11	631	665	695	722	746	767	805	835	848	899	932	11
12	580	618	652	683	710	735	777	812	827	886	923	12
13	525	568	607	641	672	700	748	788	805	871	913	13
14	466	515	558	597	632	663	717	761	781	854	902	14
15	402	456	505	548	587	623	683	733	754	837	890	15
16	333	394	448	496	540	579	647	702	726	818	878	16
17	259	326	387	440	489	532	607	669	695	798	864	17
18	179	254	320	380	434	482	565	633	663	776	850	18
19	93	175	249	315	374	427	519	595	627	753	834	19
20		91	172	245	310	369	470	553	589	727	817	20
21			89	169	241	306	417	508	548	700	799	21
22				88	167	238	360	460	504	671	779	22
23					86	164	298	408	456	639	758	23
24						85	232	352	404	605	735	24
25							160	292	349	568	710	25
26							83	227	289	528	683	26
27								157	225	486	655	27
28								81	155	440	624	28
29									81	390	590	29
30										336	554	30
31										279	516	31
32										217	474	32
33										150	429	33
34										78	381	34
35											328	35

7¾% LOAN PROGRESS CHART
Showing dollar balance remaining on a $1,000 loan

Age of Loan	5	10	11	12	13	14	15	16	17	18	19	Age of Loan
1	830	931	940	947	954	959	963	967	970	973	976	1
2	646	857	875	891	903	914	924	932	939	945	950	2
3	447	776	805	829	849	866	881	893	904	914	922	3
4	232	689	730	763	791	814	834	852	867	880	892	4
5		595	648	691	727	758	784	807	827	844	859	5
6		494	560	614	659	697	730	759	783	805	823	6
7		334	464	530	585	632	672	706	736	762	785	7
8		266	361	440	506	561	609	650	685	717	744	8
9		138	250	342	419	485	541	589	631	667	699	9
10			130	237	326	402	467	523	571	614	651	10
11				123	226	313	387	452	507	556	599	11
12					117	217	301	375	438	494	543	12
13						112	209	292	364	427	482	13
14							108	202	283	354	416	14
15								105	196	275	345	15
16									102	191	269	16
17										99	186	17
18											97	18

Age of Loan	20	21	22	23	24	25	27	29	30	35	40	Age of Loan
1	978	980	982	984	985	986	989	990	991	994	996	1
2	955	959	963	966	969	972	976	980	982	988	992	2
3	929	936	942	947	952	956	963	969	971	981	988	3
4	902	911	919	926	933	939	949	957	960	974	983	4
5	872	884	895	904	912	920	933	944	948	966	978	5
6	840	855	868	880	891	900	916	930	936	958	972	6
7	806	824	840	854	867	878	898	915	922	949	966	7
8	768	790	809	826	841	855	879	898	907	939	959	8
9	728	753	775	796	814	830	858	880	890	928	952	9
10	684	713	739	763	784	802	835	861	873	916	944	10
11	637	671	701	727	751	773	810	841	854	904	936	11
12	586	624	659	689	716	741	783	818	833	890	927	12
13	531	574	613	648	679	707	755	794	811	876	918	13
14	471	520	564	603	638	670	724	768	787	860	907	14
15	407	462	511	555	594	629	690	740	761	843	896	15
16	338	399	454	503	547	586	654	709	733	825	884	16
17	263	331	392	446	495	539	614	676	703	805	870	17
18	182	258	325	386	440	490	572	641	670	784	856	18
19	94	178	253	320	380	434	526	602	635	760	841	19
20		93	175	249	315	375	477	561	597	735	824	20
21			91	172	245	311	424	516	556	708	806	21
22				89	170	242	366	467	511	679	787	22
23					88	167	304	415	463	648	766	23
24						87	236	359	411	614	743	24
25							163	297	355	577	719	25
26							85	231	295	537	692	26
27								160	229	494	664	27
28								83	159	448	633	28
29									82	398	600	29
30										343	564	30
31										285	525	31
32										222	483	32
33										153	438	33
34										80	389	34
35											336	35

LOAN PROGRESS CHART
Showing dollar balance remaining on a $1,000 loan

8%

Age of Loan	5	10	11	12	13	14	15	16	17	18	19	Age of Loan
1	831	932	941	948	954	960	964	968	971	974	977	1
2	647	858	877	892	905	916	925	933	940	946	951	2
3	448	778	808	831	851	868	883	895	906	916	924	3
4	233	692	732	766	794	817	837	854	869	883	894	4
5		598	651	694	731	761	788	810	830	847	862	5
6		497	563	617	663	701	734	762	787	808	827	6
7		387	468	534	589	636	676	710	740	766	789	7
8		268	364	443	509	565	613	654	690	721	749	8
9		139	252	345	423	489	545	593	635	672	704	9
10			131	239	330	406	471	528	576	619	656	10
11				124	228	316	391	456	512	561	604	11
12					119	219	305	379	443	499	548	12
13						114	211	295	368	432	487	13
14							110	205	287	358	421	14
15								106	199	279	350	15
16									103	193	273	16
17										101	189	17
18											98	18

Age of Loan	20	21	22	23	24	25	27	29	30	35	40	Age of Loan
1	979	981	983	984	986	987	989	991	992	995	996	1
2	956	960	964	967	970	973	977	981	983	989	993	2
3	931	938	943	949	953	957	964	970	973	982	988	3
4	904	913	921	929	935	941	951	959	962	975	984	4
5	875	887	897	907	915	923	936	946	951	968	979	5
6	844	859	872	883	894	903	919	933	938	960	974	6
7	810	828	844	858	871	882	902	918	925	951	968	7
8	773	794	813	830	846	859	883	902	910	942	962	8
9	733	758	780	800	818	834	862	885	894	931	955	9
10	689	719	745	768	789	808	840	866	877	920	948	10
11	642	676	706	733	757	779	816	846	859	908	940	11
12	592	630	664	695	722	747	789	824	839	895	931	12
13	537	580	619	654	685	713	761	800	817	881	922	13
14	477	526	570	609	645	676	730	774	793	866	912	14
15	413	468	517	561	601	636	697	746	768	849	901	15
16	343	405	460	509	553	593	661	716	740	831	889	16
17	267	336	398	453	502	546	622	684	710	812	876	17
18	185	262	330	391	446	495	579	648	678	791	862	18
19	96	181	257	325	386	440	534	610	643	768	847	19
20		94	178	253	320	381	484	568	605	743	831	20
21			93	175	250	316	430	523	564	716	814	21
22				91	173	246	372	475	519	688	795	22
23					90	171	309	422	471	656	774	23
24						89	241	365	418	622	752	24
25							157	303	362	557	728	25
26							87	236	301	546	701	26
27								164	234	502	673	27
28								85	162	456	642	28
29									84	405	609	29
30										350	573	30
31										291	534	31
32										227	492	32
33										157	446	33
34										82	397	34
35											343	35

8¼% LOAN PROGRESS CHART

Showing dollar balance remaining on a $1,000 loan

Age of Loan	5	10	11	12	13	14	15	16	17	18	19	Age of Loan
1	831	933	942	949	955	960	965	969	972	975	977	1
2	648	860	878	894	907	917	927	934	941	947	953	2
3	450	781	810	834	854	871	885	897	908	918	926	3
4	234	695	735	769	796	820	840	857	872	885	897	4
5		601	654	698	734	765	791	814	833	850	865	5
6		500	566	621	666	705	738	766	791	812	831	6
7		390	470	537	593	640	680	715	745	771	794	7
8		271	367	447	513	570	617	659	695	726	753	8
9		141	255	349	427	493	549	598	640	677	709	9
10			133	242	333	410	476	532	581	624	662	10
11				126	231	320	395	461	517	567	610	11
12					120	222	308	383	448	504	554	12
13						115	214	299	372	436	493	13
14							111	207	290	363	427	14
15								108	201	283	355	15
16									105	196	277	16
17										102	192	17
18											100	18

Age of Loan	20	21	22	23	24	25	27	29	30	35	40	Age of Loan
1	979	981	983	985	986	987	990	991	992	995	997	1
2	957	961	965	968	971	974	978	982	983	989	993	2
3	933	939	945	950	955	959	966	972	974	983	989	3
4	907	916	924	931	937	943	953	960	964	977	985	4
5	878	890	900	910	918	925	938	948	953	970	980	5
6	847	862	875	887	897	906	922	935	941	962	975	6
7	814	832	848	862	874	886	905	921	928	954	970	7
8	777	799	818	835	850	863	887	906	914	945	964	8
9	738	763	785	805	823	839	866	889	898	935	958	9
10	695	724	750	773	794	813	845	871	882	924	951	10
11	648	682	712	739	763	784	821	851	864	912	943	11
12	597	636	670	701	728	753	795	829	844	900	935	12
13	542	586	625	660	691	719	767	806	823	886	926	13
14	483	532	576	616	651	683	737	781	800	871	916	14
15	418	474	523	568	607	643	704	753	774	855	906	15
16	347	410	466	515	560	600	668	723	747	837	894	16
17	271	341	403	459	508	553	629	691	717	818	882	17
18	188	266	335	397	452	502	587	656	685	798	869	18
19	98	184	261	330	391	447	541	617	650	775	854	19
20		96	181	257	326	387	491	576	613	751	838	20
21			94	179	254	321	437	531	571	724	821	21
22				93	176	251	378	482	527	696	802	22
23					92	174	314	429	478	665	782	23
24						91	245	371	426	631	760	24
25							170	309	368	594	736	25
26							89	241	306	554	710	26
27								167	239	511	682	27
28								87	166	464	651	28
29									86	413	618	29
30										357	582	30
31										297	543	31
32										232	501	32
33										161	455	33
34										84	404	34
35											350	35

LOAN PROGRESS CHART

Showing dollar balance remaining on a $1,000 loan 8½%

Age of Loan	ORIGINAL TERM IN YEARS											Age of Loan
	5	10	11	12	13	14	15	16	17	18	19	
1	832	934	943	950	956	961	966	969	973	975	977	1
2	650	861	880	895	908	919	928	936	943	949	954	2
3	451	783	812	836	856	873	887	899	910	919	928	3
4	235	697	738	771	799	823	843	860	875	888	899	4
5		604	657	701	737	768	794	817	836	853	868	5
6		503	570	624	670	709	742	770	794	816	834	6
7		393	474	541	597	644	684	719	749	775	798	7
8		273	370	450	517	574	622	663	699	730	758	8
9		142	257	352	431	497	554	603	645	682	714	9
10			134	244	336	414	480	537	586	629	667	10
11				127	233	323	400	465	522	572	615	11
12					122	224	312	387	452	509	559	12
13						117	217	302	377	441	508	13
14							113	210	294	367	432	14
15								109	204	287	359	15
16									106	199	280	16
17										104	195	17
18											102	18

Age of Loan	ORIGINAL TERM IN YEARS											Age of Loan
	20	21	22	23	24	25	27	29	30	35	40	
1	980	982	984	985	987	988	990	992	992	995	997	1
2	958	962	966	969	972	975	979	983	984	990	994	2
3	935	941	947	952	956	960	967	973	975	984	990	3
4	909	918	926	933	939	945	954	962	966	978	986	4
5	881	893	903	912	921	928	940	951	955	971	982	5
6	851	865	878	890	900	909	925	938	943	964	977	6
7	818	836	851	865	878	889	909	924	931	956	972	7
8	782	803	822	839	854	867	890	909	917	947	966	8
9	743	768	790	810	828	844	871	893	902	938	960	9
10	700	729	755	778	799	818	849	875	886	928	953	10
11	654	687	717	744	768	790	826	856	868	916	946	11
12	603	642	676	707	734	759	801	835	849	904	938	12
13	548	592	631	666	697	725	773	812	828	891	930	13
14	488	538	583	622	657	689	743	787	806	876	921	14
15	423	479	529	574	614	649	710	760	781	861	910	15
16	352	415	472	522	566	606	675	730	754	843	899	16
17	275	346	409	465	515	559	636	698	725	825	887	17
18	191	270	340	403	458	508	594	663	693	805	874	18
19	99	187	266	335	397	453	548	625	658	782	860	19
20		98	184	262	331	392	498	583	620	758	845	20
21			96	182	258	327	443	538	579	732	828	21
22				95	179	255	384	489	534	705	810	22
23					93	177	320	436	486	673	790	23
24						92	250	378	432	639	768	24
25							173	314	375	605	744	25
26							90	245	312	562	719	26
27								170	244	519	691	27
28								89	169	472	660	28
29									88	420	627	29
30										364	591	30
31										303	552	31
32										237	509	32
33										164	463	33
34										86	412	34
35											357	35

8¾% LOAN PROGRESS CHART

Showing dollar balance remaining on a $1,000 loan

Age of Loan	ORIGINAL TERM IN YEARS											Age of Loan
	5	10	11	12	13	14	15	16	17	18	19	
1	833	935	943	951	957	962	966		973	976	979	1
2	651	863	882	897	910	920	929	937	944	950	955	2
3	453	785	814	838	858	875	889	901	912	921	930	3
4	236	700	741	774	802	825	845	862	877	890	902	4
5		607	660	704	741	771	797	820	839	856	871	5
6		506	573	628	674	712	745	774	798	819	838	6
7		396	477	545	601	648	688	723	753	779	802	7
8		275	373	454	521	578	626	668	704	735	762	8
9		144	259	355	434	501	558	607	650	687	719	9
10			135	247	339	418	484	542	591	634	672	10
11				129	236	326	404	470	527	577	621	11
12					123	227	315	391	457	514	565	12
13						118	219	306	381	446	503	13
14							114	213	298	372	437	14
15								111	207	291	364	15
16									108	202	284	16
17										105	198	17
18											103	18

Age of Loan	ORIGINAL TERM IN YEARS											Age of Loan
	20	21	22	23	24	25	27	29	30	35	40	
1	981	983	984	986	987	988	990	992	993	995	997	1
2	964	967	970	973	976	980	983	985		991	994	2
3	937	943	949	953	958	962	969	974	976	985	991	3
4	912	920	928	935	941	947	956	964	967	979	987	4
5	884	896	906	915	923	930	943	953	957	973	983	5
6	854	869	882	893	903	912	928	940	946	966	978	6
7	822	839	855	869	882	893	912	927	934	958	973	7
8	786	807	826	843	858	871	894	913	920	950	968	8
9	747	773	795	815	832	848	875	897	906	941	962	9
10	705	734	760	784	804	823	854	879	890	931	956	10
11	659	693	723	750	773	795	831	860	873	920	949	11
12	609	647	682	713	740	765	806	840	854	908	942	12
13	554	598	637	678	704	731	779	817	834	895	934	13
14	494	544	589	628	664	695	749	793	811	881	925	14
15	428	485	535	580	620	656	717	766	787	866	915	15
16	357	421	477	528	573	613	681	737	761	849	904	16
17	279	351	414	471	521	566	643	705	732	831	897	17
18	194	274	345	408	465	515	601	670	700	811	880	18
19	101	191	270	340	403	459	555	632	665	789	866	19
20		99	188	266	336	398	505	591	628	766	851	20
21			98	185	263	332	450	546	587	740	835	21
22			96	183	259	390	496	542	712	817		22
23				95	180	325	443	493	681	797		23
24					94	254	384	439	647	776		24
25						177	320	381	611	753		25
26							92	250	318	571	727	26
27								174	248	527	699	27
28								91	173	479	669	28
29									90	428	636	29
30										371	600	30
31										309	561	31
32										242	518	32
33										168	471	33
34										88	420	34
35											364	35

LOAN PROGRESS CHART 9%

Showing dollar balance remaining on a $1,000 loan

Age of Loan	ORIGINAL TERM IN YEARS											Age of Loan
	5	10	11	12	13	14	15	16	17	18	19	
1	834	935	944	951	958	963	967	971	974	977	979	1
2	653	865	883	898	911	922	931	939	945	951	956	2
3	454	787	816	840	860	877	891	903	914	923	931	3
4	237	703	743	777	805	828	848	865	880	893	904	4
5		610	664	707	744	775	801	823	843	859	874	5
6		509	576	631	677	716	749	777	802	823	841	6
7		398	481	548	605	652	692	727	757	783	806	7
8		277	376	457	525	582	630	672	708	739	767	8
9		145	262	358	438	505	563	612	654	691	724	9
10			137	249	343	422	489	546	596	639	677	10
11				130	239	330	408	474	532	582	626	11
12					125	230	319	396	462	520	570	12
13						120	222	310	385	451	509	13
14							116	216	302	376	442	14
15								113	210	294	368	15
16									110	205	288	16
17										107	201	17
18											105	18

Age of Loan	ORIGINAL TERM IN YEARS											Age of Loan
	20	21	22	23	24	25	27	29	30	35	40	
1	981	983	985	986	988	989	991	992	993	996	997	1
2	961	965	968	971	974	977	981	984	986	991	994	2
3	938	945	950	955	959	963	970	975	978	986	991	3
4	914	923	930	937	943	949	958	965	969	980	988	4
5	887	898	909	918	926	933	945	955	959	974	984	5
6	858	872	885	896	906	915	931	943	948	968	980	6
7	826	843	859	873	885	896	915	930	936	960	975	7
8	791	812	831	847	862	875	898	916	924	952	970	8
9	752	777	799	819	837	852	879	900	910	944	965	9
10	710	740	766	789	809	827	850	884	894	934	959	10
11	664	698	728	755	779	800	836	865	878	924	952	11
12	614	653	688	718	746	770	812	845	859	912	945	12
13	559	604	643	678	710	737	785	823	839	900	937	13
14	499	550	595	634	670	702	755	799	817	886	929	14
15	433	491	541	587	627	662	723	772	793	871	919	15
16	362	426	483	534	579	620	688	743	767	855	909	16
17	283	355	420	477	527	573	650	712	738	837	898	17
18	197	278	350	414	471	522	608	677	707	818	885	18
19	103	194	274	345	409	466	562	640	673	796	872	19
20		101	191	270	341	404	512	598	635	773	857	20
21			100	188	267	337	457	553	594	747	841	21
22				98	186	264	397	504	549	719	824	22
23					97	184	331	449	500	698	805	23
24						96	252	390	446	655	783	24
25							180	323	388	619	761	25
26							94	255	323	579	735	26
27								177	253	535	708	27
28								93	176	487	678	28
29									92	462	645	29
30										378	609	30
31										315	570	31
32										247	527	32
33										172	479	33
34										90	428	34
35											372	35

9¼% LOAN PROGRESS CHART
Showing dollar balance remaining on a $1,000 loan

Age of Loan	5	10	11	12	13	14	15	16	17	18	19	Age of Loan
					ORIGINAL TERM IN YEARS							
1	835	936	945	952	958	963	968	971	975	977	980	1
2	654	866	835	900	913	923	932	940	947	952	957	2
3	456	790	819	842	862	879	893	905	916	925	933	3
4	238	705	746	780	807	831	851	868	882	895	906	4
5		613	667	710	747	778	804	826	846	862	877	5
6		512	579	635	681	720	753	781	805	826	845	6
7		401	434	552	608	656	696	731	761	787	810	7
8		280	379	461	529	586	635	676	712	744	771	8
9		146	264	361	442	509	567	616	659	696	729	9
10			138	252	346	425	493	551	604	644	682	10
11				132	241	333	412	479	537	587	631	11
12					126	232	322	400	467	525	575	12
13						121	225	313	390	456	514	13
14							118	218	305	381	447	14
15								114	213	298	373	15
16									111	208	292	16
17										109	204	17
18											107	18

Age of Loan	20	21	22	23	24	25	27	28	30	35	40	Age of Loan
					ORIGINAL TERM IN YEARS							
1	982	984	985	987	988	989	991	993	994	996	998	1
2	962	966	969	972	975	978	982	985	986	992	995	2
3	940	946	952	957	961	965	971	976	979	987	992	3
4	916	925	932	939	945	951	960	967	970	982	989	4
5	889	901	911	920	928	935	947	957	961	976	985	5
6	861	875	888	899	909	918	933	945	950	969	981	6
7	830	847	863	876	889	899	918	933	939	962	977	7
8	795	816	835	851	866	879	901	919	927	955	972	8
9	757	782	804	824	841	857	883	904	913	947	967	9
10	715	745	771	793	814	832	863	888	896	937	961	10
11	670	704	734	760	784	805	841	870	882	927	955	11
12	620	659	693	724	751	776	817	850	864	916	948	12
13	565	610	649	684	715	743	790	828	844	904	941	13
14	505	556	601	641	676	708	761	805	823	891	932	14
15	439	496	547	593	633	669	730	779	799	876	923	15
16	366	431	489	540	586	626	695	750	773	861	913	16
17	287	360	425	483	534	579	657	719	745	843	903	17
18	200	282	355	420	477	528	615	684	714	824	891	18
19	105	197	278	350	415	472	569	647	680	803	878	19
20		103	194	274	346	410	518	605	643	780	863	20
21			101	191	271	342	463	560	602	755	846	21
22				100	189	268	403	511	557	727	830	22
23					99	187	336	456	507	697	812	23
24						98	263	347	453	663	791	24
25							184	331	394	627	768	25
26							96	259	329	587	743	26
27								181	258	543	716	27
28								95	180	495	686	28
29									94	442	654	29
30										384	618	30
31										321	578	31
32										252	535	32
33										175	488	33
34										92	436	34
35											379	35

LOAN PROGRESS CHART

Showing dollar balance remaining on a $1,000 loan 9½%

Age of Loan	ORIGINAL TERM IN YEARS											Age of Loan
	5	10	11	12	13	14	15	16	17	18	19	
1	836	937	946	953	959	964	968	972	975	978	980	1
2	656	868	886	901	914	925	934	941	947	954	959	2
3	457	792	821	845	864	881	895	907	918	927	935	3
4	240	708	749	782	810	833	853	870	885	898	909	4
5		616	670	714	750	781	807	829	849	865	880	5
6		515	583	638	684	723	756	784	809	830	848	6
7		404	487	555	612	660	700	735	765	791	813	7
8		282	382	464	533	590	639	681	717	748	775	8
9		148	267	364	445	513	571	621	664	701	733	9
10			140	254	349	429	497	555	606	649	687	10
11				133	244	337	416	483	542	592	636	11
12					128	235	326	404	471	530	581	12
13						123	227	317	394	461	519	13
14							119	221	309	385	452	14
15								116	216	302	378	15
16									113	211	296	16
17										110	207	17
18											108	18

Age of Loan	ORIGINAL TERM IN YEARS											Age of Loan
	20	21	22	23	24	25	27	29	30	35	40	
1	982	984	986	987	989	990	992	993	994	996	998	1
2	963	967	970	973	976	978	982	986	987	992	995	2
3	942	948	953	958	962	966	972	977	980	988	992	3
4	918	927	934	941	947	952	961	968	971	983	989	4
5	893	904	914	923	930	937	949	958	962	977	986	5
6	864	879	891	902	912	921	936	947	953	971	982	6
7	833	851	866	880	892	903	921	935	942	964	978	7
8	799	820	839	855	870	883	905	922	930	957	974	8
9	762	787	809	828	845	861	887	908	917	949	969	9
10	720	750	775	798	819	837	867	892	902	940	963	10
11	675	709	739	766	789	810	846	874	886	931	957	11
12	625	664	699	730	757	781	822	855	869	920	951	12
13	570	615	655	690	721	749	796	834	850	908	944	13
14	510	561	607	647	682	714	767	810	828	896	936	14
15	444	502	553	599	639	675	736	785	805	881	927	15
16	371	437	495	546	592	633	701	756	780	866	918	16
17	291	365	431	489	540	586	663	725	752	849	907	17
18	203	286	360	425	483	535	622	691	721	830	896	18
19	106	200	282	355	420	478	576	654	687	809	883	19
20		105	197	279	351	416	525	613	650	787	869	20
21			103	194	276	348	470	567	609	762	854	21
22				102	192	273	409	518	564	735	837	22
23					101	190	342	463	514	704	818	23
24						100	268	403	460	671	798	24
25							187	337	400	450	776	25
26							98	264	335	595	751	26
27								184	262	551	724	27
28								96	183	503	695	28
29									96	450	662	29
30										391	626	30
31										327	587	31
32										256	543	32
33										179	496	33
34										94	443	34
35											386	35

LOAN PROGRESS CHART
Showing dollar balance remaining on a $1,000 loan

Age of Loan	ORIGINAL TERM IN YEARS											Age of Loan
	5	10	11	12	13	14	15	16	17	18	19	
1	837	938	947	954	960	965	969	973	976	978	981	1
2	657	869	888	903	915	926	935	943	949	955	960	2
3	459	794	823	847	867	883	897	909	920	929	937	3
4	241	711	751	785	813	836	856	873	887	900	911	4
5		619	673	717	753	784	810	832	852	868	883	5
6		518	586	642	688	727	760	788	812	833	852	6
7		407	490	559	616	664	704	739	769	795	817	7
8		284	385	468	536	594	643	685	721	752	780	8
9		149	269	367	449	518	576	626	668	706	730	9
10			141	257	352	433	501	560	610	654	692	10
11				134	246	340	420	488	546	597	642	11
12					129	238	330	408	476	535	586	12
13					125	230	320	398	466	524	13	
14						121	224	313	390	457	14	
15							117	218	306	382	15	
16								115	214	300	16	
17									112	210	17	
18										110	18	

(Note: for rows 13–18 the rightmost populated columns are 16, 17, 18 and 19 respectively; values read: 13: 125 230 320 398 466 524; 14: 121 224 313 390 457; 15: 117 218 306 382; 16: 115 214 300; 17: 112 210; 18: 110.)

Age of Loan	ORIGINAL TERM IN YEARS											Age of Loan
	20	21	22	23	24	25	27	29	30	35	40	
1	983	985	986	988	989	990	992	994	994	996	998	1
2	964	968	971	974	977	979	983	986	988	993	995	2
3	943	949	955	959	964	967	973	978	981	988	993	3
4	921	929	939	943	949	954	963	970	973	984	990	4
5	895	906	916	925	933	940	951	960	964	978	987	5
6	868	882	894	905	915	923	938	950	955	973	983	6
7	837	854	870	883	895	906	924	938	944	966	980	7
8	803	824	843	859	873	886	908	925	933	959	975	8
9	766	791	813	832	850	865	891	911	920	952	971	9
10	725	755	780	803	823	841	871	896	906	943	966	10
11	680	714	744	771	794	815	850	878	890	934	960	11
12	631	670	705	735	762	786	827	860	873	924	954	12
13	576	621	661	696	727	755	801	839	855	912	947	13
14	515	567	612	653	688	720	773	816	834	900	939	14
15	449	508	559	605	645	681	742	791	811	886	931	15
16	376	442	501	552	598	639	708	763	786	871	922	16
17	295	370	436	495	546	592	670	732	758	854	912	17
18	206	291	365	431	489	541	628	698	728	836	900	18
19	108	203	287	361	426	484	582	661	694	816	888	19
20		106	200	283	357	422	532	620	657	793	875	20
21			105	198	280	353	476	575	616	769	860	21
22			104	196	277	415	525	571	742	843		22
23				103	194	347	470	522	712	825		23
24					101	273	409	467	679	805		24
25						190	342	407	643	783		25
26							100	269	340	603	759	26
27								188	267	559	732	27
28								98	187	510	703	28
29									98	457	670	29
30										398	634	30
31										333	595	31
32										261	551	32
33										183	504	33
34										96	451	34
35											393	35

LOAN PROGRESS CHART   10%

Showing dollar balance remaining on a $1,000 loan

Age of Loan	5	10	11	12	13	14	15	16	17	18	19	Age of Loan
1	838	939	947	955	960	965	970	973	976	979	981	1
2	658	871	889	904	917	927	936	944	950	956	961	2
3	460	796	825	849	869	885	899	911	922	930	938	3
4	242	713	754	788	815	839	858	875	890	902	913	4
5		622	676	720	756	787	813	835	855	871	885	5
6		521	589	645	691	730	763	791	816	837	855	6
7		410	494	562	620	668	708	743	773	799	821	7
8		286	388	471	540	598	647	689	725	757	784	8
9		150	271	370	453	522	580	630	673	710	743	9
10			142	259	356	437	506	565	615	659	699	10
11				136	249	343	424	492	551	602	647	11
12					131	240	333	412	481	540	591	12
13						126	233	324	403	471	530	13
14							122	227	316	394	462	14
15								119	221	310	387	15
16									116	217	304	16
17										114	213	17
18											112	18

Age of Loan	20	21	22	23	24	25	27	29	30	35	40	Age of Loan
1	983	985	987	988	989	991	992	994	994	997	998	1
2	965	969	972	975	978	980	984	987	988	993	996	2
3	945	951	956	961	965	969	975	979	982	989	993	3
4	923	931	938	945	951	956	964	971	974	985	991	4
5	898	909	919	927	935	942	953	962	966	980	988	5
6	871	885	897	908	918	926	940	952	957	974	984	6
7	841	858	873	886	898	909	927	941	946	968	981	7
8	807	828	847	863	877	890	911	928	935	961	977	8
9	771	796	817	837	854	869	894	913	923	954	972	9
10	730	759	785	808	828	846	876	899	909	946	968	10
11	685	719	749	776	799	820	855	883	894	937	962	11
12	636	675	710	741	768	792	832	864	878	927	956	12
13	581	627	666	702	733	760	807	844	859	916	950	13
14	521	573	618	659	694	726	779	821	839	904	942	14
15	454	513	565	611	652	688	748	796	817	891	934	15
16	380	447	506	559	605	645	714	769	792	876	926	16
17	299	375	442	500	553	599	677	738	765	860	916	17
18	209	295	370	436	495	547	635	705	734	842	905	18
19	110	206	291	366	432	491	569	670	701	822	893	19
20		108	203	287	362	428	539	627	664	800	880	20
21			107	201	284	358	483	582	623	776	865	21
22				105	199	282	421	532	578	749	849	22
23					104	197	353	476	529	719	832	23
24						103	277	413	474	687	812	24
25							194	348	413	651	790	25
26							102	273	346	611	766	26
27								191	272	567	740	27
28								100	190	518	711	28
29									100	464	678	29
30										405	643	30
31										339	603	31
32										266	560	32
33										186	511	33
34										98	458	34
35											400	35

10¼% LOAN PROGRESS CHART
Showing dollar balance remaining on a $1,000 loan

Age of Loan	| ORIGINAL TERM IN YEARS											Age of Loan
	5	10	11	12	13	14	15	16	17	18	19	
1	839	939	948	955	961	966	970	974	977	980	982	1
2	660	872	891	906	918	929	937	945	952	957	962	2
3	462	798	827	851	871	887	901	913	923	932	940	3
4	243	716	757	790	818	841	861	878	892	904	915	4
5		625	679	723	760	790	816	838	857	874	888	5
6		524	592	648	695	734	767	795	819	840	858	6
7		412	497	566	623	671	712	747	777	802	825	7
8		289	391	475	544	602	651	693	730	761	788	8
9		152	274	373	456	526	584	634	678	715	747	9
10			144	261	359	441	510	569	620	672	702	10
11				137	251	347	428	497	556	607	652	11
12					132	243	337	417	485	545	596	12
13						128	236	328	407	475	535	13
14							124	229	320	399	467	14
15								121	224	314	391	15
16									118	220	308	16
17										115	216	17
18											113	18

Age of Loan	ORIGINAL TERM IN YEARS											Age of Loan
	20	21	22	23	24	25	27	29	30	35	40	
1	984	986	987	989	990	991	993	994	995	997	998	1
2	966	970	973	976	979	981	985	988	989	993	996	2
3	947	952	958	962	966	970	976	980	982	990	994	3
4	925	933	940	947	952	957	966	972	975	985	991	4
5	901	912	921	930	937	944	955	964	967	981	989	5
6	874	888	900	911	920	929	943	954	959	976	986	6
7	844	861	876	890	901	912	929	943	949	970	982	7
8	812	832	850	867	881	893	914	931	938	964	978	8
9	775	800	822	841	858	873	898	918	926	957	974	9
10	735	764	790	812	832	850	880	901	913	949	970	10
11	691	725	754	781	804	825	859	887	898	940	964	11
12	641	681	715	746	773	797	837	869	882	931	959	12
13	587	632	672	707	738	766	812	849	864	920	953	13
14	526	578	624	664	700	732	785	827	844	908	946	14
15	459	519	571	617	658	694	754	802	822	895	938	15
16	385	453	512	565	611	652	720	775	798	881	929	16
17	303	380	447	506	559	605	683	745	771	865	920	17
18	212	299	375	442	501	554	642	711	741	847	909	18
19	112	209	295	371	437	497	596	675	708	828	898	19
20		110	207	292	367	433	545	634	671	806	885	20
21			109	204	289	364	489	589	630	782	871	21
22			107	202	286	427	538	585	756	855		22
23				106	200	358	483	536	727	838		23
24					105	282	422	480	694	818		24
25						197	354	419	658	797		25
26							104	278	352	618	773	26
27								195	277	574	747	27
28								102	194	525	718	28
29									102	471	686	29
30										411	651	30
31										345	611	31
32										271	568	32
33										190	519	33
34										100	466	34
35											407	35

LOAN PROGRESS CHART

Showing dollar balance remaining on a $1,000 loan **10½%**

Age of Loan	ORIGINAL TERM IN YEARS											Age of Loan
	5	10	11	12	13	14	15	16	17	18	19	
1	839	940	949	956	962	967	971	975	978	980	982	1
2	661	874	892	907	920	930	939	946	953	958	963	2
3	463	800	829	853	873	889	903	915	925	934	941	3
4	244	719	759	793	821	844	863	880	894	907	917	4
5		628	682	726	763	793	819	841	860	877	891	5
6		527	596	652	698	737	770	798	822	843	861	6
7		415	500	570	627	675	716	751	780	806	828	7
8		291	394	478	548	606	656	698	734	765	792	8
9		153	276	377	460	530	589	639	682	719	752	9
10			145	264	362	445	514	574	625	669	707	10
11				139	254	350	432	501	561	612	657	11
12					134	245	340	421	490	550	601	12
13						129	238	331	411	480	540	13
14							125	232	324	403	472	14
15								122	227	318	396	15
16									119	223	312	16
17										117	219	17
18											115	18

Age of Loan	ORIGINAL TERM IN YEARS											Age of Loan
	20	21	22	23	24	25	27	29	30	35	40	
1	984	986	988	989	990	991	993	994	995	997	998	1
2	967	971	974	977	979	982	985	988	989	994	996	2
3	948	954	959	963	967	971	977	981	983	990	994	3
4	927	935	942	948	954	959	967	974	976	986	992	4
5	903	914	923	932	939	946	957	965	969	982	989	5
6	877	891	903	913	923	931	945	956	960	977	986	6
7	848	865	880	893	904	915	932	945	951	971	983	7
8	816	836	854	870	884	897	917	934	941	965	980	8
9	780	804	826	845	862	876	901	921	929	959	976	9
10	740	769	794	817	837	854	883	907	916	951	971	10
11	696	730	760	786	809	829	864	891	902	943	967	11
12	647	686	721	751	778	802	842	873	886	934	962	12
13	592	638	678	713	744	771	817	853	869	924	955	13
14	532	584	630	670	706	737	790	832	849	912	948	14
15	464	524	577	623	664	700	760	808	828	900	941	15
16	390	458	518	570	617	658	727	781	804	886	933	16
17	307	385	452	512	565	612	689	751	777	870	924	17
18	215	303	380	448	507	560	648	718	747	853	914	18
19	113	212	299	376	443	503	603	681	714	834	902	19
20		112	210	296	372	439	552	641	678	812	890	20
21			110	207	293	369	495	595	637	789	876	21
22				109	205	290	433	525	592	763	861	22
23					108	204	363	490	534	734	844	23
24						107	286	428	487	701	825	24
25							201	359	426	666	804	25
26							106	283	357	626	781	26
27								198	281	582	755	27
28								104	197	533	726	28
29									104	478	694	29
30										418	659	30
31										351	619	31
32										276	575	32
33										194	527	33
34										102	473	34
35											413	35

10¾% LOAN PROGRESS CHART

Showing dollar balance remaining on a $1,000 loan

Age of Loan	5	10	11	12	13	14	15	16	17	18	19	Age of Loan
1	840	941	950	957	963	967	972	975	978	981	983	1
2	663	875	894	909	921	931	940	947	954	959	964	2
3	465	802	831	855	875	891	905	917	927	935	943	3
4	245	721	762	795	823	846	866	882	897	909	920	4
5		631	685	729	766	796	822	844	863	879	893	5
6		530	599	655	702	741	774	802	826	846	864	6
7		418	503	573	631	679	720	754	784	810	832	7
8		293	397	482	552	610	660	702	738	769	796	8
9		154	279	380	464	534	593	643	687	724	756	9
10			147	266	366	449	519	578	629	673	711	10
11				140	256	354	436	506	566	617	662	11
12					135	248	344	425	495	555	607	12
13						131	241	335	416	485	545	13
14							127	235	328	408	477	14
15								124	230	321	401	15
16									121	226	316	16
17										119	222	17
18											117	18

Age of Loan	20	21	22	23	24	25	27	29	30	35	40	Age of Loan
1	985	987	988	989	991	992	993	995	995	997	998	1
2	968	972	975	978	980	982	986	989	990	994	997	2
3	950	955	960	965	969	972	978	982	984	991	995	3
4	929	937	944	950	956	960	969	975	978	987	993	4
5	906	916	926	934	941	948	958	967	970	983	990	5
6	880	894	906	916	925	933	947	958	962	978	987	6
7	851	868	883	896	907	918	936	948	953	973	984	7
8	820	840	858	874	888	900	920	936	943	967	981	8
9	784	809	830	849	866	880	905	924	932	961	977	9
10	745	774	799	821	841	858	887	910	919	954	973	10
11	701	735	764	791	814	834	868	894	906	946	969	11
12	652	691	726	756	783	807	846	877	890	937	963	12
13	598	643	683	718	749	777	822	858	873	927	958	13
14	537	590	636	676	712	743	795	837	854	916	951	14
15	470	530	583	629	679	706	766	813	833	906	944	15
16	395	463	524	576	623	664	733	787	809	890	936	16
17	311	389	458	518	571	618	696	757	783	875	928	17
18	218	307	385	453	513	566	655	724	754	858	918	18
19	115	215	303	381	449	509	609	688	721	839	907	19
20		113	213	300	377	445	558	647	685	819	895	20
21			112	211	297	374	502	602	644	795	881	21
22				111	209	295	439	552	599	769	866	22
23					110	207	369	496	549	741	850	23
24						109	291	434	494	709	831	24
25							204	365	432	673	810	25
26							107	288	363	633	787	26
27								202	286	589	762	27
28								106	201	540	733	28
29									106	485	702	29
30										424	666	30
31										357	627	31
32										281	583	32
33										197	535	33
34										104	480	34
35											420	35

LOAN PROGRESS CHART

Showing dollar balance remaining on a $1,000 loan **11%**

Age of Loan	ORIGINAL TERM IN YEARS											Age of Loan
	5	10	11	12	13	14	15	16	17	18	19	
1	841	942	950	957	963	968	972	976	979	981	983	1
2	664	877	895	910	922	933	941	949	955	960	965	2
3	466	805	833	857	877	893	907	918	928	937	945	3
4	246	724	765	798	826	849	868	885	899	911	922	4
5		634	688	732	769	799	825	847	866	882	896	5
6		533	602	659	705	744	777	805	829	850	867	6
7		421	507	577	634	683	724	758	788	813	836	7
8		296	400	485	555	614	664	706	742	773	800	8
9		156	281	383	467	538	597	648	691	728	760	9
10			148	269	369	452	523	583	634	678	716	10
11				142	259	357	440	510	570	622	667	11
12					137	251	347	429	499	560	612	12
13						132	244	339	420	490	553	13
14							129	238	332	412	482	14
15								125	233	325	405	15
16									123	229	320	16
17										121	225	17
18											119	18

Age of Loan	ORIGINAL TERM IN YEARS											Age of Loan
	20	21	22	23	24	25	27	29	30	35	40	
1	985	987	989	990	991	992	994	995	995	997	999	1
2	969	973	976	979	981	983	987	989	990	995	997	2
3	951	957	962	966	970	973	979	983	985	991	995	3
4	931	939	946	952	957	962	970	976	979	988	993	4
5	908	919	928	936	943	950	960	968	972	984	991	5
6	883	896	908	919	928	936	949	960	964	979	988	6
7	855	872	886	899	910	920	937	950	955	974	985	7
8	823	844	862	877	891	903	923	939	945	969	982	8
9	788	813	834	853	869	884	908	927	935	963	979	9
10	749	778	803	826	845	862	891	913	923	956	975	10
11	706	740	769	795	818	838	872	898	909	948	970	11
12	657	697	731	762	788	812	851	881	894	940	965	12
13	603	649	689	724	755	782	827	863	877	930	960	13
14	542	595	641	682	717	749	801	842	859	920	954	14
15	475	535	588	635	676	712	771	818	838	908	947	15
16	399	469	529	582	629	670	739	792	815	895	940	16
17	315	394	463	524	577	624	702	763	789	880	931	17
18	221	311	390	459	519	572	661	731	760	863	922	18
19	117	219	308	386	454	515	616	694	727	845	911	19
20		115	216	305	382	451	565	654	691	824	899	20
21			114	214	302	379	508	609	651	801	886	21
22				113	212	299	445	559	606	776	872	22
23					112	210	374	503	556	747	855	23
24						111	295	440	500	717	837	24
25							207	370	438	680	817	25
26							109	292	368	641	794	26
27								205	291	596	769	27
28								108	204	547	741	28
29									108	492	709	29
30										431	674	30
31										363	635	31
32										286	591	32
33										201	542	33
34										106	488	34
35											427	35

LOAN PROGRESS CHART

11¼%
Showing dollar balance remaining on a $1,000 loan

Age of Loan	ORIGINAL TERM IN YEARS															Age of Loan
	5	10	11	12	13	14	15	16	17	18	19					
1	842	943	951	958	964	969	973	976	979	982	984					1
2	666	878	897	911	924	934	942	950	956	961	966					2
3	468	807	836	859	879	895	909	920	930	939	946					3
4	247	726	767	801	828	851	871	887	901	913	924					4
5		636	691	735	772	802	828	850	869	885	899					5
6		536	605	662	709	748	780	808	832	853	870					6
7		424	510	580	638	687	727	762	792	817	839					7
8		298	403	488	559	618	668	710	746	777	804					8
9		157	283	386	471	542	601	652	695	733	765					9
10			150	271	372	456	527	587	639	683	721					10
11				143	262	361	444	514	575	627	672					11
12					138	254	351	433	504	564	617					12
13						134	247	342	424	495	555					13
14							130	241	335	417	487					14
15								127	236	329	410					15
16									124	231	324					16
17										122	228					17
18											120					18

Age of Loan	ORIGINAL TERM IN YEARS											Age of Loan
	20	21	22	23	24	25	27	29	30	35	40	
1	986	988	989	990	991	992	994	995	996	998	999	1
2	970	974	977	979	982	984	987	990	991	995	997	2
3	952	958	963	967	971	974	980	984	986	992	995	3
4	933	941	947	953	959	963	971	977	980	989	994	4
5	911	921	930	938	945	951	962	970	973	985	991	5
6	886	899	911	921	930	938	951	961	966	981	989	6
7	858	875	889	902	913	923	939	952	957	976	986	7
8	827	847	865	881	894	906	926	941	948	971	983	8
9	793	817	838	857	873	887	911	930	937	965	980	9
10	754	783	808	830	849	866	894	917	926	958	976	10
11	711	745	774	800	823	843	876	902	913	951	972	11
12	662	702	736	767	793	816	855	885	898	943	967	12
13	608	654	694	729	760	787	832	867	882	933	962	13
14	548	601	647	687	723	754	806	846	863	923	956	14
15	480	541	594	640	681	717	777	823	843	912	950	15
16	404	474	535	588	635	676	744	798	820	899	943	16
17	319	399	469	530	583	630	708	769	794	884	934	17
18	225	315	395	464	525	579	667	737	766	868	925	18
19	119	222	312	391	460	521	622	701	734	850	915	19
20		117	219	309	367	456	571	661	698	830	904	20
21			116	217	306	384	514	616	658	808	891	21
22				115	215	304	451	565	613	782	877	22
23					114	214	379	509	563	754	861	23
24						113	300	446	507	723	843	24
25							211	376	444	687	823	25
26							111	297	374	648	801	26
27								209	296	604	776	27
28								110	208	554	748	28
29									110	499	716	29
30										437	681	30
31										368	642	31
32										291	599	32
33										205	550	33
34										108	495	34
35											434	35

LOAN PROGRESS CHART

Showing dollar balance remaining on a $1,000 loan   **11½%**

Age of Loan	ORIGINAL TERM IN YEARS											Age of Loan
	5	10	11	12	13	14	15	16	17	18	19	
1	843	943	952	959	965	969	973	977	980	982	984	1
2	667	880	898	913	925	935	944	951	957	962	967	2
3	470	809	838	861	880	897	910	922	932	940	947	3
4	248	729	770	803	831	854	873	889	903	915	926	4
5		639	694	738	775	805	831	853	871	887	901	5
6		539	609	665	712	751	784	812	835	856	873	6
7		426	513	584	642	690	731	766	795	821	843	7
8		300	406	492	563	622	672	714	750	781	808	8
9		159	286	389	474	546	606	656	700	737	769	9
10			151	274	375	460	531	592	643	687	725	10
11				145	264	364	448	519	580	632	677	11
12					140	256	354	437	508	569	622	12
13						135	249	346	429	499	560	13
14							132	244	339	421	492	14
15								129	239	333	414	15
16									126	234	328	16
17										124	231	17
18											122	18

Age of Loan	ORIGINAL TERM IN YEARS											Age of Loan
	20	21	22	23	24	25	27	29	30	35	40	
1	986	988	989	991	992	993	994	995	996	998	999	1
2	971	974	977	980	982	984	988	990	991	995	997	2
3	954	959	964	968	972	975	980	985	986	992	996	3
4	935	942	949	955	960	965	972	978	981	989	994	4
5	913	923	932	940	947	953	963	971	974	986	992	5
6	889	902	913	924	932	940	953	963	967	982	990	6
7	861	878	892	905	916	925	941	954	959	977	987	7
8	831	851	869	884	897	909	929	944	950	972	984	8
9	797	821	842	860	877	891	914	932	940	967	981	9
10	759	787	812	834	853	870	898	920	929	960	978	10
11	716	749	779	805	827	847	880	905	916	953	974	11
12	617	707	741	772	798	821	859	889	902	945	969	12
13	613	659	699	734	765	792	837	871	886	936	964	13
14	553	606	652	693	728	759	811	851	868	926	959	14
15	485	546	600	646	687	723	782	829	848	915	953	15
16	409	479	540	594	641	682	750	803	825	903	946	16
17	323	404	474	535	589	636	714	775	800	889	938	17
18	228	319	400	470	531	585	674	743	772	873	929	18
19	120	225	316	396	466	527	628	707	740	855	919	19
20		119	223	313	393	462	577	667	704	836	908	20
21			118	220	311	390	520	622	664	813	896	21
22				117	219	308	457	572	620	789	882	22
23					116	217	385	515	570	761	866	23
24						115	304	452	513	729	849	24
25							214	381	450	694	829	25
26							113	302	380	655	807	26
27								212	300	611	782	27
28								112	211	561	755	28
29									112	506	723	29
30										444	689	30
31										374	650	31
32										296	606	32
33										208	557	33
34										110	502	34
35											440	35

LOAN PROGRESS CHART
Showing dollar balance remaining on a $1,000 loan

Age of Loan	ORIGINAL TERM IN YEARS											Age of Loan
	5	10	11	12	13	14	15	16	17	18	19	
1	844	944	953	960	965	970	974	977	980	983	985	1
2	668	881	899	914	926	936	945	952	958	963	968	2
3	471	811	840	863	882	898	912	924	933	942	949	3
4	249	731	772	806	833	856	875	891	905	917	927	4
5		642	697	741	778	808	834	855	874	890	903	5
6		542	612	669	715	754	787	815	839	859	876	6
7		429	516	587	645	694	735	769	799	824	846	7
8		302	409	495	567	626	676	718	754	785	812	8
9		160	288	392	478	550	610	661	704	741	773	9
10			152	276	379	464	535	596	648	692	730	10
11				146	267	367	452	523	584	636	681	11
12					141	259	358	442	513	574	627	12
13						137	252	350	433	504	566	13
14							133	246	343	425	497	14
15								130	242	337	419	15
16									128	237	332	16
17										126	234	17
18											124	18

Age of Loan	ORIGINAL TERM IN YEARS											Age of Loan
	20	21	22	23	24	25	27	29	30	35	40	
1	987	988	990	991	992	993	994	996	996	998	999	1
2	972	975	978	981	983	985	988	991	992	996	998	2
3	955	961	965	969	973	976	981	985	987	993	996	3
4	936	944	951	957	962	966	973	979	982	990	994	4
5	915	925	934	942	949	955	965	972	975	987	993	5
6	891	905	916	926	935	942	955	965	969	983	990	6
7	865	881	895	908	919	928	944	956	961	978	988	7
8	835	855	872	887	900	912	931	946	952	974	985	8
9	801	825	846	864	880	894	917	935	942	968	982	9
10	763	792	817	838	857	873	901	923	931	962	979	10
11	720	754	784	809	832	851	884	909	919	956	975	11
12	672	712	746	776	803	826	864	893	905	948	971	12
13	619	665	705	740	770	797	841	875	890	939	966	13
14	558	611	658	698	734	765	816	856	872	930	961	14
15	490	552	605	652	693	729	788	834	852	919	955	15
16	413	484	546	600	647	688	756	809	830	907	948	16
17	327	409	479	541	595	642	720	780	805	893	941	17
18	231	324	404	475	537	591	680	749	777	878	932	18
19	122	228	320	401	471	533	635	713	746	860	923	19
20		121	226	317	398	468	584	674	711	841	912	20
21			119	224	315	395	527	629	671	819	900	21
22				118	222	313	462	578	626	795	886	22
23					117	220	390	522	576	767	871	23
24						117	309	458	520	736	854	24
25							218	387	456	701	835	25
26							115	306	385	662	813	26
27								216	305	618	789	27
28								114	215	568	761	28
29									114	513	730	29
30										450	696	30
31										380	657	31
32										301	613	32
33										212	564	33
34										112	509	34
35											447	35

LOAN PROGRESS CHART

Showing dollar balance remaining on a $1,000 loan **12%**

Age of Loan	ORIGINAL TERM IN YEARS											Age of Loan
	5	10	11	12	13	14	15	16	17	18	19	
1	845	945	953	960	966	971	975	978	981	983	985	1
2	670	883	901	915	928	938	946	953	959	964	969	2
3	473	813	842	865	884	900	914	925	935	943	950	3
4	250	734	775	808	836	858	877	894	907	919	929	4
5		645	700	744	781	811	837	858	877	892	906	5
6		545	615	672	719	758	790	818	842	862	879	6
7		432	519	590	649	698	738	773	802	828	849	7
8		305	412	499	570	630	680	722	758	789	815	8
9		161	291	395	482	554	614	665	708	745	777	9
10			154	279	382	468	540	600	652	696	735	10
11				148	270	371	456	528	589	641	686	11
12					143	262	361	446	518	579	632	12
13						139	255	353	437	509	571	13
14							135	249	347	430	501	14
15								132	245	341	424	15
16									130	240	336	16
17										127	237	17
18											126	18

Age of Loan	ORIGINAL TERM IN YEARS											Age of Loan
	20	21	22	23	24	25	27	29	30	35	40	
1	987	989	990	991	992	993	995	996	996	998	999	1
2	973	976	979	982	984	986	989	991	992	996	998	2
3	956	962	966	970	974	977	982	986	988	993	996	3
4	938	946	952	958	963	967	975	980	982	990	995	4
5	917	928	936	944	951	957	966	974	977	987	993	5
6	894	907	918	928	937	944	957	966	970	984	991	6
7	868	884	898	910	921	930	946	958	963	980	989	7
8	838	858	875	890	903	915	934	948	954	975	986	8
9	805	829	850	868	884	897	920	938	945	970	984	9
10	767	796	821	842	861	878	905	926	934	964	980	10
11	725	759	788	814	836	855	887	912	922	958	977	11
12	677	717	751	781	807	830	868	897	909	950	973	12
13	624	670	710	745	775	802	846	880	894	942	968	13
14	563	617	663	704	739	770	821	860	876	933	963	14
15	495	557	611	657	698	734	793	838	857	922	958	15
16	418	489	551	605	652	694	761	814	835	910	951	16
17	332	413	485	547	601	648	726	786	811	897	944	17
18	234	328	409	480	542	597	686	755	782	882	936	18
19	124	231	325	406	477	539	641	720	752	865	926	19
20		123	229	322	403	473	590	680	717	846	916	20
21			121	227	319	400	533	635	677	825	904	21
22				120	225	317	468	585	633	800	891	22
23					119	224	395	528	583	773	876	23
24						119	314	464	526	742	859	24
25							221	392	462	708	840	25
26							117	311	391	669	819	26
27								219	310	625	795	27
28								116	219	575	768	28
29									116	519	737	29
30										457	703	30
31										386	664	31
32										306	621	32
33										216	571	33
34										114	516	34
35											453	35

12¼% LOAN PROGRESS CHART
Showing dollar balance remaining on a $1,000 loan

Age of Loan	ORIGINAL TERM IN YEARS											Age of Loan
	5	10	11	12	13	14	15	16	17	18	19	
1	846	946	954	961	967	971	975	979	981	984	986	1
2	671	864	902	917	929	939	947	954	960	965	970	2
3	474	815	844	867	886	902	915	927	936	945	952	3
4	251	736	777	811	838	861	880	896	909	921	931	4
5		648	703	747	783	814	839	861	879	895	908	5
6		548	618	675	722	761	794	821	845	865	882	6
7		435	523	594	653	701	742	777	806	831	852	7
8		307	415	502	574	634	684	726	762	793	819	8
9		163	293	399	485	558	618	669	713	750	782	9
10			155	282	385	471	544	605	657	701	739	10
11				149	272	374	460	532	593	646	691	11
12					144	264	365	450	522	584	637	12
13						140	258	357	441	514	576	13
14							137	252	350	434	506	14
15								134	247	345	428	15
16									131	243	340	16
17										129	240	17
18											127	18

Age of Loan	ORIGINAL TERM IN YEARS											Age of Loan
	20	21	22	23	24	25	27	29	30	35	40	
1	988	989	990	992	993	994	995	996	997	998	999	1
2	974	977	980	982	984	986	989	992	993	996	998	2
3	958	963	968	972	975	978	983	987	990	994	997	3
4	940	947	954	959	964	969	976	981	983	991	995	4
5	920	930	938	946	952	958	968	975	978	988	994	5
6	897	910	921	930	939	946	958	968	971	985	992	6
7	871	887	901	913	924	933	948	960	964	981	990	7
8	842	862	879	893	906	918	936	950	956	976	987	8
9	809	833	853	871	887	901	923	940	947	972	985	9
10	772	800	825	846	865	881	908	928	937	966	982	10
11	730	763	793	818	840	859	891	915	925	960	978	11
12	682	722	756	786	812	835	872	900	912	953	974	12
13	629	675	715	750	780	807	850	884	897	945	970	13
14	568	622	649	709	744	775	826	865	880	936	965	14
15	500	562	616	663	704	740	798	843	862	926	960	15
16	423	495	557	611	658	699	767	819	840	914	954	16
17	336	418	490	552	606	654	732	791	816	901	947	17
18	237	332	414	486	548	603	692	761	789	887	939	18
19	126	234	329	411	482	545	647	726	758	870	930	19
20		126	234	326	408	479	596	686	723	851	920	20
21			123	230	324	405	539	642	684	830	908	21
22			122	229	322	474	591	639	806	895		22
23				121	227	401	534	589	779	881		23
24					120	318	470	532	749	864		24
25						225	397	468	714	846		25
26							119	315	396	676	825	26
27								223	314	632	801	27
28								118	222	582	774	28
29									118	526	744	29
30										463	710	30
31										391	671	31
32										311	628	32
33										219	578	33
34										116	523	34
35											460	35

LOAN PROGRESS CHART

Showing dollar balance remaining on a $1,000 loan **12½%**

Age of Loan	ORIGINAL TERM IN YEARS											Age of Loan
	5	10	11	12	13	14	15	16	17	18	19	
1	846	946	955	962	967	972	976	979	982	984	986	1
2	673	886	904	918	930	940	948	955	961	966	971	2
3	476	817	846	869	888	904	917	928	938	946	953	3
4	253	739	780	813	840	863	882	898	911	923	933	4
5		651	705	750	786	817	842	863	882	897	910	5
6		551	621	678	725	764	797	824	848	868	885	6
7		438	526	597	656	705	746	780	809	834	856	7
8		309	418	506	578	638	688	730	766	797	823	8
9		164	295	402	489	561	622	673	717	754	786	9
10			157	284	389	475	543	609	661	705	743	10
11				151	275	378	464	536	598	651	696	11
12					146	267	368	454	527	589	642	12
13						142	261	361	446	518	580	13
14							138	255	354	439	511	14
15								135	250	349	433	15
16									133	246	344	16
17										131	243	17
18											129	18

Age of Loan	ORIGINAL TERM IN YEARS											Age of Loan
	20	21	22	23	24	25	27	29	30	35	40	
1	988	990	991	992	993	994	995	996	997	998	999	1
2	974	978	980	983	985	987	990	992	993	996	998	2
3	959	964	969	973	976	979	984	987	989	994	997	3
4	942	949	955	961	966	970	977	982	984	992	996	4
5	922	932	940	948	954	960	969	976	979	989	994	5
6	899	912	923	933	941	948	960	969	973	986	992	6
7	874	890	904	916	926	935	950	961	966	982	990	7
8	845	865	882	896	909	920	939	952	958	978	988	8
9	813	837	857	875	890	904	926	942	949	973	986	9
10	776	804	829	850	869	885	911	931	939	968	983	10
11	735	768	797	822	844	863	894	918	928	962	980	11
12	687	727	761	791	816	839	876	904	915	955	976	12
13	634	680	720	752	785	811	854	887	901	947	972	13
14	573	627	674	714	750	780	830	869	884	939	967	14
15	505	567	622	668	709	745	803	848	866	929	962	15
16	427	500	562	617	664	705	772	824	845	918	956	16
17	340	423	495	558	612	660	737	797	821	905	949	17
18	240	336	419	491	554	608	698	766	794	891	942	18
19	128	238	333	416	488	550	653	731	764	875	933	19
20		126	235	330	413	485	602	692	729	856	923	20
21			125	234	328	410	545	648	690	835	912	21
22				124	232	326	480	597	660	812	900	22
23					123	230	406	540	596	785	885	23
24						122	323	476		755	869	24
25							228	403	474	721	851	25
26							121	320	402	682	830	26
27								226	319	638	807	27
28								120	226	589	781	28
29									120	533	751	29
30										469	717	30
31										397	678	31
32										315	635	32
33										223	585	33
34										113	529	34
35											466	35

12¾% LOAN PROGRESS CHART
Showing dollar balance remaining on a $1,000 loan

Age of Loan	ORIGINAL TERM IN YEARS											Age of Loan
	5	10	11	12	13	14	15	16	17	18	19	
1	847	947	955	962	968	972	976	980	982	985	987	1
2	674	887	905	919	931	941	949	956	962	967	972	2
3	477	819	847	871	890	906	919	930	939	947	954	3
4	254	741	782	815	843	865	884	900	913	925	935	4
5		653	708	753	789	819	845	866	884	899	913	5
6		554	624	682	729	767	800	827	851	870	887	6
7		440	529	601	660	708	749	784	813	838	859	7
8		312	421	509	581	641	692	734	770	800	826	8
9		166	298	405	493	565	626	677	721	758	790	9
10			158	287	392	479	552	613	665	710	748	10
11				152	277	381	468	541	603	655	700	11
12					147	270	372	458	531	593	647	12
13						143	263	364	450	523	585	13
14							140	258	358	443	516	14
15								137	253	352	437	15
16									135	249	348	16
17										133	246	17
18											131	18

Age of Loan	ORIGINAL TERM IN YEARS											Age of Loan
	20	21	22	23	24	25	27	29	30	35	40	
1	988	990	991	992	993	994	995	996	997	998	999	1
2	975	978	981	983	986	987	990	993	993	997	998	2
3	960	965	970	974	977	980	984	988	989	994	997	3
4	943	950	957	962	967	971	978	983	985	992	996	4
5	924	934	942	949	956	961	972	977	980	989	994	5
6	902	915	925	935	943	950	962	970	974	986	993	6
7	877	893	906	918	928	937	952	963	967	983	991	7
8	849	868	885	899	912	923	941	954	960	979	989	8
9	817	840	861	878	893	907	928	945	951	975	987	9
10	780	809	833	854	872	888	914	934	942	969	984	10
11	739	773	801	826	848	867	898	921	931	964	981	11
12	692	732	766	795	821	843	879	907	918	957	977	12
13	639	685	725	760	790	816	859	891	904	950	974	13
14	579	633	679	720	755	785	835	873	888	941	969	14
15	510	573	627	674	715	750	808	852	870	932	964	15
16	432	505	568	622	669	710	778	829	850	921	958	16
17	344	428	500	563	618	645	743	802	826	909	952	17
18	243	340	424	496	559	614	700	772	800	895	945	18
19	129	241	337	421	493	556	637	737	769	879	936	19
20		128	239	335	418	490	608	698	735	861	927	20
21			127	237	332	415	551	654	696	841	916	21
22				126	235	330	485	604	652	817	904	22
23					125	234	411	547	602	791	890	23
24						124	327	482	545	761	874	24
25							232	408	480	727	856	25
26							123	325	407	689	836	26
27								230	324	645	813	27
28								122	229	595	787	28
29									122	539	757	29
30										475	723	30
31										403	685	31
32										320	641	32
33										227	592	33
34										121	536	34
35											473	35

LOAN PROGRESS CHART
Showing dollar balance remaining on a $1,000 loan **13%**

Age of Loan	ORIGINAL TERM IN YEARS											Age of Loan
	5	10	11	12	13	14	15	16	17	18	19	
1	848	948	956	963	968	973	977	980	983	985	987	1
2	675	888	906	921	932	942	950	957	963	968	972	2
3	479	821	849	873	892	907	920	931	941	949	956	3
4	255	744	785	818	845	867	886	902	915	927	936	4
5		656	711	756	792	822	847	869	887	902	915	5
6		557	627	685	732	771	803	830	854	873	890	6
7		443	532	604	663	712	753	787	816	841	862	7
8		314	424	512	585	645	695	738	774	804	830	8
9		167	300	408	496	569	630	682	725	762	794	9
10			160	289	395	483	556	618	670	714	752	10
11				154	280	384	472	545	607	660	705	11
12					149	272	376	462	536	598	651	12
13						145	266	368	448	528	590	13
14							142	261	362	447	521	14
15								139	256	356	442	15
16									136	253	352	16
17										134	249	17
18											133	18

Age of Loan	ORIGINAL TERM IN YEARS											Age of Loan
	20	21	22	23	24	25	27	29	30	35	40	
1	989	990	991	993	994	994	996	997	997	998	999	1
2	976	979	982	984	986	988	991	993	994	997	998	2
3	961	966	971	974	978	981	985	989	990	995	997	3
4	945	952	958	964	968	972	979	984	986	993	996	4
5	926	936	944	951	957	963	971	978	981	990	995	5
6	905	917	928	937	945	952	963	972	975	987	993	6
7	880	896	909	921	931	940	954	965	969	984	992	7
8	852	871	888	902	915	926	943	956	962	980	990	8
9	821	844	864	881	896	910	931	947	954	976	987	9
10	785	813	837	858	876	891	917	936	944	971	985	10
11	744	777	806	831	852	871	901	924	934	966	982	11
12	697	736	770	800	825	847	883	910	922	959	979	12
13	644	690	730	765	795	820	863	895	908	952	975	13
14	584	638	684	725	760	790	839	877	892	944	971	14
15	515	573	632	679	720	755	813	857	874	935	966	15
16	437	510	573	628	675	716	783	833	854	924	961	16
17	348	432	506	569	623	671	748	807	831	912	954	17
18	246	344	429	502	565	620	709	777	805	899	947	18
19	131	244	341	426	499	562	665	743	775	883	939	19
20		130	242	339	423	496	614	704	741	866	930	20
21			129	240	337	420	557	660	702	846	920	21
22				128	239	335	491	610	658	823	908	22
23					127	237	417	553	608	797	894	23
24						126	332	488	551	767	879	24
25							235	414	486	733	861	25
26							125	329	412	695	841	26
27								233	328	652	818	27
28								124	233	602	793	28
29									124	546	763	29
30										481	730	30
31										408	692	31
32										325	648	32
33										230	599	33
34										123	543	34
35											479	35

13¼% LOAN PROGRESS CHART

Showing dollar balance remaining on a $1,000 loan

Age of Loan	ORIGINAL TERM IN YEARS											Age of Loan
	5	10	11	12	13	14	15	16	17	18	19	
1	849	949	957	964	969	974	977	981	983	986	987	1
2	677	890	908	922	934	943	952	958	964	969	973	2
3	480	823	851	874	893	909	922	933	942	950	957	3
4	256	746	787	820	847	870	888	904	917	929	938	4
5		659	714	758	795	825	850	871	889	904	917	5
6		559	631	688	735	774	806	833	856	876	893	6
7		446	535	608	667	716	756	791	819	844	865	7
8		316	427	516	589	649	699	742	777	809	833	8
9		169	303	411	500	573	634	686	729	766	797	9
10			161	292	398	487	560	622	674	719	756	10
11				155	283	388	476	549	612	664	710	11
12					151	275	379	466	540	603	656	12
13						147	269	372	458	532	595	13
14							143	264	365	452	526	14
15								141	259	360	446	15
16									138	256	356	16
17										136	252	17
18											134	18

Age of Loan	ORIGINAL TERM IN YEARS											Age of Loan
	20	21	22	23	24	25	27	29	30	35	40	
1	989	991	992	993	994	995	996	997	997	999	999	1
2	977	980	982	985	987	988	991	993	994	997	998	2
3	963	967	972	975	979	981	986	989	991	995	997	3
4	946	953	960	965	969	973	980	984	986	993	996	4
5	928	937	946	953	959	964	973	979	982	991	995	5
6	907	919	930	939	947	954	965	973	976	988	994	6
7	883	898	912	923	933	942	956	966	970	985	992	7
8	856	875	892	905	917	928	945	958	963	981	990	8
9	824	848	867	885	900	912	933	949	956	977	988	9
10	789	817	841	861	879	895	920	939	946	973	986	10
11	748	781	810	835	856	874	904	927	936	967	983	11
12	702	741	775	804	829	851	887	914	924	961	980	12
13	649	695	735	769	799	825	867	898	911	954	977	13
14	589	643	690	730	765	795	844	881	896	947	972	14
15	520	583	638	685	725	760	818	861	878	938	968	15
16	441	515	578	633	680	721	788	838	858	927	963	16
17	352	437	511	574	629	677	754	812	836	916	957	17
18	250	348	434	507	571	626	715	782	810	903	950	18
19	133	247	346	430	504	567	671	749	780	887	942	19
20		132	245	343	428	501	620	710	747	870	933	20
21			131	243	341	425	562	666	708	850	923	21
22				130	235	336	497	616	664	828	911	22
23					129	241	422	559	614	802	898	23
24						128	336	493	557	773	883	24
25							238	419	492	740	866	25
26							127	334	418	702	846	26
27								237	333	658	824	27
28								126	236	608	798	28
29									126	552	769	29
30										487	736	30
31										414	698	31
32										330	655	32
33										234	606	33
34										125	549	34
35											485	35

LOAN PROGRESS CHART
Showing dollar balance remaining on a $1,000 loan 13½%

Age of Loan	5	10	11	12	13	14	15	16	17	18	19	Age of Loan
1	850	949	957	964	970	974	978	981	984	986	988	1
2	678	891	909	923	935	945	953	959	965	970	974	2
3	482	825	853	876	895	911	924	934	944	951	958	3
4	257	749	790	823	850	872	890	906	919	930	940	4
5		662	717	761	798	828	853	874	891	906	919	5
6		562	634	691	738	777	809	836	859	879	895	6
7		449	538	611	670	719	760	794	823	847	868	7
8		319	430	519	592	653	703	745	781	811	837	8
9		170	305	414	503	577	638	690	733	770	801	9
10			163	294	402	490	564	626	679	723	761	10
11				157	285	391	480	554	616	669	714	11
12					152	278	383	470	544	607	661	12
13						148	272	375	463	537	600	13
14							145	267	369	456	530	14
15								142	262	364	451	15
16									140	259	360	16
17										138	255	17
18											136	18

Age of Loan	20	21	22	23	24	25	27	29	30	35	40	Age of Loan
1	989	991	992	993	994	995	996	997	997	999	999	1
2	977	980	983	985	987	989	992	994	994	997	999	2
3	964	969	973	976	979	982	986	990	991	995	998	3
4	948	955	961	966	970	974	981	985	987	993	997	4
5	930	939	947	954	960	965	974	980	983	991	996	5
6	909	921	932	941	949	955	966	974	978	989	994	6
7	886	901	914	925	935	944	957	968	972	986	993	7
8	859	878	894	903	920	930	947	960	965	982	991	8
9	828	851	871	888	902	915	936	951	957	978	989	9
10	793	821	844	865	883	898	923	941	949	974	987	10
11	753	786	814	839	860	878	907	930	939	969	984	11
12	707	746	779	806	834	855	890	917	927	963	981	12
13	654	700	740	774	804	829	871	902	914	957	978	13
14	594	648	695	735	769	799	846	885	899	949	974	14
15	525	588	643	690	730	765	822	865	882	940	970	15
16	446	520	584	638	686	727	793	843	863	930	965	16
17	356	442	516	580	635	682	759	817	840	919	959	17
18	253	353	438	512	576	631	720	788	815	906	952	18
19	135	250	350	435	509	573	676	754	786	891	945	19
20		134	248	347	433	507	626	716	752	874	936	20
21			133	247	345	431	568	672	714	855	926	21
22				132	245	343	502	622	670	833	915	22
23					131	244	427	565	620	808	902	23
24						130	341	507	563	779	887	24
25							242	424	498	746	871	25
26							129	338	423	708	851	26
27								240	338	664	829	27
28								128	240	615	804	28
29									128	558	775	29
30										493	742	30
31										419	705	31
32										335	661	32
33										238	612	33
34										127	555	34
35											491	35

13¾% LOAN PROGRESS CHART

Showing dollar balance remaining on a $1,000 loan

Age of Loan	ORIGINAL TERM IN YEARS											Age of Loan
	5	10	11	12	13	14	15	16	17	18	19	
1	851	950	958	965	970	975	978	981	984	986	988	1
2	679	892	910	924	936	946	954	960	966	971	975	2
3	483	827	855	878	897	912	925	936	945	953	959	3
4	258	751	792	825	852	874	893	908	921	932	941	4
5		665	720	764	800	830	855	876	894	908	921	5
6		565	637	694	741	780	812	839	862	881	898	6
7		452	542	614	674	723	763	797	826	850	871	7
8		321	433	523	596	657	707	749	785	815	840	8
9		171	308	417	507	581	642	694	737	774	805	9
10			164	297	405	494	568	630	683	727	765	10
11				159	288	395	483	558	620	673	719	11
12					154	281	386	474	549	612	666	12
13						150	275	379	467	541	605	13
14							147	269	373	461	535	14
15								144	265	368	455	15
16									142	262	364	16
17										140	258	17
18											138	18

Age of Loan	ORIGINAL TERM IN YEARS											Age of Loan
	20	21	22	23	24	25	27	29	30	35	40	
1	990	991	992	993	994	995	996	997	998	999	999	1
2	978	982	984	986	988	989	992	994	995	997	999	2
3	965	970	974	977	980	983	987	990	991	996	998	3
4	949	956	962	967	972	975	981	986	988	994	997	4
5	932	941	949	956	962	967	975	981	983	992	996	5
6	912	924	934	943	950	957	967	975	979	989	995	6
7	889	904	917	928	937	946	959	969	973	986	993	7
8	862	881	898	911	922	933	949	962	967	983	992	8
9	832	855	874	891	905	918	938	953	959	980	990	9
10	797	824	848	868	886	901	925	943	951	975	988	10
11	757	790	818	842	863	881	911	932	941	971	985	11
12	711	750	784	813	838	859	894	920	930	965	982	12
13	659	705	745	779	808	833	874	905	917	959	979	13
14	599	653	700	740	774	804	852	888	903	951	976	14
15	530	593	648	695	735	770	827	869	886	943	971	15
16	450	525	589	644	691	732	798	847	867	933	966	16
17	360	447	521	585	640	688	764	822	845	922	961	17
18	256	357	443	517	582	637	726	793	820	910	955	18
19	137	254	354	440	515	579	682	760	791	895	947	19
20		135	252	352	438	512	632	722	758	879	939	20
21			134	250	350	436	574	678	720	860	929	21
22				134	249	348	508	628	676	838	919	22
23					133	247	432	571	626	813	906	23
24						132	345	505	569	784	892	24
25							245	429	504	751	875	25
26							131	343	428	714	856	26
27								244	342	671	834	27
28								130	243	621	810	28
29									130	564	781	29
30										499	748	30
31										425	711	31
32										339	668	32
33										241	619	33
34										129	562	34
35											497	35

LOAN PROGRESS CHART

Showing dollar balance remaining on a $1,000 loan **14%**

Age of Loan				ORIGINAL TERM IN YEARS								Age of Loan
	5	10	11	12	13	14	15	16	17	18	19	
1	851	951	959	965	971	975	979	982	985	987	989	1
2	681	894	911	926	937	947	955	961	967	971	975	2
3	485	829	857	880	899	914	927	937	946	953	960	3
4	259	754	794	827	854	876	895	910	923	934	943	4
5		667	722	767	803	833	858	878	896	911	923	5
6		568	640	697	744	783	815	842	865	884	900	6
7		454	545	618	677	726	767	801	829	853	874	7
8		323	436	526	600	660	711	753	788	818	844	8
9		173	310	420	511	585	646	698	741	778	809	9
10			166	299	408	498	572	635	687	731	769	10
11				160	291	398	487	562	625	678	723	11
12					155	283	390	479	553	617	670	12
13						152	277	383	471	546	609	13
14							148	272	377	465	540	14
15								146	268	372	460	15
16									143	265	367	16
17										141	262	17
18											140	18

Age of Loan				ORIGINAL TERM IN YEARS								Age of Loan
	20	21	22	23	24	25	27	29	30	35	40	
1	990	992	993	994	995	995	996	997	998	999	999	1
2	979	982	984	986	988	988	992	994	995	998	999	2
3	966	971	975	978	981	984	988	991	992	996	998	3
4	951	958	963	968	973	976	982	987	988	994	997	4
5	934	943	951	957	963	968	976	982	984	992	996	5
6	914	926	936	945	952	959	969	977	980	990	995	6
7	891	906	919	930	939	948	961	970	974	987	994	7
8	865	884	900	913	925	935	951	963	968	984	992	8
9	835	858	877	894	908	921	940	955	961	981	990	9
10	801	828	852	872	889	904	928	946	953	977	986	10
11	761	794	822	846	867	885	913	935	943	972	986	11
12	716	755	788	817	842	863	897	922	933	967	983	12
13	664	710	749	783	812	836	878	908	920	961	980	13
14	603	658	705	745	779	809	856	892	906	954	977	14
15	534	598	653	700	740	775	831	873	890	945	973	15
16	455	530	594	649	696	737	802	851	871	936	968	16
17	364	451	526	590	645	693	769	826	849	925	963	17
18	259	361	448	523	587	642	731	799	824	913	957	18
19	138	257	358	445	520	584	688	765	796	899	950	19
20		137	255	356	443	517	627	727	763	883	942	20
21			136	253	354	441	580	684	725	864	933	21
22			135	252	352		513	634	682	843	922	22
23				135	251		437	576	632	818	910	23
24					134		350	510	575	790	896	24
25						249	435	509		757	879	25
26							133	347	434	720	861	26
27								247	347	677	839	27
28								132	247	627	815	28
29									132	571	787	29
30										505	754	30
31										430	717	31
32										344	674	32
33										245	625	33
34										131	568	34
35											503	35

14¼% LOAN PROGRESS CHART
Showing dollar balance remaining on a $1,000 loan

Age of Loan	5	10	11	12	13	14	15	16	17	18	19	Age of Loan
1	852	951	959	966	971	976	979	982	985	987	989	1
2	682	895	913	927	938	948	956	962	968	972	976	2
3	436	830	859	882	900	915	928	939	948	955	961	3
4	260	756	797	830	856	878	897	912	925	935	945	4
5		670	725	770	806	836	860	881	898	913	925	5
6		571	643	701	748	786	818	845	868	887	903	6
7		457	548	621	680	729	770	804	832	856	877	7
8		326	439	529	603	664	714	756	792	822	847	8
9		174	313	424	514	589	650	702	745	782	813	9
10			167	302	411	502	576	639	691	735	773	10
11				162	293	401	491	566	629	682	727	11
12				157	286	393	483	558	621	675		12
13					153	280	386	475	551	614		13
14						150	275	380	469	544		14
15							147	271	376	464		15
16								145	268	371		16
17									143	265		17
18										142		18

Age of Loan	20	21	22	23	24	25	27	29	30	35	40	Age of Loan
1	990	992	993	994	995	995	997	997	998	999	999	1
2	980	982	985	987	989	990	993	995	996	998	998	2
3	967	972	975	979	982	984	988	991	992	996	998	3
4	952	959	965	970	974	977	983	987	989	995	997	4
5	936	945	952	959	964	969	977	983	985	993	996	5
6	916	928	938	945	954	960	970	978	981	991	995	6
7	894	909	921	932	941	949	962	972	975	988	994	7
8	868	887	902	916	927	937	953	965	970	985	993	8
9	839	861	880	897	911	923	942	957	963	982	991	9
10	805	832	855	875	892	907	930	948	955	978	989	10
11	766	798	826	850	870	888	916	937	946	973	987	11
12	720	759	793	821	846	867	900	925	938	968	984	12
13	668	715	754	788	817	842	882	911	923	962	982	13
14	608	663	709	749	784	813	860	895	909	956	978	14
15	539	603	658	705	745	780	836	877	893	948	974	15
16	460	535	599	654	701	742	807	855	875	939	970	16
17	368	456	531	595	651	698	774	831	854	928	965	17
18	262	365	453	528	592	648	737	803	829	916	959	18
19	140	260	362	450	525	590	693	770	801	903	952	19
20		139	258	360	448	523	643	733	768	887	944	20
21			138	257	358	445	585	689	731	868	935	21
22				137	255	357	519	640	688	847	925	22
23					137	254	442	582	638	823	913	23
24						136	354	516	581	795	899	24
25							252	440	515	763	884	25
26							135	352	439	726	865	26
27								251	351	683	844	27
28								134	250	633	820	28
29									134	577	792	29
30										511	760	30
31										436	723	31
32										349	680	32
33										248	631	33
34										133	575	34
35											509	35

LOAN PROGRESS CHART
Showing dollar balance remaining on a $1,000 loan **14½%**

Age of Loan	5	10	11	12	13	14	15	16	17	18	19	Age of Loan
1	853	952	960	967	972	976	980	983	985	987	989	1
2	684	896	914	928	939	949	957	963	968	973	977	2
3	488	832	861	883	902	917	930	940	949	956	963	3
4	261	758	799	832	859	880	899	914	926	937	946	4
5		673	728	772	808	838	863	883	900	915	927	5
6		574	646	704	751	789	821	848	870	889	905	6
7		460	551	624	684	733	773	807	835	859	880	7
8		328	441	533	607	668	718	760	795	825	850	8
9		176	315	427	518	592	654	706	749	785	816	9
10			169	304	415	505	580	643	695	740	777	10
11				163	296	405	495	570	634	687	732	11
12					159	289	397	487	562	626	679	12
13						155	283	390	480	555	619	13
14							152	278	384	474	549	14
15								149	274	379	468	15
16									147	271	375	16
17										145	268	17
18											144	18

Age of Loan	20	21	22	23	24	25	27	29	30	35	40	Age of Loan
1	991	992	993	994	995	996	997	998	998	999	999	1
2	980	983	985	987	989	991	993	995	996	998	999	2
3	968	972	976	980	982	985	989	992	993	996	998	3
4	954	960	966	971	975	978	984	988	990	995	998	4
5	937	946	954	960	966	970	978	984	986	993	997	5
6	918	930	940	948	955	962	971	979	982	991	996	6
7	897	911	924	934	943	951	964	973	977	989	995	7
8	871	890	905	918	930	939	955	966	971	986	993	8
9	842	865	884	900	914	926	945	959	964	983	992	9
10	809	836	859	878	895	910	933	950	957	979	990	10
11	770	802	830	854	874	891	919	940	948	975	988	11
12	725	764	797	825	849	870	903	928	938	970	985	12
13	673	719	759	792	821	846	885	914	926	964	983	13
14	613	668	714	754	788	817	864	899	912	958	979	14
15	544	608	663	710	750	785	840	881	897	950	976	15
16	464	540	604	659	707	747	812	860	879	941	972	16
17	372	460	536	601	656	703	779	835	858	931	967	17
18	265	369	457	533	598	653	742	807	834	920	961	18
19	142	263	366	455	530	595	699	775	806	906	955	19
20		142	261	364	452	528	649	738	774	891	947	20
21			140	260	362	450	591	695	736	873	938	21
22				139	259	361	524	645	694	852	928	22
23					139	257	447	588	644	828	917	23
24						138	358	522	587	800	903	24
25							256	445	520	768	888	25
26							137	357	444	731	870	26
27								254	356	689	849	27
28								136	254	640	825	28
29									136	583	798	29
30										517	766	30
31										441	729	31
32										353	686	32
33										252	637	33
34										135	581	34
35											515	35

185

14¾% LOAN PROGRESS CHART

Showing dollar balance remaining on a $1,000 loan

Age of Loan	|	|	|	ORIGINAL TERM IN YEARS	|	|	|	|	|	|	Age of Loan
	5	10	11	12	13	14	15	16	17	18	19	
1	854	953	961	967	972	977	980	983	986	988	990	1
2	685	898	915	929	940	950	957	964	969	974	978	2
3	489	834	862	885	904	919	931	941	950	957	964	3
4	262	761	801	834	861	882	901	916	928	939	948	4
5		675	731	775	811	841	865	885	902	917	929	5
6		577	649	707	754	792	824	851	873	892	907	6
7		463	554	628	687	736	777	810	839	862	882	7
8		330	445	536	610	671	722	764	799	828	853	8
9		177	317	430	521	596	658	710	753	789	820	9
10			170	307	418	509	584	647	700	744	781	10
11				165	299	408	499	575	638	691	736	11
12					160	292	400	491	566	630	684	12
13						156	286	394	484	560	624	13
14							153	281	388	478	554	14
15								151	277	383	473	15
16									149	274	379	16
17										147	271	17
18											145	18

Age of Loan	ORIGINAL TERM IN YEARS	|	|	|	|	|	|	|	|	|	|	Age of Loan
	20	21	22	23	24	25	27	29	30	35	40	
1	991	992	993	994	995	996	997	998	998	999	999	1
2	981	984	986	988	990	991	993	995	996	998	999	2
3	969	973	977	980	983	986	989	992	993	997	998	3
4	955	962	967	972	976	979	984	988	990	995	998	4
5	939	948	955	962	967	972	979	984	987	994	997	5
6	921	932	942	950	957	963	973	980	982	992	996	6
7	899	914	926	936	945	953	965	974	978	989	995	7
8	874	892	908	921	932	941	957	968	972	987	994	8
9	846	868	886	903	916	928	947	960	966	984	992	9
10	812	839	862	882	898	912	935	952	959	980	991	10
11	774	806	834	857	877	894	922	942	950	976	989	11
12	729	768	801	829	853	874	906	931	940	971	986	12
13	678	724	763	796	825	850	889	917	929	966	984	13
14	618	673	719	759	793	822	868	902	915	960	981	14
15	549	613	668	715	755	789	844	884	900	952	977	15
16	469	545	609	664	712	752	816	864	882	944	973	16
17	376	465	541	606	661	709	784	840	862	934	968	17
18	268	373	462	538	603	658	747	812	838	923	963	18
19	144	266	371	459	535	600	704	780	811	910	957	19
20		143	265	369	457	533	654	743	779	894	949	20
21			142	263	367	455	596	700	742	877	941	21
22				141	262	365	530	651	699	856	931	22
23					141	261	452	594	650	833	920	23
24						140	363	527	592	805	907	24
25							259	450	526	774	892	25
26							139	361	449	737	874	26
27								258	360	695	854	27
28								138	257	645	830	28
29									138	589	803	29
30										523	771	30
31										446	735	31
32										358	692	32
33										256	643	33
34										137	587	34
35											521	35

LOAN PROGRESS CHART 15%

Showing dollar balance remaining on a $1,000 loan

Age of Loan	\[ORIGINAL TERM IN YEARS\] 5	10	11	12	13	14	15	16	17	18	19	Age of Loan
1	855	953	961	968	973	977	981	984	986	988	990	1
2	686	899	916	930	942	951	958	965	970	975	978	2
3	491	836	864	887	905	920	933	943	957	965	972	3
4	264	763	804	836	863	885	902	917	930	940	949	4
5		678	733	778	814	843	863	888	905	919	931	5
6		580	652	710	757	795	827	853	875	894	910	6
7		465	557	631	691	740	780	813	842	865	885	7
8		333	447	539	614	675	725	767	802	832	856	8
9		179	320	433	525	600	662	713	757	793	823	9
10			172	310	421	513	588	651	704	748	785	10
11				166	301	412	503	579	642	695	740	11
12					162	294	404	495	571	635	688	12
13						158	289	397	488	564	628	13
14							155	284	392	482	558	14
15								153	280	387	477	15
16									150	277	383	16
17										149	274	17
18											147	18

Age of Loan	\[ORIGINAL TERM IN YEARS\] 20	21	22	23	24	25	27	29	30	35	40	Age of Loan
1	991	993	994	995	995	996	997	998	998	999	999	1
2	981	984	986	988	990	991	994	995	996	998	999	2
3	970	974	978	981	984	986	990	992	993	997	999	3
4	956	963	968	973	977	980	985	989	991	996	998	4
5	941	949	957	963	968	973	980	985	987	995	997	5
6	923	934	943	952	958	964	974	981	983	992	996	6
7	902	916	928	938	947	955	967	975	979	990	995	7
8	877	895	910	923	934	943	958	969	973	987	994	8
9	849	871	889	905	919	930	949	962	967	985	993	9
10	816	843	865	885	899	915	937	954	960	983	991	10
11	778	810	838	861	881	898	924	944	952	977	989	11
12	734	772	805	833	857	877	909	933	942	973	987	12
13	682	728	767	801	829	853	892	920	931	968	985	13
14	623	677	724	763	797	826	872	905	918	962	982	14
15	554	618	673	720	760	794	848	888	903	954	978	15
16	473	549	614	669	717	757	821	867	886	946	975	16
17	380	470	546	611	666	714	789	844	866	937	970	17
18	272	367	467	543	608	664	752	817	842	926	965	18
19	146	270	375	464	541	606	709	785	815	913	959	19
20		145	268	373	462	538	660	749	784	898	952	20
21			144	266	371	460	602	706	747	881	944	21
22				143	264	369	535	656	705	861	934	22
23					142	262	457	599	655	837	923	23
24						142	367	532	598	810	910	24
25							262	455	532	779	895	25
26							141	365	454	743	878	26
27								261	365	700	858	27
28								140	261	651	835	28
29									140	594	808	29
30										528	777	30
31										452	740	31
32										363	698	32
33										259	649	33
34										139	593	34
35											527	35

15½% LOAN PROGRESS CHART

Showing dollar balance remaining on a $1,000 loan

Age of Loan	5	10	11	12	13	14	15	16	17	18	19	Age of Loan
				ORIGINAL TERM IN YEARS								
1	856	955	963	969	974	978	982	985	987	989	991	1
2	689	902	919	933	944	953	960	966	972	976	980	2
3	494	840	868	890	908	923	935	945	954	961	967	3
4	266	768	808	841	867	889	906	921	933	943	952	4
5		684	739	783	819	848	872	892	909	923	934	5
6		585	658	716	763	801	833	859	880	899	914	6
7		471	563	637	697	746	786	820	847	871	890	7
8		337	453	546	621	682	732	774	809	838	862	8
9		182	325	439	532	607	670	721	764	800	830	9
10			175	315	428	520	596	659	712	756	792	10
11				169	306	418	511	587	651	704	748	11
12					165	300	411	503	579	643	697	12
13						161	294	404	496	573	637	13
14							158	290	399	491	567	14
15								156	286	395	486	15
16									154	283	391	16
17										152	280	17
18											151	18

Age of Loan	20	21	22	23	24	25	27	29	30	35	40	Age of Loan
				ORIGINAL TERM IN YEARS								
1	992	993	994	995	996	996	997	998	998	999	999	1
2	983	985	987	989	991	992	994	996	996	998	999	2
3	972	976	979	982	985	987	991	993	994	997	999	3
4	959	965	970	975	978	981	986	990	992	996	998	4
5	944	952	959	965	970	975	982	987	988	995	998	5
6	927	938	947	955	961	967	976	982	985	993	997	6
7	907	920	932	942	951	958	969	977	981	991	996	7
8	883	900	915	928	938	947	961	972	976	989	995	8
9	856	877	895	911	924	935	952	965	970	986	994	9
10	823	850	872	891	907	920	942	957	964	983	992	10
11	786	818	845	868	887	903	929	948	956	980	991	11
12	742	781	813	841	864	884	915	938	947	975	989	12
13	692	737	776	809	837	861	898	926	936	971	986	13
14	632	687	733	772	806	834	879	911	924	965	984	14
15	563	628	683	729	769	803	856	895	910	958	981	15
16	482	559	624	679	726	766	829	875	893	951	977	16
17	388	479	556	621	677	724	798	852	874	942	973	17
18	278	385	476	553	618	674	762	826	851	931	968	18
19	150	276	383	474	551	616	720	795	824	919	963	19
20		149	274	381	472	549	670	759	793	905	956	20
21			148	273	379	470	613	717	757	888	948	21
22				147	272	378	546	667	715	869	939	22
23					146	271	467	610	666	846	929	23
24						146	376	543	609	820	917	24
25							269	465	542	789	903	25
26							145	374	465	753	886	26
27								268	374	712	867	27
28								144	268	663	844	28
29									144	606	818	29
30										539	787	30
31										462	752	31
32										372	710	32
33										266	661	33
34										143	604	34
35											538	35

LOAN PROGRESS CHART

Showing dollar balance remaining on a $1,000 loan

16%

Age of Loan	ORIGINAL TERM IN YEARS											Age of Loan
	5	10	11	12	13	14	15	16	17	18	19	
1	858	956	964	970	975	979	983	985	988	990	991	1
2	692	904	921	935	946	955	962	968	973	977	981	2
3	497	843	871	893	911	926	938	948	956	963	969	3
4	268	772	813	845	871	892	910	924	936	946	954	4
5		689	744	788	824	853	877	896	913	926	938	5
6		591	664	722	769	807	838	864	885	903	918	6
7		476	570	644	704	753	793	826	853	876	895	7
8		342	459	553	628	689	739	781	816	844	868	8
9		185	330	445	539	615	677	729	771	800	837	9
10			178	320	434	527	604	667	720	763	800	10
11				173	312	425	518	595	659	712	757	11
12					168	305	418	511	588	652	706	12
13						165	300	412	504	582	646	13
14							162	296	407	499	576	14
15								159	292	402	495	15
16									158	289	399	16
17										156	286	17
18											154	18

Age of Loan	ORIGINAL TERM IN YEARS											Age of Loan
	20	21	22	23	24	25	27	29	30	35	40	
1	993	994	995	995	996	997	998	998	999	999	999	1
2	984	986	988	990	992	993	995	996	997	999	999	2
3	973	978	981	984	986	988	992	994	995	998	999	3
4	961	967	972	976	980	983	988	991	992	997	998	4
5	947	955	962	968	973	977	983	988	990	995	998	5
6	931	941	950	958	964	969	978	984	986	994	997	6
7	911	925	936	946	954	961	972	979	983	992	996	7
8	889	905	920	932	942	951	964	974	978	990	996	8
9	862	883	901	916	928	939	956	968	973	988	994	9
10	831	856	878	897	912	925	946	961	967	985	993	10
11	794	825	852	874	893	909	934	952	959	982	992	11
12	751	789	821	848	871	890	920	942	951	978	990	12
13	700	746	785	817	845	868	904	931	941	973	988	13
14	641	696	742	781	814	842	885	917	929	968	986	14
15	572	637	692	739	778	811	863	901	916	962	983	15
16	491	568	634	689	736	775	837	882	900	955	980	16
17	396	488	565	631	686	733	807	860	881	946	976	17
18	284	393	485	563	629	684	771	834	859	937	971	18
19	153	282	391	483	561	626	730	804	833	925	966	19
20		152	281	389	481	559	681	768	803	911	960	20
21			152	280	388	479	623	727	767	895	953	21
22				151	278	387	556	678	726	877	944	22
23					150	278	477	621	677	855	935	23
24						150	385	574	620	829	923	24
25							276	475	553	799	909	25
26							149	383	475	764	894	26
27								275	383	722	875	27
28								148	275	674	853	28
29									148	617	827	29
30										550	797	30
31										472	762	31
32										381	721	32
33										273	672	33
34										148	616	34
35											549	35

17% LOAN PROGRESS CHART

Showing dollar balance remaining on a $1,000 loan

Age of Loan	5	10	11	12	13	14	15	16	17	18	19	Age of Loan
1	861	958	966	972	977	981	984	987	989	991	992	1
2	697	909	926	939	950	958	965	971	976	980	983	2
3	503	850	878	900	917	932	943	953	960	967	972	3
4	272	781	822	853	879	900	917	931	942	951	959	4
5		699	755	799	834	862	886	905	920	933	944	5
6		602	676	734	780	818	849	874	895	912	926	6
7		487	582	657	717	765	805	837	866	886	905	7
8		352	471	566	642	703	753	794	828	856	879	8
9		191	340	458	553	629	692	743	785	820	849	9
10			184	330	447	542	619	683	735	778	814	10
11				179	322	439	533	611	675	728	772	11
12				175	316	432	526	604	669	722		12
13					171	311	426	520	599	664		13
14						169	307	421	516	594		14
15							167	304	417	512		15
16								165	301	414		16
17									163	299		17
18										162		18

Age of Loan	20	21	22	23	24	25	27	28	29	30	35	40	Age of Loan
1	993	995	995	996	997	997	998	999	999	999	999	999	1
2	986	988	990	992	993	994	996	997	997	999	999	999	2
3	977	980	984	986	988	990	993	995	996	998	999	999	3
4	966	971	976	980	983	986	990	993	994	997	999	999	4
5	953	961	967	972	977	980	986	990	992	996	998	999	5
6	938	948	956	963	969	974	981	987	989		995	998	6
7	920	933	944	952	960	966	976	983	986		994	997	7
8	899	915	929	940	949	957	970	978	982		992	997	8
9	874	894	911	925	937	947	962	973	977		990	996	9
10	844	869	890	907	922	934	953	967	972		988	995	10
11	809	839	865	886	904	919	943	959	966		985	994	11
12	767	804	835	862	883	902	930	950	958		982	992	12
13	718	763	801	832	859	881	915	940	949		978	991	13
14	659	714	759	778	830	856	898	927	939		974	989	14
15	590	656	711	756	795	822	877	913	926		968	986	15
16	508	587	653	708	754	793	853	895	912		962	984	16
17	411	506	584	650	706	752	824	875	894		955	981	17
18	297	409	503	582	648	704	789	850	874		946	977	18
19	161	295	407	501	580	646	749	821	849		935	972	19
20		160	294	406	500	574	701	787	820		923	968	20
21			159	293	404	498	644	746	786		908	961	21
22				159	292	403	576	698	746		891	953	22
23					158	291	496	642	698		870	944	23
24						158	402	574	641		846	934	24
25							290	495	574		817	922	25
26							157		400	494	783	907	26
27									289	400	743	890	27
28									156	288	695	869	28
29										156	639	845	29
30											572	816	30
31											492	782	31
32											398	742	32
33											287	694	33
34											156	638	34
35												571	35

LOAN PROGRESS CHART

Showing dollar balance remaining on a $1,000 loan **18%**

Age of Loan	ORIGINAL TERM IN YEARS											Age of Loan
	5	10	11	12	13	14	15	16	17	18	19	
1	864	961	968	974	979	983	986	988	990	992	993	1
2	702	914	930	943	953	962	968	974	978	982	985	2
3	509	857	884	906	923	939	948	957	964	970	975	3
4	277	790	830	861	887	907	923	937	947	956	964	4
5		710	765	808	843	871	894	912	927	940	950	5
6		613	687	745	791	828	859	883	903	920	933	6
7		498	594	669	729	777	817	848	874	896	913	7
8		361	483	578	655	716	766	807	840	867	890	8
9		197	349	470	566	643	706	757	799	833	861	9
10			190	340	460	556	634	706	750	792	827	10
11				185	333	452	548	627	695	744	787	11
12					181	327	445	542	620	685	738	12
13						178	323	440	536	615	681	13
14							176	319	436	532	611	14
15								174	316	432	528	15
16									172	313	429	16
17										170	311	17
18											169	18

Age of Loan	ORIGINAL TERM IN YEARS											Age of Loan
	20	21	22	23	24	25	27	29	30	35	40	
1	994	995	996	997	997	998	998	999	999	999	999	1
2	988	990	991	993	994	995	997	998	998	999	999	2
3	980	983	986	988	990	992	994	996	997	999	999	3
4	970	975	979	983	985	988	992	994	995	998	999	4
5	958	965	971	976	980	983	988	992	993	997	999	5
6	945	954	962	968	973	978	984	989	991	996	998	6
7	928	940	950	958	965	971	980	986	988	995	998	7
8	908	924	936	947	956	963	974	982	985	994	997	8
9	885	904	920	933	944	954	968	977	981	992	997	9
10	857	881	900	917	931	942	960	972	977	990	996	10
11	823	852	877	898	915	929	950	965	971	988	995	11
12	782	819	849	874	895	912	939	957	964	985	994	12
13	734	779	816	846	872	893	925	948	957	982	993	13
14	677	731	776	813	844	870	909	937	947	978	991	14
15	608	673	728	773	811	842	890	923	936	974	989	15
16	525	605	671	726	771	809	867	907	922	968	987	16
17	427	523	603	669	724	769	839	888	906	962	984	17
18	309	425	521	601	667	722	806	865	887	954	981	18
19	168	308	423	519	599	665	767	837	864	944	977	19
20		168	306	422	518	598	719	804	836	933	973	20
21			167	305	421	517	663	765	803	920	967	21
22				166	305	420	595	718	764	904	961	22
23					166	304	515	661	717	885	953	23
24						166	418	594	665	862	943	24
25							303	514	593	834	932	25
26							165	417	513	801	919	26
27								302	417	762	903	27
28								165	302	715	884	28
29									164	659	861	29
30										592	833	30
31										512	800	31
32										416	761	32
33										301	714	33
34										164	658	34
35											591	35

RATE %	PAYMENT $	LOAN $
7.00	207.92	10,500.00

TERM: YEARS	MONTHS	PERIODS
5		60

Prepared by Financial Publishing Company, Boston

PAYMENT NUMBER	PAYMENT ON INTEREST	PRINCIPAL	BALANCE OF LOAN
1	61.25	146.67	10,353.33
2	60.39	147.53	10,205.80
3	59.53	148.39	10,057.41
4	58.67	149.25	9,908.16
5	57.80	150.12	9,758.04
6	56.92	151.00	9,607.04
7	56.04	151.88	9,455.16
8	55.16	152.76	9,302.40
9	54.26	153.66	9,148.74
10	53.37	154.55	8,994.19
11	52.47	155.45	8,838.74
12	51.56	156.36	8,682.38
13	50.65	157.27	8,525.11
14	49.73	158.19	8,366.92
15	48.81	159.11	8,207.81
16	47.88	160.04	8,047.77
17	46.95	160.97	7,886.80
18	46.01	161.91	7,724.89
19	45.06	162.86	7,562.03
20	44.11	163.81	7,398.22
21	43.16	164.76	7,233.46
22	42.20	165.72	7,067.74
23	41.23	166.69	6,901.05
24	40.26	167.66	6,733.39
25	39.28	168.64	6,564.75
26	38.29	169.63	6,395.12
27	37.30	170.62	6,224.50
28	36.31	171.61	6,052.89
29	35.31	172.61	5,880.28
30	34.30	173.62	5,706.66
31	33.29	174.63	5,532.03
32	32.27	175.65	5,356.38
33	31.25	176.67	5,179.71
34	30.21	177.71	5,002.00
35	29.18	178.74	4,823.26
36	28.14	179.78	4,643.48
37	27.09	180.83	4,462.65
38	26.03	181.89	4,280.76
39	24.97	182.95	4,097.81
40	23.90	184.02	3,913.79
41	22.83	185.09	3,728.70
42	21.75	186.17	3,542.53
43	20.66	187.26	3,355.27
44	19.57	188.35	3,166.92
45	18.47	189.45	2,977.47
46	17.37	190.55	2,786.92
47	16.26	191.66	2,595.26
48	15.14	192.78	2,402.48
49	14.01	193.91	2,208.57
50	12.88	195.04	2,013.53
51	11.75	196.17	1,817.36
52	10.60	197.32	1,620.04
53	9.45	198.47	1,421.57
54	8.29	199.63	1,221.94
55	7.13	200.79	1,021.15
56	5.96	201.96	819.19
57	4.78	203.14	616.05
58	3.59	204.33	411.72
59	2.40	205.52	206.20
60	1.20	206.20	207.40*

The final payment is usually somewhat different from the regular payment, and is shown starred on the last line.

Amortization Schedules

Starting with the payment as shown in this book an amortization schedule can be constructed showing the allocation of each payment into interest and principal, also the balance outstanding after each payment has been made. Proceed by (1) computing the interest on the previous balance; (2) deducting this from the payment; and (3) crediting the remainder as a repayment of principal. As a specimen in the column to the left we give the amortization schedule for a loan of $10,500 at 7% payable over 5 years by monthly payments of $207.92.

Note that the final payment is usually several cents smaller than the regular payment. This is because the tabulated payment is always a fraction of a cent too large. (If, however, the payment were 1¢ less, the final payment would be slightly larger.)

Amortization schedules for loans of any amount, interest rate, and term or payment may be obtained from the publisher of this booklet.